AMERICAN SOCIETY
An Introductory Analysis

AMERICAN
SOCIETY

An Introductory Analysis

by LUKE EBERSOLE
University of Tennessee

McGRAW-HILL BOOK COMPANY, INC.

New York   Toronto   London   1955

AMERICAN SOCIETY

Library of Congress Catalog Card Number 55–7274

For my parents

Preface

American Society is designed for courses in introductory sociology and general social science. It is hoped that it will be useful also in courses in the field of American studies.

As an introductory textbook this work is in concurrence with the frequently expressed need for more understanding of our own society. It seeks to bring to that understanding selected insights, concepts, and methods of social analysis. The focus of attention, however, is on American society rather than on concepts as such. Principles and concepts are stated, but their inclusion is always determined by their usefulness in describing and analyzing particular data.

The purpose of the book is decidedly pedagogical. It is planned for use by teachers who do not choose to bring their students into sociology by sudden submergence into the depth of sociological abstraction. Whatever logical merit it may otherwise have, the procedure of beginning with discussions of population is intended as a means of starting with things concrete. The inclusion of social history is required by the theme of social change which runs throughout. It also makes possible the use of a method of social analysis with which nearly all students have some familiarity. In all regards an attempt has been made to be guided by teaching considerations and by the requirements of a sound sociological orientation.

LUKE EBERSOLE

Contents

x *Contents*

Introduction

CHAPTER ONE

An Approach to American Society

Society as a condition exists when an aggregation of individuals is bound together by a system of relationships, that is, by organized mutual responsiveness. A society is the largest territorial group in which this condition exists. Thus society within human groups involves a complex web of social relationships.

The complexity of American society is evident. More than 150 million people are involved in its "web of social relationships." These people are distributed over a vast territory. In some places millions live together within a relatively small area; in other places the population is widely and thinly scattered. The people are of many kinds: young, old, white, black, yellow, rich, poor, neither rich nor poor, Catholic, Jewish, Protestant, laborers, white-collar workers, professionals, Republicans, Socialists, and Democrats. They are of many nationality backgrounds. They live in the country, in cities, and in suburbs. They engage in myriad activities associated with work, play, family, religion, education, and government. Some activities are similar and some are wholly different. Some of the customs practiced are alike; others are quite unlike. Ideas, beliefs, and values are of all varieties and shades.

Yet despite this complexity, which we have merely begun to describe, social life goes on with regularity and order. The man who drives to work in the morning expects that other people will drive on the right side of the street. He expects that when he arrives at his place of work there will be other people there to perform their usual duties. Parents who send their children to school expect that teachers will teach them certain knowledge, skills, and attitudes. The farmer who goes twenty miles to town expects merchants to give him the things he needs in exchange for money. The family that goes to church expects the service to be conducted in an accustomed manner. Examples of this sort could be given indefinitely, but the point is that social behavior is not haphazard and independent. It is, rather, interdependent and ordered. Human beings do not live alone. They are involved in an intricate web of social relations. They are mutually aware of each other, and their behavior is modified and regulated accordingly. Moreover, as these relations continue they become established in rather definite patterns.

Viewed in this way American society, or any other society, may be seen as a social system. Within the social system there is disorder as well as order, irregularity as well as regularity, but there must be a greater degree of order than disorder if a society is to function. In pursuing their interests human beings take account of one another's actions in innumerable ways. They form an endless number of small and large groups. The relationships of individuals with individuals, of individuals with groups, and of groups with groups are regulated by mutual expectations. Social interaction is ordered by customary, moral, legal, and traditional rules. Above the rules as they are actually observed are ideal standards for social relations which are only approximated in practice. Within the larger groups are smaller groups and still smaller groups. Within the larger beliefs and traditions are the detailed customs, practices, and expectations by which behavior is regulated. In brief, society is elaborately organized. Although to a large degree the groups, the rules, the ideals, and the patterns of relations emerge without deliberate planning, they nonetheless provide an effective organization for social living.

For our purposes it is important to observe that the patterned relations which give order to society are continuous. The family system within the larger social system is not created new in each generation; it is ongoing from generation to generation. Each new husband is not faced with the necessity of deciding whether he will be housekeeper or whether he will be breadwinner. The pattern of expectations is transmitted to husbands ready-made. Similarly, economic organization is not made brand-new in each decade or in each century. There are many economic matters which require almost no decision because the patterns are established. This is by way of indicating that social organization persists indefinitely. The membership of a society is always being replaced, but the organization of society continues.

Although the organization of society is persisting and continuous, it is also constantly changing. Expectations concerning the behavior of women are not the same as they were one hundred years ago even though social organization has continued without interruption. Likewise the patterns of relations in almost every area of society have been altered. Some changes are so slow and subtle as to be practically imperceptible; other changes are painfully perceptible.

Both the continuing and the changing nature of society are of particular significance in the study of American society. In many respects the American social system is similar to what it was a century or more ago, but in many important respects it has undergone remarkable change. In this book we are guided both by continuity and by change. American society is to be understood in terms of what it has been, how it has changed, and what it is now.

It would, of course, be impossible in a medium-size textbook to describe and analyze American society in detail. Nor is this the intent. It is our purpose rather to characterize the major components of our society and to indicate the manner of their functioning. In the perspective of continuity and change we shall at many points turn to the past in order better to understand the present.

Our first inquiry has to do with population. People constitute the medium of society. The population of a society is more than a mere agglomeration of individuals. It is at the same time a diversity and a unity. It is made up of people having unlike and like, contrasting and common, characteristics. Further, the nature of a social population is always undergoing modification. The characteristics of the people, size and density of population, and trends in growth are alterable. Population characteristics and changes help to determine the nature of a society, and the nature of a society helps to bring about population changes. In the study of American society it is therefore necessary to give attention to population. We shall describe and analyze the sources, backgrounds, composition, growth, distribution, and other characteristics of the population of the United States.

We turn second to the community aspect of American society. Communities are basic systems within the larger social system. American communities are not all-inclusive (the social relations of a person are not all within his community) and they are not self-contained (they are not independent of other communities). The web of social relations extends beyond any particular community, and communities are dependent and interdependent. Still, the great majority of relations directly involving an individual are found within his community. Within communities are found the multiplicity of groups through which needs and interests are provided for. Within communities behavior is regulated and status is given. Moreover, although communities are not replicas of each other, their groups, patterns of relations, and forms of regulation are often markedly similar. We shall identify and describe various types of communities and observe similarities and differences among them.

Social classes constitute the third major component of the American social system which we shall consider. Social classes may not at first appear to be so concrete as communities because they are not territorially defined. They are, however, real and important social units. Whereas the area of community influence can be delimited geographically, class lines cut horizontally across communities and across society as a whole. Thus social populations may be regarded as stratified or divided into levels or layers. The stratification system functions as part of the organization of society by which relationships are defined, roles and responsibilities assigned, and behavior regulated. We shall direct attention to the functioning of the American system of social stratification and to the movement of people from one class to another.

Finally, we turn to social institutions. The institutional structure is a primary factor in imposing form and order on the activities and relationships of a society. The functioning of most societies seems to require family life, economic activity, government, education, and religion. There are other kinds of activity but these are basic. How these activities are carried on is controlled by systems of values and norms (standards, rules, and expected ways of behaving). By means of the value-norm structure responsibilities, roles, statuses, rights, privileges, and expected behaviors are defined. Not all action is institutionally regulated. But actions that appear to be related to the continuing fulfillment of the functional needs of a society are thus regulated. We shall deal with the development and the present structure of family, economic, government, education, and religious institutions in American society.

Two further points should perhaps be made concerning the nature of society and its organization. First, the organization of a society is an integrated whole. We shall look at the parts separately —social population, communities, classes, and institutions. But in operation they function together as a vast, complex, and intricate system. Second, the social system of a society is never completely integrated. Some societies are more highly integrated than others. But complexity and change seem to preclude the possibility of complete integration. American society is notably complex and changing.

SELECTED REFERENCES

Bennett, John W., and Melvin M. Tumin: *Social Life*, New York, Knopf, 1948.

Davis, Kingsley: *Human Society*, New York, Macmillan, 1949.

Green, Arnold W.: *Sociology*, New York, McGraw-Hill, 1952.

Linton, Ralph: *The Study of Man*, New York, Appleton-Century, 1936.

MacIver, R. M., and Charles H. Page: *Society*, New York, Rinehart, 1949.

Ogburn, William F., and Meyer F. Nimkoff: *Sociology*, New York, Houghton Mifflin, 1950.

Williams, Robin M., Jr.: *American Society*, New York, Knopf, 1951.

Wilson, Logan, and William L. Kolb: *Sociological Analysis*, New York, Harcourt, Brace, 1949.

PART ONE: People

CHAPTER TWO

Population Origins

Throughout the history of the United States, the population of this country has been characterized by rapid growth and by heterogeneity. Both characteristics were in evidence from the beginning. In 1650 the total population of the colonies, not counting the Indians, was about 52,000. Fifty years later this number had increased to 275,000; and by 1750 the population of the colonies was more than 1,000,000. When the first census was taken, in 1790, a total population of 3,929,000 was reported.

The diversity of the national origins of the inhabitants of the American colonies is well recognized. There were English, Scotch, Irish, Germans, Dutch, French, Welsh, Swedes, Finns, and a variety of others. From many nations came many languages, many skills, many customs, and many beliefs. But the heterogeneity of the early settlers did not derive solely from national origins. It was a diversity born of many and mixed motives for leaving the Old World to come to the New. The colonists included those who were seeking economic opportunity, adventurers, fugitives from religious oppression, military deserters, criminals, debtors, and bond laborers. Thus, although life on the new continent may have done much to minimize the distinctions, there were representatives of practically all social classes. This disparity of class origins must be held in mind during the following survey of the more important nationality groups which contributed to the colonial population.

NATIONAL ORIGINS OF THE POPULATION

The leading nationality groups in colonial America were the English, Dutch, Germans, Scotch-Irish, and French, with the English far outnumbering all others.

English

The onset of the flow of Englishmen to the North American Continent was marked by the formation of two companies in the year 1606. These companies, having charters from James I, were the London Company and the Plymouth Company. The London Company was granted the right to colonize and trade in the region between the thirty-fourth and the forty-first parallels. The Plymouth Company was granted the same rights between the thirty-eighth and the forty-fifth parallels. In the overlapping area between the thirty-eighth and the forty-first parallels, neither company was to establish a settlement within one hundred miles of the other. As business enterprises both companies were unsuccessful and gave up their charters, but they did play a part in opening the way for colonization.

The mood of the first London Company adventurers was one of romance and great expectation. Virginia, they believed, would be a land of easy wealth. In May, 1607, they founded the first permanent English settlement in America at Jamestown. The undue optimism was short-lived. The promised gold and jewels did not materialize. Although Virginia in the summer appeared to be a dreamland of beauty, it was soon discovered that this was not a land to be exploited to gain quick wealth; it was a land to be developed by hard work.

After the initial disillusionment the Virginia colony set itself to the necessary task of making the most of the resources discovered. More than a decade of painfully severe struggle followed. By 1616 some of the first arrivals, having completed the terms of service to which they were committed, began to acquire their own land, and renewed vitality was engendered. In 1616–1617 a policy was adopted by which organized groups of Englishmen who agreed to settle servants were granted definite tracts of land. Within the limits of its means the Company continued to assist migrants. In spite of the efforts of the Company, the Indians, disease, and hunger took a heavy toll. In 1624 the Virginia Company (the reorganized London Company) was dissolved, and Virginia became the first royal province in America.

At the same time that the London Company was struggling to settle Virginia, the Plymouth Company was trying its hand in New England. Almost immediately a failure, the Plymouth Company was abandoned in 1608 and in 1620 was reorganized as the Council of New England. No colonies were founded by the Council, but in the same year that it was organized a shipload of religious separatists landed on the *Mayflower* to establish the first permanent settlement in New England at Plymouth. In time the Plymouth Colony was incorporated in the Massachusetts Bay Colony.

It was with the founding of the Massachusetts Bay Company in 1630 that colonization in New England began on a significant scale. After the crowning of Charles I in 1625, prospects for the Puritans in England were not pleasant; and in 1630 a large migration began. In that year about one thousand colonists arrived. It is estimated that during the next decade approximately twenty thousand persons crossed the Atlantic to join the Massachusetts colony. The rapidly growing population of this colony soon overflowed into the regions which became Rhode Island, New Hampshire, and Connecticut. The process of geographical expansion was encouraged by the exclusiveness of the Massachusetts colony. Although they themselves had taken flight from persecution, the Puritans were not inclined to welcome Baptists, Quakers, and other rebels against tradition and orthodoxy.

In addition to those of Virginia and New England, the colonizing enterprises in Maryland and Pennsylvania should be mentioned. In 1632 Sir Cecilius Calvert received a grant of land which had been cut out for his father, Lord Baltimore. The second Lord

Baltimore was interested in providing a refuge for Catholics in the new colony of Maryland. The first group landed in 1634 and founded St. Marys City. The growth of the Maryland colony was slow because few Catholics migrated and because Protestants preferred Protestant colonies. In 1681 William Penn started his "holy experiment" in Pennsylvania. Backed by wealthy Quakers, this turned out to be one of the most successful and prosperous colonies.

Mainly from the settlements here named, English colonization expanded until the thirteen colonies under English control were formed. Although many nationality groups were represented in the population of colonial America during the first seventy-five years of its history, the dominance of the English was decided. Until 1680 at least nine-tenths of the colonists were English.

Dutch

While the English were taking possession of Virginia and New England, the Dutch were moving into the central region between these colonies. In 1621 New Netherlands was organized by the Dutch West India Company. A few years later the first settlers came to Manhattan Island to make New Amsterdam the center of Dutch expansion in America. Dutch jurisdiction over the country around the Hudson and Delaware Rivers was relatively brief. The gap in English control was closed in 1664 when, during a war with Holland, a fleet was sent over to take possession of all Dutch territory. Probably at the time of this capitulation to the English, the population of New Netherlands was not in excess of eight thousand.

Dutch authority was lost, but the cultural influence remained. The language, the architecture, the cleanliness of housewives, the methods of farming—these survived for generations. Historians have made frequent reference to the clannishness of the Dutch and to the persistence of their customs. But if the Dutch hinterland was imbued with a degree of provincialism, the same cannot be said of New Amsterdam. Very early the cosmopolitan character of this community seemed to foretell the type of city that it was to become. Swedes, Finns, French, Portuguese Jews, Scots, Spanish traders, Norwegians, Danes, Bohemians, Negroes, Poles, Germans, Italians, and English were numbered among its residents along with the Dutch. In all, eighteen languages were spoken in New Amsterdam.

German

After the beginning of the eighteenth century two groups of immigrants gained and held the center of the stage until the end of the colonial period. They were the Germans and the Scotch-Irish. Although there had been a few small German settlements in America prior to the turn of the century, it was not until then that German immigration began in earnest. And in earnest they were, for while the hardships of moving to a distant continent were formidable, they seemed less fearsome than the perils of staying at home.

During and following the Thirty Years' War Germany was a seething center of political, economic, and religious unrest. In the Palatinate, from which most of the immigrants came, life was especially oppressive. As a result of the Protestant Reformation loyalty to a single church was a thing of the past, and with each change of rulers the people were expected to shift their religious loyalties. The rise of a multitude of pietistic and mystical sects was greeted with intolerance and persecution. An attempt was made to force a mass return to Catholicism. Meanwhile ship companies were seductively seeking immigrant cargo. The rising trend was further promoted by the advertisements of William Penn and others who were urging migration. The culminating decision was to seek relief in America, and the exodus from Germany began.

In 1683 Francis Daniel Pastorius brought thirteen German families to Pennsylvania. Germantown, now a part of Philadelphia, was established as the first permanent German settlement in this country and became the chief point of entry and distribution of German immigrants throughout the colonial period. They quickly spread into the regions of eastern and southern Pennsylvania and westward to the valley of the Susquehanna, practicing their careful and productive methods of farming wherever they went. By 1766 Benjamin Franklin estimated that the Germans constituted one-third of the Pennsylvania population. The German overflow from Pennsylvania moved south through the Shenandoah Valley of Virginia into North Carolina and even to Georgia. Almost all the Germans of the Shenandoah Valley can trace their ancestry to these eighteenth-century forebears, since few of the later German immigrants reached this section.

German attempts to locate in colonial New England were negligible. The German influx in New York, however, was of considerable consequence. The party of three thousand Germans who came to New York in 1710 was probably the largest group of immigrants to arrive at one time during the whole colonial period. Maryland did not receive a significant German contingent until after 1725. Baltimore acquired a German element, as did western Maryland, where the overflow from Pennsylvania was shared.

Although the Germans were best known for their skilled and intensive cultivation of the soil, there were many artisans among them. Everywhere they earned the reputation of being a thrifty and industrious people. Nevertheless they were not universally liked. They were accused of being clannish, opposed to education, and unwilling to participate in public affairs. It is probable that in part these accusations were valid and in part they did an injustice. Like other people, the Germans were not altogether good and not altogether bad, nor were they all cut to the same pattern. Even Benjamin Franklin, who seems to have reserved a special distaste for the Germans and who said that "those who come to us are the most stupid of their own nation," later admitted that they were "a people who brought with them the greatest of all wealth—industry and integrity, and characters that have been superpoised and developed by years of persecution." Certainly the reluctance of the Germans to give up their native language was a factor which helped to set them apart from the English-speaking colonists. Also it is true that a contempt for education existed among some of them; on the other hand, notable contributions to the dissemination of knowledge were made by German printing and publishing interests. It is likely that to some extent the charge of nonparticipation in public affairs was stimulated by the refusal of numerous Germans to take part in the American Revolution because of conscientious objections to fighting. On this matter the Germans were clearly divided. The members of the various religious sects were generally pacifistic, whereas the members of the established Lutheran and Reformed Churches had no scruples against war. One group of Germans who ultimately contributed to the population of the United States were soldiers by profession. These were the German mercenaries who fought for the British, of whom it is estimated that twelve thousand stayed in the United States after the American Revolution.

Scotch-Irish

The second great wave of eighteenth-century immigration brought the Scotch-Irish. They were so called because they came to America from Ulster, to which place they had moved from Scotland about one hundred years earlier. The Scottish Presbyterians were invited to migrate to Ulster during the period when James I was attempting to make a Protestant country of Catholic Ireland. After a stay of about a century the once-favored Scottish Presbyterians found themselves in most unfavorable circumstances in Ireland. Now it was the Presbyterians who were being persecuted by the Episcopalian authorities seeking to achieve uniformity of religious worship. At the same time the wool industry in Ireland was practically destroyed by laws passed by the British-controlled Irish Parliament. It is difficult to discover the relative importance of the causes of emigration, but it is the judgment of a number of scholars that the economic factor was more important than the religious factor in this case.

There were some Ulster Catholics, natives of Ireland, among the emigrants, but by far the greater number were of the less native Scotch-Irish. It is reported that 4,200 set sail for American shores in 1718, and that after 1740 they were leaving Ireland at the rate of 12,000 a year. Altogether the Scotch-Irish added between 150,000 and 200,000 to the colonial population before 1776. They outnumbered all others except, of course, the English, who were in a class by themselves.

The Scotch-Irish landed at ports up and down the Atlantic Coast, but since the land along the coast was already well occupied, they pushed into the interior. Their reception by the Puritans of Massachusetts was extremely cool, and therefore Maine, New Hampshire, Vermont, and western Massachusetts became their places of settlement in New England. They forged into the foothill regions of Virginia and the Carolinas and, driven by what would appear to be a Calvinistic craving for the difficult, set themselves to the conquest of the unvanquished regions of Ohio, Kentucky, and Tennessee. The chief stronghold of the Scotch-Irish, however, was Pennsylvania with its abundance of land, its attractive climate, and its liberal citizenship laws. By the time of the Revolution it was supposed that they constituted one-third of the total population of Pennsylvania. They moved north along the Delaware River and west to the Susquehanna and Cumberland Valleys. By 1776 the Scotch-Irish were well established in the American colonies. They were distributed in some 500 communities, of which there were about 70 in New England; 40 to 50 in New York; 50 to 60 in New Jersey; more than 130 in Pennsylvania and Delaware; more than 100 in Virginia, Maryland, and Tennessee; about 50 in North Carolina; and about 70 in South Carolina and Georgia.

Of the various contributions to American culture made by the Scotch-Irish, their introduction of Presbyterianism was one of the most outstanding. Wherever they went they built Presbyterian churches and preached the theology and ethics of Calvinism. In many ways their communities were church-centered. It is worthy of note that in contrast to the many poorly educated ministers of the day, the Presbyterian clergy were distinguished by their erudition. The religion of Calvin was not merely something to be experienced; it had to be learned. The emphasis on education resulted in the establishment of schools as well as churches. A

great number of the Scotch-Irish achieved prominence in a variety
of fields including the ministry, law, journalism, and politics.
The fighting Scotch-Irish played a leading role in frontier skir-
mishes with the Indians, as they did also in the American Revolution, which many of them entered with a deep hatred of the English.

French

In comparison to other groups, the number of French in colonial
America was small, but in terms of influence they are not to be
forgotten. As early as the Dutch settlement of New Netherlands,
French Huguenots were to be found in its diverse population.
Later, New Rochelle, widely known for its schools, became the
leading center of French culture in New York and was considered
an excellent place to learn the language and manners of the French.
The migration of French Huguenots was speeded after 1685,
when the toleration of Protestants in France was brought to an
end by the revocation of the Edict of Nantes. Within two years
after this event about 150 Huguenot families came to New England, where they located in spite of the absence of an enthusiastic
welcome. These first Frenchmen and those who followed them
to New England were rapidly assimilated and soon were lost in
the English population. It is difficult to evaluate the influence of
the French in Pennsylvania because many of them came after living for a time in Germany or Holland, where some of their French
characteristics and even their French names had been lost. The
Huguenots were brought to Virginia to direct the production of
wine, to introduce silk culture, and to experiment with the cultivation of rice, but instead they quickly became successful growers
of tobacco. The greatest number of French Huguenots settled in
South Carolina. Here they became prosperous planters of rice,
indigo, and cotton. They built homes displaying refined tastes,
maintained private schools, and frequently became moneylenders
to their English neighbors. As elsewhere, the assimilation of the
French in South Carolina was rapid, so that by 1776 the process
was practically complete.

The French Huguenots did not come to the colonies destitute and dispossessed. If some of them were poor, their poverty was temporary. As a thrifty, progressive, and enlightened people, they were quick to recreate the prosperity, the comforts, and the refinements to which they had been accustomed. In New Orleans the children of the wealthy had French dancing masters, and French operas were being produced before the end of the eighteenth century. While the entire Huguenot immigration probably did not exceed fifteen thousand, their contribution to colonial culture was quite out of proportion to their numbers. It has been estimated that they contributed about eight times as many outstanding leaders as might have been expected in view of their numbers.

There were some Catholics among the French immigrants, but they were relatively few. Little trading-post settlements of French Catholics were established in the old Northwest and in the valley of the Mississippi. The Acadians of *Evangeline* fame were deported from Nova Scotia in 1755. Many of the Acadians found their way into Louisiana, while others were scattered throughout the English colonies along the coast.

An exhaustive treatment of the origins of the population of the United States would include Swedes, Welsh, Spanish, and others, in addition to the groups already discussed. However, since they made up such a very small percentage of the colonial population, we shall consider it sufficient for our purposes to call attention to the fact that there were immigrants from other nations.

CLASS ORIGINS OF THE POPULATION

It is a cherished tradition among families in some parts of the country that their forebears were originally members of a transplanted aristocracy. This belief has been especially widespread with regard to the first citizens of Virginia. The truth of the matter is that one seeks in vain to find many representatives of the old aristocracies of Europe among the New World settlers. A few families of noble blood fled to Virginia after the execution of

Charles I rather than live under the rule of Cromwell, but the tales that are told of a general royalist exodus are entirely mythical. Virginia did produce an aristocracy, but most of the aristocrats were descendants of merchants, retired sea captains, and plantation owners whose wealth was newly acquired.

Before coming to this country most of the colonists belonged to the middle and lower classes. Although we could turn to any region to find examples of middle-class membership, we shall consider the case of New England because of the rather clearly defined upper-middle-class and lower-middle-class groups found there. The Puritans proper had been of the upper middle class in England. Their leaders were of the wealthier commercial groups; some of them were involved in the high finance of their nation; some had commercial interests in the colonies; they were successful men. The separatists, on the other hand, were of the lower middle class. They were poorer; they were little shop owners and tradesmen. Whatever else the Puritans may have contributed, it is interesting to speculate about how much democratic spirit there would have been in the new nation if the matter had been left to the Puritans. Unlike the separatists, the Puritans did not believe in religious freedom for all groups within their jurisdiction. Unlike the separatists, they believed that some men are born to rule and that others are born to be ruled.

Finding representatives of the lower social classes among the first settlers is not a difficult task. The indentured servants are most easily identified. It was a common practice for persons without funds for the voyage to America to sign a contract agreeing to work as virtual slaves for a period of from three to seven years in order to pay their transportation. Such an agreement was entered into by many poor but respectable persons. Not all the indentured servants, however, came of their own free will. Women, children, and able-bodied men were frequently kidnaped and sent to the colonies to be sold into servitude. Likewise, the policy of transporting criminals to work in the colonies swelled the number of indentured servants. It is estimated that the number of criminals sent to America from England reached fifty thousand. To be sure, the only offenses of which some of these criminals were guilty were those of indebtedness and extreme poverty.

Indentured servants of all varieties, the criminal and the non-criminal, those who came voluntarily and those who came under compulsion, were brought from England and from the other countries of Europe as well. Upon receiving their freedom indentured servants could take their place in society without being stigmatized. Usually they were given a sum of money and granted the rights of citizenship. Most of them became worthy members of their communities, and a few climbed to positions of outstanding leadership.

The problem of the Negro slave had its beginning very early in colonial history. In 1619 twenty Negroes were landed from a Dutch vessel at Jamestown, Virginia. They were bought by white settlers who made indentured servants of them. In time some Negroes achieved their freedom while others were made permanent slaves. At the time of the first census, in 1790, there were 757,000 Negroes in the United States, about 92 per cent of whom were slaves.

ASSIMILATION

It has been noted that the population of this country was heterogeneous from the start; even so, over against this fact must be placed another which was of major significance in controlling the process of assimilation within the colonies. It must be remembered that the English greatly outnumbered all other nationalities. There is little agreement about the exact percentage of each nationality, but the general proportions are fairly well known. Based on a study of surnames, the census volume *A Century of Population Growth* reports the percentage composition for nationality groups in the white population at the end of the colonial period as follows: English, 82.1 per cent; Scottish, 7.0 per cent; Irish, 1.9 per cent; German, 5.6 per cent; Dutch, 2.5 per cent; and all other groups, 0.9 per cent. The primacy of the English people was cultural as well as numerical. Other nationalities contributed to and influenced cultural developments in the colonies, but the basis of social, economic, and political life was essentially English. It has been observed that it was probably because the English were sufficiently preeminent quickly to reduce other elements to their type that assimilation was so easy, quick, and complete.

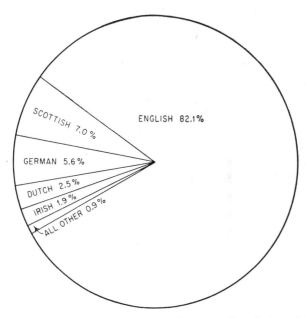

Figure 1. Estimate of National Origins of the White Population of the United States around 1790.

There was only slight interest in the regulation of immigration. The concern, of course, was not that there would be too many immigrants; but the colonies were not altogether happy to be made a depository for the paupers and criminals of Europe. From all indications the fear of economic competition, which appeared so frequently in later centuries, was not present at this time. Generally the attitude was one of encouraging as many as could to come to the colonies.

Doubtless there is a good deal of romanticism in the following lines from the *Letters of An American Farmer* by Hector St. John de Crèvecoeur; nevertheless, they tell something about the process of assimilation as it was going on in America in the seventeenth and eighteenth centuries: [1]

"The rich stay in Europe, it is only the middling and the poor that emigrate. . . . Every thing tended to regenerate them; new laws, a new mode of living, a new social system; here they are become men: in Europe they were so many useless plants, wanting vegetable mould, and refreshing showers; they withered and were mowed down by want, hunger, and war: but now by the power of transplantation, like all other plants, they have taken root and flourished! Formerly they were not numbered in any civil list of their country, except in those of the poor; here they rank as citizens."

SUMMARY

From the beginning the population of this country was characterized by rapid growth and by heterogeneity. Colonial Americans were of diverse national and class origins. The English constituted by far the largest single group. Among the other important groups were the Scotch-Irish, Germans, Dutch, and French. Each group brought rather distinctive cultural characteristics. There were representatives of various social classes among the colonists, particularly the middle and lower classes. Representatives of the old aristocracies of Europe were very few. Assimilation proceeded rapidly. Because the English made up such a large proportion of the population, the cultural base was essentially English. There was very little concern about controlling immigration. As many as could were encouraged to come.

SELECTED REFERENCES

Adams, James Truslow: *The American*, New York, Scribner, 1943.
Davie, Maurice R.: *World Immigration*, New York, Macmillan, 1936.
Fairchild, H. P.: *Immigration*, New York, Macmillan, 1928.

[1] Quoted in V. L. Parrington, *The Colonial Mind, 1620–1800*, New York, Harcourt, Brace, 1927, vol. 1, pp. 142, 143.

Hansen, Marcus Lee: *The Atlantic Migration, 1607–1860*, Cambridge, Mass., Harvard University Press, 1940.

Parrington, V. L.: *The Colonial Mind, 1620–1800*, New York, Harcourt, Brace, 1927.

Ross, Edward A.: *The Old World in the New*, New York, Century, 1914.

Wittke, Carl: *We Who Built America*, New York, Prentice-Hall, 1939.

CHAPTER THREE

Immigrant Americans

In the preceding chapter an account was given of the settlement of colonial America. Those who made their arrival before the American Revolution are usually referred to as *colonists*. Those who came after the founding of the nation are referred to as *immigrants*.

In the present chapter we shall trace the immigration movement from the beginning of the national period down to the middle of the present century. During this period approximately 40 million immigrants entered the United States. Of this number about 85 per cent came from Europe, about 11 per cent from other American countries, about 3 per cent from Asia, and the remaining 2 per cent from other parts of the world. When the first official immigration count was made in 1820, immigration was proceeding at the rate of around 8,000 a year. From that date forward there was a steady increase until in six of the years in the peak decade between 1905 and 1914, immigration exceeded 1 million annually.

FROM 1783 TO 1830

Since no official record of persons arriving in the United States was kept until 1820, it becomes necessary to rely on estimates. It is estimated that 250,000 immigrants came here from the close of the Revolutionary War up to 1820. During the War of 1812 immigration fell off, but in the years after the war there was a significant increase. By 1830 immigration had reached more than 20,000 a year.

Immigration policy during this early period of our national history was not well defined. The interest of the Federal government was extremely slight, and practices varied from state to state. The states made some attempt to select immigrants on the basis of religious beliefs and physical, mental, moral, and economic fitness. It seems that there existed a fear of foreign influence in our politics. This was the case in 1798 when the Federal government passed the Alien Act. Prompted by the possibility of war with France, the law, which was to expire in two years, gave the President the power to deport aliens who were regarded as dangerous to the country. While this piece of legislation reveals something about the mood of the new government, it may hardly be called an immigration law. It is significant that when the Federal government did concern itself with immigration, the first law that it passed was not to restrict immigration, but rather to protect immigrants. In 1819 the United States Congress took cognizance of the overcrowding of ships and enacted a law which was primarily designed to better the conditions of transportation to this country. The same act provided for the recording of new arrivals.

Although immigration was not a live issue there was some feeling that it ought to be controlled. Foreigners were not considered to be as good citizens as the native-born. Thomas Jefferson questioned the wisdom of encouraging immigration from countries having monarchical governments. George Washington took a cautious view of unrestricted immigration. When John Quincy Adams was Secretary of State he declared that inasmuch as the government had never officially encouraged emigration from Europe, immigrants were not to look for favors, but if they became citizens they were to expect the same rights as all citizens.

In the main, immigration was approved and newcomers were well received. The need for increasing the population was recognized. In local communities more people strengthened the safety of life and property. Occupation of large land tracts added to the value of property. There was no scarcity of land, and there was work for everyone. The fact that assimilation was rapid further made it unlikely that many natives would become preoccupied with opposing immigration.

THE OLD IMMIGRATION: 1830 TO 1882

Around 1830 the lull in the flow of Europeans to America which followed the Revolution came to an end, and the great Atlantic migration began. Conditions in Europe and in the United States worked together to produce a massive movement of people. By 1854 immigration swelled to 427,833 for one year. After dropping to 72,183 in 1862, it again increased until in 1873 it reached 459,803, the record figure for the period from 1830 to 1882. Most of the immigrants came from northern and western Europe, the Irish and the Germans having the greatest numbers. The other principal northwestern European countries supplying immigrants were England, France, the Netherlands, Norway, and Sweden.

Despite the importance of the urge to secure religious freedom and of the desire to escape from political oppression, the hope of finding greater economic opportunity has always been a chief cause of migration. Indeed, throughout the history of the United States, the economic motivation for migration to this country has probably been of paramount importance. The record shows that, whatever the conditions in Europe and in other parts of the world, times of prosperity in America brought more immigrants, and times of depression brought fewer immigrants. Even when this country was not enjoying the heights of prosperity the economic motivation was active, for land speculators looking for prospects, industrialists rounding up cheap labor, and steamship agents soliciting passengers were tirelessly active in attracting the hopeful of Europe. Through them and from reports sent back by those who had already come, the United States gained the reputation of being the land of economic opportunity for all. Often the promised rewards were gained painfully slowly. Even so, because of the rapid expansion of industry and the exceptional agricultural possibilities, on the whole this country was able to live up to its reputation for some time.

It was good that fortune eventually smiled on many of the immigrants, for an Atlantic crossing was not a pleasurable experience. In his work, *The Atlantic Migration*, Marcus Hansen says

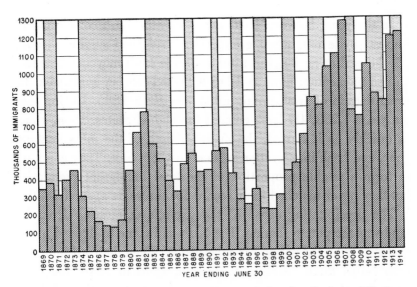

Figure 2. Immigration into the United States as Related to Periods of Business Expansion and Business Contraction: 1869–1914. Shaded areas represent periods of business contraction; white areas represent periods of business expansion. Between the Civil War and the First World War immigration tended to increase in periods of prosperity and to decline during depressions. (From A. Ross Eckler and Jack Zlotnick, "Immigration and the Labor Force," *The Annals*, vol. 262, March, 1949, p. 95.)

that many captains went to sea with only a collection of proverbs regarding the weather and a thermometer with which to locate the Gulf Stream. In many instances the voyage was a frightful ordeal. Overcrowding, limited sanitation facilities, and lack of food made for extreme hardship. The dreaded outbreaks of cholera, typhus, and smallpox took their toll. As late as 1870, six weeks was required for sailing vessels to make a crossing. With the coming of the steamship, conditions improved and the trip was reduced from six weeks to two weeks. In 1865 sailing vessels carried 96 per cent of the passengers who came to New York, while 4 per cent traveled by steamship. By 1873 the ratio was reversed. The shift from sail- to steam-driven ships did not cause migration, but it certainly facilitated it.

Irish

In the years between 1830 and 1882, the Irish constituted the largest single immigrant group. They had been coming through- out the earlier period, but after 1830 the Irish movement steadily gained momentum until in 1846 it turned into an avalanche. The great decade of Irish immigration was 1846–1855. During these ten years 1,288,300 Irish entered the United States. Then, almost as quickly as it started, the main strength of the movement was gone, and Irish immigration was cut to about half. They continued to form a sizable proportion of the total immigrant population, but they never matched their record for the years around 1850.

The precipitating cause of the gigantic emigration from Ire- land was the potato famine. The Irish had come to depend almost exclusively on the potato for subsistence. When their all-important crop failed three years in succession, 1846 to 1848, the entire agricultural population was threatened with extinction. All who could fled from the country. As a result of the potato famine the character of the Irish immigration changed. Whereas earlier nine- teenth-century immigrants were, in the main, persons with a reasonable degree of education and economic self-sufficiency, the mid-century Irish were untrained and usually without means. They were small tenant farmers, farm laborers, and other unskilled workers.

For many of the Irish the hardships of the voyage across the Atlantic were as nothing compared to the disappointing destiny which was their lot in America. As a people who had survived on little more than easily grown potatoes, they were ill fitted for life in the urban centers of this country. They had no money and few skills. The literature on Irish immigration is replete with accounts of the deplorable circumstances in which they lived. Some of the

Irish went into agriculture; however, most of them turned to manual labor in factories, in mines, and on the railroads. Many went into domestic and personal service. They tended to congregate in cities, where wage workers were in greatest demand and where they could be in close association with their countrymen. New York, Pennsylvania, Massachusetts, Illinois, Ohio, and New Jersey were the favorite first sanctuaries of the sons of Ireland.

Although for some time the Irish in America were doomed to a menial existence, their advance was rapid. Within a few generations they had turned over the pick and shovel to later immigrants. They moved from construction gangs into factories as workers, bosses, and employers. They gave up domestic and personal service in favor of saleswork, stenography, schoolteaching, clerking, bookkeeping, and business. Thousands achieved success in the professions, especially in law, politics, and the church.

There is rather general agreement that while the Irish underwent a remarkable transformation in this country, in several ways they remained basically unchanged. Whatever his station in life, the Irishman has been known for his extravagant use of words. He continued to be convivial, and his generosity and even improvidence did not quickly forsake him. His loyalty to family and friends remained. All in all, as has been said,[1] he "helped to modify the Puritan heritage of America. He has tempered its somber colors and more gloomy outlook with the joys of life."

Germans

As Irish immigration declined in the middle of the nineteenth century, German immigration increased. While the Irish outnumbered the Germans in the period from 1830 to 1882, for the nineteenth century as a whole more immigrants came to the United States from Germany than from any other country. After 1848 there was a movement from Germany which reached its maximum in 1854, when 215,000 Germans arrived here. Whereas in 1850 about 26 per cent of the foreign-born population was of German

[1] Carl F. Wittke, *We Who Built America*, New York, Prentice-Hall, 1939, p. 186.

origin, by 1860 the percentage had raised to 31. In appreciable numbers the Germans continued to enter America throughout the rest of the 1800's and during the early 1900's. Over 5,300,000 Germans came to the United States in the century before the First World War. In 1910 the census reported 8,282,618 persons in this country who were born in Germany or one or both of whose parents were born in Germany.

The causes of German immigration were both economic and political, but as was true in the case of the Irish, the economic factor was of primary importance. Many Germans were excellent farmers; others were thoroughly trained artisans. They thought they saw in the uncultivated soil and in the expanding industrialism of America a chance to utilize their skills to greater advantage. In the acquisition of this belief they were ably assisted by American agents and promoters in Germany, whose business it was to present the best possible picture of the promised land. Political motivation for leaving Germany was provided by the failure of the liberal uprising in 1848. The period after 1815 was one of reactionary control during which newly claimed freedoms were curtailed. Protest efforts were suppressed with an iron hand. In 1848 the liberals made an attempt at rebellion only to fail and to incur further oppression. Thereafter the United States received many political refugees from Germany.

The Germans who found their place in America were of many types: Prussians and Saxons, peasants and mechanics, Protestants and Catholics. Among the political refugees were men of means and of superior education, men prepared to give economic and intellectual leadership. It should not be concluded, however, that as a result of the unsuccessful revolution of 1848 most of the immigrants were either intellectuals or persons of wealth. Instead, most of the Germans were expectant, ambitious, and hard-working farmers and artisans in quest of new economic opportunities.

Of all the immigrant groups, the Germans came to be the most generally distributed throughout the country. Their influence is found in both urban and rural areas. In great numbers they moved into the Middle West, where they had much to do with opening the region to agriculture. They had little difficulty making their way economically. They made excellent farmers and farm laborers, and those who practiced their trades in the city found a ready demand for their skills. The patient, philosophic, industrious, and provident Germans presented a rather marked contrast to the Irish.

Much of the hostility toward immigrants was directed at the Irish, but the Germans did not escape criticism. Like the Germans who settled in America in the eighteenth century, the principal charge made against the nineteenth-century German immigrants was that of clannishness and unwillingness to become "Americanized." In part the accusations arose because the Germans brought with them a language, a literature, and customs of their own. Time is always required for any group to give up old customs and to accept new ones. This is true even when the people whose language and customs are foreign intermix readily with the native population; it is doubly true when there is a degree of segregation. When the Germans were scattered their assimilation was rapid; when their numbers were great enough to make it possible for them to use their own language and to maintain their own churches and schools, their assimilation proceeded more slowly. The inability of the older Americans to understand the Germans and their customs derived from a fundamental difference between the American expression of Puritanism and the Continental way of life. Along with hard work, the Germans were fond of dancing, art, drama, bowling, cards, beer, and Sunday picnics. The joys of living were enhanced by good food, drink, and music. To many of the natives the cultivation of such frivolous and "worldly" interests was anathema. Particularly in the Middle West, the conflict between the advocates of the Continental Sunday and of the Puritan Sabbath continued for long years. Some Germans appeared to invite disapproval. German intellectuals looked upon the Americans as a people with few refined tastes, and they delighted in shocking the Puritanical. It was known that many of the "Forty-eighters" lived in the hope of returning to Germany to carry through political reforms. Nor did the movement to create a German state in Texas, Missouri, Illinois, or Wisconsin win friends for the Germans.

Conflict between the Germans and the native Americans should not be overemphasized. That there was clannishness among the Germans is evidenced by the admonitions of German leaders like Carl Schurz urging them to be less clannish and to hold less strongly to their old customs. On the other hand, before the First World War a number of German groups voiced concern because Germans were too quickly losing their cultural identity in this country. On the whole, the assimilation of Germans proceeded rapidly. This is signally noteworthy since in many respects they represented a more advanced culture. Their cultural contributions were among the greatest.

Scandinavians

The Scandinavian immigration, which included Swedes, Norwegians, and Danes, was of little moment until after the Civil War. Small groups had entered the United States during the first half of the nineteenth century, but by 1850 there were only 18,000 of Scandinavian birth. The Norwegians, who came first, did not reach 5,000 a year until 1866. Five thousand a year was reached by the Swedes in 1868, and by the Danes in 1880. In 1873 the Scandinavians composed 7.7 per cent of the year's total immigration, and at the height of their influx, in 1882, they accounted for 13.4 per cent of the immigrants to this country. Between 1820 and the First World War the total Scandinavian immigration has been estimated at over 2 million.

Religious and political factors played only a minor part in causing emigration from the Scandinavian countries. There were no revolutions, and government to a fair degree was democratic. Again in this instance, the primary causes of emigration were economic. The limited amount of land available for cultivation could not easily support an expanding population. The climate was severe, and the growing season was short. A series of crop failures occurred between 1850 and the 1880's, and from 1866 to 1870 there was a general financial depression. Under these circumstances, agents extolling life in America found receptive and responsive listeners.

Most of the Scandinavian immigrants were of the lower economic classes. As a people accustomed to farming, they moved into the Northwest to participate in the agricultural conquest of the prairie. Although they were poor, and although not more than one in six was a skilled laborer, they held education in high regard and illiteracy was practically nonexistent among them. They were in no sense a burden to the country of their adoption. Not noted for spectacular achievement, they were a sturdy, thrifty, honest, and orderly people.

French, Dutch, and Others

Irish, German, and Scandinavian immigrants far outnumbered all others during the nineteenth century. There were, however, several smaller contingents of immigrants from other countries. The French were the largest of these smaller groups. Nearly 353,000 French immigrants came to the United States between 1820 and 1920. Most of the French immigrants were of the working class or professional men, and as such preferred life in the city. They placed their mark on American manners and customs and, especially in the port towns, established centers of French culture.

Other groups included the Dutch, Russian-Germans, Welsh, and Swiss. Dutch immigration did not quite equal French immigration. From 1820 to 1920 there were nearly 340,000 Dutch immigrants. The German-speaking immigrants who migrated to America from Russia were fundamentally German in culture in spite of long residence in Russia. The region between the Mississippi River and the Rocky Mountains became the home of many of the Russian-Germans. Most of the Welsh who came to this country engaged in farming or continued in their old occupation of mining. Pennsylvania received more of the Welsh than any other state. The

Swiss immigrants, whose culture was essentially German, founded communities in the Middle Western states and a few in the Far West and the Southwest.

Immigration Policy

Attitudes toward immigration during the period from 1830 to 1882 were varied. There were attempts to restrict immigration, and there were attempts to encourage its speed-up. There was opposition and also a great deal of indifference. Like the law passed in 1819, others passed in 1847, 1848, and 1855 were intended to improve conditions on passenger vessels. For example, by the Act of 1848, vessels carrying passengers were required to load an adequate supply of food, and a cooking range had to be provided for the use of steerage passengers. There was opposition to immigration on economic grounds, but the effectiveness of this opposition was insignificant because labor was not well organized and because industrialists were seeking cheap labor and labor that could be used to outmaneuver the unions. The fact that at times there existed an actual manpower shortage further weakened opposition based on economic reasons. This was true during the Civil War, when immigration declined. In part because President Lincoln wanted to increase the labor supply, an act was passed in 1864 establishing an Immigration Bureau in the Department of State. The law continued in effect until 1868, during which time immigration rose from over 193,000 in 1864 to nearly 316,000 in 1867.

Since authority to control immigration was not clearly defined, several states took matters into their own hands and enacted legislation. As would be expected, those states most affected took the initiative. Among these states were New York, Massachusetts, and California. The passage of laws by the various states produced one significant, though indirect, result. When the state laws were declared unconstitutional by the United States Supreme Court, responsibility for the regulation of immigration thereby was placed with the Federal government. As in the case of state laws, in seeking to secure the passage of Federal legislation the advocates of restriction were especially concerned about paupers, criminals, and other "undesirables" among the aliens. The policy of Federal regulation of immigration was initiated in 1875 with the passage of an act which excluded certain groups named as undesirables.

Of the groups that agitated against immigration, the one that attracted the most attention and the largest number of followers was the Native American Party, which became the Supreme Order of the Star-Spangled Banner or Know-Nothing Party. A combination of economic, political, and religious reasons was used to justify its activities. This movement is of particular interest in view of the recurrence from time to time of similar criticisms of foreigners. It illustrates the respectability with which prejudice can cloak itself. Founded in 1835, the Native American Party claimed by 1845 that it had 48,000 members in New York, 42,000 in Pennsylvania, 14,000 in Massachusetts, and 6,000 in other states. It was represented in Congress by six members from New York and two from Pennsylvania. When a national platform was adopted in 1845 the demand was made that none but native Americans be placed in public office. In 1850 the Supreme Order of the Star-Spangled Banner took up the cause. Candidates for membership in the order had to be descended from at least two generations of American ancestors; and no one could join the organization who was himself a Catholic, whose wife was a Catholic, or whose ancestors for two generations had been Catholics. When a member of the order was queried concerning the activities of the organization, the answer was "I know nothing," hence the byname "Know-Nothing Party."

Notwithstanding the original pose of taciturnity, the purposes of the Know-Nothing Party came to be widely known. It called for more stringent immigration laws, advocated the deportation of foreign paupers, demanded the repeal of all naturalization laws, opposed for public office persons who were not native Americans, and fought against every form of Catholic influence in the United States. From all indications it was the last objective, that of opposing Catholicism, which gave the movement its drive. In a predominantly Protestant country the erection of Catholic churches, schools, and convents gave rise to a deeply rooted set of suspicions, hates, and fears. The Irish Catholics bore the brunt of the attack. Nativists resorted to violence in their misguided endeavors to keep America from being corrupted by foreigners. Whatever they did, they did in the name of "our country, our whole country, and nothing but our country."

The Know-Nothing Party may have succeeded in intimidating some of the foreign-born, but it was wholly unsuccessful in securing the passage of any legislation. While we shall not turn again to the description of such organizations, it may be noted that later generations have produced similar groups of prejudiced zealots, among them the American Protective Association and the Ku Klux Klan. It is doubtful whether these had any more effect upon immigration policy than did the nativists.

Despite the agitation of small interested groups, it may be assumed that most of the citizens were not much concerned about immigration and its possible consequences. Indifference is not so easily reported as opposition and protest; still, it may be equally important in determining policy.

ORIENTAL IMMIGRATION

Since the designations *old immigration* and *new immigration* refer almost exclusively to the movement of Europeans to the United States, Oriental immigration must be treated separately. In many respects the influx from the Orient was a flow apart from the main stream of immigration.

Immigration on the West Coast of the United States was dominated first by the Chinese. By 1852 there were about 25,000 Chinese on the Pacific Coast, with the greatest concentration in California. Approximately 200,000 came in the years between 1850 and 1880. Nearly 40,000 arrived in the year 1882, when Chinese immigration reached its peak. Thereafter immigration from China declined sharply. In 1890 there were 107,488 Chinese immigrants in this country. By 1920 the number had dropped to 61,639, over half of whom were living on the West Coast.

Along with conditions in China, the chief causes of the sudden immigration of Chinese to the United States were the discovery of gold in California and the building of American railroads. News of gold brought some Oriental adventurers, but most of the immigrants were happy to be promised employment as gold-mining laborers. Railroad builders were quick to recognize the possibility of exploiting the Chinese as a cheap source of labor. Of the 10,000 men employed by the Central Pacific Railroad in 1869, nine-tenths were Chinese laborers. They were industrious and tractable and could be assigned to the most disagreeable tasks. Railroad builders asserted that without Chinese coolies the transcontinental railroads could not have been built.

It is interesting to note the American change of attitude toward the Chinese. At first the Chinese were welcomed because of their usefulness. Their customs and dress, although different and strange, were regarded with amusement or curiosity. Chinese traditions with their long history aroused some admiration. But these attitudes did not long prevail. Antagonism mounted swiftly. The underlying basis of opposition seems to have been economic. It was charged that Chinese laborers competed unfairly with American labor. The accusation was not entirely without basis. Some of the Chinese lived on wages of $30 or $35 a month and were able to put something aside as savings. That these wages seemed good to many Chinese and that the Chinese performed tasks that others were reluctant to accept made little difference. When the great period of railroad construction drew to a close, American laborers wanted no more competition from the Chinese. A number of additional factors came into play to lend support to the opposition. Cultural differences between the Orient and the Occident were pronounced, and the Chinese did not assimilate readily. Living in segregation, they came to be looked upon with suspicion. The weirdest sort of tales were circulated concerning their customs and ceremonies. Because of their racial characteristics and distinctive dress, their presence in American communities was conspicuous. In California anti-Negro feeling was strong, and persons originally from the South were inclined to place all dark-skinned people in one class. There is not much to be proud of in the record of American treatment of the Chinese. Every variety of ill was laid to their charge, and assurance of action against the Chinese was a standard political promise.

Treated as a local problem at first, Chinese immigration gained national attention in 1876 when a congressional committee was appointed to investigate. The result of the investigation was a treaty with China in 1880 which allowed the mutual exclusion of immigrants except teachers, students, merchants, and travelers. The treaty was followed by the passage in 1882 of a law which provided for the exclusion of Chinese laborers for a period of ten years. The law was reenacted and the time extended in 1892 and again in 1902. In 1904 the time limit was removed and Chinese exclusion became a permanent policy. It was not until 1943 that this legislation was repealed and an annual quota of 105 Chinese immigrants was established.

When Chinese immigration was cut off, the Japanese moved in to take their place. Japanese immigration was small before 1890, in which year the total number of Japanese in the United States was reported to be only 2,637. In the next ten years more than 27,000 came, and the total Japanese immigration for the decade from 1901 to 1910 exceeded 58,000.

As early as 1900 there was agitation for the extension of the exclusion law in order to prevent the Japanese from entering this country. The matter was dramatically given national publicity in 1906, when the San Francisco school board barred Japanese pupils from white schools. Although this action was rescinded, it led to the "gentleman's agreement," which became effective in 1908. The Japanese government promised to stop granting passports to laborers, except former residents of the United States or wives or children of such persons. The policy of Oriental exclusion was carried to completion in 1924. The general immigration act of that year provided that "aliens ineligible to citizenship" should be barred as immigrants.

THE NEW IMMIGRATION: 1882 TO 1917

After 1882 there was a significant shift in the source of the immigrant population of the United States. In the years before the 1880's about 95 per cent of the European immigrants to this country had come from the countries of northern and western Europe; by 1910 the proportion of European immigrants from the northern and western countries had dropped to about 20 per cent. By that time the volume of European immigration was from the countries of southern and eastern Europe. It is because of this change in the make-up of the immigrant population that the term *new immigration* has come to be used to distinguish this movement from the *old immigration* of northwestern Europeans.

A number of factors brought about the shift in the source of immigrants. Conditions in northern Europe were improving. The reduction of famine and of political and religious intolerance in Ireland and in Germany weakened the desire to emigrate from those countries. The industrialization of England, Germany, and other countries provided new opportunities for employment. On the other hand, in the countries of southern and eastern Europe there was a lag in agricultural, political, and social reforms. Industrialization proceeded slowly. Thus, as compared to opportunities offered in their own countries, southern Europeans had more to gain by migrating to the United States than did the northern Europeans.

There is another factor which helps to account for the increase in the movement of southern Europeans. During the first three-quarters of the nineteenth century transportation and communication between the United States and north European countries were much better than between the United States and southern Europe. The establishment of numerous steamship routes direct to Mediterranean ports provided the easy and cheap transportation without which mass migration would not have been possible. Once started, the movement gained momentum at a tremendous rate. As northern Europeans showed less inclination to migrate, steamship agents and American employers directed their efforts to stimulate immigration to another part of the continent.

It has sometimes been reasoned that changing conditions in the United States were an important factor in producing the new immigration trend. The period under consideration was one of unparalleled industrial development in this country. The demand for workers could not be supplied by the native population. It has been said, therefore, that south Europeans came because they were attracted by factories. It is true, of course, that the need for industrial workers provided the greatest attraction to those who were predisposed to migrate; but the inference that industrialization was of great importance in determining the character of immigration is open to question. It must be remembered that many north Europeans remained in their own countries not because of a distaste for industrial employment, but because of new opportunities for such employment at home. Moreover the Irish, who constituted a large segment of the old immigration, showed little interest in agriculture in this country. Then too, south Europeans could hardly have had a positive preference for work in factories since, like north Europeans, many of them were peasants without experience in industrial labor. It is probably nearer the truth to conclude that immigrants seized employment where they could find it. By the time the south Europeans arrived public lands suitable for agriculture had been taken up. The greatest opportunities for work were in industry; therefore in industry they worked.

Slavic Immigrants

Immigrants to the United States from the slavic countries of Europe included Russians, Ukrainians, Poles, Czechoslovaks, Yugoslavs, and Bulgarians. Statistics regarding slavic immigrants are complex and confusing and could add little to this brief discussion. The general outline will suffice. There was a wave of about 39,000 immigrants from Russia between 1870 and 1880, but it is impossible to know how many of these were ethnic Russians and how many were Ukrainians, Lithuanians, Latvians, Estonians, Finns, Germans, and others. A second rush of immigration came as a result of the revolution of 1909, and another followed the establishment of the Soviet regime after the First World War. Coupled with economic conditions, political and religious persecution was an important cause of emigration from Russia. The Russians located in greatest numbers in Pennsylvania, Connecticut, New Jersey, New York, and Ohio. The Ukrainians, known also as "Ruthenians" and as "Little Russians," began to arrive in significant numbers in the 1870's. They moved into the soft-coal and the hard-coal regions of Pennsylvania, to Philadelphia, to New York City and the industrial cities in its environs, and later to almost all large industrial centers. The great inflow of Poles, which started in the 1880's and was encouraged by Russian economic and political troubles between 1900 and 1910, reached its full volume in the fifteen years preceding the First World War. The Poles concentrated in industrial cities along the Great Lakes, in the mining and industrial centers of Pennsylvania, and on the Northeastern coast. A goodly number of Czechs came to this country in the two decades following 1848. The Slovaks began to come near the end of the nineteenth century. About half of the Slovaks in the United States live in Pennsylvania, where Pittsburgh is their center. There was a mass immigration of Yugoslavs after 1890. Although most of them had been farmers at home, the Yugoslavs turned to heavy industrial labor in the East and the Middle West. Most of the Bulgarian immigrants came during the first two decades of the present century. It should be noted that while the major migration from the Slavic countries occurred after 1882, there had been some immigrants from these countries during earlier periods.

East European Immigrants

Among the east European immigrants were the Latvians, Lithuanians, Estonians, Finns, Austrians, Hungarians, and Rumanians. The records of east European immigration are somewhat meaningless because of numerous changes in political control and because of the creation of new states after the First World War. Hungarians, who constituted a large segment of the immigration from this part of Europe, began to migrate to the United States after 1880. Their movement reached its peak in 1907, when 60,071 were admitted. Although they established some agricultural communities, the Hungarians, like other new immigrants, found it easier to make their way in the city as industrial laborers. The Magyar group of Hungarians especially gained a reputation for being thrifty, neat, and intelligent. Some of their number achieved success as tailors, small storekeepers, and restaurant proprietors. There was practically no Rumanian immigration to America before 1880. The Rumanians came in greatest numbers from 1900 to 1910 to take their places in mills, factories, and mines. Of the thousands of Lithuanians who came to the United States after 1880, the great majority live in big cities or work in the mines. Half of the Latvians in this country live in the four cities of New York, Boston, Philadelphia, and Baltimore.

South European Immigrants and Others

The immigration from southern Europe brought Italians, Greeks, Spanish, Portuguese, and Albanians. The Italian group was the largest. Between 1820 and 1930 over 4,628,000 Italians came to the United States, of which number over 3,500,000 arrived in the present century. The steady and swift flow of emigrants out of Italy after 1870 may be attributed to population pressure, heavy taxes, retarded agriculture, an oppressive system of land control, and insufficient industrialization. By the time of the First World War there were large groups of Italians in New York, Philadelphia, Chicago, Baltimore, Detroit, Omaha, and the textile centers of New England, as well as in agricultural communities all across the continent. Not all Italians, however, stayed in this country. Almost 1,216,000 Italians left the United States between 1908 and 1916.

In American cities the Italians gathered in colonies in which they perpetuated their own culture. There were Italian societies, Italian bakeries, Italian stores, Italian festivals, and Italian newspapers. Many of the immigrants had little direct contact with the culture of the new land to which they had come. Occupationally the first generation of Italians did about the same things that the Irish had done plus new menial work created by more industrialization. They worked on the railroads, in the mines, on construction gangs, as street cleaners, in the stockyards, in the brickyards, and in the steel mills. But like the Irish, their lowly position was not permanent. The second generation moved toward more skilled occupations. Most but not all of the expatriates of sunny Italy clung to the cities. As independent farmers and as farm laborers they became involved in raising berries, apples, peaches, grapes, cotton, sugar cane, and rice.

Attention should be called to the non-European immigrants from the Levant. Altogether over 100,000 Armenians, Arabs, Turks, and Syrians had migrated to the United States by 1920.

Selective Immigration Legislation

The only effect of immigration laws passed during the period from 1882 to 1917 was to make immigration more selective. There was some discussion of ways by which the volume of immigration might be restricted, but no legislative action was taken to achieve this end. In 1882 a selective immigration law was passed which is usually considered to be the first important general immigration legislation. The act barred the admission of idiots, lunatics, convicts, and persons likely to become public charges. The exclusion of Chinese laborers also came at this time. In 1885 the first contract-labor law was adopted. Its purpose was to protect American labor by preventing the importation of cheap foreign labor

under contract. Later paupers, polygamists, and persons suffering
from loathsome or contagious diseases were added to the classes
of aliens who could be barred from entering the country. All arriving aliens were required to undergo a medical inspection. In
time, the excludable classes came to include epileptics, insane persons, professional beggars, anarchists, feeble-minded persons,
alien children under sixteen unaccompanied by their parents, persons suffering defects that might affect their ability to earn a living, and those who admitted the commission of a crime involving
moral turpitude. In 1917 Congress passed a basic immigration
law that contained all previous grounds for exclusion plus two
additional ones. A literacy requirement was written into the statute,
and persons coming from a designated geographical zone were
excluded. This zone included India, Siam, Indochina, Afghanistan,
parts of Siberia, Iran, and Arabia; and the islands of Java, Suma-
tra, Ceylon, Borneo, New Guinea, Celebes, and other lesser groups.

FROM THE FIRST WORLD WAR TO 1950

After the First World War the era of almost unlimited immigration came to a close. The period that followed was characterized
by restriction and by stronger regulation of immigration.

Immigration Restriction

Not all the reasons given in favor of restriction were valid, but
they helped to give expression to a widespread feeling that the
United States could not and should not indefinitely absorb millions
of people from other countries. In the postwar period the usual
concern about employment competition from "outsiders" was
heightened. Would there be enough jobs to go around? Why admit
more immigrants when there is uncertainty about the employment
possibilities of those already here? Always the issue of unfair
competition from immigrants willing to work at low wages was
raised. Awareness of the presence of large numbers of new immigrants was increased by their concentration in cities. Late arrivals

from Europe were blamed for many of the ills of city life: crime, disease, dirt, physical deterioration, and poverty. High crime rates, especially, were held to be a result of immigration. Because southern Europeans did not assimilate so readily as northern Europeans, they were believed to be innately inferior to the earlier immigrants from the countries of northern Europe. Then too, participation in the First World War produced a fear of foreign ideologies and a distrust of foreign-born persons who might be a threat to American ideas and to American government. There was, among some, a desire to have as little as possible to do with persons of foreign birth, particularly those who had been wartime enemies.

Some of the criticisms of immigration were justified; others were only half true or wholly false. We cannot know what would have been the economic consequences, whether desirable or undesirable, of continuing the policy of nonrestriction. However much immigrants may have been involved in the maladies of cities, it is certain that undesirable conditions would have developed in rapidly growing American cities even if there had been no immigration. Available evidence seems to indicate that significant differences in crime rates disappear when rates for the foreign-born and their children are compared with rates for the native-born of comparable socioeconomic levels. The slower assimilation of southern Europeans is not to be explained in terms of innate inferiority. Over against the possibility of the introduction of ideas threatening to a free society must be considered the fact that many of the immigrants had fled to this country to find freedom. But whether true or false, the charges made against immigrants gave effective support to restrictive measures.

The first immigration law that had the effect of limiting the number of immigrants was passed in 1921. Earlier legislation had attempted to prevent the entrance of less desirable individuals, but it did not reduce the volume of immigration. The purpose of the 1921 law was to restrict the high flow of immigration after the First World War. A total annual quota of 357,803 was established for Europe, Africa, Australia, and a large part of Asia. The quota of any nationality was limited to 3 per cent of the number of foreign-born of that nationality resident in the United States in 1910. The act was temporary and expired in 1924.

In 1924 a new law was passed which limited total immigration from all countries except independent countries in the Western Hemisphere to 164,667 annually. This act carried provisions for immigration restriction which were to become effective in 1927. It also provided an interim formula for determining quotas until 1927. From 1925 to 1927 the number of immigrants from any country was limited to 2 per cent of the number of foreign-born of that nationality resident in the United States in 1890. The intent of the change from 1910 to 1890 as the base year for determining quotas is obvious. The new formula favored immigration from northern and western Europe, since southern and eastern Europeans did not come in greatest numbers until after 1890.

Because of various delays, the national-origins provisions of the immigration act of 1924 did not become effective until 1929. The maximum total immigration was fixed at approximately 153,700 per year. The quota of each nationality was determined on the basis of the national origins of the white population. The proportion of immigration from a particular country was to be the same as the proportion of the population of the United States having that national origin in 1920. Estimating the national origins of the population of the entire country was a difficult and thankless task. When provisional quotas were first submitted to Congress there were loud protests because of the "considerable element of uncertainty" in the classification. Those nationalities whose quotas were cut most were especially unhappy. A six-man board of experts worked for five years before their recommendations were finally accepted. There were some quota changes after 1929 because of shifts in political boundaries and because of the admission of groups that were barred at the time the law went into effect. The National Origins Law dealt with the practical problem of deciding how many immigrants should be admitted from each country, and in so doing it gave expression to the desire to preserve the culture of the United States by selecting as potential citizens those whose traditions, languages, and political systems were most like those of this country.

Quota Immigration

The National Origins Law was not notably successful in achieving the selection for which it was designed. Only about half the anticipated proportion of northern and western Europeans came to the United States. Although 79 per cent of the white population of this country was of northern and western European origin, only 41.9 per cent of the immigrants admitted between 1930 and 1949 came from that part of Europe. On the other hand, persons of southern and eastern European ancestry constituted 15.1 per cent of the white population of the United States in 1920, but 28.2 per cent of the immigrants between 1930 and 1949 came from southern and eastern Europe. Other quota countries had 0.3 per cent of the white population in 1920, but they contributed 3.3 per cent of the immigrants. Under the national-origins plan it might have been expected that nonquota countries would furnish 5.6 per cent of the immigrants. Actually, their proportion was 26.6 per cent between 1930 and 1949.

It is difficult to evaluate the effect of legislation passed in the 1920's on the volume of immigration. Even after the 1921 law total immigration rose to over 700,000 during a twelve-month period in 1923–1924. By 1933 total immigration was down to 23,000. Although without a doubt quota legislation was instrumental in bringing about this decline, there were other contributing influences. The most important of these forces was the economic depression of the 1930's which to some extent rendered restrictive legislation unnecessary. After 1930 quotas themselves only restricted immigration from countries having very small quotas, since the quotas of many other countries frequently were not filled.

At the same time that the degression began to lift in the United States, Fascism and Naziism were driving a number of Europeans out of their homelands. Quota immigration started to rise in 1934 and reached a peak in 1939. In the latter year and in 1940, almost all of the German quota was filled, as were also the quotas for Bulgaria, Danzig, Greece, Hungary, Rumania, and Spain. In 1939 quota immigration was over 62,000. During the Second World War quota immigration dropped to a low of 9,045 in 1943. In 1949 almost three-fourths of the annual quota of 153,929 was filled.

Nonquota Immigration

The Immigration Act of 1924 provided for certain classes of nonquota immigrants, but it was not expected at that time that nonquota immigration would be as great as it has been. Since 1924 nonquota immigration has nearly equaled quota immigration. More than one-fifth of the immigration from countries having quotas has been outside the quota limits. Most of the nonquota immigrants from quota countries were wives, husbands, or children of American citizens. Many men who had preceded their families brought their wives and children to this country in the late 1920's. After the Second World War war brides were brought to the United States as nonquota immigrants.

The countries of the Western Hemisphere have provided the chief source of nonquota immigration. When the first quota act was passed in 1921 only one year of residence in a country of the Western Hemisphere was required for quota exemption. In 1922 the required period of residence was increased to five years. The 1924 act provided that persons born in independent countries in the American continents should not come under quota restrictions. This does not leave Western Hemisphere immigration without controls. Excluding provisions and visa and head-tax requirements are maintained.

From nonquota countries Canadians and Mexicans have come in greatest numbers, the former exceeding the latter. There has always been an exchange of people between Canada and this country, more people entering than leaving the United States. For a number of years Canada furnished more immigrants to the United States than any other country. The 1930 census reported more than 1,200,000 Canadian-born persons living in this country. Canadian immigration dropped during the years of the depression, but it was not influenced by the Second World War to the same extent as quota immigration. Mexican immigration was affected by the depression to such a degree that more Mexicans left the United States than entered. The records show that since the Second World War Mexican immigration has averaged less than 8,000 per year, but it is believed that there are many illegal entries. There appears to be a general increase in immigration from the West Indies, Central America, and South America.

ASSIMILATION OF IMMIGRANTS

The new immigrants did not assimilate as readily as the old immigrants. The reasons for this situation are not difficult to find. In the first place, they came in greater numbers than the old immigrants. With one million new arrivals a year it was to be expected that assimilation problems would multiply. The urban concentration of these people intensified the difficulties. Those who came from the same country frequently lived together in one part of the city, where they perpetuated the language and the customs of of their homeland. To some extent this segregation was forced upon them. They had to live together because they were unwelcome in residential areas inhabited by the native-born. Much of the segregation, however, was voluntary. They lived together because they preferred to be with their relatives, friends, and countrymen. Under these circumstances the experience of living in a strange land was less painful. Language was another barrier to speedy assimilation. Eastern and southern Europeans brought with them a great variety of languages and dialects. Finally, the new immigrants brought with them a culture in many ways unlike that of this country. In this regard southeastern Europeans were at a

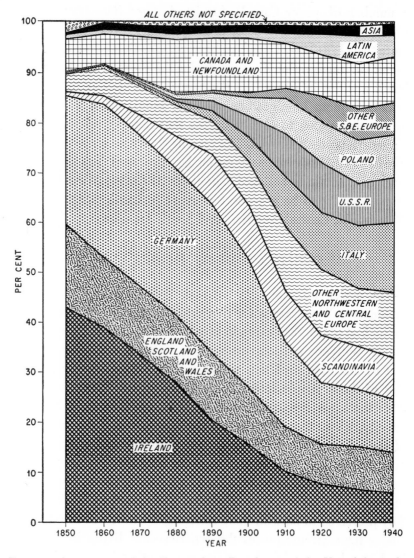

Figure 3. Composition of the Foreign-born Population of the United States by Country of Birth: 1850–1940. (From Clyde V. Kiser, "Cultural Pluralism," *The Annals*, vol. 262, March, 1949, p. 122.)

52

greater disadvantage than northwestern Europeans had been, for the culture of the old immigrants was not so different from that of the United States as was the culture of the new immigrants.

Despite the slower assimilation of new immigrants, today these groups, along with the descendants of old immigrants, have moved far in the direction of losing their identity as groups having separate cultures. In the last quarter of a century the process of assimilation has been relatively rapid. The marked reduction of immigration has been a most important factor in hastening the trend. Old World traits transplanted in a new setting were sustained by later arrivals who sought out their fellow countrymen in America for moral and economic support, and who, in turn, gave renewed strength to the customs of their native land. Then, almost abruptly, direct contact with the Old World through immigration diminished, and this source of culture renewal ran low. Sentiments associated with the past became weaker. Memories of the homeland grew dim in the minds of those who were young when they came here. Among the native-born children of immigrants there were no memories of the homeland and Old World sentiments were second hand. Old World patterns held little attraction for them. In the third generation preference for New World patterns is practically complete. Thus as the time since the beginning of immigration restriction grows longer, as the foreign-born live in this country more years, and as new generations are born, the process of assimilation is accelerated.

Assimilation is not, however, merely a result of the passing of time. Many factors have influenced the process. Public schools have played an extremely important part. Through schools the children of immigrants quickly come in contact with American culture. They not only acquired formal education; they were exposed to the values, attitudes, manners, customs, and activities of American communities. Through schools the new culture was soon placed in steady competition with the old. Children attempted to adopt new ways and often interpreted them to their parents. Although there sometimes was resistance to the breakdown of established customs, immigrant parents, in many instances, were willing and eager to learn.

The change from one culture to another was, of course, advanced by numerous influences which affected adults directly. Occupational associations usually provided the first regular contacts with native citizens and with their habits of living. Even among the most reluctant of the foreign population, in the course of earning a living there were inevitable adjustments which had to be made. As the foreign-born moved from place to place to work, and as opportunities for employment expanded, assimilation occurred more rapidly. To occupational contacts must be added the effects of participation in clubs, churches, recreation, and government. The development through these activities of interests in common with those of native Americans was a powerful assimilative force. The trend was furthered by economic prosperity and by the financial success of some immigrants. As incomes increased, standards of living changed. Imitation of the money-spending habits of Americans led to imitation in other ways. Higher incomes tended to produce participation in a greater number of activities. Even the institutions of immigrant communities sometimes fostered assimilation, for although the original purpose was to reproduce the culture of the past, the objective was never fully achieved. Old institutions were modified by the requirements of a new environment.

Intermarriage is both a cause and a measure of assimilation. When marriage occurs between persons having different nationality backgrounds, it may be taken as an indication that assimilation is in process. Such intermarriage is a cause of still further assimilation. In the United States, marriage outside their cultural groups was not uncommon among the children of European immigrants. In the third generation it is still more frequent. This is a most telling evidence of the development of greater cultural unity.

Assimilation in the United States is not complete. It is stayed by strong forces. Religion is one of the most important. In connection with religion the culture of the past has persisted. Use of the native language is cherished by some churches. Marriage outside the cultural group is often prevented, not by nationality differences, but by religious differences. Moreover, assimilation never has and does not now occur with equal rapidity among all groups. Just as there was a difference in this regard between north Europeans and south Europeans, so there are differences among the various south European groups. The assimilation of Orientals is moving much more slowly than that of Europeans.

In viewing the assimilation which has occurred as a result of the landing of millions of immigrants on American shores, it must be observed that accommodation has been two-way. Foreign-born Americans have adjusted to the culture which they found here, but in turn the culture which they found has been changed by their coming. The action must not be thought of as the imposition of a fixed culture upon new members of our society. Rather it may be considered as the constant, but hardly radical, modification of a basic pattern of culture. Such unity of culture as exists in America today includes elements introduced by immigrants. There are vast differences within our culture, but less and less can these differences be identified with national cultures. There are some community, sectional, religious, class, and political contrasts the origins of which are associated with the diversity of the national sources of our population. But it may be expected that these differences will survive long after the descendants of immigrants have been fully assimilated.

SUMMARY

As a new nation the United States welcomed immigrants. There was some feeling that immigration should be controlled, but interest in restriction was slight. For a number of decades after the close of the colonial period there was a lull in immigration to this country.

Around 1830 a great new influx of people from Europe began. The years from 1830 to 1882 are referred to as the period of the *old immigration*. Outstanding among the immigrants who came during these years were the Irish, Germans, and Scandinavians. The assimilation of these groups proceeded rather rapidly. Attitudes toward immigration varied. There were attempts both to encourage immigration and to restrict it. Restrictive efforts were ineffective.

The Chinese and the Japanese were the two chief Oriental immigrant groups. Chinese immigration increased rapidly after 1850 and reached its peak around 1882. Welcomed first as workers, the Chinese were later prevented from entering the United States. When Chinese immigration was cut off the Japanese moved in to take their place. After a few decades of immigration the Japanese also were excluded.

The *new immigration* from Europe began around 1882. At about this time the source of the immigrant population began to shift from northern and western Europe to southern and eastern Europe. Conditions in Europe and increased transportation were important factors in bringing about the change. Slavic groups and Italians were among the largest new immigrant groups. The new immigrants tended to settle in cities. Significant selective immigration legislation was passed in 1882 and thereafter.

The era of relatively free immigration came to an end after the First World War. During the 1920's important restrictive laws were passed. The intent of this legislation was both to cut down immigration and to select the countries from which the largest numbers of new citizens should come. People from some areas of the world were excluded from entrance into the United States; people from other areas were placed under quota arrangements; still others were permitted to enter more freely.

The assimilation of new immigrants was not so rapid as that of the old immigrants. By now, however, both the old and the new European Americans have moved far in the direction of losing their cultural identity. Their assimilation is not complete but it is proceeding rapidly, although not equally rapidly for all groups.

SELECTED REFERENCES

Adams, James Truslow: *The American*, New York, Scribner, 1943.

Bernard, W. S., et al.: *American Immigration Policy: A Reappraisal*, New York, Harper, 1950.

Davie, Maurice R.: *Refugees in America*, New York, Harper, 1947.

Fairchild, Henry Pratt: *Immigration*, New York, Macmillan, 1928.

———: *Melting Pot Mistake*, Boston, Little, Brown, 1926.

Hansen, Marcus Lee: *The Atlantic Migration, 1607–1860*, Cambridge, Mass., Harvard University Press, 1940.

———: *The Immigrant in American History*, Cambridge, Mass., Harvard University Press, 1940.

Smith, William Carlson: *Americans in the Making*, New York, Appleton-Century, 1939.

Taft, Donald R.: *Human Migration*, New York, Ronald, 1936.

Warner, W. Lloyd, and Leo Srole: *Social Systems of American Ethnic Groups*, New Haven, Conn., Yale University Press, 1945.

Wittke, Carl: *We Who Built America*, New York, Prentice-Hall, 1939.

Woofter, T. J., Jr.: *Races and Ethnic Groups in American Life*, New York, McGraw-Hill, 1933.

CHAPTER FOUR

American Minority Peoples

We have seen that the assimilation of European immigrants in American society is proceeding rapidly. The process is not complete; but whereas in earlier years many of the immigrant groups from Europe constituted subgroups within our society, now they are losing their identity as separate groups. They are achieving a sense of belonging to the dominant group. Their inferior status as "outsiders" is disappearing. They are less and less identified as "Irish Americans," "German Americans," or "Italian Americans"; they are becoming simply "Americans."

There remain, however, a number of unassimilated subgroups in American society. These groups have not lost their identity. They are assigned inferior status and are not permitted the privileges of full participation in American society. These subgroups having inferior status are referred to as *minority groups*. Even now, not all European immigrant groups can be classified outside the minority category; but on the whole, European immigrants and their children are accorded a place in the dominant group which has not been granted to certain other groups. The chief minority groups in American society today are the Indians, Orientals, Spanish-speaking Americans, and Negroes.

AMERICAN INDIANS

It has been estimated that in 1492 there were from 700,000 to 1 million Indians in the area which is now the United States. By 1871, when the Indians became official wards of the Federal government, their population had decreased to less than half a million. The decline continued until around 1900, when an upward trend began. In 1950 the Indian population was 343,410.[1]

The distribution of groups of Indians in the United States has been summarized by Charles Marden as follows: [2]

"(1) *The Southwest.* Primarily Arizona and western New Mexico. Major groups are the Navaho, Hopi, Papago, Pueblo, and Apache.

"(2) *California and the Northwest.* An intermittent scattering of Indian tribes through California, Nevada, and Utah, including many Shoshone and Paiute. A further intermittent but less wide scattering of reservations in Washington, Oregon, Idaho, Montana, and Wyoming.

"(3) *The North Central.* The area of greatest concentration here is in South Dakota with its large Sioux population, followed by substantial reservations in North Dakota and Minnesota and scattered small bands in Nebraska and Iowa on the south and in Wisconsin and Michigan on the east.

"(4) *Oklahoma.* It is not surprising that this former Indian territory has more Indians than any other state, only exceeded by the Southwest region. Linked with this area may be considered the small bands in northern Kansas.

"(5) *North Carolina.* While some small Indian groups are located in widely scattered places in Texas, Louisiana, Mississippi, Alabama, Florida, South Carolina, and Virginia, the Cherokee tribes of North Carolina far outdistance in total population all other Indian groups combined in the South.

"(6) *New York.* Of the relatively few Indians to be found in the Northeast, most of them are located in the rural areas of New York State, including the Seneca, the Onondaga, and the Tonawanda. Very small bands may be found in Rhode Island and in Maine."

---

[1] Census returns for Indians are subject to some uncertainty, inasmuch as definitions have varied. Many authorities regard the census count as being too low.

[2] Charles F. Marden, *Minorities in American Society*, New York, American Book, 1952, pp. 319, 320; based on a map in G. E. E. Lindquist, *The Indian in American Life*, New York, Friendship, 1944.

Bureau of Indian Affairs

Polson, Montana, on the Flathead Indian Reservation. This community has modern homes and stores. It is a manufacturing and resort town and the trade center of a fertile farming area.

Today most Indians live on reservations. The Navaho reservation is the largest. It covers about 25,000 square miles, an area larger than Connecticut, Rhode Island, Massachusetts, and New Jersey combined. In contrast are the small plots of one or two square miles in California and elsewhere. There are some unsegregated Indians who live in urban centers as self-supporting citizens. We are primarily interested in those who live as Indians in groups.

The recognition of reservations began during the colonial period and continued throughout a large part of the nineteenth century. The problem was long looked upon as being largely a military one. In 1824 an Indian Office was established under the War Department. The white man sought to devise means whereby he could occupy new land without being too much molested by Indians. Under treaty arrangements Indians were permitted to live in territories ceded to them. As the white population encroached on Indian territory, frequently in violation of treaties, the areas occupied by Indians grew smaller. The result was a large number of widely scattered separate areas in which Indians could practice their way of life relatively free from white interference.

In 1871 the period of treaties came to an end. The Indians lost their status as independent tribes and nations. They were made wards of the United States. A new policy emerged. Indians were to be civilized and Americanized. The aim of the policy was the ultimate liquidation of reservations and the assimilation of Indians in American society. To this end the Dawes Act or General Allotment Act was passed in 1887. The purpose of the Act was to make it possible for Indians to become individual landowners. Land could be allotted to family heads, who after twenty-five years became full owners. It was soon discovered that most Indians were not eager to give up their tribal ties and customs. They preferred to continue as Indian communities. They found individualistic agriculture confusing. The new property system was strange to groups accustomed to the ways of communal tribes. They lacked knowledge and skill in the type of agriculture envisaged for them. The only use that many Indians could find for their land was to lease it to white men; and white men were more than willing to administer such transactions. Pressure was brought on the government to sell unallotted land to farmers and ranchers. The failure of the allotment plan was recognized, and in 1933 it was practically given up.

A reversal of policy in the conduct of Indian affairs was initiated in 1933. The way was opened during the Hoover administration by the establishment of the Bureau of Indian Affairs in the Department of the Interior and by the active interest of that department in a more humane approach. In the first years of the Roosevelt administration a new policy was developed, and in 1934 the Indian Reorganization Act was passed. The intent of the Act was to grant Indians the right to manage their own affairs. Self-government was offered to those tribes which elected to accept the

Post Office at Kenel, South Dakota, on the Standing Rock Reservation of the Sioux Indians. Reservations vary greatly in physical appearance and in the degree to which the inhabitants are self-supporting.

provisions of the Act. Unlike earlier efforts to destroy the distinctive culture of Indians and to break up their communities and tribes, the purpose of the new program was to make it possible for Indians to preserve their customs and their unity, and at the same time to provide a place for them as Indians in the larger American society.

The results of the new policy have not been extraordinary, but there have been gains. The principle of self-government has been accepted in more than two-thirds of the tribes; agriculture has been expanded; and education has been improved. On the other hand, despite the machinery for self-government which has been provided, there is very little political autonomy in Indian tribes. Although the Federal government has made serious attempts to withdraw from Indian affairs, Federal authority is everywhere evident, even in the creation of tribal constitutions. Schools are

American Red Cross

Grinding Corn Meal by Primitive Methods on the Cherokee Indian Reservation, North Carolina. The extent to which Indians perpetuate their traditional practices varies from one group to another. Both modern and primitive ways are often found on the same reservation.

largely controlled and administered by white men. Ownership and use of agricultural land is still a major problem.

It is, of course, incorrect to consider all Indian groups as similar in their relations with white Americans and in their adjustment to the majority culture. Some Indians are economically self-sufficient; others are wholly dependent. Some tribes exercise a high degree of self-regulation; others are controlled almost entirely from without. Some are Americanized; many have a preliterate pattern of living.

The status of Indians as voting citizens appears finally to be defined. Although citizenship was conferred upon all Indians in 1924, the right to vote was regulated by the various states. In 1940 there were still seven states which interpreted their state laws as barring Indians from voting, but the restrictive measures were not enforced in five of these states. In 1948, as a result of court decisions in the two remaining states in which Indians were disfranchised, Arizona and New Mexico, all Indians gained the right to vote.

There is a difficult dilemma in the present policy toward Indians. If tribes, particularly the more primitive, are only encouraged to strengthen their own customs and solidarity, they will achieve no greater qualification for participation in the affairs of American society as a whole, for common participation is based on common understandings. Moreover, the Indian who has grown up in a dissimilar minority culture will find it difficult to adjust to the majority culture if he chooses to leave his home community. But the policy, in reality, has never been thought of as granting Indians the right to maintain a culture wholly unlike that of the dominant majority. It has been assumed that in many areas of living the Indian way of life would tend toward that of the white majority. It has been assumed, too, that the dominant majority would give guidance in this direction. This means supervision, and the supervision which the white man prefers to think of as guidance is experienced as regulation and control by Indians. Against this control they protest. And yet at the same time that Indians object to interference in their affairs, they accuse the Federal government of not doing as much as it could. Many Indians, while coveting self-regulation, cannot be and sometimes do not care to be self-sufficient.

Thus American Indians remain as unassimilated groups, both geographically and culturally separate from the majority group in our society. The geographical isolation of the reservation system may be expected to continue for many years. The cultural isolation, also, will probably not soon disappear. For this the Indian feels little regret. He is convinced of and defensive of the superiority of his own ways. Notwithstanding the many honest attempts that have been made to aid the Indian, his reluctance to embrace the white man and his culture should not be difficult to understand in view of the abuse that he has suffered.

ORIENTALS

In continental United States in 1950 there were 141,365 Japanese, 117,140 Chinese, 61,636 Filipinos, and small numbers of Asiatic Indians, Koreans, Polynesians, and other Asiatics. Because of the insignificant numbers in the other groups, we shall consider only the Chinese, Japanese, and Filipinos.

Chinese

The Chinese population in the United States is concentrated in cities. In 1940 over 71 per cent were living in cities having populations of 100,000 or over, and 20 per cent were in cities of 25,000 to 100,000. The largest concentration is found on the West Coast, but there are some Chinese in most cities of 100,000 or over. In size of Chinese population San Francisco ranks first, New York City second, and Los Angeles third.

In cities many Chinese are segregated in Chinatowns. These sections are usually relatively small and compact. Residents live crowded in areas filled with restaurants, laundries, and shops. Here the language, customs, and traditions of China are perpetuated. Social organization is strongly familistic. Associations for mutual aid and protection are maintained. Chinatowns often serve as social centers for Chinese who live elsewhere in cities. Although Chinatowns are culturally isolated, they are never economically self-sufficient. In a study of Chinatowns, Rose Hume Lee observes that the services of the "ghetto" must be demanded by the larger society.[3] Curiously, two of the leading services provided by Chi-

---

[3] Rose Hume Lee, "The Decline of Chinatowns in the United States," *American Journal of Sociology*, vol. 54, March, 1949, pp. 422–432.

nese are unrelated to their national culture. Chinese restaurants and laundries are of American origin and represent the attempt of Chinese to enter businesses in which they would not greatly compete with the white population. They have also learned to capitalize on tourist interest in their culture through the establishment of curio shops.

Although Chinatowns have been the centers of Chinese culture in American cities, many Chinese live scattered throughout urban areas. Relations between these widely distributed Chinese and their white neighbors vary. Some are almost isolated from the people who live around them, but they are in close association with their countrymen in Chinatown. Others participate regularly in the activities of the communities in which they live and have practically no contact with Chinatown. A few are culturally isolated both from their white neighbors and from Chinatown.

Further dispersion of Chinese is resulting from the development of new occupational opportunities. They are finding employment as industrial workers, clerks, and professionals. They are entering businesses such as real estate, manufacture of home decorations, and wholesaling Chinese food to American restaurants. The need for finding new occupations has arisen, in part, because of competition from non-Chinese laundries and from non-Chinese restaurants serving Chinese food. The search for different types of work is also motivated by the desire to be dissociated from traditional Chinese-American occupations.

Chinatowns are not found in cities of less than 50,000 population, and in 1940 there were only 28 Chinatowns in the United States. The number of Chinese annually admitted to this country for permanent residence is too small to be significant as a source of population for Chinese colonies in cities. Chinatowns, therefore, must hold their children or decline. Rose Hume Lee believes that because of the occupational and residential redistribution which is occurring, Chinatowns are declining and that eventually they will almost disappear. Chinese colonies will survive only in commercial cities such as San Francisco and New York, where a concentrated Chinese population will be needed in connection with trade between this country and the Orient.[4]

Japanese

Before the Second World War the Japanese population in the United States was highly concentrated on the West Coast. Of the 126,947 Japanese in this country in 1940, 88.5 per cent lived in the three Pacific states; 73.8 per cent lived in California alone; and 29.1 per cent lived in Los Angeles County. It is apparent that in other parts of the country contact with Japanese was extremely limited.

Japanese on the West Coast remained largely within their own communities. High social barriers stood between them and the white population. The position of the Japanese as an outside group was definite, and was made all the more so by the ineligibility of the foreign-born for citizenship. Even second-generation Japanese, who were citizens by birth, were almost wholly dependent upon Japanese communities for security and for status. Traditions of family and community loyalty were strong. The tendency to engage in family economic enterprises gave additional support to group solidarity. The leading occupations of agriculture (45.2 per cent) and wholesale and retail trade (23.6 per cent) required a minimum of continuing contact with the majority group. For those who worked in personal services (17.1 per cent), social distance was clearly defined.

The outbreak of war between the United States and Japan brought about the complete disruption of Japanese communities on the West Coast. Immediately after Pearl Harbor financial and travel restrictions were placed on enemy aliens. Although Japanese born in this country were American citizens, they were treated as aliens. Fear and hatred of Japanese Americans mounted; many lost their jobs; they were economically boycotted; some were driven from their homes. Soon after war was declared John L. DeWitt, Commanding General of the Western Defense Command,

[4] *Ibid.*

urged the removal of enemy aliens from designated zones. The proposal was accepted and was redefined to include not only aliens, but "all Japanese." The evacuation of Japanese in California, Oregon, Washington, and Arizona was quickly begun. They were relocated in centers in isolated areas of the Southwest and elsewhere, where they lived under military guard throughout the war.

At the end of the war, relocation centers were emptied as quickly as they had been filled. Some Japanese were reluctant to leave because of rumors of prejudice and discrimination awaiting them if they attempted to return home. Nevertheless, in order to prevent the centers from becoming permanent reservations, all residents were removed and all regular centers were closed by December 1, 1945. Most of the Japanese went back to the West Coast, facing strong resistance to their return. Attempts were made to prevent them from reclaiming their homes and their businesses. Many suffered severe losses through property sales at the time of evacuation and through damage or destruction of goods, homes, and equipment during their absence.

Organized resistance was not sustained, and the intense hatred which existed in the war period subsided. Groups, some of which had been active throughout the war, came forward to give aid to returning families. Abatement of prejudice was influenced by factors such as the record of units of Japanese-American soldiers in the United States Army, official policy toward defeated Japan, and considerable feeling that the relocation program had been without just cause and that it constituted a violation of democratic principles. Public shame generated sympathy.

Today a large proportion of the Japanese are living again in the areas in which they were before the war. Poor housing, employment problems, and financial losses changed the mode of living of many, but the essential unity of community groups has been restored. Those who did not return to their homes are widely distributed throughout the country. In some communities assimilation of Japanese individuals and families is taking place. In the main, however, Japanese on the West Coast and elsewhere are unaccepted by the dominant group. They remain relatively isolated in American society.

Filipinos

Most of the Filipinos in the United States have come in the years since the First World War. The 1920–1930 decade was the period of most rapid immigration. There were 5,603 Filipinos in this country in 1920, about 45,000 in 1930, and between 60,000 and 65,000 at the beginning of the Second World War. The migration was largely of men; in 1930 males resident in this country outnumbered females about 15 to 1. Filipino immigration was practically cut off by legislation enacted by Congress in 1934, although a small quota was allowed.

Filipinos have been concentrated on the West Coast, where they have faced discrimination similar to that of the Chinese and the Japanese. In addition they have had their own peculiar problems. They have been a highly mobile labor force and as such have lacked group stability and cohesion. During the depression of the 1930's they had the enmity of labor organizations attempting to preserve the labor market. Their mobility and the unbalanced sex ratio have retarded the establishment of family life. The inevitable association of Filipinos with women of other races has been a further source of antagonism. The way of life of Filipinos who have located in cities has been more stable than that of the migratory agricultural workers.

SPANISH-SPEAKING AMERICANS

The size of the Spanish-speaking population of the United States is not accurately known, but it is estimated as being around 3,000,-000 or 3,500,000. This constitutes the second largest ethnic minority group in our population, the Negro group being the largest. Uncertainty concerning the number of Spanish Americans arises because of the heterogeneous character of the group and because of the varying definitions that have been employed for census purposes. The above estimate includes all Spanish-speaking people in the United States, whether immigrants, descendants of immigrants, or descendants of original settlers. These people are concentrated in Texas, California, New Mexico, Arizona, and Colorado. Some live in the cities of the Middle West and the Northeast.

Among the Spanish-speaking groups in this country are the descendants of people who lived in territories annexed by the United States. In the years before annexation Texas, New Mexico, Arizona, and parts of California and of Colorado were inhabited largely by Spanish-speaking people. The great majority of these people were of mixed Spanish and Indian stock. The culture that they developed was predominantly a rural village culture. With the growth of cities in the Southwest a considerable number have located in urban centers. The proportion of the Spanish-speaking population descendant from the indigenous Spanish Americans is notably large in New Mexico and in southern Colorado.

Native Spanish Americans in the United States are to be distinguished from recent and earlier Mexican immigrants and their descendants. Immigration from Mexico has been going on and increasing steadily since the middle of the last century. The greatest influx of Mexicans occurred in the 1920's. After the formation of the Border Patrol in 1929 the movement of Mexicans into this country was almost halted. Today the majority of Mexicans in the United States who are identified as belonging to the "immigrant" group are actually native-born. An indeterminate number of Mexicans continue to migrate illegally into the Southwestern states to find employment. They are called *wetbacks* because frequently they cross the border by swimming a river. The stay of many of these workers is temporary.

The distinction between Mexican immigrants and the native Spanish-speaking population is recognized by these groups themselves. The native Spanish-speaking people are particularly interested in maintaining the separation. They reserve for themselves the name "Spanish Americans" as distinguished from "Mexicans."

In view of their present situation, as well as historically, there is considerable justification for the distinction. Many Spanish Americans have achieved a higher economic and educational level than have Mexican immigrants. In some communities Spanish Americans are identified largely with the middle class. In other communities poverty is the common lot of both groups. But whether they occupy the same or different social levels, Spanish Americans and Mexican immigrants regard each other with mutual antipathy.

The mixed character of the Spanish-speaking population is more complex than the differentiation described above. There are rural-urban, occupational, and class differences. Also, Mexican immigrants must be distinguished from immigrants from other Latin-American countries. But despite the heterogeneity of the Spanish-speaking people in the United States, there are certain conditions of living and elements of culture which they have in common: they speak the same language, they practice the same religion, and they have minority social status. In the eyes of the Anglo-American population they are an out-group. In the Southwest discrimination is probably less marked in New Mexico than in other states of the region. Elsewhere in the United States the status of Spanish-speaking people appears to be somewhat higher than in the Southwest. In recent years both Spanish-speaking and English-speaking people have put forth an increasing effort to improve economic conditions. But almost everywhere Spanish-speaking Americans continue to have minority status.

Brief attention should be given here to the Puerto Ricans. They, too, are Spanish-speaking, but their situation in the United States differs from that of other Americans in their language group. Since Puerto Rico is a territory of the United States, Puerto Ricans are citizens of the United States. They are free to migrate to this country without restriction and they are entitled to full civic rights. Racially, they have Negro, white, and some Indian ancestry. On the continent, because of their language and recent arrival, they are treated as immigrant aliens; because of their racial similarity to the Negro, many of them are treated like American Negroes.

More than 90 per cent of the Puerto Ricans on the mainland have congregated in New York City. Most of them live in areas of deteriorated housing under conditions of extreme overcrowding. Many work in the lowest-paid jobs. The discrimination that they encounter because of their Negroid physical characteristics is new to them. At the present they constitute the least assimilated large group in New York City. It remains to be seen whether there will develop a pattern of assimilation similar to that of European immigrants. It appears likely, however, that because of their identification with Negroes, Puerto Ricans for some time will experience the same type of discrimination as that faced by the American Negro.

NEGROES

Negroes constitute the largest ethnic minority group in the United States. In 1950 they numbered 15,042,286, or 10 per cent of the total population. Their prominence as a minority group is more than numerical. Readily observable physical characteristics set them apart from the white majority. The "Negro problem" has been with us for many decades. Repeated attention has been called to discrimination and to the low level on which Negroes frequently live. This has served to create a special awareness of the status of Negroes. Moreover, the slave position which Negroes once occupied has resulted in attitudes which make the situation of the Negro different in certain respects from that of other minority groups in this country.

Negro Population

At the time of the first census, in 1790, one out of five persons in the United States was a Negro. At present one out of ten persons is a Negro. The percentage of Negroes in the total population declined from 19.3 in 1790 to a low of 9.7 in 1930. The chief reason for the change in the proportion of Negroes and whites was the differential source of population growth. Until 1930 the white population was increased by immigration as well as by an excess of births over deaths. There was no significant immigration of Negroes after 1808, and natural increase alone accounted for growth in the Negro population. Between 1930 and 1950 the proportion of Negroes in the population increased 0.3 per cent. This increase is too small to indicate a trend, but it is possible that the increase will continue. Since immigration is no longer an important source of white population growth, hereafter the proportion of Negroes and whites will be determined by birth and death rates in each group. In the past, contrary to popular opinion, Negroes have not reproduced themselves more rapidly than have whites. In recent years there appears to be evidence that Negroes have been reproducing themselves somewhat more rapidly than have whites. If the difference in rate continues an increase in the proportion of Negroes in the population of the United States may be anticipated. If there is such an increase it may be expected to occur slowly, and it will not necessarily be of indefinite duration.

The Negro population of the United States at one time was largely rural and Southern. In 1790 only a few Negroes lived outside the South. As late as 1940 about 77 per cent of all Negroes still lived south of the Mason-Dixon line. After the Civil War the geographical distribution of Negroes changed little until the First World War. Some movement from rural to urban areas occurred within the South, but large migration did not take place until 1915. The movement of Negroes which began at that time was toward the city and toward the North. In the South the proportion of Negroes living in cities increased from 22 to 37.3 per cent between 1910 and 1940. Most of the Negroes who migrated to the North became concentrated in cities, particularly in the largest cities. Since 1940 there has been a significant movement of Negroes to the West Coast, again to the largest cities. Of the total Negro population, 62.4 per cent lived in urban areas in 1950. In spite of their redistribution American Negroes are still concentrated in the South; 68 per cent of the Negro population was in the South in 1950.

Negroes in the United States are not to be regarded as a "pure" racial group. Racial crossing had an early beginning. Slave traders fathered offspring by their female cargo. In the colonies there was miscegenation between Negro and white indentured servants and between Negroes and Indians. Under slavery Negro women were expected to comply with the sexual demands of their white masters. This pattern survived for some time after emancipation. The Northern army in the South further contributed to the admixture. Intermarriage was a factor in racial mixing, although only to a limited degree. By 1910 one out of five Negroes was considered to be of mixed ancestry. Evidence concerning the present extent of interracial sex relations is not reliable, but it appears that such relations have declined. Also prostitution and contraception have reduced the reproductiveness of interracial sex relations.

Historical Background for Minority Status

When the first Negroes were brought to colonial America their legal status was similar to that of white indentured servants. From the beginning, however, their ethnic background and racial visibility marked Negroes for differential treatment, including longer periods of servitude. Eventually permanent and hereditary servitude was recognized by law and slavery became established. Under the plantation type of agriculture the demand for cheap labor was great, and as the plantation system expanded so did slavery. Following the Revolutionary War slavery came under the strong criticism of a number of prominent national leaders. At the same time slavery became less important in states that were turning to diversified farming and in those areas in which the soil had been exhausted. Many owners were freeing their slaves, and for a time the voluntary abolition of slavery seemed to be a real possibility. But after the invention of the cotton gin in 1793 the demand for labor in raising cotton brought an end to the voluntary abolition movement before it was more than started. The slave status of the Negro was fixed until it was forcibly disrupted by the Civil War.

The Civil War raised the legal status of the Negro, but his social status in general was unchanged. The war left destruction and bitterness. The South had been forced to grant freedom to its slaves. The loss of slave labor was rendered doubly onerous by the manner in which it was brought about. The memory of military defeat was not pleasant. Some Southern states were in a condition of economic ruin. Many once-prosperous citizens were almost entirely dispossessed. In addition to carrying the stigma of his earlier slave status, the Negro was an ever-present reminder of defeat. Before emancipation Negroes were regarded with a degree of indifference; after emancipation they became the object of active antagonism. The hope of returning to things as they were before the war found most active expression in the determination to "keep the Negro in his place."

The situation was not improved during the period of Reconstruction from 1865 to 1879. Former slaveowners were not compensated for their loss. Negroes were free, but they had no money to buy land, nor were they given land in order to become economically independent. The action taken by the Federal government was just drastic enough to be irritating to the South, but not bold enough to contribute to the solution of the problems of either whites or Negroes. At a time when the primary need was for economic reconstruction, a second "war" was being fought for political power. From this struggle emerged the politically united "solid South," in which the Negro was practically disfranchised.

Although there was an increase in Negro land ownership in the South until around 1900, under the economic system that developed in the postwar period many Negroes were bound to the land almost as strongly as under slavery. As *sharecroppers* Negroes worked on allotted plots of land and returned to their landlords a portion of the crops which they produced. Negroes who under slavery had been trained in skilled work were frequently forced to leave these jobs in order to make place for white workers. They turned to the lowest unskilled work, or to the land.

The end of slavery affected Negroes who had been free along with those who had been slaves. There always had been some free Negroes, and in 1860 about 10 per cent of all Negroes were free.

Free Negroes were concentrated in those areas of the South in which the plantation system did not flourish and in certain Southern and Northern cities. The economic conditions under which they lived varied from one section to another. In the main, free Negroes were more economically secure in Southern cities than in rural areas. Their situation was somewhat more favorable in Southern cities than in Northern cities. Only a few free Negroes became prosperous. The emancipation of slaves did not necessarily change the economic conditions of all Negroes who had been free before the Civil War, but their social status was redefined. Whereas earlier they enjoyed the status of a nonslave group, after emancipation in the thinking of whites the distinction between Negro groups tended to break down. Whether they had been slave or free, Negroes came to be placed in one class; they were all identified as belonging to an inferior race.

The North freed the slaves, but it was not ready to engage in a sustained struggle to establish economic, political, and social rights for Negroes. By their own experience, Northerners were not well prepared for such an effort. While it seemed obvious to them that slavery was a contradiction of their basic beliefs concerning human rights, most Northerners were too far separated from Negroes to be concerned about Negro welfare indefinitely. In many Northern communities there were no Negroes. Moreover, even at the time of the Civil War, Northern Negroes were consigned to an inferior status. With the migration into their region of unskilled and uneducated Negroes, Northerners came to accept the inevitability of low status for Negroes.

Economic Adjustment

At the end of the Civil War, the great majority of Negroes fell into the unskilled agricultural class. Some were domestic servants and a few had been trained as skilled artisans. There were almost no proprietors or professionals. From this beginning, small Negro professional, proprietor, clerical, and craft occupational groups have developed; but the great mass of Negroes still work in unskilled agricultural, industrial, service, and domestic occupations. In these occupations they have had no economic security. Incomes have been low; employment has been irregular; Negroes have been the last hired and the first fired. Only since the Second World War has significant improvement taken place, and that very slowly.

The plight of Negroes in agriculture is related to the difficulty in acquiring land ownership. For most Negro farmers owning land has not been even a remote possibility. They have been fortunate to subsist. There has been little opportunity to acquire capital or credit. But the scarcity of land ownership is only one of a number of interrelated problems. Much of the land cultivated by Negroes is unproductive. The soil is eroded, light, and lacking in fertility. It has been neglected for decades, and Negroes do not have the knowledge or the motivation to improve the land. Methods of farming are primitive and holdings are small. Overpopulation and the resultant oversupply of workers has helped to retard the introduction of improved methods of farming. Levels of living in plantation areas are generally lower than in other agricultural areas. Dire necessity has driven many Negroes from the soil. Today the majority of Negroes do not work in agriculture, and it is clear that more Negroes will need to turn to nonagricultural occupations.

Outside of agriculture the effects of minority status are likewise evident. The expansion of industry has not resulted in a proportionate increase in the number of better positions for Negroes. In the South competition from white workers has pushed Negroes into the least desirable types of work, which are defined specifically as "Negro jobs." The employment of white women in industry has further limited the types of work for which Negroes are eligible, since, according to long-established custom, white women and Negroes cannot work together. In the North, also, most Negroes are found in the lower occupational groups, and, in a sense, they are less protected from competition. Inasmuch as jobs are not clearly defined as "Negro jobs," Northern whites are more willing to work in the lowest occupations. In all parts of the country, as machines have made certain types of work less difficult and less undesirable, the place of the Negro in these jobs has been challenged by white competition.

Although the status of Negro labor remains generally low, there are exceptions and signs of change. Labor unions are contributing to the rise of the Negro. Older trade-unions excluded Negroes from membership, but industrial unions have tried to establish a new pattern. They have admitted Negroes as members and have attempted to break down occupational racial barriers. Negroes moved into new occupations as a result of the labor shortage during the Second World War. Opportunities for Negroes and other minority workers were increased by the creation of a Fair Employment Practice Committee. By executive order of the President it was required that there be no discrimination because of race, creed, color, or national origin in the employment of workers in defense industries or in government. The function of the committee was to investigate violations of the order. The satisfactory experience of employers coupled with the absence of marked unemployment pressure after the war made it possible for a considerable number of Negroes to remain in the types of work which they entered in wartime. Greatest gains were made in skilled and semi-skilled occupations.

Negroes who have entered the professions, business, clerical work, and other white-collar occupations constitute a relatively small group. Extremely limited opportunities together with the normal processes of selection make Negroes in white-collar occupations a highly privileged class. Exclusion of Negroes from skilled work is strong, but it is not as rigidly fixed as exclusion from white-collar work. New jobs appear to be opening for unskilled and skilled Negro workers; in the white-collar occupations, with the possible exceptions of clerical work and government service, there is only slight evidence of change.

A significant difference between wage earners and white-collar workers among Negroes is that the former have a place in the white-dominated economy, whereas the latter must depend to a large extent upon Negro communities. Negro businessmen and professionals have almost no opportunity to work in white communities, and they must compete with whites for the patronage of Negroes. Negroes buy at white stores in Negro neighborhoods and elsewhere, but Negro stores attract few white customers. Negroes seek the services of white doctors and lawyers, but Negroes in these professions are almost entirely dependent upon Negro clients. The two professions in which Negroes have faced least competition from whites are the ministry and teaching, although in the North Negro teachers have not had a monopoly in teaching Negroes. Clergymen are the only Negro professionals who have practically no competition from whites.

How is the present economic status of the American Negro to be explained? Four basic factors are involved: (1) lack of conditioning for economic responsibility; (2) inadequate opportunity for occupational training; (3) extremely limited sources of capital and credit; (4) discriminatory treatment even of responsible, well-trained, and resourceful Negroes. Slavery did not provide much experience for economic responsibility. There was little opportunity or need for learning thrift, industry, and self-reliance. Instead, habits of dependence were cultivated. Among many Negroes, living without prospect of better conditions, patterns of irresponsibility and dependence have survived as part of their culture. Indeed, these patterns have often been encouraged by whites who prefer irresponsibility to independence in Negroes. The Negro who is motivated to achieve a higher occupational and economic level meets with difficulty in acquiring adequate training. Training provided through public funds has been inferior in quality. The cost of education above the elementary level places it out of the reach of many Negroes whose innate capacities would qualify them for further training. The difficulty of gaining entrance into schools has presented still another education problem. Negroes who wish to enter business are hard put to find capital or credit. Slavery did not contribute to the accumulation of wealth among Negroes. There are few wealthy Negro families and few Negro financial organizations. Negroes have not fared well in their efforts to obtain capital and credit from white organizations.

The most difficult aspect of the Negro's economic situation is the tendency for low economic status to perpetuate itself. Negroes who are irresponsible and untrained are regarded as inferior; they are considered unworthy both of good employment and of further training. But unless the circle of influences is broken, poverty begets poverty, dependence begets dependence, and ignorance begets ignorance. When Negroes succeed in breaking out of this circle of influences they have won only half of the struggle. They encounter obstacles which are unrelated to motivation and qualification. Even when Negroes are highly motivated and well trained, they do not compete with whites on an equal basis.

Political Adjustment

The United States Constitution grants to Negroes the full rights of citizens. Since the Civil War there has been no serious effort in the North to deprive Negroes of their voting rights. In the South there was a hard-fought battle to prevent Negroes from voting and from otherwise exerting political power. For a period following emancipation, Negroes participated actively in politics in the South, but during and after the Reconstruction a number of means were devised for disfranchising Negroes. Until declared unconstitutional by the United States Supreme Court, "grandfather clauses" were used to exclude from voting those persons whose ancestors had not been eligible to vote or who had not voted before 1861. Negroes have been discouraged or prevented from voting by poll-tax requirements and by literacy tests, which frequently have been unenforced in the case of white voters. The establishment of the Democratic solid South was both a protest against the Republican Party, under whose administration slaves were freed, and a defense against the political participation of Negroes. In many Southern elections the Republican Party has had almost no chance of victory. The real contest has been within the Democratic Party. It was only necessary, therefore, to prevent Negroes from voting in Democratic primaries in order to deprive them of an effective vote. This was done by treating state Democratic parties as private organizations to which Negroes could not belong in the South. In 1944 the United States Supreme Court ruled that the Democratic Party is a public organization and that citizens eligible to vote cannot be excluded from membership.

It has not always been necessary actually to use the various devices for preventing Negroes from voting. The knowledge that they would be blocked at the polls has been enough to keep many Negroes from attempting to vote. Voting practices are part of an over-all effort to keep Negroes from exerting an influence in public affairs. They provide a semilegal basis for a nonlegal program of intimidation. The intimidation affects all the civil rights of Negroes. In the North, although his right to vote is almost never challenged, the Negro is discouraged from claiming his full civil rights.

In no part of the country is the political position of the Negro fixed and unchanging. A number of effective national organizations have been developed through which Negroes are asserting their civil rights. More experienced and better-trained Negro lawyers are meeting with increasing success in presenting civil-rights cases before the courts. Civil rights has become a national political issue, and public debate has served to make a greater number of people aware of the situation as it exists. Further, it is possible that the South is moving in the direction of a two-party system. If the two-party system should become a reality in the South, a change in the political participation of the Negro might be anticipated.

The Negro Community

The economic and political life of the Negro is not separate from American life as a whole. There is a close relation between over-all economic conditions and the economic welfare of the Negro. The general political climate of the country influences the political status of the Negro. In many ways the culture of the Negro is similar to that of whites. But notwithstanding his involvement in American society, the Negro has lived a life apart from the main stream of our culture. His culture is almost entirely American in origin, and it is characteristically American in content; nevertheless, to a degree it is different from white culture. The difference is a result of the distance which is maintained between whites and Negroes. Frequently the distance is geographical; in most cities Negroes live in segregated areas. In rural areas the lines of geographical separation are not so clearly drawn. But although residential segregation has been instrumental in keeping Negroes and whites apart, social distance is of equal importance in sustaining the separation. Even when Negroes and whites live in close proximity, social distance is maintained. There is a minimum of communication; the interaction that takes place is in accordance with definitely defined patterns of aloofness; most activities are separate. In their family life, religion, and recreation, Negroes although influenced by white culture are almost entirely removed from white association.

Negro family life never has conformed fully to conventional white patterns. As slaves, Negroes were bought and sold with little concern for family ties; marriage was not considered essential for mating; whatever family unity there was centered around Negro women. Survivals of this transient family organization are evident today. Negro families tend to be unstable and matriarchal. Sexual behavior is not closely regulated, and illegitimate children are freely accepted in established families. There are several prominent exceptions to Negro family instability: rural "black puritans" and upper- and middle-class Negroes are no less conventional and no less stable in their family relationships than are whites.

Within the Negro community the church has a place of signal importance. It is a community center in which are held meetings of all types—religious, political, and recreational. It is the most all-involving group to which the Negro belongs, and in it he is untouched by white interference. Through the church Negroes gain a sense of solidarity and of hope. Religion offers comfort in the face of trouble. Within the church status may be achieved. There are Negroes who are not associated with the church, but they are in the minority.

Negro isolation from the dominant culture has been supported by separate education for Negroes and for whites. In the South the separation has been practically complete. In the past in public education Negro and white children could not attend the same schools, and only Negro teachers were permitted to teach Negro students. Normally schools tend to serve as agencies through which the prevailing cultural patterns are transmitted. When, however, an already insular group is educationally isolated, the result is continuing cultural separation. In the North, where separate Negro schools have been fewer, education has been an important avenue of cultural contact.

The isolation of the Negro community is reflected in its social and civic life. There are an even greater number of social, fraternal, occupational, and civic organizations and clubs than in white communities. Americans are much inclined to form and join organizations, but the existence of such a large number of associations in Negro communities has been interpreted as an unhealthy situation. In *An American Dilemma* it was pointed out that [5] "The situation must be seen as a pathological one: Negroes are active in associations because they are not allowed to be active in much of the other organized life of American society."

Trends in Negro-White Relations

The minority status of the Negro is well defined. The Negro is unassimilated in American society. His culture, though American, is unique. He does not enjoy rights and privileges comparable to those of whites. On the whole, his economic position is singularly low. Even so, the status of the Negro is not inalterably fixed. Rather it is constantly being redefined, very slowly in some communities

[5] Gunnar Myrdal et al., *An American Dilemma*, New York, Harper, 1944, p. 952.

and more rapidly in others. In thinking and in practice the place of the Negro in American society is in process of change.

It is apparent that a sizable segment of the Negro population has ceased to accept the inevitability of their low status. They have come to reject the validity of ideas concerning black inferiority and white superiority which have been used to support discriminatory behavior toward them. As some Negroes have gained new rights and opportunities, others have been motivated to imitate their efforts. The relatively few Negroes who have achieved prominence outside the Negro group have become symbols of possible success. Negroes aspire to attain economic and occupational goals which at one time would have seemed hopeless. In some communities the traditional docility and subservience of Negroes in the presence of whites has markedly diminished. Long exposure to the democratic ideology has helped to create among Negroes a desire to share in the rewards of a democratic society. Although they have not received the full benefits of democracy, Negroes are committed to the beliefs of democracy. Indeed, democratic thinking is for them a necessity, for it keeps alive the hope of improved status. Thus an increasing number of Negroes view their minority position, not with reference to ideas of racial inferiority, but with reference to democratic beliefs concerning rights and opportunities.

As individuals and in organized groups Negroes are attempting to gain the rights and opportunities which they believe should be theirs. Apart from any concerted campaign many individual Negroes are struggling to secure education, better employment, respectable housing, legal protection, and recognition in Negro and in non-Negro groups. They are making friends among whites and participate with them in community enterprises. Some Negroes, particularly entertainers, artists, and intellectuals, have frequent and close association with non-Negro groups.

Only a small number of Negroes give active support to organized attempts to improve their welfare and status; nevertheless these efforts are important in redefining the place of the Negro.

The National Association for the Advancement of Colored People and the Urban League are the two organizations which have been most effective in working in the interest of Negroes. The NAACP, founded in 1909, is concerned primarily with civil liberties. Its chief strategy is to employ political and judicial methods in fighting against discriminatory treatment of Negroes. It has been active in legislative battles over lynching, poll taxes, and fair employment practices, and in many court cases, including those concerning segregation in education, travel, and housing. The National Urban League, formed in 1911, promotes a general social-welfare program among Negroes. The work is carried on through local Urban Leagues, which engage in a variety of activities such as nurseries, child-placement agencies, clubs, training programs, study groups, health work, delinquency prevention, and employment services. It is through the latter activity that the league performs its most important function. All local Urban Leagues attempt to find more and better jobs for Negroes and encourage and aid Negroes to secure necessary training. Both the National Association for the Advancement of Colored People and the Urban League were founded on white initiative, but their strength today derives from the action of Negroes themselves. Negro self-improvement and protest efforts receive the sustained support of the Negro press. The Negro press has very little effect on whites, but for the Negro it is a constant stimulus in his struggle for new status.

The white conscience has never been altogether at rest concerning the Negro. Periodically groups of whites have attempted to find ways whereby the Negro might be aided and by which he might help himself. Northern and Southern white leadership in the formation of Negro self-help and protest groups is evidence of this motivation. In 1919 a group of Southern white liberals founded the Commission on Interracial Cooperation, which, according to Myrdal,[6] *"rendered interracial work socially respectable in the conservative South."* In local communities many small groups have identified themselves with the problems of the Negro. But

[6] *Ibid.,* p. 847.

most whites have not been preoccupied with race relations. They have been willing to "let time solve the problems."

In recent decades, at the same time that the Negro has been rejecting the traditional definition of his position, an increasing number of whites have become sensitive to the contradiction between American values and the status of the Negro. The mobility of the Negro has heightened the awareness of the problems of the Negro and of the problems of race relations. The service of Negroes in the armed forces has dramatized their contrasting position in their home communities. Frequent political debate has focused more than usual attention on the issue of Negro status.

The measurable results of Negro protest and white concurrence, though far from spectacular, are indicative of a trend. Employment opportunities have increased. To a greater degree Negroes have been integrated into community life. They hold more offices in government than previously. They have been admitted to schools from which they were formerly excluded. A serious attempt has been made to abolish segregation in the armed services. Segregation in public places has declined. It appears that slowly the Negro is being integrated into American society.

A momentous decision affecting Negro and white relations was handed down by the Supreme Court of the United States on May 17, 1954. In a unanimous opinion the Court held that racial segregation in the public schools is a violation of the Federal Constitution. For many years the policy of segregation was defended by the "separate but equal" rule recognized by the Court since 1896. The effect of the new decision was to disestablish the "separate but equal" principle, for the Court declared that separated educational facilities are "inherently unequal." It is clear that for the future of Negro and white relations much depends upon the manner in which the decision of the Court is implemented.

The over-all view must not be distorted by the somewhat more rapid changes which have occurred in recent years. The movement toward integration of the Negro into American society is counteracted by strong forces. Patterns of Negro-white accommodation have been modified, but many separating barriers remain.

SUMMARY

The assimilation of European immigrants in American society is proceeding rapidly. There are, however, a number of other groups which are unassimilated. These unassimilated subgroups are referred to as minority groups. The chief minority groups in the United States are the Indians, Orientals, Spanish-speaking Americans, and Negroes.

Most Indians live on reservations scattered throughout the country. The largest concentrations are in the Southwestern and North Central states. On reservations Indians are encouraged to preserve their own customs and to practice self-government. The degree of self-sufficiency varies greatly, but in many groups there is much regulation from outside. The isolation of American Indians is both geographical and cultural.

The largest Oriental groups in the United States are the Japanese, Chinese, and Filipinos. Most Chinese live in cities, where they have usually been segregated in Chinatowns. Some Chinese live scattered throughout urban areas, and the trend appears to be toward further dispersion. Chinatowns will probably eventually disappear. Until the Second World War most Japanese Americans lived on the West Coast, where they remained largely within their own communities. During the war they were relocated in isolated areas. After the war a large proportion of the Japanese returned to the areas in which they had lived before; others are widely distributed. Both the Chinese and the Japanese are held socially distant by the dominant group.

Spanish-speaking Americans include immigrants, descendants of earlier immigrants, and descendants of people who lived in territories annexed by the United States. Native Spanish Americans and Mexican immigrants make a distinction between their groups and view each other with antipathy. But by the Anglo-American population both are regarded as out-groups; both have minority status.

The Negro population is the largest ethnic minority in the United States. One out of every ten Americans is a Negro. Although there has been considerable mobility among Negroes, they are still concentrated in the South. The low status of the Negro derived from his position as a slave. Racial visibility made it easily possible to set him apart for differential treatment. Low status has resulted in poor training and extremely limited opportunities. Economically, educationally, occupationally, and politically the Negro level of training and achievement has been low. The present status of the Negro is, therefore, a product of discriminatory treatment and of the self-perpetuating nature of low status. Nevertheless many Negroes have succeeded in achieving higher levels. Moreover an increasing number of Negroes are rejecting the traditional definition of their position. In this rejection they are joined by an also increasing number of whites. The eventual integration of the Negro into American society appears to be indicated by the present trend. But this end is hardly immediate. The minority status of the Negro is still definite.

SELECTED REFERENCES

Bloom, Leonard, and Ruth Riemer: *Removal and Return*, Berkeley, Calif., University of California Press, 1949.

Frazier, E. Franklin: *The Negro Family in the United States*, New York, Dryden, 1948.

Johnson, Charles S.: *Growing up in the Black Belt*, American Council on Education, 1941.

———: *Patterns of Negro Segregation*, New York, Harper, 1943.

Leonard, Olen, and C. P. Loomis: "Culture of a Contemporary Rural Community, El Cerrito, New Mexico," *Rural Life Studies* 1, U.S. Bureau of Agricultural Economics, 1941.

Marden, Charles F.: *Minorities in American Society*, New York, American Book, 1952.

Myrdal, Gunnar, et al.: *An American Dilemma*, New York, Harper, 1944.

Rose, Arnold, and Caroline Rose: *America Divided—Minority Group Relations in the United States*, New York, Knopf, 1948.

Schermerhorn, R. A.: *These Our People*, Boston, Heath, 1949.

Simpson, George Eaton, and J. Milton Yinger: *Racial and Cultural Minorities*, New York, Harper, 1953.

Warner, W. Lloyd, Buford H. Junker, and Walter A. Adams: *Color and Human Nature*, Washington, American Youth Commission, 1941.

Wissler, Clark: *Indians in the United States*, New York, Doubleday, 1946.

Young, Donald: *American Minority Peoples*, New York, Harper, 1932.

CHAPTER FIVE

Population Composition and Distribution

The study of population is an important phase of social analysis. Population studies can contribute much to the understanding of a society. Trends in population frequently reflect related social changes. In turn, population changes may help to bring about other changes. In the present chapter we shall discuss the composition and distribution of the population of the United States.

POPULATION COMPOSITION

The characteristics and problems of a community are in part determined by the make-up of its population. How many people there are in each race, sex, or age group are not merely interesting facts. The proportion of the population in each group influences the customs, practices, attitudes, values, needs, and organization of communities and of a society as a whole.

Nativity and Racial Composition

We have already described the ethnic origins and make-up of the population of the United States. It remains here to summarize the present nativity and race composition.

The proportion of foreign-born persons in this country is declining. In 1880 the white foreign-born constituted 13.1 per cent of the population. They constituted 11.4 per cent in 1930 and 6.7 per cent in 1950. Unless there is a change in immigration policy the decline will continue.

The races of mankind are classified on the basis of measurable physical characteristics such as hair texture, degree of hairiness of the body, nasal index, skin color, and stature. The three major

Table 1. Nativity and Racial Composition of the Population of the United States, 1930 and 1950

Race or nativity	1930		1950	
	Number	*Per cent*	*Number*	*Per cent*
All classes	122,775,046	100.0	150,697,361	100.0
White	110,286,740	89.8	134,942,028	89.5
Native	96,303,335	78.4	124,780,860	82.8
Foreign-born	13,983,405	11.4	10,161,168	6.7
Negro	11,891,143	9.7	15,042,286	10.0
Other races	597,163	0.5	713,047	0.5

SOURCE: U.S. Bureau of the Census, *U.S. Census of Population: 1950*, vol. 2, *Characteristics of the Population*, 1953, part 1.

racial groups are the Caucasoid, Negroid, and Mongoloid. In census taking the popular, but not accurate, term "white" is used instead of Caucasoid. Also the method of self-identification is employed; that is, an individual is white if he regards himself as white, and Negro if he regards himself as Negro.

Racially almost 90 per cent of all Americans are white. Negroes make up 10 per cent of the total population. Other nonwhite groups constitute only 0.5 per cent of the total population.

The nativity and racial composition of the population varies significantly from one region to another. In the Northeast the foreign-born constitute 13.1 per cent of the regional population as contrasted to only 1.6 per cent in the South. Negroes constitute 21.7 per cent of the population in the South but only 2.9 per cent of the population in the West. In Vermont the Negro population is about 0.1 per cent, whereas in Mississippi Negroes make up 45.3 per cent of the population. In Georgia, Alabama, Louisiana, and South Carolina Negroes constitute between 30 and 40 per cent of the population.

Table 2. Nativity and Racial Composition of the Population by
Regions, Divisions, and States, 1950

Region, division, and state	White			Nonwhite	
	Total	Native	Foreign-born	Negro	Other races
Northeast	94.7	81.6	13.1	5.1	0.2
New England	98.4	84.5	13.8	1.5	0.1
Maine	99.7	91.5	8.1	0.1	0.2
New Hampshire	98.8	88.9	10.9	0.1	0.1
Vermont	99.9	92.2	7.6	0.1	
Massachusetts	98.3	83.1	15.2	1.6	0.1
Rhode Island	98.1	83.8	14.3	1.8	0.1
Connecticut	97.3	82.4	14.8	2.6	0.1
Middle Atlantic	93.6	80.7	12.9	6.2	0.2
New York	93.5	76.7	16.8	6.2	0.3
New Jersey	93.3	80.3	13.0	6.6	0.1
Pennsylvania	93.9	86.5	7.4	6.1	
North Central	94.7	88.6	6.1	5.0	0.3
East North Central	93.9	86.8	7.1	5.9	0.2
Ohio	93.5	87.9	5.6	6.5	
Indiana	95.5	93.0	2.5	4.4	
Illinois	92.4	83.4	9.0	7.4	0.2
Michigan	92.9	83.4	9.5	6.9	0.2
Wisconsin	98.8	92.4	6.4	0.8	0.4
West North Central	96.5	92.5	4.0	3.0	0.4
Minnesota	99.0	92.0	7.0	0.5	0.5
Iowa	99.2	96.0	3.2	0.7	0.1
Missouri	92.4	90.1	2.3	7.5	
North Dakota	98.2	90.3	7.9		1.8
South Dakota	96.3	91.6	4.7	0.1	3.6
Nebraska	98.2	93.9	4.3	1.4	0.4
Kansas	96.0	94.0	2.0	3.8	0.2
South	78.1	76.5	1.6	21.7	0.2
South Atlantic	75.7	74.0	1.7	24.1	0.2
Delaware	86.1	81.7	4.4	13.7	0.2
Maryland	83.4	79.8	3.6	16.5	0.1
District of Columbia	64.5	59.6	4.9	35.0	0.4
Virginia	77.8	76.7	1.1	22.1	0.1
West Virginia	94.2	92.5	1.7	5.7	
North Carolina	73.4	73.0	0.4	25.8	0.8
South Carolina	61.1	60.7	0.4	38.8	0.1
Georgia	69.1	68.6	0.5	30.9	
Florida	78.1	73.7	4.4	21.7	0.1
East South Central	76.4	75.9	0.5	23.5	0.1
Kentucky	93.1	92.6	0.5	6.9	

Table 2. Nativity and Racial Composition of the Population by
Regions, Divisions, and States, 1950 (*Continued*)

Region, division, and state	White			Nonwhite	
	Total	*Native*	*Foreign-born*	*Negro*	*Other races*
Tennessee	83.9	83.4	0.5	16.1	
Alabama	67.9	67.5	0.4	32.0	0.1
Mississippi	54.6	54.2	0.4	45.3	0.1
West South Central	82.8	80.5	2.3	16.7	0.5
Arkansas	77.6	77.1	0.5	22.3	0.1
Louisiana	67.0	65.9	1.1	32.9	0.1
Oklahoma	91.0	90.2	0.8	6.5	2.5
Texas	87.2	83.6	3.6	12.7	0.1
West	95.0	87.3	7.7	2.9	2.1
Mountain	95.5	90.8	4.7	1.3	3.2
Montana	96.8	89.5	7.3	0.2	3.0
Idaho	98.8	95.5	3.3	0.2	1.0
Wyoming	97.8	93.2	4.6	0.9	1.3
Colorado	97.9	93.4	4.5	1.5	0.6
New Mexico	92.5	90.0	2.5	1.2	6.3
Arizona	87.3	81.2	6.1	3.5	9.2
Utah	98.2	93.9	4.3	0.4	1.3
Nevada	93.6	87.0	6.6	2.7	3.7
Pacific	94.8	86.1	8.7	3.5	1.7
Washington	97.3	89.3	8.0	1.3	1.3
Oregon	98.4	92.9	5.5	0.8	0.8
California	93.7	84.4	9.3	4.4	1.9

SOURCE: U.S. Bureau of the Census, *U.S. Census of Population: 1950*, vol. 2, *Characteristics of the Population*, 1953, part 1.

Sex Composition

The sex ratio of a population is stated in terms of the number of males per 100 females. A sex ratio of more than 100 indicates an excess of males, and a sex ratio of less than 100 indicates an excess of females.

The proportion of the sexes is an important characteristic of a population. The sex ratio is a factor in determining birth rates and death rates. How many people in the population can get married depends upon the proportion of men and women. A scarcity of women or a scarcity of men can affect the customs and manners of a community. Even the mores may be influenced.

Until 1950 there has always been an excess of males in the United States as a whole. In 1850 the sex ratio was 104.3. In 1910 it reached a high of 106. There was a gradual decline to 100.7 in 1940 and to 98.6 in 1950.

Table 3. Sex Ratio in the United States by Nativity and Race, 1850–1950

Year	All classes	Native white	Foreign-born white	Negro
1850	104.3	103.1	123.8	99.1
1860	104.7	103.7	115.1	99.6
1870	102.2	100.6	115.3	96.2
1880	103.6	102.1	115.9	97.8
1890	105.0	102.9	118.7	99.5
1900	104.4	102.8	117.4	98.6
1910	106.0	102.7	129.2	98.9
1920	104.0	101.7	121.7	99.2
1930	102.5	101.1	115.1	97.0
1940	100.7	100.1	111.1	95.0
1950	98.6	98.6	103.8	94.3

SOURCE: U.S. Bureau of the Census, *U.S. Census of Population: 1950*, vol 2, *Characteristics of the Population*, 1953, part 1.

Two factors especially account for the excess of males in the past. As the table above indicates, there were more men than women among the immigrants who came to this country. The other factor was the high death rate among women of childbearing age. The decline in immigration and the decline in maternal mortality rates have resulted in a lowering of the sex ratio. Since the death rate for males is now higher than that for females the present excess of females may be expected to continue.

While the imbalance in the sex ratio for the population as a whole has not been great, within particular groups the disproportion has been significant. Even higher than the former sex ratios among foreign-born whites were those among other groups. In 1890 the sex ratio of the Chinese in the United States was 2,678.9; in 1900 that for the Japanese was 2,369.6. Even in 1950 the Chinese ratio was 189.6, or almost twice as many men as women.

Areal variations in sex ratios may also be observed. Rural farm areas have more men than women. The 1950 ratio was 110.1. In rural nonfarm areas the ratio was 103.6. The excess of women in urban areas is indicated by the 1950 ratio of 94.6. For cities of over 100,000 population the lowest sex ratio was 79.8 in Pasadena. All other cities in this class having sex ratios of less than 90 were Southern cities: Atlanta, Birmingham, Charlotte, Chattanooga, Jacksonville, Little Rock, Memphis, Mobile, Montgomery, Nashville, Richmond, Savannah, Shreveport, and Washington, D.C.

Age Composition

The age composition of the population has been changing steadily for more than a century. Larger proportions of the population are in the older age groups. In 1880 the median age of the population was 20.9; that is, half the population was older and half the population was younger than 20.9. In 1950 the median age of the population was 30.2.

Table 4. Median Ages of the Population of the United States by Color, 1880–1950

Year	All classes	White	Nonwhite
1880	20.9	21.4	18.0
1890	22.0	22.5	18.5
1900	22.9	23.4	19.9
1910	24.1	24.5	21.1
1920	25.3	25.6	22.5
1930	26.5	26.9	23.5
1940	29.0	29.5	25.2
1950	30.2	30.8	26.1

SOURCE: U.S. Bureau of the Census, *U.S. Census of Population: 1950*, vol. 2, *Characteristics of the Population*, 1953, part 1.

Table 5 shows that in 1880 those under 10 years of age constituted 26.7 per cent of the population; in 1950 the percentage in this group was 19.5. Between the same years the proportion in the oldest age group more than doubled. In 1880 the percentage 65 years of age and over was 3.4; in 1950 it was 8.1.

Table 5. Percentage of United States Population by Age, 1950 and 1880

Year	Under 10	10–19	20–29	30–39	40–49	50–64	Over 65
1950	19.5	14.4	15.7	15.1	12.8	14.3	8.2
1880	26.7	21.4	18.3	12.7	9.1	8.4	3.4

SOURCE: U.S. Bureau of the Census, *U.S. Census of Population: 1950*, vol. 2, *Characteristics of the Population*, 1953, part 1.

Regional differences in age composition, although diminishing, are still evident. The South has a higher proportion of young people than have other regions. In 1950 the proportion under 20 years of age was 38 per cent in the South, 33 per cent in the North Central region, 33 per cent in the West, and 30 per cent in the Northeast. This means that the South is faced with the task of providing education for a higher proportion of its population than other regions. On the other hand the South has a lower proportion of its population in the 30 to 65 age group. In 1950 the percentages in this group were 38 per cent in the South, 43 per cent in the North Central region, 43 per cent in the West, and 45 per cent in the Northeast.

The population pyramids in Figure 4 show the age structure of the United States and urban, rural nonfarm, and rural farm areas. Rural farm and urban differences are most conspicuous. In 1950 those under 20 years of age comprised 42 per cent of the population in rural farm areas and 30 per cent in urban areas. Urban areas have higher proportions in the middle years. In the ages 20 to 49 urban areas have 46 per cent as compared to 36 per cent in rural farm areas.

The changing age composition of the population is affecting American social life. Whether people are young or old helps to determine the kinds of goods produced. The buying habits of the various age groups are not the same. Methods of advertising and selling are influenced by the characteristics of buyers. Similarly amusement and recreation patterns differ with age, and more attention is being given to the interests of older people. All the effects are not fully evident. It is possible that older people will tend to associate more on an age basis for recreation and for other purposes. The aged may become an important pressure group. It has been suggested frequently that social life in general, including economic and political behavior, may become increasingly con-

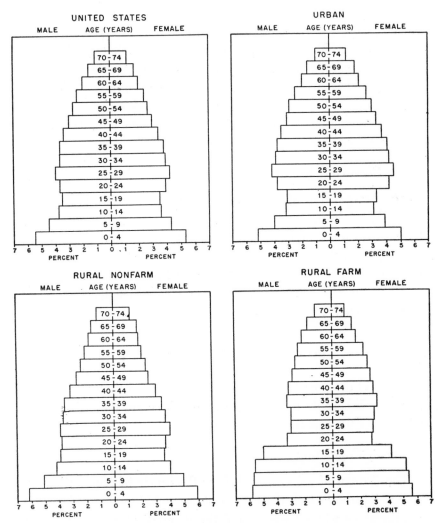

Figure 4. Per Cent Distribution of the Population of the United States, Urban and Rural, by Age and Sex: 1950. (Source: U.S. Bureau of the Census.)

servative as a larger proportion of the population moves into the older group.

As the percentage of older people increases the question of how the aged are to be cared for becomes more serious. Awareness of the need for helping the aged to maintain a satisfactory economic position is growing. In many occupations young workers are preferred. Workers are made to retire while they are still physically and mentally able, thus requiring a difficult psychological as well as economic readjustment. Pension plans and government-sponsored social-security programs are long-term efforts to make it possible for individuals to receive income after retirement. There may be occupational changes which will provide suitable employment for the older age group.

Other Characteristics of the Population

The composition of the population of the United States might be analyzed in many other ways. Data are available concerning the occupational, marital, religious, and educational composition of the population. These and other characteristics are important, but we have reserved them for treatment in other chapters in connection with the particular social areas to which they are most closely related.

POPULATION DISTRIBUTION

In 1950 the population of continental United States was 150,-697,361. Where do these people live? How are they distributed throughout the country?

Center of Population

The Bureau of the Census defines the center of population [1] as "the point upon which the United States would balance, if it were a rigid plane without weight and the population were distributed

---

[1] U.S. Bureau of the Census, *U.S. Census of Population: 1950*, vol. 2, *Characteristics of the Population*, 1953, part 1, p. 9.

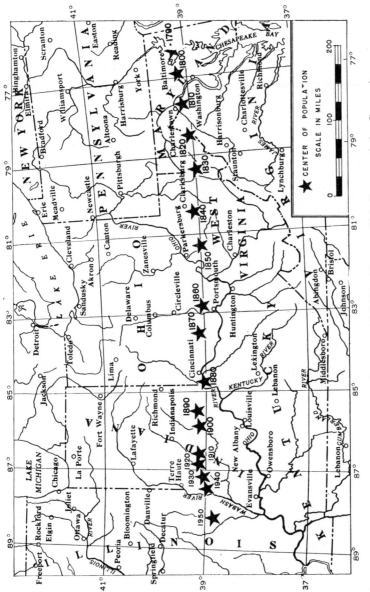

Figure 5. Centers of Population: 1790–1950. (Source: U.S. Bureau of the Census.)

99

thereon with each individual being assumed to have equal weight and to exert an influence on a central point proportioned to his distance from that point." This point has been moving steadily westward. In 1790 the center of population was 23 miles east of Baltimore, Maryland. By 1940 it had reached a point south of Terre Haute near the western boundary of Indiana. In 1950 it moved 42 miles westward and 7.6 miles southward into Illinois. This was the largest westward movement of the center of population in the present century.

Distribution of Population by Regions and Other Divisions

The map on page 101 shows the geographic breakdown made by the Bureau of the Census for purposes of population analysis. In total population the South ranks first, the North Central region second, the Northeast third, and the West fourth.

Table 6. Population by Regions and Divisions, 1950

Region and division	Population
Northeast	39,477,986
New England	9,314,453
Middle Atlantic	30,163,533
North Central	44,460,762
East North Central	30,399,368
West North Central	14,061,394
South	47,197,088
South Atlantic	21,182,335
East South Central	11,477,181
West South Central	14,537,572
West	19,561,525
Mountain	5,074,998
Pacific	14,486,527

SOURCE: U.S. Bureau of the Census, *U.S. Census of Population: 1950*, vol. 2, *Characteristics of the Population*, 1953, part 1.

Regional populations acquire additional meaning when related to land areas. The Northeast has approximately 26 per cent of the population but only about 5 per cent of the land area; the North Central region has about 30 per cent of the population and about

Figure 6. Regions and Geographic Divisions of the United States. (Source: U.S. Bureau of the Census.)

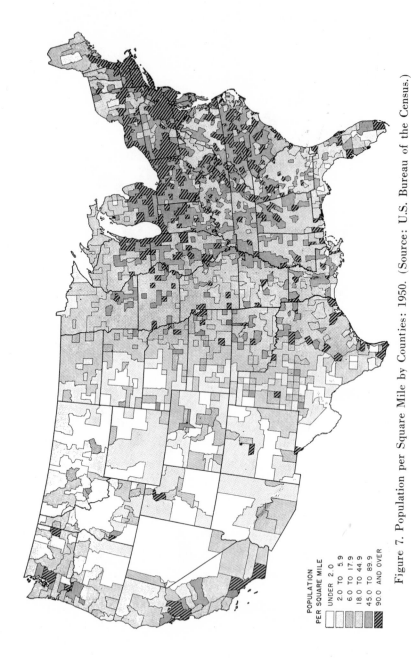

POPULATION
PER SQUARE MILE

UNDER 2.0
2.0 TO 5.9
6.0 TO 17.9
18.0 TO 44.9
45.0 TO 89.9
90.0 AND OVER

Figure 7. Population per Square Mile by Counties: 1950. (Source: U.S. Bureau of the Census.)

25 per cent of the land area; the South has about 30 per cent of the population and also about 30 per cent of the land area; and the West has only 13 per cent of the population and approximately 40 per cent of the land area. In 1950 there were 241.2 persons per square mile in the Northeast, 58.8 in the North Central region, 53.7 in the South, and 16.6 in the West.

The Middle Atlantic division led the other divisions with 300.1 persons per square mile of land area. The number of persons per square mile in the other divisions were as follows: New England, 147.5; East North Central, 124.1; West North Central, 27.5; South Atlantic, 79.0; East South Central, 63.8; West South Central, 33.8; Pacific, 45.3; Mountain, 5.9.

Changes in Population Distribution

The distribution of the population is constantly changing. The proportion of the population in the Northeast and the South has declined over the years, whereas the proportion in the North Central region and the West has increased. Over a 100-year period the greatest percentage decline was in the Northeast region, from 37.2

Table 7. Percentage Distribution of Population by Regions and Divisions, 1850, 1900, 1940, 1950

Regions and divisions	1950	1940	1900	1850
Northeast	26.2	27.3	27.7	37.2
New England	6.2	6.4	7.4	11.8
Middle Atlantic	20.0	20.9	20.3	25.4
North Central	29.5	30.5	34.7	23.3
East North Central	20.2	20.2	21.0	19.5
West North Central	9.3	10.3	13.6	3.8
South	31.3	31.6	32.3	38.7
South Atlantic	14.1	13.5	13.7	20.2
East South Central	7.6	8.2	9.9	14.5
West South Central	9.6	9.9	8.6	4.1
West	13.0	10.5	5.4	0.8
Mountain	3.4	3.2	2.2	0.3
Pacific	9.6	7.4	3.2	0.5

SOURCE: U.S. Bureau of the Census, *U.S. Census of Population: 1950*, vol. 2, *Characteristics of the Population*, 1953, part 1.

per cent in 1850 to 26.2 per cent in 1950. The greatest increase was in the West, from 0.8 per cent in 1850 to 13.0 in 1950.

The trend of population redistribution is further indicated by the rates of growth between 1940 and 1950. By far the highest rate of growth was in the West, where the increase was 40.9 per cent. The South was second with a 13.3 per cent increase. In the North Central region and the Northeast the rates were 10.8 per cent and 9.7 per cent respectively. Among the states California's increase of 53.3 per cent was highest. Oregon had an increase of 39.6 per cent, and Washington had an increase of 37.0 per cent. The gains for Arizona, Nevada, New Mexico, and Utah ranged from 25.2 per cent for Utah to 50.1 per cent for Arizona. Florida had an increase rate of 46.1 per cent. In and around the nation's capital, the District of Columbia, Maryland, and Virginia had increases of more than 20 per cent. Other states that showed gains of more than 20 per cent were Michigan and Texas. Four states, Arkansas, Mississippi, North Dakota, and Oklahoma, had population losses.

The growth or decline of population in a region or in a state is accounted for by two factors: (1) the natural rate of increase, that is, the balance of births and deaths; and (2) net migration, that is, the loss or gain from outmigration and inmigration. A study of Table 8 shows that the seven states having the greatest percentage increases in population between 1940 and 1950 were also states in which the rates of increase from migration were higher than the rates of natural increase. In one of these states, Maryland, the difference between the natural rate of increase and the net migration rate was very small. In all the other forty-one states natural-increase rates were higher than increases from migration. In New Mexico and in Utah, both having relatively high increase rates, the gains resulted largely from high rates of natural increase. The four states which declined in total population were the states having the greatest percentage losses from migration. States having high rates of natural increase and also high losses from migration were North Carolina, Louisiana, Tennessee, South Carolina, Georgia, Alabama, West Virginia, Kentucky, Mississippi, Arkan-

Table 8. Rate of Population Increase and Its Components, by States, 1940–1950

(*States arrayed in descending order of magnitude according to population growth, 1940 to 1950*)

States which grew faster than average	Net change in total population 1940 to 1950	Natural increase	Net migration
	Per cent of 1940 population *		
California	53.3	14.8	38.5
Arizona	50.1	22.5	27.6
Florida	46.1	16.5	29.6
Nevada	45.2	14.5	30.9
Oregon	39.6	13.5	26.1
Washington	37.0	14.6	22.4
Maryland	28.6	13.7	14.9
New Mexico	28.1	26.0	2.1
Utah	25.2	23.8	1.3
Virginia	23.9	17.7	6.2
Michigan	21.2	14.8	6.4
District of Columbia	21.0	15.1	6.0
Texas	20.2	19.8	0.4
Delaware	19.4	11.6	7.9
Colorado	18.0	14.2	3.7
Connecticut	17.4	10.9	6.5
New Jersey	16.2	9.1	7.2
Wyoming	15.9	16.3	− 0.4
Ohio	15.0	11.7	3.3
Indiana	14.8	12.1	2.7
United States	14.5	13.7	0.8
States which grew slower than average	*Per cent of 1940 population* *		
North Carolina	13.7	21.9	− 8.1
Louisiana	13.5	20.1	− 6.6
Tennessee	12.9	19.2	− 6.3
Idaho	12.2	17.3	− 5.1
South Carolina	11.4	25.0	−13.6
Rhode Island	11.0	9.7	1.4
Illinois	10.3	9.3	1.0
Georgia	10.3	20.6	−10.3
New York	10.0	8.0	2.0
Wisconsin	9.5	12.2	− 2.7
Massachusetts	8.7	8.2	0.5
New Hampshire	8.5	8.7	− 0.2

(*Cont.*)

Table 8. Rate of Population Increase and Its Components, by States, 1940–1950 (*Continued*)

States which grew slower than average	Net change in total population 1940 to 1950	Natural increase	Net migration
	Per cent of 1940 population *		
Alabama	8.1	21.0	−12.9
Maine	7.9	11.0	− 3.2
Minnesota	6.8	12.9	− 6.1
Pennsylvania	6.0	9.7	− 3.6
Kansas	5.8	10.9	− 5.1
Montana	5.6	12.9	− 7.2
West Virginia	5.4	18.3	−12.9
Vermont	5.2	10.9	− 5.6
Missouri	4.5	10.0	− 5.5
Kentucky	3.5	16.6	−13.1
Iowa	3.3	11.2	− 8.0
South Dakota	1.5	13.7	−12.3
Nebraska	0.7	11.1	−10.3
Mississippi	− 0.2	20.6	−20.8
Arkansas	− 2.0	20.2	−22.3
North Dakota	− 3.5	15.3	−18.8
Oklahoma	− 4.4	14.7	−19.1

* Components will not necessarily add up to net population change because of rounding. Source: U.S. Department of Commerce, Bureau of the Census.

SOURCE: Charles A. R. Wardwell, *Regional Trends in the United States Economy* Washington, 1951, Appendix Table 10.

sas, and Idaho. If the effects of migration were excluded, the South would be the most rapidly growing region. As it is, the most rapidly growing region is the West.

Significance of Internal Migration

It would be hazardous to predict how far the redistribution of population will go, but it is evident that many Americans are on the move. Between 1940 and 1950, without counting the inmigrants whose moves were offset by outmigrants, twenty-two states and the District of Columbia realized a net gain of about 5 million from internal migration. This represented a net loss of an equal number for the other twenty-six states.

Further evidence on migration comes from studies of civilian population movements after the Second World War. In these studies, made by the Bureau of the Census, migration was defined as moving outside the county and consisting of moves within the same state and between states. Moves within the same county were not defined as migration. From April, 1947, to April, 1948, some 20 per cent of the people of the United States moved: 14 per cent moved to another house in the same county; 3 per cent migrated to another county in the same state; 3 per cent migrated to another state.[2]

The postwar studies showed that on the average the persons who migrate are younger than those who do not, that more women than men migrate, that a higher proportion of nonwhites than whites move, and that mobility increases with education. Economic opportunity appears to be the chief motivation for migration. More frequently than for any other single reason people move to new localities to take jobs or to look for them. Other reasons given for migration are housing problems, changed marital status, and health.

The reasons for migration are not to be oversimplified. In the 1930's after extensive research Carter Goodrich and his colleagues concluded that migration tends to be out of areas of low economic opportunity and into areas of high economic opportunity.[3] The economic impetus of many important population movements is well recognized. The long migration westward, the massive movement from country to city, the rapid flow of population in response to the expansion of defense industries, and the seasonal shift of migratory workers are all examples of migration in quest of economic opportunity. But the nature of economic opportunity varies, and the areas of opportunity change. Moreover noneconomic cultural factors are often inseparably associated with the economic. That Americans will continue to move in great numbers seems evi-

[2] Charles A. R. Wardwell, *Regional Trends in the United States Economy*, 1951, p. 65.
[3] Carter L. Goodrich et al., *Migration and Economic Opportunity*, Philadelphia. University of Pennsylvania Press, 1936.

dent. Inasmuch as the areas of economic and other opportunities may be changing, the direction that the movement of population will take is far less evident.

SUMMARY

The proportion of foreign-born persons in the United States is declining and will continue to do so. In 1950, 6.7 per cent of the population was foreign-born. The nonwhite population was 10.5 per cent. There are significant regional variations in nativity and racial composition.

Until 1950 there have always been more males than females in this country. The 1950 census reported more females than males. Rural areas have an excess of males; urban areas have an excess of females.

The age composition of the American population is changing. The older age groups are becoming proportionately larger. The median age of the population is increasing. Rural and urban differences in age composition are significant. Regional differences are diminishing. The changing age structure of the population is influencing American social life. The problem of making economic provision for the aged is of particular importance.

The distribution of the population is never stable; redistribution is a continuing process. The center of population has been moving steadily westward and is now in eastern Illinois. The Northeast is still the most densely populated region, and the West the least densely populated. However, the proportion of the population in the Northeast has been declining, and the proportion in the West has been increasing. Among the states California has the most rapidly growing population.

Population redistribution is in part a result of differing natural-increase rates and in part a result of migration. A large number of Americans are migrating. The causes of migration are numerous, but economic causes are outstanding. In the past the movement of people has tended to be out of areas of low economic opportunity and into areas of high economic opportunity. Thus the direction of migration changes with geographic shifts in economic opportunity.

SELECTED REFERENCES

Coudry, E. V., ed.: *Problems of Ageing*, Baltimore, Md., Williams & Wilkins, 1942.

Dublin, Louis I., Alfred J. Lotka, and Mortimer Spiegelman: *Length of Life*. New York, Ronald, 1949.

Goodrich, Carter, et al.: *Migration and Economic Opportunity*, Philadelphia, University of Pennsylvania Press, 1936.

Landis, Paul H., and Paul K. Hatt: *Population Problems*, New York, American Book, 1954.

National Resources Committee: *The Problems of a Changing Population*, 1938.

Smith, T. Lynn: *Population Analysis*, New York, McGraw-Hill, 1948.

Thompson, Warren S.: *Population Problems*, New York, McGraw-Hill, 1953.

Wardwell, Charles A. R.: *Regional Trends in the United States Economy*, Washington, GPO, 1951.

Willcox, Walter F.: *Studies in American Demography*, Ithaca, N.Y., Cornell University Press, 1940.

CHAPTER SIX

Population Growth

The growth of the population of the United States has been phenomenal. At the time of the first census, in 1790, the population was 3,929,000. The number had increased to 23,192,000 by 1850 and to 75,995,000 by 1900. The 1950 census reported a population of 150,697,361 for continental United States. It may be noted that between 1850 and 1900 the population more than tripled, and between 1900 and 1950 it almost doubled.

In accounting for this tremendous growth of population three factors must be given consideration: *migration*, the *birth rate*, and the *death rate*.

MIGRATION

Immigration

The story of the great migration to our shores was told in earlier chapters. It remains now to consider the extent to which the forty million immigrants who came since the founding of the nation contributed to population growth. To ask whether they added to the total population may seem to be a needless question, but exactly this issue was raised about seventy years ago by General Francis A. Walker. Walker's theory was that the immigrant and his children do not represent a net addition to the population. Instead, since the birth rate declines most rapidly in those areas in which immigrants are most numerous, immigrants and their children are only substitutes for the unborn children of native parents. He held that the lower birth rate among the natives resulted from an unwillingness to have their children compete with foreigners.

Population students have given attention to Walker's theory largely to reject it. We shall summarize the arguments against the

110

theory as given by Warren S. Thompson, a leading population authority. Thompson agrees that native birth rates have been lower in the Northeastern states, where immigrants were most numerous. He concedes that many natives did not want their children to do heavy construction and factory work after such labor was taken over by the immigrants. But he is not willing to grant that it follows that immigration is the chief cause of the lower birth rate among the natives. Other factors such as urbanization and industrialization are related to the declining birth rate. It may be reasonable to inquire whether immigration hastened urbanization and industrialization and thus made for a decline in the birth rate, but that is a matter quite different from Walker's assertion that immigrant competition caused a reduction in the birth rate. Immigration may have speeded up industrialization and urbanization, but on the other hand, industrialization and urbanization are causes of immigration, since immigrants would not have come if jobs had not been available. Inasmuch as the development of industries and cities would have brought about a decline in the birth rate even if there had been no immigration, the lower birth rate may hardly be attributed to immigration. Thompson's conclusion is that although the drop in the birth rate may have been hastened by immigration, the coming of millions of people has contributed materially to our growth, and that if there had been no immigration the population of this country would not be as large as it is today.[1]

Emigration

While immigration statistics are most impressive, it must be remembered that the effect of immigration on population increase has always been counteracted to a degree by emigration. The flow of people has been two-way. Not all the aliens who entered this country remained to become permanent residents. Some came to seek only temporary refuge from political troubles; others came with the purpose of acquiring enough money to make life more comfortable in their native land; still others came expecting to

[1] Warren S. Thompson, *Population Problems*, 3d ed., New York, McGraw-Hill, 1942, pp. 181, 182.

stay, but either because life here was not all that they had hoped for or because they were overcome with homesickness returned to the land from which they came. In addition to emigrating aliens there have been some citizens, native-born or naturalized, who have left the United States to find homes in other countries. How many citizens have emigrated is not known.

Information concerning emigration from this country is extremely limited. Record of departures from the United States was not made until 1908, and even then only aliens and not citizens were counted. However, by comparing these records of aliens leaving with those of aliens entering the country, it is possible to gain an impression of the balance between immigration and emigration. In the decade 1905–1914, when immigration was at its height, the number of aliens admitted annually was approximately one million. During the same period aliens leaving the country numbered almost one-half as many as those admitted, so that the average net gain was over half a million. As a result of the First World War, between 1915 and 1919 both immigration and emigration fell off markedly, but the balance favored a gain for the United States. After the end of the war there was a significant increase in immigration but not in emigration. Following the passage of the immigration legislation of the 1920's there was a steady decrease in the net gain which continued to 1930. Then came the depression. For the first time in the history of the United States the migration balance changed. In each of the six years from 1931 to 1936 more people left this country than entered from foreign countries. During 1931 and 1932 from three to five persons departed for every one who entered. In 1937 the normal trend was resumed. Conditions prevailing just before, during, and since the Second World War have not been conducive to emigration from this country.

THE BIRTH RATE

Information concerning the rate of births in the United States is limited. Until the present century the collection of birth statistics was left entirely to the states. The results were incomplete and chaotic. It was not until 1915 that a national birth registration area was established, and then only ten states and the District of Columbia were included. State after state was added until finally with the addition of the last state, Texas, in 1933, the birth registration area covered all of continental United States. For the many years for which no adequate birth statistics exist, birth rates have been estimated on the basis of the census enumeration of children, available for every tenth year from 1800 to the present. It is customary to define the birth rate as the number of births per thousand population per year. This is the *crude birth rate* and is not to be confused with refined rates for specific groups in the population.

The Long Trend and Its Causes

Limited though the accurate statistics may be, from estimates that have been made the birth-rate trend for about a century and a half is clearly evident. After 1800 the secular trend in the rate of births in the United States was downward. It has been estimated that in 1800 the birth rate was over 50 per 1,000 population. By 1900 the rate had dropped to around 30, and by 1940 it was about 18. The birth-rate decline in the United States is not unique. Similar trends have occurred in other countries.

The list of postulated causes of the birth-rate decline is long, but it must be recognized that much that has been written, while plausible and even probable, lacks real proof. There are, however, at least two concrete facts that have provided clues in the search for causes. The first fact is that the decrease in the birth rate in the United States did not occur everywhere at the same time. At the beginning of the nineteenth century the rate of births was uniformly high throughout the United States. The process of decline started first in the older communities in the Northeastern region of the country, particularly in the more highly urbanized areas. From these centers the decline moved across the country until it was evident almost everywhere. Even so, the Southern states, several of the Rocky Mountain states, and the Dakotas showed relatively high birth rates as late as 1930. By 1940 birth rates as high as those of a century ago were reported for only the most isolated rural areas.

A second telling fact, which is related to the first, is that birth rates have been and continue to be higher in rural areas than in urban areas. It would be misleading merely to indicate the difference between crude birth rates in rural areas and in urban areas, for in some years the differences are not significant. In part this is because the proportion of women of childbearing age in rural areas is reduced by migration to the city. For our purposes *net reproduction rates* are more revealing. The net reproduction rate indicates the number of daughters that would be born during the course of their lifetime to the survivors of 100 newborn females. A rate of 100 is just enough to replace the group. In 1940 the urban net reproduction rate was 74; the rural nonfarm rate was 114; and the rural farm rate was 144. Thus, the urban population was not replacing itself, while the rural population was more than replacing itself. The difference between the rural farm and the rural nonfarm rates should be noted.

The conclusion to be drawn from the foregoing evidence is obvious. The decline in the birth rate is related to urbanization. As American cities have increased in number and in size the rate of births has dropped. Even the fertility of rural women, which is still higher than that of urban women, has decreased as urban influences have extended into rural regions. When the attempt is made to identify the specific causes of lower birth rates in urbanized areas, the results are less certain. We shall consider a few of the factors which appear to be associated with the long-time declining trend.

The change from a predominantly rural and agricultural way of life to an essentially urban and industrial way of life has transformed the economic functions of the family. Traditionally the family constituted an economic production unit. Many needs were provided for by the family itself. Food was grown, processed, and consumed by the members of the family. Clothing, also, was often homemade. Each family attempted to be as economically self-sufficient as possible. Many families saw little actual money in a year. Their economic security was dependent upon their capacity to produce. Under these circumstances, in which the co-operative activity of a number of people was essential, it is not difficult to see why large families were desirable.

All this was changed by conditions created by industrialization and urbanization. The transition was not abrupt, but it was definite. The principal economic activity of the family was no longer production but consumption. Economic security was based upon the ability to earn money to be used to purchase the necessities of life. Earning money became the responsibility of a limited number, usually one, of the family members. While all members of the family did not contribute earning power, they all participated in consumption. Thus was provided an economic motivation for the limitation of family size.

Our problem is to explain why modern families have become smaller, not why traditional families were larger; however, the contrast between past and present is helpful. It is not to be inferred from the preceding discussion that traditional rural folk were calculating individuals who planned their families with one eye on farm acreage. It would probably be more nearly correct to say that large families were assumed in earlier years and that family finances did not require any limitation of numbers. The family economy permitted numerous children, but there were many noneconomic reasons why families were large. A family-centered mode of living was practiced. It was taken for granted that an important objective of marriage was to "raise a family." Establishing a family gave status in the community. Where opportunities for social contact were limited, the associational value of children was enhanced. Of necessity many interests and activities centered around the home and involved the entire family.

This situation was altered by urbanization. Towns and cities provided a variety of attractive activities outside the home. In the pursuit of occupational and recreational interests, having many children entailed inconvenience. Instead of being objects of esteem, large families came to be regarded as somewhat unusual and peculiar. Whereas in traditional families numerous children had been anticipated, in the modern family it became customary to have only a few children, if any. The belief crystallized that two or three children were enough.

The acquisition of new interests outside the home is especially marked among women. The wide scope of women's activities is remarkable in contrast to their earlier rather circumscribed existence. Although it is doubtful whether women experienced much sense of restriction, it was in the domestic sphere that they formerly secured their satisfactions, achieved success, and received recognition. To a great degree a woman was judged by her ability as a homemaker and a mother. The demands made upon her by her family left little time for anything else. Recent inventions, however, have made housework less time-consuming; countless nondomestic avenues of expression are open; and modern ideas allow women to play new roles. In the expanded area of feminine activities, having few children means greater freedom. Even in carrying out household duties women are taken out of the home more frequently. Doing the family shopping accompanied by seven children would be no small accomplishment.

Up to this point our discussion has been concerned with the reasons for the lower rate of births in urbanized areas as contrasted to rural areas. In order further to understand the birth-rate trend in the United States attention must be given to a phenomenon found within urban areas. In cities there are *differential birth rates;* that is, there are different rates of increase for different groups in the population. It has been demonstrated by many studies that fertility rates are not the same for all socioeconomic groups. In general it is found that in lower- and middle-class groups especially, as social and economic status increases, the rate of reproduction decreases. In occupational terms this means that skilled workers have fewer children than unskilled workers, that business and clerical groups have fewer children than skilled workers, and that the rate of births in the professional class is the lowest of all. Variations in the fertility of educational groups are also discovered. For example, a study made in Indianapolis in 1941 reported that the number of children born to that date per 100 married women grouped by the highest school grade completed were as follows: below eighth grade, 270; eighth grade, 194; one to three years of high school, 171; four years of high school, 113; one to three years of college, 113; and four or more years of college, 88.[2] Similar evidence is offered by numerous other studies.

In part, the reasons for this differential birth rate are economic, but we are not dealing here with the simple economics of cost per child. If it were merely a matter of cost per child, then of course the lowest-income groups would have the fewest children and the highest-income groups would have the most children. Why, then, is the situation reversed? The answer is to be found in the differential desire to achieve certain standards and to reach definite goals. It would be difficult to guess how many children could be supported on a salary of $10,000 a year if only the essentials for healthy living were provided. However, as socioeconomic status increases, the felt need for maintaining a higher standard of living also increases. Desires and wants seem to be multiplied rather than added. Insomuch as the effort to attain a given standard involves parents' desires for themselves, they are motivated to have few children so that they may have more to spend on themselves. Insomuch as their ambitions involve their children, parents are motivated to limit the size of their family in order to have more to spend on the children they do have. Persons in the lower-income groups have the costs of living to meet, but they are less controlled by the compulsion to raise their standard of living. Therefore they are less concerned about the number of their children.

The goals of persons in the higher socioeconomic groups are not all material. They may be social or professional. Nevertheless the

[2] P. K. Whelpton and Clyde V. Kiser, "Social and Psychological Factors Affecting Fertility: I. Differential Fertility among 41,498 Native-white Couples in Indianapolis," Milbank Memorial Fund *Quarterly*, vol. 21, no. 3, July, 1943, pp. 252, 253.

consequences are the same. To the degree that it is believed that children will be a hindrance to the realization of ambitions, families are small. Again, the reproductive behavior of persons in the lower occupational and educational groups appears to be less regulated by such ambitions.

Having considered the influence of urbanization and some of the reasons for differential birth rates within cities, we come finally to the possible effect upon birth rates of the use of contraceptive devices. It is definitely known that among groups in which contraception is practiced the birth rate is low, whereas in groups in which it is not practiced the birth rate is higher. This could lead to the conclusion that the use of contraceptive devices causes the lower rate of fertility. However, it must be remembered that the decline in the rate of reproduction was well underway before the use of modern commercialized methods of contraception. Further, it has frequently been pointed out that even primitive groups employed means of limiting the size of their families. Apparently when there was a desire to control reproduction a way was found. This suggests that the role of contraceptives has not been so much to cause the birth-rate decline as to facilitate it. The primary causes of the decline were those factors which created the desire to limit the number of children. Given this desire, the use of contraceptives became the easy means of controlling births. Of course, the availability of modern contraceptives cannot be completely discounted as a cause of the decline of births. It is possible that their ready availability has encouraged regularity in the control of conception.

The higher rate of births in the lower income and educational groups has sometimes been attributed to a lack of knowledge concerning contraception. This reasoning seems to invest the members of these groups with a degree of ignorance which probably does not exist. It is possible that they are uninformed with regard to clinically prescribed methods of birth control, but it is unlikely that they are ignorant of popular methods. Again the matter appears to be one of attitudes. Because persons in the lower income and educational groups are less motivated to limit births, they pay less attention to contraception.

Birth Rates since 1940

A significant change in birth rates occurred in the 1940's. After reaching a low of 16.6 in 1933, crude birth rates in the latter half of the 1930's fluctuated around 17. From 17.9 in 1940 the crude birth rate rose to a high of 25.8 in 1947. After 1947 rates fluctuated around 24.

Table 9. Crude Birth Rates, United States, 1940–1950

Year	Crude birth rate
1940	17.9
1941	18.8
1942	20.8
1943	21.5
1944	20.2
1945	19.5
1946	23.3
1947	25.8
1948	24.2
1949	23.9
1950	23.6

SOURCE: National Office of Vital Statistics, *Vital Statistics—Special Reports,* vol. 37, no. 7.

There is no real agreement about the meaning of the change in birth rates in the 1940's. After the Second World War many population authorities believed that the rise in birth rates was temporary and that rates would quickly move toward the level of the late 1930's. Although the expected decline has not taken place, some population students maintain that the higher rates do not represent a significant change in the size of families. They hold that factors such as age at marriage and child spacing account for the higher rates. Other students of population take the view that families have become larger and that birth rates above the level of those of the thirties may be expected to continue for some time. In any case, it is evident that in projecting population trends birth rates are not accurately predictable at present.

THE DEATH RATE

The death rate is usually expressed in terms of the number of deaths per thousand population per year. Death statistics, like birth statistics, are far from complete in the United States. A few states have recorded deaths for more than one hundred years, but it was not until 1900 that the annual collection of mortality statistics began, and not until 1933 that the death registration area became nationwide. Although records for early years are only fragmentary, it is clear that the reduction in mortality rates has been considerable. In Massachusetts, for example, the death rate was reduced from 27.8 per 1,000 in 1789 to 11.9 in 1940. Except for the influenza epidemic of 1918, in which year the death rate reached 18.1, the death-rate trend has been downward since 1900. In the states included in the registration area the death rate was 17.6 in 1900, 13.0 in 1920, 11.3 in 1930, 10.7 in 1940, and 9.6 in 1950. Since 1921, when the rate was 11.6, the change has not been great.

Medical, economic, and social factors have worked together to bring about the decline in the death rate. Diseases which were important causes of death 50 years ago have been greatly reduced, and some have been almost eliminated. From 1900 to 1902, typhoid fever and diphtheria each killed more than 28 persons a year out of every 100,000 of the population. The death rate for measles, scarlet fever, and whooping cough was more than 10 for each, but now is not more than 1 or 2. During the same period, the rate for bronchitis has been reduced from over 40 to less than 3, and the pneumonia and influenza rate has dropped from nearly 190 to less than 65. The largest reduction of all is in tuberculosis, which has been cut from over 165 to less than 35 deaths per 100,000 persons per year.

The significance of the progress that has been made in the saving of life is all the greater because of the marked decline in the infant mortality rate which has been achieved. In 1915 there were approximately 100 deaths per 1,000 infants under one year of age. Thus one infant in ten died before reaching the age of one. The infant death rate was steadily lowered until in 1942 there were only 40.8 deaths per 1,000 live births in a year.

Along with advances in medicine and surgery, improved sanitation has contributed much to the death-rate decline among both children and adults. A broad campaign of education has made individuals aware of the need for sanitary practices in the home. Community programs for the maintenance of cleanly and healthful conditions have produced results. The removal of wastes, the purification of sewage, the protection of water supplies, and the elimination of breeding places for insect carriers of disease have aided in the struggle to prolong life.

Control and utilization of natural resources to provide a plentiful and constant supply of food and other necessities of life have also influenced the death rate. The food supply has become more abundant and more diversified. The development of better food processing, storage, and transportation has made for healthful living. The general standard of living has been raised, and the amount of income which can be spent for medical care, for food, and to improve general living conditions is higher.

But the picture is not altogether bright. Since 1900 the rate for accidental deaths has remained almost unchanged. Cancer and diseases of the heart cause about twice as many deaths as formerly. It should be stated, however, that the increase in cancer and certain of the so-called degenerative diseases may in part be due to more accurate diagnosis. Furthermore, as life has been prolonged there has been an increase in the proportion of the population in the older age groups, in which these causes of death are most common. Nevertheless the seriousness of these increases is not to be minimized.

What can be predicted concerning the future of the mortality trend? Since eventually everyone must die, the death rate cannot go down indefinitely. As death is postponed a greater proportion of the population comes within the older age group. As this group grows larger in proportion to other groups, the downward death-rate trend must cease. It is expected that the further reduction of death rates among children and young adults will be greater than in the older age groups. This fact is important because mortality improvement in the younger groups has more effect upon the average length of life than improvement at old age. It is also important because reduction of the number of deaths among young people means that more persons reach the reproductive years and thus contribute to population growth.

TRENDS IN POPULATION GROWTH

The Past

The past importance of the three factors involved in population growth may be stated briefly. Throughout the history of the United

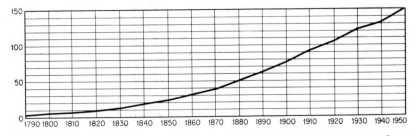

Figure 8. Population Growth in the United States. The seventeen censuses have measured the growth of the United States population from 3.9 million in 1790 to 150.7 million in 1950. The population at each census is given here in millions. (From Philip M. Hauser, "The Census," *Scientific American*, April, 1951, p. 15.)

States migration has contributed to the rapid growth of our population, but the extent of its effect remains unknown. Since the enactment of restrictive laws immigration has ceased to be a significant source of population growth in this country. But whatever the effect of immigration, far more important was the balance of births and deaths. We have seen that the trend of birth rates was down for many years. Nevertheless because there were many more births than deaths the population continued to grow. Rapidly declining death rates permitted a considerable excess of births over deaths even though birth rates were going down. Of course if birth rates had remained high while death rates declined, the population of the United States would be much larger than it is today.

Although our population has continued to grow, the declining birth rate has had a marked effect. The rate of growth declined steadily. Between 1800 and 1810 the population increased 36.4 per cent; between 1880 and 1890 the increase was 25.5 per cent; and between 1930 and 1940 the increase was 7.2 per cent.

Table 10. Population and Per Cent of Increase, United States, 1790–1950

Year	Population	Decennial per cent increase
1790	3,929,214	
1800	5,308,483	35.1
1810	7,239,881	36.4
1820	9,638,453	33.1
1830	12,866,020	33.5
1840	17,069,453	32.7
1850	23,191,876	35.9
1860	31,443,321	35.6
1870	38,558,371	22.6
1880	50,155,783	30.1
1890	62,947,714	25.5
1900	75,994,575	20.7
1910	91,972,266	21.0
1920	105,710,620	14.9
1930	122,775,046	16.1
1940	131,669,275	7.2
1950	150,697,361	14.5

SOURCE: U.S. Bureau of the Census *U.S. Census of Population: 1950*, vol. 1, *Number of Inhabitants*, 1952.

The Future

In the 1920's and 1930's the trend of population growth in the United States appeared clear. The rate of growth was steadily declining. The great immigration was past, birth rates were going down, and death rates could not go down indefinitely. Under these conditions it seemed reasonable to expect that the rate of population growth would continue to decline until there would be no growth at all. This was the conclusion to which demographers (professional students of population) came after careful analysis of the combined influence of migration, birth rates, and death rates. Numerous predictions were made. The predictions varied as to the peak size and date, but there was general agreement that in the latter part of the present century the population of the United States would cease to grow. Some analysts expected population to reach the point at which it would become stable as early as 1960.

It is evident now that earlier predictions were in error. In the middle 1950's total population, still growing, reached the point at which earlier some analysts expected it would stabilize. The rate of growth between 1940 and 1950 was twice as great as between 1930 and 1940. The chief reason for the errors in prediction was the change in the birth-rate trend.

At best it is difficult to project long-time trends of population growth. The uncertainty of future birth rates has induced marked caution. Most demographers agree, however, that a stable population is far less immediate than was believed in the thirties. A conservative prediction is that if the population becomes stable it will not be until well into the next century. However, if birth rates are high in the future, a stable population is not in sight.

Population *growth* and *rate of growth* are not to be confused. Although our total population is expected to grow for many years, unless birth rates are high the long-time trend of the rate of growth will be downward. In viewing the effects of population trends attention must be given to the rate of growth as well as to numerical growth.

IMPLICATIONS OF TRENDS IN POPULATION GROWTH

For many Americans words like "stability" and "decline" are objectionable in the extreme. They much prefer to think in terms of "growth" and "increase." Thus schools are expected to increase their enrollments, churches seek to add new members, businesses struggle to expand, and old organizations consider it a sign of success when they can form new subsidiary organizations. In view of the strong attachment to the idea of growth in America it is not surprising that the prospect of a decline in the rate of population growth has been viewed with alarm by some individuals. They

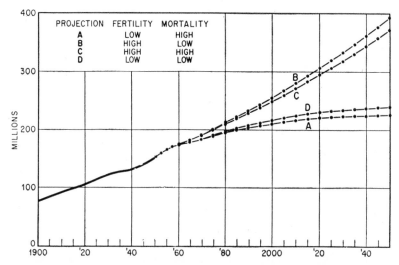

PROJECTION	FERTILITY	MORTALITY
A	LOW	HIGH
B	HIGH	LOW
C	HIGH	HIGH
D	LOW	LOW

Figure 9. United States Total Population: 1900–2050. This chart shows four possible trends of future population growth in the United States. Long-range prediction is made especially difficult by the uncertainty of future birth-rate trends. (From Robert J. Myers and E. A. Rasor, *Illustrative United States Population Projections*, 1952, Actuarial Study 33, Federal Security Agency, November, 1952, p. 25.)

have felt that the only good population is a rapidly expanding one. However, since it is possible that the population of the United States will not continue to increase indefinitely, it becomes necessary to understand the implications of a declining rate of population growth and of ultimate, although far from immediate, stability of population.

Economic Implications

The economic consequences of population change are outstanding. It may be anticipated that the total national economy will be affected. Almost by definition our economy has been an expanding economy. Certainly in practice it has been expansive. The business that merely holds its own is not regarded as a successful business. A thriving enterprise is supposed to get bigger and bigger. The aim is to sell more products so that more profit can be made so that more plants can be built so that more goods can be produced so that more products can be sold, and so expansion rolls on. It would be folly to think and act in this manner if at the same time that production is increased the market is not increased also. To a large degree we have been able to take an expanding market for granted. One of the important reasons why this has been true is that at the same time that more goods have been produced, population growth has provided an ever-increasing number of customers. There have always been more people to help to create a greater demand for more goods.

The expansion of our economy, of course, cannot be attributed to population growth alone, for there are many countries with large populations which maintain low levels of economic production. Nor have all the years of population growth been years of prosperity. Nevertheless, the rapid increase in the number of people in the United States has had widespread effects, and many segments of the economy have been involved. It has been necessary to build houses, pave streets, and provide power, light, water, and sewer systems. New factories, transportation and communication facilities, offices, and stores have had to be constructed. These enterprises have offered opportunities for investment and have furnished employment for a large number of people.

In a country, then, in which the assumption of economic expansion has in part been based upon the assumption of population increase, it seems desirable to consider the possible consequences of diminishing population growth. The population will continue to increase for many years, but what will happen if the rate of growth again slows? A somewhat gloomy situation might be anticipated. Considerable logic could be used to support the pessimistic prediction that less rapid population expansion might stall our economy. Relatively fewer additional people could mean less incentive for expansion of business. Less expansion could result in a reduction of opportunities for investment. It could also reduce the need for workers, which in turn might operate to lower wages and to bring on unemployment. Reduction of the aggregate income of consumers would lessen the demand for goods, thus causing a further decline in production and still more unemployment. Once started, such a downward spiral could be calamitous. Fortunately there is nothing inevitable about this untoward series of events. They could but they probably need not occur. If a state of mind is created which recognizes the need for adjustment it may be assumed that the transition to a less rapidly growing population can be made without disaster. It is impossible to know just what the nature of future economic changes will be. Adjustments will be made from time to time as the need arises. Although only time will reveal the details, it appears probable that a diminution of population growth will to a degree hitherto unknown draw attention to the importance of consumers as such in maintaining economic stability and a high level of production. Providing purchasing power will be a major economic concern. The producer may find it necessary to safeguard the purchasing power of the consumer in order to survive himself.

The Demographic Position of the United States

Will population trends in any way modify the position of the United States among the nations of the world? Ours is not the only country with a declining rate of growth. Other economically advanced and urbanized nations are moving in the direction of population stability. Included in this group are the countries of Europe except those in the eastern and southern parts, Canada, Australia, New Zealand, and the white population of the Union of South Africa. Together these countries contain less than one-fifth of the world's population. Another fifth of the people of the world are in countries which are not so highly industrialized and urbanized and in which birth rates have not dropped so far. Included in this group are the Soviet Union, Japan, eastern and southern Europe, and parts of Latin America. It is expected that in these countries population stability or even decline will occur in time, but not so soon as in the first group. The great agrarian regions of Asia and Africa present a marked contrast. The factors which cause fertility rates to drop have not yet had an effect, whereas mortality rates have been reduced in some areas. Since this circumstance does not make for a declining rate of population growth it may be some time before industrialization and urbanization slow down population growth in these parts of the world.

The position of the United States has never been determined by population size. A combination of population, industrial potential, scientific advance, and military might have given to the United States a position of power unique in the history of the world. It is possible that populationwise the United States will become relatively less important in the world. What the future industrial prominence of this country will be is not ours to know. It is to be hoped that as the United States continues to make its contribution in world society any demographic deficiency can be compensated for by a high level of culture.

SUMMARY

The growth of population in the United States has been rapid. Three factors determine population growth or decline: migration, the birth rate, and the death rate.

The massive migration to America contributed materially to population growth, but how much it contributed is not known. To some degree the effect of immigration on population growth was counteracted by emigration.

The trend in the birth rate was downward for almost a century and a half. The decline occurred first and most rapidly in urbanized and industrialized areas. By now birth rates have declined everywhere in the United States, but rates are lower in urban areas than in rural areas. Birth rates are not equally low in all economic classes. Rates are highest in the lower-income groups. Interrelated economic, status, and interest factors are involved in causing birth-rate decline and birth-rate differences. Birth rates were lowest in the 1930's. Since 1940 the rates have been somewhat higher.

The death-rate trend has been downward for many years. Medical, economic, and social factors have worked together to bring about the decline. The death rate cannot go down indefinitely, and it may be expected to rise above the present level. In the past the declining death rate has been the most important factor causing rapid population growth.

Before 1940 it seemed evident that the population of the United States was moving toward stability. The birth rate was going down, immigration was largely cut off, and the death rate could not continue to go down. But the upturn in birth rates has made the future trend of population growth less certain. It is expected, however, that although the population will continue to grow beyond the end of the present century, the long-term trend in the rate of growth will be downward.

A declining rate of population growth has economic and international implications. Inasmuch as rapid population growth has been assumed in our economy, a declining rate of growth will probably require economic adjustments. Moreover it appears that the future world position of the United States will not derive from superior numbers of people.

SELECTED REFERENCES

Kiser, Clyde V.: *Group Differentials in Urban Fertility*, Baltimore, Md., Williams & Wilkins, 1942.

Kuczynski, Robert R.: *The Balance of Births and Deaths*, New York, Macmillan, 1928.

Landis, Paul H., and Paul K. Hatt: *Population Problems*, New York, American Book, 1954.

Lorimer, Frank, Ellen Winston, and Louise K. Kiser: *Foundations of American Population Policy*, New York, Harper, 1940.

National Resources Committee: *The Problems of a Changing Population*, 1938.

Smith, T. Lynn: *Population Analysis*, New York, McGraw-Hill, 1948.

Thompson, Warren S.: *Population Problems*, New York, McGraw-Hill, 1953.

Willcox, Walter F.: *Studies in American Demography*, Ithaca, N.Y., Cornell University Press, 1940.

PART TWO: Communities

CHAPTER SEVEN

Rural Communities

The United States began as, and during a large part of its history has been, a rural nation. Even though urbanization is now occurring rapidly the influence of rural culture on the American way of life is considerable. American culture is a combination of rural and urban elements. The present chapter deals with the rural setting and with the factors related to the distribution of people in rural communities. The following chapter is a discussion of typical patterns of group life in rural areas.

THE MEANING OF RURAL

The meaning of *rural* is not defined by a single attribute; it involves a combination of characteristics. It is proposed here to consider some of the characteristic features of rural society.

Size of the Population

For census purposes in 1950 all territory other than that in places having 2,500 inhabitants or more was regarded as rural. In earlier censuses, unincorporated places having 2,500 inhabitants or more were also classified as rural. The new definition is superior to the old inasmuch as under the old definition some large and densely populated places were counted as rural merely because they lacked legal municipal boundaries.

The Bureau of the Census divides the rural population into two major groups: rural farm and rural nonfarm. The farm population for 1950 included all persons living on farms, as determined by the question, "Is this house on a farm (or ranch)?" The classi-

133

fication depended upon the respondent's conception of what is meant by the word "farm." Farm residence was determined without regard to occupation. The rural nonfarm population included all persons living outside urban areas who did not live on farms.[1]

In taking the census clear-cut categories must be created. If counting is to be done it must be known at precisely what point one group is divided from another. It must be recognized, however, that definitions of rural and of urban in terms of numbers of people are necessarily arbitrary. The dividing line between rural and urban is set at 2,500 population. Why not 2,000 or 3,000? It is possible that a place having a population of 3,000 might be as rural in its way of life as a place having 2,000 population.

This is by way of indicating that although population size is helpful in making the rural-urban distinction, from a sociological point of view other factors are involved. Rurality is a way of living. A rural community is one that has particular social characteristics. It is a community in which certain occupations predominate. When these criteria are employed an exact definition of rural is difficult. The break between rural and urban is gradual rather than abrupt. Of many places it is only possible to say that they are more or less rural or urban.

Nevertheless from a sociological point of view population is significant, for rural sociologists have used the nature of social relationships as one important basis for distinguishing rural from urban. In a rural area population density is low enough so that the inhabitant can know a large proportion of the persons in the area in which he lives. The presence of a stranger is recognized by almost everyone in a rural community. Anonymity is not characteristic of rural life as it is of urban life.

The Importance of Agriculture

"Rural" and "agriculture" are not synonymous terms, but the primary importance of agriculture is one of the outstanding char-

---

[1] U.S. Bureau of the Census, *U.S. Census of Population: 1950*, vol. 2, *Characteristics of the population*, 1953, part 1, pp. 33, 35.

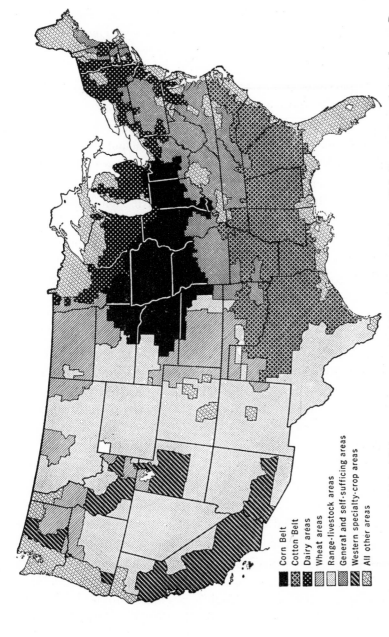

Corn Belt
Cotton Belt
Dairy areas
Wheat areas
Range-livestock areas
General and self-sufficing areas
Western specialty-crop areas
All other areas

Figure 10. Regionalized Types of Farming in the United States. (Source: U.S. Department of Agriculture, Bureau of Agricultural Economics.)

135

acteristics of most rural communities. In 1950, of the employed
workers living on rural farms, 70.8 per cent were engaged in agriculture. Of the employed rural nonfarm residents, 8.5 per cent
were engaged in agriculture.

The importance of agriculture in rural life cannot be indicated
fully by giving statistics on the number of persons who work at
farming. Farming is more than an occupation to be engaged in
for a set number of hours each day and then put aside until the
return to work on the next day. Farming is a way of life as well
as an occupation. Directly and indirectly it regulates the activities
of the family. It dominates conversation. It influences patterns of
thought. The farm child does not grow up "not sure what Dad
does at work." He knows the importance of rainfall and of daily
changes in the weather. He is aware of commodity prices and what
their fluctuations mean for him. The child as well as the adult
understands the need, albeit sometimes irksome, for doing work
at the appropriate time. Frequently recreation is related to the
main business of farming. Farm-women meetings, 4-H clubs, fairs,
and demonstrations are regarded as recreational, but they are also
agricultural. Farming is not an interest exclusively for adult
males. The occupational tie is a family tie. Further, the all-encom-
passing agricultural milieu is shared by most families. The common occupation creates a common environment. Men, women, and
children have an occupational tie throughout the community.

The dominance of agriculture in rural areas extends beyond the
occupation of farming. Many of the nonagricultural occupations
are closely related to agriculture; some are dependent upon agriculture. Grain and feed businesses are an integral part of the agricultural enterprise. Farm-implement dealers are prosperous or not
depending on farm prosperity. Many residents of rural villages
gain a livelihood by providing services for farm families. They
operate the gas stations, automobile agencies, stores, banks, and
transportation facilities. Economically they are dependent upon
agriculture, for the farmer's income becomes their income.

Table 11. Percentage Distribution of Employed Persons by Industry Groups for the United States, Rural Nonfarm and Rural Farm: 1950

Industry group	United States	Rural nonfarm	Rural farm
Agriculture	12.2	8.5	70.8
Forestry and fisheries	0.2	0.7	0.2
Mining	1.7	4.9	1.3
Construction	6.1	8.9	3.1
Manufacturing	25.9	25.6	9.4
Transportation, communication, and other public utilities	7.8	7.4	2.1
Wholesale and retail trade	18.8	18.0	4.3
Finance, insurance, and real estate	3.4	1.9	0.5
Business and repair service	2.5	3.1	0.8
Personal services	6.2	5.9	1.7
Entertainment and recreation services	1.0	0.8	0.1
Professional and related services	8.3	8.4	2.7
Public administration	4.4	4.0	1.2
Industry not reported	1.5	1.9	1.8

SOURCE: U.S. Bureau of the Census, *U.S. Census of Population: 1950*, vol. 2, *Characteristics of the Population*, 1953, part 1.

Nonagricultural Occupations

Although agricultural employment is dominant in rural society, nonagricultural occupations have an important place. Even the population living on farms is not wholly dependent upon agriculture. Some members of farm families are engaged in farming while others are not; some persons living on farms have both agricultural and nonagricultural employment; and some farm residents make a seasonal change from agriculture to nonagricultural work. In 1950, 9.4 per cent of the workers living on rural farms were engaged in manufacturing; 4.3 per cent were in wholesale and retail trade; 3.1 per cent were in construction; and 2.7 per cent were in professional and related services. About 35 per cent of the families living on rural farms in April, 1951, indicated that the major source of their earnings in 1950 was from nonfarm work.[2] Thus the distinction between the farm and nonfarm populations becomes less definite.

[2] *Ibid.*, p. 34.

The occupational attachments of rural nonfarm people are chiefly in nonagricultural industries. Manufacturing ranks first, in 1950 accounting for 25.6 per cent of the employed workers. The second largest group of rural nonfarm workers were the 18 per cent in wholesale and retail trade. Other important nonagricultural industries are construction (8.9 per cent); professional and related services (8.4 per cent); and transportation, communication, and public utilities (7.4 per cent).

The importance of nonagricultural occupations in rural areas suggests that the meaning of rural is changing. We shall see that isolation, limited services, self-sufficiency, and localism are far less characteristic of rural society than in the past. The changes are manifest in the occupational structure.

SETTLEMENT PATTERNS

In the study of rural communities attention must be given to the manner in which the population is distributed on the land. The arrangement of people on the land affects other phases of rural life. The way in which land is used, the availability of economic and other services, and the nature of social relationships are conditioned by settlement patterns.

Historical View

In many parts of the world throughout the history of agriculture it has been customary for persons engaged in farming to live together in villages. From villages the inhabitants go out to cultivate the land in the surrounding territory. Sometimes the distance from the village to the fields is short, but villagers have been known to go a number of miles to till the soil and reap their crops.

In the settlement of colonial America there was a tendency to try to establish the farm-village pattern. Early New England towns had farm-village characteristics. The first settlers usually remained in the groups in which they came. They battled together against the elements and against the Indians. The village system was the one under which they had lived before coming to this country, and they transplanted the form of settlement with which they were familiar. Almost all of the early New England settlements were unmodified reproductions of the English type of village.

The village pattern was found throughout the colonies. In Pennsylvania there were various forms of settlement, but a definite effort was made to promote the establishment of villages. It appears that William Penn preferred them over scattered farms. There were numerous early attempts to form villages in New Jersey, Delaware, and Maryland. In the South the plantation system had some village characteristics. Workers' quarters were in clusters rather than scattered. Planters' homes were often in villages from which they commuted to their plantations. Even in the back country attempts were made to develop villages.

Only in New York, under the influence of the Dutch, was the single farmstead the original pattern of settlement. In this instance Dutch authorities during one period concluded that the English village settlement was superior and attempted to bring about a change. Their efforts were largely unsuccessful.

While greatest encouragement was given to the formation of villages, in no region of early America was the village the only form of settlement. New England had some isolated farmsteads. From the beginning both villages and scattered farmsteads were established in the Middle Colonies. In the South isolated small farms were found, particularly among the displaced poor whites. Frontier farms were frequently isolated.

Scattered Farmsteads

The great majority of farmers in the United States today do not live in villages. Unlike their European and early American predecessors, they live apart from their partners in agriculture. They live on the land that they cultivate, and farm homes are widely scattered. This arrangement is referred to as the *isolated-farm, single-farmstead,* or *scattered-farmsteads* pattern of settlement.

The probable reasons for the decline of the village as a place

USDA

Dairy Farm in Lancaster County, Pennsylvania. American farms are of many types. Tradition, land resources, climate, and work requirements combine to produce a variety of farm cultures.

of residence for persons engaged in agriculture are many. Convenience in caring for livestock was one factor that led to the dispersion of farms. Tending and providing water for livestock could be done with less difficulty by living on the land, away from the village. The desire for land and cattle was great. More land was required than was available in the immediate vicinity of the village. Further, the agricultural village is usually composed of a homogeneous population. The creation of villages in America required the cooperation of families having common purposes and like culture. The first settlements were inhabited by persons of similar backgrounds and objectives. But the families that met on the Western frontier were not notably homogeneous. They represented a great variety of backgrounds, beliefs, and objectives. They did not spontaneously congregate in villages, and they seemed uninclined to organize and put forth an effort to achieve

Submarginal Farm in Washington. The cultivation of such land does not yield a profit. Some farms of this type are found in nearly all parts of the United States.

this end. Life on the frontier fostered individualism. Indeed, the frontier selected individualists as its inhabitants. The settlers of the West were men on a quest. They were a striving variety of men, eager for land. For the most part they pushed westward in families rather than in village-size groups. They had individual and family values, not village values.

In large portions of the United States the way in which land was divided contributed to the development of scattered farmsteads. The Land Ordinance of 1785 provided that land surveyed thereafter should be divided into units having thirty-six sections, each section one mile square. The sections often were divided into quarter sections of 160 acres. The rectangular pattern covers most of the territory west of the Alleghenies. This method of land division promoted the isolation of farms. The trend was furthered when,

USDA

Cattle Ranch and Range in the Yampa River Valley, Colorado. The range-livestock area includes farms that are extremely large and others that are relatively small. The topography of the area is also notably varied.

after 1841, it was required that in order to acquire unsettled land it was necessary to establish residence on such land.

Transportation has an interesting bearing on the appearance and the survival of scattered farmsteads. When transportation was poor it was more convenient for the farmer to live on the land than to live in a village and travel to his farm to work. At that time the rural family was relatively self-sufficient, and visits to the village to buy supplies could be few. Today the farm family is much dependent upon the town and must visit it regularly. Improved transportation makes it possible to maintain frequent contact with the town while living at a considerable distance from it. Thus, while at one time poor transportation encouraged the development of the single farmstead, good transportation is now contributing to its perpetuation.

A number of writers have lamented the existence of the isolated-farm type of settlement. It limits, they say, the social contacts of the farmer. He does not benefit from the cultural and material advantages of the town. Children, having few playmates and few opportunities for association with the outside world, grow up ill prepared for social intercourse. Although such may have been the situation in the past, this is hardly an accurate description of the present. Farmsteads are still scattered, but they are far less isolated.

Types of Farms

Observation of the relation of the farmer to the land must not be distorted by the prevalence of scattered farmsteads. *Single farmstead* is a term that may evoke an image of a particular type of farm. There are, however, great differences in the types of farms. Farms range in size from less than 3 acres to more than 100,000 acres. Farms may be classified as (1) commercial family farms, (2) subsistence family farms, (3) plantations, and (4) factory farms.

1. The family farm is generally thought of as the typical agricultural enterprise. It is the family farm that the advocates of rural living have idealized. Most of the labor and management on this type of farm are provided by the family. The term *commercial family farm* is used to denote the farm on which the income is sufficient to support the family at a satisfactory level. The operator lives on the land, and agriculture is his primary pursuit. This is the most common type of farm in the United States. The size of these farms varies. Family poultry, fruit, and truck farms are usually under 50 acres. Most of the general, animal-specialty, and grain farms are over 100 acres. There are many farms of over 500 acres which would classify as family farms.

2. Subsistence farms are those which do not provide sufficient income from the sale of farm products for family support. Included in this category are self-sufficient farms, that is, those in which the family consumes more of its products than it sells. Many of these farms are small, and the existence eked out on them is

USDA

Texas Mexican Cotton Pickers in Arkansas. Cotton has created a distinctive type of agriculture. Dependence upon a large supply of cheap labor has been an important feature of the traditional cotton culture.

meager. Another type of subsistence farm is the part-time farm. In this case off-farm work is the chief source of family income. The agricultural-industrial combination appears to be increasing.

3. The plantation is the oldest type of large-scale farm in the United States. In a study of 646 plantations in seven Southeastern states, T. J. Woofter defined a plantation as a tract with five or more families, including the landlord, laborers, and share tenants or renters. The average size was 907 acres. Fourteen families, not counting the landlord's family, lived on the typical plantation. The average amount of land cultivated by families was 20 acres for sharecroppers, 25 acres for tenants, and 45 acres for wage hands.[3] Plantations are a Southern phenomenon, and their distribution has remained much as it was at the time of the Civil War. Plantation

[3] T. J. Woofter, Jr., "Landlord and Tenant on the Cotton Plantation," Works Progress Administration Research Monograph V, 1936.

control is usually in the hands of individuals rather than corporations.

4. Factory farms are the nonplantation, large-scale farms. They are operated entirely as business enterprises. Labor is hired and work is organized and supervised much as it is in a modern factory. The labor force frequently is hired on a seasonal basis. Large-scale farms usually specialize in one crop or in one type of crop. Factory farms often are owned by corporations rather than by individuals or by families.

Villages

There are in the United States a few survivals of the traditional farm village. Belief in communal life has always been a tenet of Mormonism. Early Mormon settlements were almost exclusively village communities. Those who tilled the soil were expected to live with their brethren in towns. Requirements have been relaxed, but in several states of the West, Mormon communities are found which are essentially of the farm-village type. Also, many Spanish-speaking groups in the Southwestern states have a traditional village culture. In rural areas Spanish Americans demonstrate a strong attachment to the village form of settlement. Periodically experimental farm-village communities have been organized in various parts of the country, only to be shortly disbanded.

While farm villages, inhibited by persons engaged directly in agriculture, have never been numerous in the United States, the rural village has had a most important function. The rural village is a center of business rather than a place of residence for the farm population. It is inhabited by persons many of whom are indirectly dependent upon agriculture. The trade relations of rural dwellers are facilitated by village centers. These small but important centers are part of the national network of transportation and communication which covers rural America and which connects rural and urban areas.

In recent decades there has been an increase in a type of farming which appears to have something in common with the farm-village way of life. Persons living in towns and cities engage in farming and commute as necessity demands. This practice is found particularly in grain- and fruit-growing areas. Absentee grain farmers are sometimes referred to as "suitcase farmers" because they leave the city for several weeks to plant crops, then return home until the harvest season, at which time another trip is made to gather crops. Like the residents of farm villages, these agriculturalists travel between town and country to carry on farming; but unlike farm villagers, when modern commuter farmers are at home their way of life is usually urban rather than rural.

There are other rural villages with characteristics different from those of the agriculture-dependent villages. These are the industrial villages described below: [4]

"The industrial village is usually overlooked by those interested in the amalgamation of agriculture and industry, yet it is most important. Moreover, its history is valuable to those who would bring a payroll to the support of agriculture. For three quarters of a century industrial villages have been doing this very thing, evolving a distinctive type of community, in which population is younger, with more males and children and fewer widows than in agricultural villages. There is small contact with the hinterland, partly because of location, as in lumbering centers, and partly because of independent interests. The average trade area is only four square miles, with only half as many stores as in the agricultural village. Farmers do not frequent its churches, farm children do not attend its schools. One eighth of its employees come from farm homes. Life is ordered by the factory whistle and the decision of an often distant and unknown executive. Industry dominates the social organization of the community, in which there is often a high degree of paternalism, never found in agricultural villages. In the South, where textile mills have been imported into agricultural villages, a great gulf usually exists between the old population and the new who live on 'the mill hill.' Mill-workers and

[4] J. H. Kolb and E. de S. Brunner, *The Study of Rural Society*, Boston, Houghton Mifflin, 1946, pp. 281–282.

USDA

Mining Village in Allegany County, Maryland. Although this type of community is rural, it presents a marked contrast to rural communities dominated by agriculture.

agrarians are served by different churches, although of the same denomination. So far from uniting industry and agriculture, the average case has bred social estrangement."

THE RURAL COMMUNITY

Having viewed the rural setting and the arrangement of people on the land, we turn to a consideration of the community as a major functioning unit of rural society.

The Meaning of Community

The word *community* is used in a variety of ways. In popular usage it is assumed that everyone understands what a community is, and yet there is little consistency in the manner in which the term is employed. It is therefore necessary to define community specifically for sociological purposes if there is to be a meeting of minds. In the chapters that follow the term is used to mean that a community exists when the people of a locality are served by the same institutions and services. With regard to rural areas in particular the definition given by Sanderson has gained wide acceptance: [5] "A rural community is that form of association maintained between the people and their institutions in a local area in which they live on dispersed farmsteads and in a village which usually forms the center of their common activities."

When these definitions are analyzed there are three essential elements: locality, people, and common dependence upon institutions and services. First, consider locality. There is an identifiable geographical area. The territory may be large or small, depending upon the other factors. The area of a particular community can be defined, but the limits are not clear-cut as political boundaries are. Communities can be delimited only roughly, and their boundaries frequently are unrelated to political limits. The people of a community may be few or many; they may be densely settled or widely scattered. The confines of a community are not determined by any fixed standards of population or of area size. The third element of the definition, common dependence upon institutions and services, is the determining factor. People belong to the same community because they buy at the same stores, sell at the same markets, deal at the same banks, attend the same schools and churches, and use the same recreational facilities. It is not required that everyone within a locality know everyone else in order for a community to exist. On the contrary, it is quite unlikely that all persons in a rural community will be personally acquainted, and in urban communities it is impossible. Community relatedness derives from involvement in the same network of organizations and services.

[5] Dwight Sanderson, *Rural Sociology and Rural Social Organization*, New York, Wiley, 1942, p. 278.

Delimiting Rural Communities

Given the foregoing definition of community, how could the limits of a specific community be discovered? Where does one community area end and another begin? Around 1913 C. J. Galpin invented a method for mapping rural community areas which has been used in many ways since that time. Galpin constructed a brief questionnaire which he used to discover such things as where farm families traded, where they went to school, where they went to church, and where they banked their money. He then located on a map the families trading at the center that lived farthest out on all roads radiating from the center. He drew a line around the area connecting the most remote families for each service. The bounds for all service areas did not coincide, but together they outlined approximate community limits. Galpin concluded that the trade area is the most important single determiner of community boundaries. More recently, consolidated school and high-school attendance areas have been discovered to be of outstanding importance in determining community areas. Because of the relationship between town and country, Galpin combined "rural" and "urban" into *rurban* to designate communities composed of open-country areas and town centers.

It will be recognized that the activities of a family are not always related to only one center. Certain kinds of trading may be carried on at a small center, while other trading is in a larger center. The family then belongs to two communities at the same time. In many areas rural social organization involves a system of communities in which several smaller communities are included in the larger community.

In most cases a rural community is organized around one service center; however, there are exceptions. In some communities the people of the entire locality are about equally dependent on two or three villages. Each village performs a somewhat specialized function. The community is bound together as it would be if all services were performed in one center. Also there are open-country communities that have no village centers. A school, a church, and a store located in the open country may provide common association within a locality. Such communities are found especially in parts of the South.

Service Centers

The service centers upon which rural people are dependent vary in size and in the functions they perform. On the basis of research conducted by J. H. Kolb, the typical service centers have been classified as follows: [6]

"(1) *The single, simple service type.* This type of center is usually an open-country neighborhood or hamlet center where single and comparatively simple or undifferentiated services are performed. The agencies in such centers may be school, church, general store, Grange hall, or repair shop. The centers usually fall into the hamlet classification; that is, places of less than 250 population.

"(2) *The limited, simple service type.* This type of service center may range in size from about 200 to 400 or 500 people. Villages in this class fall short of providing what may be termed a 'six-service standard'; that is, having agencies in all of the following groups of services: economic, educational, religious, social, communication, professional.

"(3) *The semi-complete, intermediate type.* This type of center averages about 800 to 1000 people with a range from about 400 to over 1200. In certain Middle-Western states it is the most frequent type. It is intermediate because it stands between the type last mentioned and the larger centers, some of which are county-seat towns. It is semi-complete because it is frequently lacking in fulfillment of the six-service standard. It may have a bus line, but no railroad; a high school, but a small one; a market, but with inadequate processing agencies for raw products. Its trade area is relatively large and its merchandising agencies frequently draw as much as 75 per cent of their business from farm sources.

[6] Kolb and Brunner, *op. cit.*, pp. 301–302.

"(4) *The complete, partially specialized type.* This type averages about 2500 or more persons and may range from 1200 to 5000, or just a little over. Its agencies are numerous enough to cover all the more common needs, and differentiated enough to take on specialized characteristics. Its services are often rendered on a less personal basis than in the small centers. Together with its tributary community area, it has some elements of functional self-sufficiency. If the population in the center ranged from 1000 to 2500, within limits and in regions of general farming, one would expect to find about an equal number of people in the tributary country area.

"(5) *The urban, highly specialized type.* This type, which needs further sub-classification, is represented by the larger town and the city. The interests assume larger proportions and are divided into such functions as manufacturing, wholesaling, and financing. They are the centers in which farmers and their wives, as well as villagers, shop when quality, variety, and opportunity for a wide and discriminating selection are wanted. They cannot cater to general trade needs as the small town can; they specialize to a higher degree. The farmer does not look for spools of barbed wire on the city square, but his wife does shop there for some of her choice, ready-to-wear clothing—at least, she likes to do her window-shopping there."

Community Services

Community has its source in common dependence upon institutions and services. The foregoing classification of types of service centers indicates that only limited reliance can be placed on small centers, whereas larger centers offer fairly complete services. Following is a summary of the leading services available to the rural population in service centers.

1. *Transportation and communication.* To a large degree, service centers owe their existence to transportation and communication. The location of a great number of villages and towns was determined by transportation facilities. Along waterways, roads,

railroads, and highways the towns developed. Transportation brings to service centers merchandise, farm supplies, and processed food. From the center these are distributed to the rural population. Food products and raw materials are brought to the center for local processing and manufacture, or to be transported to other communities. Bus and railroad lines give the rural dweller contact with near and distant places. Villages and towns are also centers of communication. Here are located the telephone exchange, the telegraph office, and the post office with its rural delivery service.

2. *Trade*. From the point of view of the rural population probably the primary function of towns is trading. More frequently than for any other reason the farmer goes to town to sell or to ship his products and to buy food, clothing, supplies, and equipment. In small centers retailing to farmers is the chief economic activity. In both small and large centers are found the middlemen who receive crops and livestock and then market them throughout the country.

3. *Professional, craft, and personal services*. Doctors, dentists, lawyers, and other professionals are located in the larger centers particularly. The choice of professional services usually increases with the size of the town. Available, too, are the services of craftsmen such as mechanics, plumbers, carpenters, and electricians. The need for these craftsmen has increased with the greater use of electricity; automobiles, trucks, and tractors; and modern plumbing and heating systems. As rural standards of living have risen, there has been a growing demand for restaurants, beauty parlors, pressing and cleaning shops, and other personal services.

4. *Banking and insurance*. The town bank is the most important agency for transacting the financial affairs of the rural resident. Here he deposits his funds, secures loans, and arranges for certain investments. The bank is often the arbiter of his credit position in the community. Demand for the banking and the more strictly insurance services of insurance agencies in towns centers is increased by farm prosperity.

5. *Manufacturing*. Before the improvement of transportation

there were local manufacturing establishments in a great number of the villages of this country. Many of these industries have moved to larger urban centers, or the villages that they occupied have grown until they have become large towns and cities. Although almost every kind of industry may be found in one village or another, a few types of manufacturing predominate among the surviving village industries. Well in advance of all others are food industries. The other two leading types of village manufacturing are in the paper (including newspaper and printing establishments) and the lumbering industries. Taken together, industries associated with agriculture account for the major portion of village manufacturing.

6. *Education.* Though always prominent, educational services in villages and towns have gained in importance in recent decades. The consolidation of rural schools brings all the children of a larger community to one place for education. Thus a strong community tie is provided through the schools. The greater popularity of education among rural people and the rise in high-school attendance increase the community functions of education. To school educational services must be added those provided by libraries, lectures, demonstrations, and farm meetings. Rural adults seem to be showing a marked willingness to learn, especially in matters relating to agriculture and homemaking.

7. *Religion.* The rural population is served both by open-country and by village and town churches. However, like economic and educational activities, rural religious activities tend to be concentrated in service centers. As the population of the center increases, so also does the number of churches, although the increases are not proportional. In general the greater the density of population, the greater the number of churches per thousand population. The smaller the town, the less the chance that its churches will survive. Open-country churches have least chance of survival.

8. *Recreational and social.* The modern farmer goes to service centers for much of his recreation and social life. In the village

he attends lodge and farm organization meetings. He is attracted to the somewhat larger centers by theaters, ball games, band concerts, and bowling alleys. Schools are social as well as educational centers. School plays, athletic events, and entertainments bring rural people together in town. The church, too, has a dual function, providing for both religious and recreational-social needs.

Changes in Rural Communities

In the present century rural communities have experienced remarkable changes. A score of influences have contributed, but insofar as dependence on services is involved, probably no single factor has done more to revolutionize rural community life than the coming of the automobile. Rapid and easily accessible means of transportation have altered life in the city also; but it is doubtful that the effects have been as striking as in rural areas. Change continues, and it is not clear what the outcome will be. Up to the present, however, a number of trends have been evident.

In the pre-automobile era the territory within which regular social intercourse could be carried on was limited by the means of transportation. Even the larger rural communities could include only relatively small areas. One of the first sociologists to study the rural community in the United States defined the community in terms of the "team haul." He wrote: [7]

"People in the country think of the community as that territory, with its people, which lies within the team haul of a given center. . . . Social customs do not proceed farther than the team haul. Imitation, which is an accepted mode of social organization, does not go any farther in the country than the customary drive with a horse and wagon. . . . Men's lives are housed and their reputations are encircled by the boundary of the team haul.

"The reason for this is economic and social. The life of the countryman is lived within the round of barter and of marketing his products. The team haul which defines the community is the

[7] Warren H. Wilson, *The Evolution of the Country Community*, Boston, Pilgrim, 1912, pp. 91–92.

radius within which men buy and sell. . . . It is the radius of social intercourse."

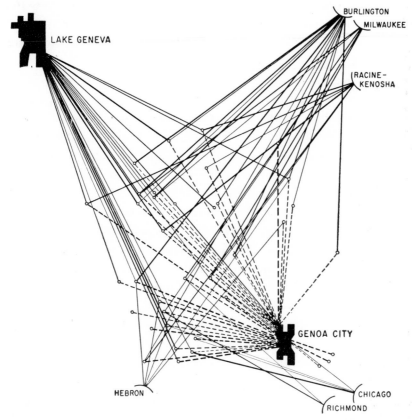

Figure 11. Sociogram Showing Competitive Character of Two Similar Centers, Lake Geneva and Burlington, Wisconsin, with Regard to Trade Contacts. Burlington, comparable in type to Lake Geneva, draws certain kinds of both men's and women's clothing shopping contacts as well as some movie contacts directly away from Lake Geneva. Other clothing shopping contacts extend to city centers such as Milwaukee and Kenosha. (From John H. Kolb and LeRoy J. Day, "Interdependence in Town and Country Relations in Rural Society," Bulletin 172, University of Wisconsin Agricultural Experiment Station, December, 1950, p. 31.)

One result of the use of the automobile was that it put rural residents in frequent contact with urban centers. The distance the farmer could travel to buy and sell was increased many times.

City stores offered better-quality goods and greater selection. Choice of professional services was extended. Local professionals no longer enjoyed monopolies created by isolation. In the city the ruralite could choose from among various doctors, dentists, oculists, and lawyers. The services of specialists became more easily available.

Marketing habits were altered. Using a car or truck, the farmer could easily market his products as far as 100 miles from home. Instead of selling to the nearest buyer he began to seek out the best markets for his products. Furthermore his production was less controlled by strictly local marketing opportunities. The marketing advantages of larger urban centers gave him greater production flexibility.

At the same time other developments were helping to turn rural attention toward the city. Communication media were modifying rural interests, attitudes, and wants. The wider circulation of city newspapers brought more rural dwellers into daily touch with life in the city. Through the press and radio they were exposed to the same ideas and advertisements as their urban cousins. Their attitudes and wants were influenced accordingly. They came to want many of the things that the city had to offer.

Alteration of rural interests and drives was facilitated by the schools. Consolidated schools and high schools reduced the rural character of education. Town schools were urbanizing agencies. Rural students came under the influence of teachers having urban backgrounds. Town and country children mingled from the elementary grades upward. A generation of young people grew up to want things quite unthinkable in the childhood years of their parents. To this phase of urbanization, again, transportation was the key. Without the school bus the consolidated school would have been impossible.

For a time some students foresaw a disappearance of the service functions of small towns as a result of the new urban orientation of rural society. It appears now that this expectation was ill founded. Large villages and small towns occupy a significant position in the constellation of centers that serve the rural population. They have not taken over certain important functions of larger urban centers, but they are in the process of making an adjustment to city competition. Cities have an established place in the facilitation of some types of farm marketing. Goods such as furniture, better clothing, and luxuries are often bought in the larger urban centers. The countryman also turns to the city for specialized professional services. But large villages and small towns are more than holding their own as the main service centers for agricultural areas. High schools, banks, lodges, craft services, professional services, local newspapers, telephone exchanges, chain grocery stores, and clothing stores are located in these centers. Merchandising has increased. There are a growing number of drugstores, novelty shops, beauty parlors, restaurants, and theaters. In short, trips to the city to secure some services have become less necessary. Many services have been brought nearer to rural people.

The automobile era has had its casualties. Hamlets and small villages are the sufferers. Many crossroads places and hamlets have ceased to have any service function. Small centers may survive, but with reduced importance and on a somewhat specialized basis. Post offices and telephone exchanges are removed to larger centers. Public transportation is curtailed. The small village must provide services that are daily required locally. Frequent need and convenience make it possible for a limited number of grocery stores, garages, and gas stations to do business. The small village may be the seat of a nonconsolidated elementary school and a church. Meetings of an agrarian nature may be held there. But although they may continue to provide a few services, many small villages are better characterized as stopping places than as centers.

In reviewing the relative importance of the very small, the intermediate, and the larger service centers, it may be observed that the intermediate center accounts for the greatest number of services. It is the community of the intermediate center to which the rural dweller "belongs" to the greatest degree. Within this community most of his needs are met. At the same time, but to a lesser degree, he has become part of a larger community of which the city is the center.

Early in the 1940's the U.S. Department of Agriculture published studies of six rural communities in this country.[8] In his study of the Sublette community in Haskell County, Kansas, E. H. Bell describes the way in which change has affected some rural areas. Haskell County is not a typical rural area. It is considered to be the most unstable and disorganized of the six communities studied. The following account is not to be regarded as representative of rural communities. It shows, however, the degree to which some areas have changed from traditional rural community patterns.[9]

"Before the days of the wheat boom and rapid transportation, communities were important realities in the life of the people. The institutional activities of the people all bore relation to the community center, which in most cases was a village. If one lived in a certain area he naturally went to the village community center to buy supplies, sell his produce, do his banking, get his mail, go to church, and take part in organized activity. Informal social participation developed in these centers as a byproduct of the institutional activities.

"Now the conquest of space by automobiles has broken the chief bond that held the people together in communities, and this, together with economic conditions, has brought about a dispersal of the institutions. People are no longer oriented toward a specific center; the individual is now the center and looks about him in all

[8] The studies were made under the general direction of Carl C. Taylor. In the foreword to each study Dr. Taylor wrote: "The six communities selected for study—El Cerrito, New Mexico; Sublette, Kansas; Irwin, Iowa; Lancaster, Pennsylvania; Landaff, New Hampshire; and Harmony, Georgia—were not selected in an attempt to obtain a geographic sampling of contemporary rural American communities, but as samples of, or points on, a continuum from high community stability to great instability. At one end of the continuum, an Amish community, Lancaster, Pennsylvania, was selected. At the other end of the continuum, a 'Dust Bowl' community in Kansas was selected. The other four communities, for one reason or another, range themselves between these extremes." Attention is called to these studies because repeated reference will be made to them hereafter in connection with rural life.

[9] Earl H. Bell, "Culture of a Contemporary Rural Community: Sublette, Kansas," *Rural Life Studies* 2, U.S. Bureau of Agricultural Economics, 1942, pp. 68–70.

directions. An examination of the activities of an individual gives a picture of the disorganization of the community.

"Mr. B. lives 10 miles northeast of Sublette, the county seat of Haskell County. He uses the bank in Sublette and occasionally goes to the courthouse to consult with the county agent or A.A.A. committee. While in town he buys some groceries the family needs at once. Most of his supplies are bought either in Copeland or Garden City, 15 and 35 miles away. He says that for the past year there has been a grocery store in Copeland where he can buy to advantage; except for it he would buy most of his supplies in Garden City. There is no physician at Sublette or Copeland so he must go elsewhere for health service. During the year he has been taking his family to an osteopath in Montezuma (20 miles), who sends him on to Dodge City (another 23 miles) in case of more serious illnesses. Many machine repair parts are not carried in stock in the smaller towns. As Dodge City is a center of distribution, Mr. B. goes directly there for repairs. He says that during some seasons more than a month may elapse between trips to Dodge City, but at other times he may go twice a week. Most of his wife's clothes are bought there. The so called community sales are held weekly in the larger towns, and during the slack seasons he likes to go to them to keep abreast of the local prices at which commodities are selling.

"His chief recreation is found at moving picture shows. He goes most often to Garden City, but frequently attends at Dodge City. Sundays are often spent at the homes of relatives who live in surrounding counties. His wife belongs to two women's clubs; the members are chosen on the basis of congeniality and are widely scattered over Haskell and the adjoining county on the east. Other informal social associations are largely with members of Mr. B.'s own age group. They are scattered about the county, but occasionally several of them get together for an evening of cards. Two or three of these families sometimes arrange to meet at a dance in Satanta.

"The farm families are attracted to several villages by the forces of business, recreation, religion, etc. At times the relative strength of these vary considerably. At present, the pulling power of Sublette is strengthened by the fact that the A.A.A. headquarters are there. When discussing Mr. B.'s activities it was noted that the prices at a certain grocery store gave Copeland a temporary ascendency with the B. family. When the children reach high-school age or if the local rural school should be closed, the village in which the children attend school may change the family's community affiliation.

"It is clear that the community is weak and the individual's life is segmented, with each segment oriented in a different direction. The businessmen of Sublette deplore the fact that their town lacks certain facilities with power to draw the families in. Several said the almost vacant streets of Sublette on Saturday afternoons and evenings were the result of not having a good movie theater— the people like to go to a movie on Saturday and so they do their shopping elsewhere. The businessmen also say that the town suffers severely by not having a physician. The people themselves say that by going to a neighboring town to shop they can save more than enough to take them to a show.

"In the old sense, the community as a geographical area which can be outlined on a map with a village center in which major business and social activities are conducted does not exist in Haskell County. The actual condition is a hybrid of rural and urban patterns. Automobiles have expanded the boundaries of the individual's activities. This occurred after the country had developed a hierarchy of towns, primarily on the basis of function in distribution, production, and assembly. Thus Dodge City was a wholesale point for southwestern Kansas and served the area through retail outlets in the smaller towns and villages. Some of these towns that were situated in more densely populated areas (in the case of Garden City in an irrigated valley) grew, and offered more services. So, superimposed upon the hierarchy of distribution was a hierarchy of size and service.

"As long as the individual was held down by distance he had to be content with the services of the local retail village. He dealt with the outer world through the local merchant, who in turn dealt largely through traveling representatives. Thus the final area of distribution was well insulated from the outside world by the fact that their contacts were mainly through the relatively impersonal, indirect, and formalized channels of trade. The same insulation limited contacts to the few people in the immediate vicinity, thus stabilizing the social organization. If certain services were not available to them, the matter of choice was not involved; they had to get along without them and were not especially unhappy about it.

"With the coming of automobiles, the picture was changed. When a farmer's machine needed repairs and the local dealer did not have a part, he had been in the habit of having the dealer order it and there might be a delay of 3 days or more. But after he owned an automobile he went to Dodge City, perhaps at the local dealer's suggestion, and got the part himself, thus saving 2 days. The barrier was immediately broken. The whole process of business was reversed. Instead of the outside world bringing the commodity to the consumer and delivering it through a local merchant, the consumer went outside and got it himself. He saw the advantages and told his friends. More and more went outside, and as the practice grew the local merchant could not afford to carry so large a stock. Now a farmer says, 'If I go to Sublette, just as likely as not I can't get what I want; so I just go to Dodge in the first place. We usually want other things anyway that we can't get in town and there is a much better stock of everything to choose from. If I buy $10 or $15 worth of stuff, I save enough to more than pay for the trip, and my wife and I can go to a show.'

"Moreover, the individual's contacts have been widened so that he can select his associates. Just as the larger towns offer a wider selection of merchandise, so does the expanded area offer a wider selection of companions and activities. The local village store has now taken on the aspects of the urban neighborhood drug and grocery stores, which are used as a convenience. The individual's experience has been expanded and he has learned where each distinct need and desire can be satisfied best.

"We may, then, picture the individual farmer as having primary experience in an area some 100 miles in diameter and within which he moves about freely. In this area are small and large zones of activity—villages, towns, and cities—each competing for his business and social activity. Each has special inducements; some excel in one segment of activity and some have monopolies on certain services. The farmer's freedom of movement permits him to use each advantage. He is in a position not unlike that of the urban shopper who goes from store to store buying the advertised 'special' at each."

SUMMARY

Defined in terms of population, rural refers to all territory except in places having 2,500 inhabitants or more. Density of population in rural areas, therefore, is low. The economy of agriculture tends to dominate rural communities. This agricultural dominance influences nonfarming as well as farming occupations and activities. Nevertheless nonagricultural pursuits are of considerable significance in rural areas.

In many parts of the world it has been customary for agricultural people to live together in villages. Attempts were made to establish farm villages in colonial America. But today the great majority of farmers in the United States live on scattered farmsteads rather than in villages. Farms are of varying types. Four major types are commercial family farms, subsistence family farms, plantations, and factory farms. Although there are only a few survivals of the traditional farm village, the nonfarm village has an important function as a service center for the rural population.

A community exists when the people of a locality are served by the same institutions and services. Most rural communities are composed of an open-country area and a town center. The community is bound together by the services and activities provided within it, especially by the services provided in the town center. The service centers upon which rural people are dependent vary in size and in the functions they perform. The important community services include transportation and communication; trade; professional, craft, and personal services; banking and insurance; manufacturing; education; religion; and recreational and social services.

In the twentieth century rural communities have changed markedly. Transportation has been a most important factor in bringing about the change. Buying and selling habits have been altered. Farmers are brought into more frequent contact with urban centers. Communication and education have contributed to breaking down the cultural isolation of rural areas. Many new services have been brought into rural communities. Some of the smallest centers have lost their service functions. The intermediate-size centers continue to perform important functions. The variety of services that they provide appears to be increasing. At the same time many rural people have become part of a larger community with a city center.

SELECTED REFERENCES

Alihan, Milla A.: *Social Ecology*, New York, Columbia University Press, 1938.

Fry, C. Luther: *American Villages*, New York, Harper, 1926.

Kolb, John H., and Edmund de S. Brunner: *A Study of Rural Society*, Boston, Houghton Mifflin, 1952.

McWilliams, Carey: *Factories in the Fields*, Boston, Little, Brown, 1939.

Sanderson, Dwight: *Rural Sociology and Rural Social Organization*, New York, Wiley, 1942.

Smith, T. Lynn: *The Sociology of Rural Life*, New York, Harper, 1947.

Sorokin, P. A., C. C. Zimmerman, and C. J. Galpin: *A Systematic Source Book in Rural Sociology*, Minneapolis, University of Minnesota Press, 1930–1932, 3 vols.

Taylor, Carl C., et al.: *Rural Life in the United States*, New York, Knopf, 1949.

———, Louis J. Ducoff, and Margaret J. Hagood: *Trends in the Tenure Status of Farm Workers in the United States, 1880–1940*, U.S. Department of Agriculture, 1948.

Williams, James M.: *Our Rural Heritage*, New York, Knopf, 1925.

Woofter, T. J., Jr.: *Landlord and Tenant on the Cotton Plantation*, Works Progress Administration Research Monograph V, 1936.

CHAPTER EIGHT

Rural Group Life

The group life of the modern rural resident is prescribed by birth, locality, and interests. Our purpose in discussing the family, neighborhood, and interest groups is to indicate the relative place of these types of association in present-day rural society.

THE FAMILY

The study of group life in rural communities must begin with the family, for much of the association of rural people is family-centered. The rural way of life has attached singular significance to the family. Emphasis has been placed on the desirability of marriage, the blessings of having many children, the advantages of family unity, and the virtue of family loyalty. The family is the primary unit around which rural society is organized.

A strong basis for association within the rural family is provided by the common occupational interest of its members. The predominant rural occupation is agriculture, and agriculture is to a large degree a family enterprise. The farm family lives with its work. Home life is intimately related to earning a living. Day and night the family is near its responsibilities. Unlike urban families, which are frequently separated by work, rural families are joined in work. Parents and children share tasks. Patterns of family association which grow out of the need for working together are particularly significant because they carry over into nonworking hours.

Despite the coming of the automobile and the decline of rural isolation, farm families spend more of their leisure hours at home than do urban families. The home environment is the playground

164

of farm children. Rural young people are at home in the evening more than city youth. Away from home, too, they are often in the company of their parents. Visiting friends and taking automobile trips are family activities.

The associational importance of the rural family is further revealed in the make-up of a number of the leading rural organizations. Many farm groups are essentially family organizations. Their programs stress better farm and home practices. In some, activities are provided for the entire family. For example, one of the purposes of the Grange is the improvement of home life. It includes husband, wife, and children over fourteen in its membership. The Farm Bureau is an association of families which has an avowed interest in all aspects of farm life. Although 4-H clubs include only young people as members, family cooperation is required to carry through projects. Special attention is given to the improvement of farm and home practices.

The rural church is a family church. Religious traditions give strong support to ideals of family unity and loyalty. In many respects church life is an extension of family life. In church-attending families children begin at an early age to accompany their parents to all varieties of church meetings. As a group the family goes to Sunday school and "church," revival meetings, business meetings, "socials," and picnics. Church membership is socially inherited through the family. Family connections play a great part in the control of churches, and in cases of divisions within churches family alignments are often evident.

Familial association in rural areas frequently extends beyond the immediate family group. Families belonging to the same kinship group visit together regularly. Family reunions are rural events. Relatives living in the same community associate with each other with greater frequency and regularity than they do with other persons. Although not typical, families in some rural areas develop a clannishness which almost eliminates informal social life with nonrelatives. Just how much more important association among relatives is in rural areas than in urban areas is not known, but there is agreement that, in general, kinship ties are stronger in the country than in the city.

One evidence of the strength of rural kinship ties is the frequency with which family unity is preserved despite geographical separation. Even when married children live some distance from the home of their parents, family association may be a most vital part of their social life. Regular family gatherings include parents, children, and grandchildren, and periodically larger kinship groups assemble. Particularly on holidays, relatives gather to eat, to exchange news and gossip, to be entertained by the younger children, and to tell again the anecdotes that have been told uncounted times before. When this type of family association survives, including persons coming from a distance, there is usually a rather closely knit nucleus group of relatives living in the home community.

In his study of Sublette, Kansas, E. H. Bell found that continuity of family ties after the marriage of the children was the general rule. The following case, which Bell considers typical of the Sublette community, illustrates how this continuity may exist even when a family is scattered.[1]

"Mr. M. is an old settler. He had four children—one son and three daughters. He now lives on his home place with the son, his youngest child, and daughter-in-law. One daughter married a local boy and now lives on a farm about 12 miles away; another daughter lives on a farm in the adjoining county, and the third lives on a farm in Colorado.

"The father has done less work during recent years. He has a few cattle, but there is not much attempt to formally divide the income. Both father and son are interested in improving the place.

"The two brothers-in-law in the county work with each other more than with anyone else, although both have closer neighbors. The families visit together more than with others. The sisters-in-law frequently spend the afternoon together, helping each other

---

[1] Earl H. Bell, "Culture of a Contemporary Rural Community: Sublette, Kansas," *Rural Life Studies* 2, U.S. Bureau of Agricultural Economics, 1942, pp. 78–79.

with work. Frequently these two families and the one in the adjoining county, more than 40 miles away, spend Sundays together. After a recent feed-crop failure in Haskell County both families hauled most of their cattle up to the farm in the other county, which is in an irrigated district, where they were cared for by the other brother-in-law, who in turn frequently has welding and other repair work done by his brother-in-law on the home place.

"They see the sister in Colorado rather frequently and speak of her as though she were only a few miles away."

The foregoing discussion of the place of the rural family group is most applicable to farm families. However, in many ways family life in the rural village resembles that on the farm. The occupational tie is less important in nonfarm families, and there are more opportunities for extrafamilial social contacts. Nevertheless the central position of the family group persists.

THE NEIGHBORHOOD

Human group life is sometimes intimate and personal and sometimes superficial and impersonal. Those groups in which contacts generally are intimate, personal, and face to face are *primary groups*. Groups in which contacts generally are not intimate and personal are *secondary groups*. The immediate family group is easily recognized as a primary group. A theater audience is definitely a secondary group. But there are many groups which are not so easily classified. Some groups are more or less primary, or more or less secondary. Probably the difference between primary and secondary groups is one of degree rather than kind. At least difficulty is encountered in attempting to place every particular group in one category or the other.

When Charles H. Cooley wrote his classic statement on primary groups,[2] he named the neighborhood, along with the family and the play group of children, as an example of a primary group. Our questions here are: To what extent do neighborhood groups exist

[2] *Social Organization*, New York, Scribner, 1915, p. 23*ff.*

in modern rural society, and to what degree are the relationships of rural neighborhoods primary in nature?

The Meaning of Neighborhood

A neighborhood is defined by Kolb and Brunner [3] as "that first group outside the family which has social significance, and which has some sense of local unity. It is conditioned both geographically and psychologically. It is an area of local association and it is a group of primary, personal, or face-to-face contacts." Dwight Sanderson [4] defines a rural neighborhood as "consisting of a small number of families in a restricted locality which are recognized as associating more closely together in certain activities than with others."

Thus, like a community, a neighborhood can be located geographically. The area that it includes can be roughly delimited. Neighborhood areas are often designated by names such as Pat's Hill, Spring Creek, Owl Hill, York Center, and Curry's Mill. These names are of local origin and significance, and only rarely appear on maps. A neighborhood area is necessarily small, for when geographical proximity is the first cause of association, primary group relations within a locality ordinarily do not extend far. Neighborhood boundaries sometimes are fixed by nature; hills, valleys, streams, and forests often help to define the area in which regular primary contact occurs.

The number of families in rural neighborhoods varies. Some neighborhoods have less than five families, while others have as many as fifty. Topography, roads, size of farms, and local institutions are factors that determine the number of families among which neighboring is carried on.

A distinction must be made between neighborhoods and communities. They are alike in that both are geographically identifiable, but they differ in the conditions necessary for their existence.

[3] J. H. Kolb and E. de S. Brunner, *A Study of Rural Society*, Boston, Houghton Mifflin, 1946, p. 225.

[4] Dwight Sanderson, *Rural Sociology and Rural Social Organization*, New York, Wiley, 1942, p. 234.

A community exists when there is common dependence upon services within an area; a neighborhood exists when there are primary group relations within an area. A community does not exist merely because families live in the same locality and know each other personally. On the other hand, services within an area are not required for the existence of a neighborhood. A school, a church, or a Grange hall in a neighborhood may foster neighboring, but such services are not essential.

In neighborhoods, as in other groups, there are differing degrees of primary contact. In some definitely delimitable locality groups neighboring is frequent and intensely intimate; in others it is infrequent and considerably less intimate. Moreover, all families in a neighborhood are not equally neighborly. There may be families within a neighborhood area who have practically no primary association with families living near them. In our day of automobiles such a situation is more likely to be found than it was when social contacts were limited more by distance.

Neighborhoods in the Past

Throughout most of our history, the neighborhood has been one of the most important groups in rural America. In colonial days the neighborhood was the basic rural locality group. Then the neighborhood and the community were practically one. Within an area of primary association most of the essential services were provided. Economically, educationally, and religiously neighborhoods tended to be homogeneous. Kinship ties often extended throughout the neighborhood. The neighborhood was thus a strongly knit group.

In the past neighboring was frequently a necessity. Although New England has a reputation for encouraging family independence, it also produced neighboring. Writing about the earlier years of the Landaff community in New Hampshire, MacLeish and Young comment: [5]

[5] Kenneth MacLeish and Kimball Young, "Culture of a Contemporary Rural Community: Landaff, New Hampshire," *Rural Life Studies* 3, U.S. Bureau of Agricultural Economics, 1942, p. 26.

"Cooperation outside the family was dictated largely by circumstances. Houses and barns could not be built by one man, and it was not efficient to do certain kinds of work unaided. The things around which such mutual aid centered were limited and definite, and although help might be given in many ways, it was not to be demanded.

"Visiting was not common because it was often impossible. Cooperative work provided occasion for friendly social intercourse, as did church meetings. There was no lack of interest in neighborhood or town events; people attended husking bees, paring bees, and berry-picking parties with great enjoyment; women visited when they could, and men stopped to talk with their neighbors when they passed by. But these things were incidental to the independent existence of the family which long remained a basic value."

In early Western settlements the neighborhood was a meaningful social group. Concerning the Irwin community in Iowa, Moe and Taylor write: [6]

"The country neighborhood was the pattern of early association which meant more to early settlers than all others combined. These neighborhoods often contained two or more families related by blood or a nucleus of families who came together to the county from some common source of origin. Even when early settlers had not previously known each other, they formed neighborhoods by family visiting, exchange of work, assistance in time of sickness, and fairly early for the purpose of establishing schools, building and care of roads, and sometimes for protection against prairie fires."

In the South, which has a higher proportion of the rural population than any other region, the neighborhood became particularly important. To a special degree association in the rural South was circumscribed by the neighborhood. Farm families living near each other visited frequently and otherwise participated in inti-

[6] Edward O. Moe and Carl C. Taylor, "Culture of a Contemporary Rural Community: Irwin, Iowa," *Rural Life Studies* 5, U.S. Bureau of Agricultural Economics, 1942, p. 22.

mate forms of association. In small-farm, white neighborhoods, kinship ties were notably strong. Many plantations constituted neighborhoods in which tenants and croppers lived together on a primary basis. Negroes and whites living in the same locality developed separate neighborhoods. It is interesting to observe that white and Negro neighborhood areas frequently did not coincide.

Changing Neighborhoods

Rural neighborhoods persist as places with names, but there are evidences of changing relationships within neighborhoods. In the Department of Agriculture *Rural Life Studies* repeated reference is made to this change. While talking about cooperative work among neighbors an old resident in Landaff, New Hampshire, recalled: [7]

"Things are all changed now from the way they used to be. When I was a boy, there'd be big gangs of men going around from farm to farm working on the harvest and they still had raising bees. You don't get that any more. Sometimes I think folks are less obliging, and then again I think it might be because work is worth a lot more money now. Nowadays, when nobody calls on the neighbors for that kind of work, folks wouldn't think much of a man that did. Nowadays you got to manage by yourself and hire work done."

On the other hand, some of the farmers of Irwin, Iowa, believe that work cooperation increased during the depression years of the 1930's. "The reasons they give are that farmers have been depressed economically and that cooperation was somewhat recreational and offered relief from individual concern, and that mechanization has so speeded up farm work that they had time to cooperate with less chance of individual loss. . . . Farmers of the community express regret that cooperation is practiced very little except in response to a specific problematical situation caused by personal troubles." [8]

[7] MacLeish and Young, *op. cit.*, p. 60.
[8] Moe and Taylor, *op. cit.*, p. 51.

But although some types of work assistance may have increased, either temporarily or permanently, it is the opinion of the older people of the Irwin community that visiting with immediate neighbors has declined since the coming of the automobile. "A few deprecate the change, but the majority feel they are now able to choose their friends on the basis of similarity of interests rather than by necessity of propinquity. They believe that association with people on adjoining farms in itself was never a virtue." [9]

Work cooperation has never been common in the South, but visiting has been a perennial symbol of the Southern way of life. Yet even in the rural South, visiting habits are changing. In his study of Harmony, Georgia, Waller Wynne reported: [10]

"The pattern of visiting within Harmony Community today contrasts sharply with that of 20 years ago. Then people—both white and colored—visited more often than now. The decrease in the frequency of visiting was attributed partly to a decline in the interest of neighbor in neighbor, but more to 'changes of the times.' Among white residents, the character of visiting has changed, also. For example, among white residents and to some extent among Negroes, the practice of paying a brief call while on the way to or from town in their automobiles has supplanted the more formal visits, or brief conversations at the trade center on Saturdays permit an exchange of information and so it does not seem necessary to visit each other in the homes."

A number of factors are related to the decline of neighboring in rural areas. As the preceding statements suggest, transportation is probably the most disruptive influence. The disappearance of dependence on local families for social contacts makes neighborhood association less frequent and less intimate. Relationships outside of the small local area compete with neighborhood contacts. As local relationships become less intimate there is less willingness to solicit work assistance, although in cases of special need aid may be volunteered.

[9] *Ibid.*, p. 52.
[10] Waller Wynne, "Culture of a Contemporary Rural Community: Harmony, Georgia," *Rural Life Studies* 6, U.S. Bureau of Agricultural Economics, 1943, p. 43.

Neighborhoods disappear first in the vicinity of villages and towns; they persist in the more isolated areas. In somewhat isolated localities service and associational functions continue to be of considerable importance, whereas in less isolated areas these functions tend to be taken over by service centers. In rural areas near towns and cities association among families living in the same locality takes on a more secondary character.

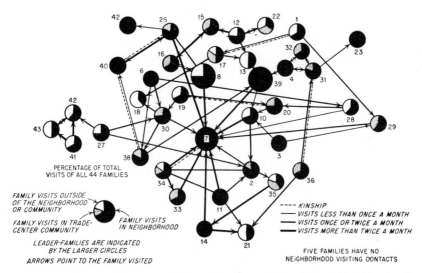

Figure 12. Visiting Pattern of Farm Families, White Plains Neighborhood, Charles County, Maryland. (From Linden S. Dodson and Jane Wooley, "Community Organization in Charles County, Maryland," Bulletin A21, University of Maryland Agricultural Experiment Station, January, 1943.)

The residential mobility of the rural population is a factor contributing to the decline of neighboring. Rural families move from one domicile to another less frequently than do city families; nevertheless, even as a result of only one move, a family may cease to have intimate contact with a neighborhood. Upon arrival in a new community a family may feel no real need for primary neighborhood association. Family contacts, friends distributed over a wide area, special-interest groups, urban contacts, and a few select friends living nearby may provide all the association desired. Having no socially inherited connection with the neighborhood, a family new to a locality may be slow to cultivate relationships. At the same time older residents, involved with their own friends and activities, may be uninclined to do anything to relate the family to the neighborhood. The apparent social self-sufficiency of the new

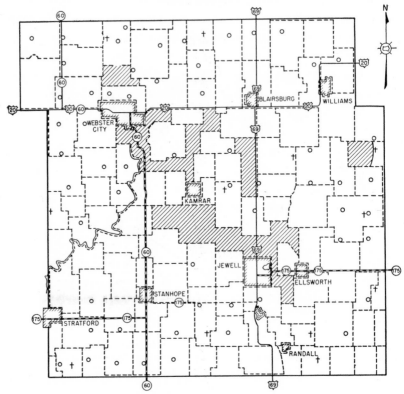

NEIGHBORHOOD BOUNDARY --- INTERSTITIAL AREA //// RURAL CHURCH + OPEN RURAL SCHOOL O

Figure 13. Neighborhoods in Hamilton County, Iowa, 1947. In a study of this county 108 open-country neighborhoods were identified. Old-time residents and those in the lower socioeconomic groups were found to be most specific about the boundaries of the neighborhoods in which they felt they belonged. Younger families and those in higher-income groups had less fully developed neighborhood awareness. Families living near the trade centers showed less identity with neighborhoods than did families living farther from the centers. In the 8 per cent of the county identified on the map as interstitial area, group life lacked sufficient cohesiveness to be thought of as neighborhoods. (From Paul J. Jehlik and Ray E. Wakeley, "Rural Organization in Process," Research Bulletin 365, Iowa State College Agricultural Experiment Station, September, 1949, p. 137.)

family may be recognized, and therefore older families may feel no great compulsion to neighbor.

In summarizing the place of the neighborhood in the associational life of rural communities today, it may be observed that neighborhood areas as places with names have tended to survive. Some disappear, but others emerge. The service functions of neighborhoods have diminished. There has been a marked decline in the number of local areas in which are found both the primary contacts of neighborhoods and the service functions of communities. On the other hand, some neighborhoods owe their survival to one or two specialized services locally provided. Although neighboring continues, in general it has declined in frequency and in intimacy, and therefore it is less primary in nature. Surviving neighborhood activities are participated in not only by families who live in the immediate locality, but by persons from other localities as well. Thus propinquity has diminished as a determiner of association.

SPECIAL-INTEREST GROUPS [11]

In the past, association within the neighborhood accounted for most of the group life of rural folk. The territory encompassed by many rural organizations coincided closely with the neighborhood area. It is evident that this situation no longer exists. Locality has become less important in the selection of rural group members. Rural society now has a great number of groups which extend beyond and cut across locality groups. There are farmers' organizations, social and recreational groups, youth organizations, educational organizations, and numerous other groups which draw their members from many localities. Membership in these groups is based not on common geography, but on common interests. Members are not born into such groups; they join them. It is these groups which rural sociologists refer to as *voluntary organizations,* or *special-interest groups.*

[11] Acknowledgment is made of special indebtedness in this section to Dwight Sanderson's treatment of interest groups in *Rural Sociology and Rural Social Organization,* New York, Wiley, 1942, pp. 506–585.

Farmers' Organizations

The oldest farmers' organization in the United States is the Grange, or Patrons of Husbandry. Organized in 1867 by a government clerk in Washington, D.C., its greatest popularity was achieved in the early 1870's. At the height of its influence, in 1875, the Grange had three-quarters of a million members in forty-three states. Thereafter it rapidly declined to a membership of about 100,000. Then, after 1890, it grew steadily to a membership of 635,000 in 1940. The Grange is strongest in the Northeastern part of the country, particularly in New England.

The Grange is a fraternal order whose membership is open to persons of both sexes over fourteen years of age. In the main, membership is made up of more prosperous farmers, although non-farmers are included. It is organized into subordinate granges (local granges), Pomona granges (the county is the usual territory), state granges, and a national grange. Membership becomes more exclusive from the local level upward. The purposes of the Grange are legislative, economic, educational, and social. Meetings are usually held every two weeks. The program consists of a business session, lecture hour, and social period. Much importance is attached to ceremonial procedures. The fraternal and social functions seem to have gained ascendance over the earlier role of the organization as a champion of causes.

The Farmers' Educational and Cooperative Union is to some of the Western and North Central states what the Grange is to the Northeast. The organization had its beginning in Texas in 1902 and spread rapidly throughout the cotton belt. At its peak, around 1907, the membership is estimated to have been around 1 million. In 1940 the membership was estimated at between 200,000 and 300,000. By that time a shift of strength away from the cotton belt had occurred.

Like the Grange, the Farmers' Union is a secret fraternal group, organized into local, county, state, and national units. It has, however, no degrees and little ritual. The Farmers' Union has attracted a less prosperous group of farmers than the Grange. It counts a large proportion of tenant farmers and middle-class farmers among its members. Membership is open to all members of the family over sixteen years of age. The activities of the organization are fraternal, economic, educational, and political. Much attention has been given to cooperative enterprises. There is a strong youth program. The recreational and social functions of the Union are important, but they have not superseded other functions to the degree that they have in the Grange.

One of the most effective farm groups throughout the country is the Farm Bureau. This organization was an outgrowth of the agricultural extension activities carried on jointly by the U.S. Department of Agriculture and the state colleges of agriculture. Today the organization of county farm bureaus varies from state to state. In some states the connection between extension services and county bureaus no longer exists, while in other states this relationship is maintained, although frequently on a voluntary basis. The national and state federations of farm bureaus have no connection with extension services; they are chiefly concerned with economic and legislative matters. The Farm Bureau has been among the strongest political pressure groups in the country.

Membership in county farm bureaus is open to anyone. The entire family is usually included. Middle-class and prosperous farmers are predominant. The organization is not closely knit, and attending meetings is the extent of the participation of many members other than officers.

Education is one of the chief functions of county farm bureaus. With the aid of county agricultural agents, county home-demonstration agents, and county agents in charge of club work, a significant program of education is promoted. Through the county organizations an abundance of practical information is made available to farm families. The Farm Bureau declares an interest in all phases of farm life. In practice the activities of county organizations have been largely educational, whereas national and state federations have been preoccupied with agricultural policy and legislative issues.

In the present century the growth of cooperative associations has been a prominent aspect of change in rural communities. Informal cooperation among farmers in primary groups was long a characteristic of the rural way of life. Formal cooperation among farmers in secondary groups is a more recent innovation. The first farm cooperatives in the United States were started around 1810, but it was not until around the turn of the twentieth century that the movement began to gain impetus. By 1943 it was estimated that about half of the farmers of this country belonged to cooperative organizations. The per cent of farmers doing business through cooperatives is lowest in the Southern states. The movement has been given appreciable support by the Grange, the Farmers' Union, and the Farm Bureau.

There are three main types of cooperatives: buying, selling, and service. Buying cooperatives include all the many kinds of consumers' cooperatives, or, as the farmers commonly call them, "cooperative purchasing associations." Among the leading marketing cooperatives are the dairy and grain associations. In close relation to these are cooperative milk-processing plants and grain elevators. Service cooperatives are those organized to provide services such as telephone, power and light, and health services.

Cooperatives are organized on a local, federated, and centralized basis. Small local cooperatives usually are interested in one commodity. Dairy products, grain, fruit, vegetables, livestock, and cotton are leading commodities in which they deal. Federated cooperative organizations are formed by the union of local associations in order to gain greater efficiency. The area of a federated association may cover a county, district, state, or larger region. Examples are the California Fruitgrowers Association and the Land O' Lakes Creameries. Centralized cooperatives unite widely scattered producers for the purpose of marketing one commodity. In this type there usually are no local associations and organization is from the top down, rather than from the local community upward.

The cooperative movement has attempted to do more than serve economic interests. Social unity, adult education, and recreation have been stressed. The economic motivation, however, has been the strongest bond uniting members. Relationships within cooperative associations tend to be impersonal and secondary in character.

Social and Recreational Groups

Farmers' clubs are among the most important local organizations of farm people. They are especially prevalent in the West North Central states, but are found also in many other states. The name *farmers' club* covers a multitude of organizations. Choral societies, literary societies, community clubs, and many other miscellaneous groups are labeled farmers' clubs. But whatever the name, the majority of these groups are interested in social life and recreation. Generally the social interest is combined with other purposes such as improvement of agriculture, education, or promotion of community welfare. Only a minority of such clubs consider themselves to be strictly social and recreational in function; nevertheless the desire for social life is the main reason for the existence of these organizations.

Farm women's clubs are of many varieties. Some have a formal organization; others are most informal. Some, such as card clubs, are admittedly social clubs. In the service and educational clubs social activities, although important, are considered to be incidental to other purposes. Homemakers clubs, organized under the Farm Bureau and the extension services, are regarded as chiefly educational organizations. These groups meet regularly in local units and develop a definite sense of group solidarity. In some instances farm women's clubs have formed federations or have joined the State Federation of Women's Clubs. A select few among farm women are admitted to women's clubs in larger villages and towns.

Notwithstanding their contributions to worthy community projects, service clubs such as Rotary, Kiwanis, Lions, and others may be listed among social and recreational groups. Promotion of sociability is one of their well-recognized functions. These organizations are typically urban business and professional in member-

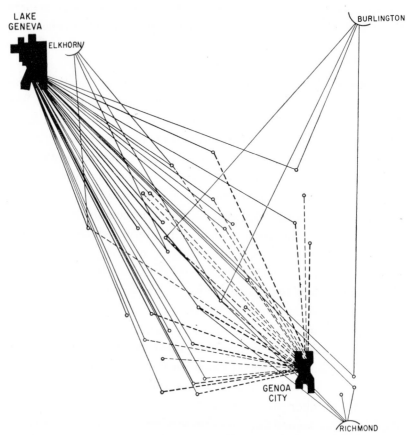

Figure 14. Sociogram Showing Complementary Character of Two Centers, Genoa City and Lake Geneva, Wisconsin, with Regard to Certain Social Contacts. Complementary relations are indicated by the concentration of contacts for clubs, parties, dances, groceries, farm machinery, and equipment in the smaller center, Genoa City, and by a convergence of contacts for high school, library, movies, and clothing in Lake Geneva. (From John H. Kolb and LeRoy J. Day, "Interdependence in Town and Country Relations in Rural Society," Bulletin 172, University of Wisconsin Agricultural Experiment Station, December, 1950, p. 30.)

ship. It appears, however, that the number of such organizations in the larger villages is increasing, and that some of the more prosperous farmers are being admitted to membership. This development is more a commentary on trends in rural-urban relationships than on rural group life as such.

In addition to the types of social and recreational organizations already listed, rural people participate in numerous other groups such as dancing clubs, musical organizations, hobby clubs, and athletic teams. Also, there are informal cliques and loafing groups which meet in homes, country stores, gas stations, and taverns. Far more time is spent by some rural dwellers in these informal groups than in the more formal organizations.

Youth Organizations

The 4-H Club, with over two million members, is the largest rural youth organization in the United States. Four-H club work is part of the program of the Agricultural Extension Service. Clubs are always organized on a local basis, and a deliberate attempt is made to keep units small. When a group becomes too large a new unit is formed. In some states boys and girls belong to the same club; in other states they have separate clubs. Each member works on a project related to farm life. Projects include enterprises in the fields of foods, clothing, farm sanitation, livestock, horticulture, farm crops, dairying, cotton, forestry and wild life, and agricultural engineering. The program stresses learning by doing, development of desirable ideals, formation of well-rounded personalities, and training for leadership. A wide variety of work, educational, and recreational activities are offered.

There are no federated state or national 4-H organizations. Joint club activities consist of state 4-H congresses and state 4-H camps. An annual national 4-H camp is held in Washington, D.C., to which delegates are sent from the states. The 4-H organization has been remarkably successful in inspiring loyalty to the movement. Only a small proportion of the eligible young people, however, belong to clubs.

The Future Farmers of America is an organization for boys which is part of the program of rural high schools. Under the leadership of the local teacher of vocational agriculture, a training and morale-building program is carried on which includes school exhibits, tours, and social and athletic events.

Boy Scouts, Girl Scouts, and Camp Fire Girls are not strong in the farming areas of rural communities. Most of the rural units of these organizations are in the larger villages. Their programs stress character building, health, handcrafts, nature study, and citizenship.

Although the Young Men's Christian Association and the Young Women's Christian Association have been chiefly urban organizations, both groups have given some attention to rural areas. The YMCA has a secretary in charge of rural work and has been more active in rural areas than the YWCA. The formation of high-school clubs has been one of the most important Christian Association activities in rural communities.

Educational Organizations

The leading educational organization in which rural adults participate is the parent-teacher association. A broad program of community education and school improvement is sponsored. Through the organization the school interprets its objectives and activities and solicits the aid and cooperation of parents. Parents, in turn, have an opportunity to indicate their wishes and to suggest and support school improvement. The consolidation of schools has contributed to an increase in the number of rural parent-teacher associations. The organization has been more successful in the consolidated and larger schools than in the one-room-school districts.

The other organizations having educational programs are the farmers' organizations which have already been discussed. Of these, the educational efforts of the Agricultural Extension Service are outstanding.

Fraternal and Civic Organizations

Fraternal orders in rural communities have varying functions. The Grange is chiefly a farmers' organization. Its purposes are broader than those of most fraternal organizations. Practically all orders have some form of mutual-aid plan. In most Negro orders, of which there are many, insurance features are particularly important. With the exception of the Grange, most rural lodges draw their members from the villages. This is especially true of those orders in which the insurance function is minor. In many village lodges the desire for a sense of belonging and for social activity are the primary motivating factors. The village lodge hall is a social center for members of the order.

Among the rural civic organizations are cemetery associations and fire companies. In some rural communities cemetery maintenance and improvement are regarded as an esteemed civic activity. The village fire company, too, is a source of community pride. Raising funds for equipment is an enterprise with innumerable possibilities for business and social meetings. Non-fire-fighting citizens join the company, and the women's auxiliary complements the endeavors of male members. Fire-company service extends into farm areas, and farm families join in the activities of the company.

TRENDS IN RURAL GROUP LIFE

The most evident change in rural group life is the decline in the importance of locality as a determiner of association. This development is perhaps so conspicuous that it is misleading. It must be noted that locality has only become less significant; it has not become insignificant. Identification with a place, a locality, an area still exists. Furthermore, the territory in which regular association occurs has merely expanded; it has not lost all limits. The group life of most rural dwellers still takes place within a limited area.

As to the nature of the social contacts of rural people, a preference for relationships of a somewhat personal character still appears to persist. Again, a difference between past and present is that geography has diminished as a factor controlling the choice of intimate and personal acquaintances. Primary contacts continue, but they are distributed over a wider area. Also the associations of rural people are no longer restricted to primary groups as, to a large degree, they were in the past. To the primary relationships have been added a great number of more impersonal secondary contacts.

Sorokin, Zimmerman, and Galpin have contributed a pair of concepts which are useful in analyzing trends in rural group life. They define two contrasting types of groups, the *cumulative group* and the *functional group:* [12]

"The cumulative social group is one whose members are bound together not by one, but by *two or more* binding ties. . . . These cumulative groups or communities may be of various degrees of complexity or integration: twofold, threefold, fourfold, etc., according to the number of ties that bind the members together. For instance, we may have a group of cultivators who dwell in the same village (territorial tie); who are kinsmen (blood tie); who have the same religion (religious tie); who are tenants of the same lord (subjection tie); and who are collectively responsible for the maintenance of order in the village (collective responsibility tie). In this particular case the rural cumulative community is bound together by five ties—those of territory, blood, tenancy, religion, and responsibility." In contrast, the functional group is one whose members are united by only one tie.

The cumulative group has never been so strong in the United States as in some other parts of the world. Moreover, rural group life in this country has always been both cumulative and functional. But in the past rural groups have tended toward the cumulative type. As social change has taken place in rural communities,

[12] P. A. Sorokin, C. C. Zimmerman, and C. J. Galpin, *A Systematic Source Book in Rural Sociology*, Minneapolis, University of Minnesota, 1930, vol. 1, p. 309.

functional groups have not destroyed cumulative groups; they continue to coexist. The trend, however, has been away from cumulative association and toward functional association.

In this description of trends it must be stated that the term *rural group life* is, in a sense, a misnomer. It suggests that rural group life is distinct and different from urban group life. This is only partly true. Between the most rural and the most urban group types, there are degrees of rural and of urban, and it is impossible to say where the point of separation lies. Urban patterns extend into the country, and to a lesser degree rural patterns influence the city.

Then too, the term is inaccurate, since some of the group life of rural residents takes place in an urban environment. The countryman's contact with the city for social life and recreation is considerable. The city dweller, in turn, has an increasing number of contacts with rural groups. Interaction between country and city must therefore be included as one of the trends in rural group life.

SUMMARY

The family is the primary unit around which rural society is organized. Among rural people family unity and loyalty have been especially strong. Farming is frequently a family enterprise and as such provides an occupational and economic basis for family solidarity. Many farm groups are organized around family interests and include the entire family as members. Likewise the rural church is to a singular degree a family church. Family unity is often preserved even when family members are geographically isolated.

The neighborhood has also been an important group in rural America. Families living in the same locality have worked and visited together on a rather intimate basis. Neighborhoods continue to exist, but there are indications that they are changing. Work cooperation and visiting habits are not the same as they were in traditional neighborhoods. Transportation has reduced the dependence of local families on each other for social contacts. Greater residential mobility than in the past hinders the development of strong neighborhood ties. Neighborhoods tend to disappear first near towns and villages.

Rural people have the opportunity to participate in a large number of special-interest groups. Among these are the Grange, Farmers' Union, Farm Bureau, cooperatives, farmers' clubs, women's clubs, service clubs, 4-H Club, Future Farmers of America, educational groups, and fraternal and civic organizations. Many of these groups draw their members from a wide area. They extend beyond and cut across the smaller locality groups.

Locality has become less important as a factor in selecting the membership of rural groups. At the same time the secondary-group contacts of rural people have increased in number. Primary contacts continue, but they are more widely distributed. The trend has been away from association in an all-involving locality group and toward association in somewhat dispersed, functional, special-interest groups. Further, much of the group life of rural people is urban-centered.

SELECTED REFERENCES

Calhoun, A. W.: *A Social History of the American Family*, Cleveland, Ohio, Clark, 1917–1919, 3 vols.

Hillman, Arthur: *Community Organization and Planning*, New York, Macmillan, 1950.

Kirkpatrick, E. L., Rosalind Tough, and May L. Cowles: "The Life Cycle of the Farm Family," Research Bulletin 121, Wisconsin Agricultural Experiment Station, 1934.

Kolb, John H., and Edmund de S. Brunner: *A Study of Rural Society*, Boston, Houghton Mifflin, 1952.

—— and Douglas G. Marshall: "Neighborhood-Community Relationships in Rural Society," Research Bulletin 154, Wisconsin Agricultural Experiment Station, 1944.

Morgan, Arthur: *The Small Community*, New York, Harper, 1942.

Sanderson, Dwight: *Rural Sociology and Rural Social Organization*, New York, Wiley, 1942.

Sorokin, P. A., C. C. Zimmerman, and C. J. Galpin: *A Systematic Source Book in Rural Sociology*, Minneapolis, University of Minnesota Press, 1930–1932, 3 vols.

Taylor, Carl C., et al.: *Rural Life in the United States*, New York, Knopf, 1949.

Terpenning, Walter A.: *Village and Open-country Neighborhoods*, New York, Appleton-Century, 1931.

Zimmerman, Carl C.: *The Changing Community*, New York, Harper, 1938.

CHAPTER NINE

Urban Communities

In 1940 and earlier the U.S. Bureau of the Census defined as *urban* all incorporated places having a population of 2,500 or more. In 1950 the census counted as urban all places, incorporated and unincorporated, of 2,500 or more. The full definition in 1950 was as follows: "the urban population comprises all persons living in (*a*) places of 2,500 inhabitants or more incorporated as cities, boroughs, and villages, (*b*) incorporated towns of 2,500 inhabitants or more except in New England, New York, and Wisconsin, where 'towns' are simply minor civil divisions of counties, (*c*) the densely settled urban fringe, including both incorporated and unincorporated areas, around cities of 50,000 or more, and (*d*) unincorporated places of 2,500 inhabitants or more outside any urban fringe. The remaining population is classified as rural." [1] Urban may be defined in terms of social characteristics as well as in terms of population. The social characteristics of urban communities will be discussed in the next chapter. In the present chapter attention is turned to the growth and the structure of urban communities.

GROWTH OF AMERICAN TOWNS AND CITIES

Urban growth in the United States has been rapid. The vast territory that 300 years ago had only a sparse and scattered population has become the land having more big cities than any other country. Urban growth, of course, is not peculiar to the United

[1] U.S. Bureau of the Census, *U.S. Census of Population: 1950*, vol. 1, *Number of Inhabitants*, 1952, p. xv.

States. Among the European nations, before the Second World War, England, Wales, and Germany had higher proportions of their populations living in urban areas than did the United States. But urban development here has been less gradual than in Europe. Transportation, industrialization, immigration, and other factors combined to cause a sudden and gigantic urban growth in this country during the last hundred years.

Statistical Summary

In 1790, 1 out of every 20 of the inhabitants of the United States lived in an urban area. In every decade thereafter, with the exception of 1810 to 1820, the urban population grew more rapidly than the rural population. By 1860, 1 out of 5 persons was included in the urban population; and by 1920 the urban population exceeded the rural population. In 1950 about 3 out of 5 persons were living in urban areas. Applying the old definition, the urban proportion of the population was 59 per cent; applying the new definition, it was 64 per cent.

The 1950 urban population according to the new urban definition consisted of (1) the 86,550,941 inhabitants of the 3,883 incorporated places of 2,500 population or more, (2) the 1,994,727 inhabitants of the 401 unincorporated places of 2,500 population or more, and (3) the 7,922,018 persons living in the urban fringe areas but outside the incorporated places of 2,500 population or more.

Population increases between 1940 and 1950 indicate continuing rapid urban growth. The old urban definition must be used to show the trend. On the basis of the old definition the urban population increased from 74,423,702 in 1940 to 88,927,464 in 1950. Using the same definition the rural population increased from 57,245,573 in 1940 to 61,769,897 in 1950. This represents an urban gain of 19.5 per cent and a rural gain of 7.9 per cent.

In 1790 no city in the United States had as many as 50,000 inhabitants; 2 cities exceeded 25,000 population; 3 cities had populations of between 10,000 and 25,000; and 28 towns and cities had populations of between 2,500 and 10,000. The first city of over 100,000 was reported in 1820. There was no city of over a million until 1880. By 1880 there were 1,054 towns and cities having populations of more than 2,500. Of this number, 77 cities had populations of more than 25,000.

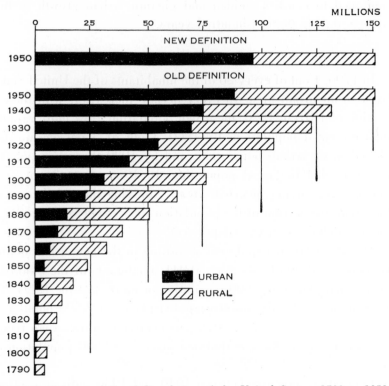

Figure 15. Urban and Rural Population of the United States: 1790 to 1950. (Source: U.S. Bureau of the Census.)

These figures stand in marked contrast to the present number and size of cities in the United States. In 1950 the largest city, New York City, had a population of 7,891,957. Five cities had populations exceeding 1 million. There were 101 cities having populations between 100,000 and 1 million. Three hundred and seventy-eight places had populations of between 25,000 and 100,-000. There were 3,800 places of 2,500 to 25,000.

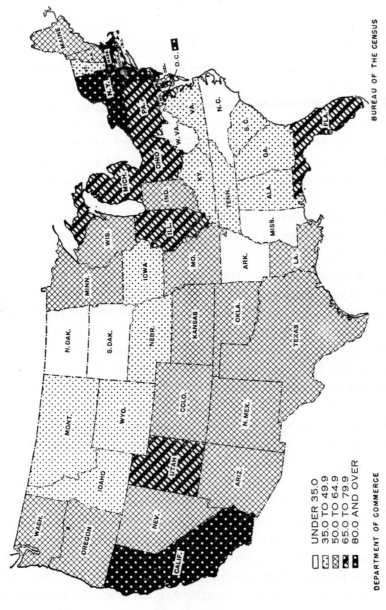

Figure 16. Urban Population Percentage by States: 1950. (Source: U.S. Bureau of the Census.)

Factors Related to Urban Growth

Why did city growth occur when it did, and what caused it to be so rapid? All the factors that bring about population growth in general—birth rates, death rates, migration—are involved, but the significant fact is that city expansion has far outrun population growth for the country as a whole. Between 1790 and 1950 the entire population of the United States increased more than thirty times, but during the same period the urban population increased more than three hundred times.

Extraordinary urban growth in the United States has not been from within the city; it has been the result of an influx from without. The improvement of agriculture coupled with urban opportunities set in motion a cityward stream of migration the steady flow of which was checked only briefly during the great depression of the 1930's. The other source of the growing urban population was immigration. A high proportion of the immigrants who came to this country up to the First World War and briefly thereafter were destined to locate in cities. In the period of the new immigration the urban concentration of the foreign-born was especially pronounced.

Urban growth, except as a part of general population increase, would hardly have been possible without advances in agriculture. The proportion of a population that can live in cities is limited by the level of agricultural production. The need for food and other products of agriculture is basic. Only those persons can live in cities whose labors are not required on the land. The city may not always attract the full number of persons who can be spared from farming, but in the long run it cannot attract a greater proportion of the population than agriculture can do without. This does not mean that within a country a perfect balance is always maintained between consumption in the city and production on the farm. Some agricultural products are imported from other countries. Nevertheless the labor demands of necessary domestic agriculture determine how many people can move to the city. When, therefore, improved and more efficient methods made it possible for fewer men to produce more on the farm, the growth of cities was facilitated.

As the farm sent a greater number of its children to the city, urban centers became prepared to absorb them. The mechanization of industry led to the urban concentration of manufacturing. The factory system centralized industry. It brought together in one place a large number of persons employed in manufacturing. Transportation and power requirements encouraged the urban clustering of industrial units.

The demand for workers in factories was only one of the types of employment that drew people to the city. Urban expansion was both a cause and an effect. The more cities grew, the more they had to grow. Larger populations were needed to provide the commercial, transportation, governmental, construction, utility, recreational, and luxury services required in urban communities. A large proportion of city people are not engaged in production but in providing services for each other. Industrialism has, in fact, diminished as a cause of city growth. After the First World War the percentage of urban persons employed in manufacturing declined.

Industry, commerce, and urban advantages and opportunities pulled the population cityward, while transportation and communication made centralization possible. Without the development of transportation and communication facilities, urban growth on a grand scale would have been most improbable. Transportation was essential to bring raw materials and commodities to the city for production or for marketing. Transportation was necessary also to take products away from the city for marketing and distribution elsewhere. In the nineteenth century steam-driven boats and trains were the chief channels of centralization. Railroads converged on the urban centers. In the twentieth century electric engines and internal-combustion engines added their influence. They expanded the area in which urban advantages could be made available; thus

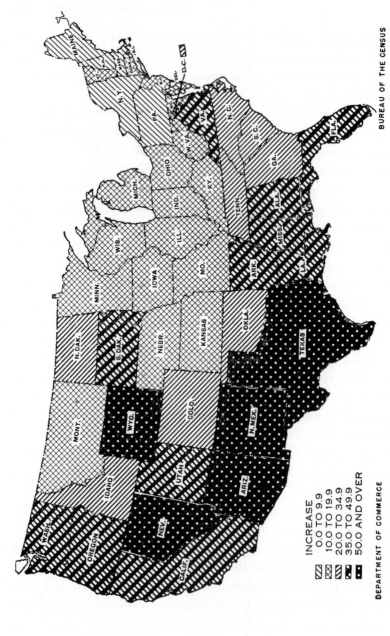

DEPARTMENT OF COMMERCE

BUREAU OF THE CENSUS

INCREASE
0.0 TO 9.9
10.0 TO 19.9
20.0 TO 34.9
35.0 TO 49.9
50.0 AND OVER

Figure 17. Per Cent Increase in Urban Population by States: 1940 to 1950. (Source: U.S. Bureau of the Census.)

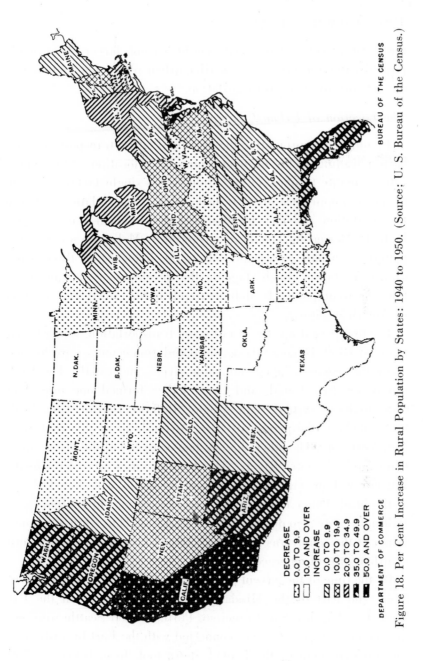

DECREASE

0.0 TO 9.9

10.0 AND OVER

INCREASE

0.0 TO 9.9

10.0 TO 19.9

20.0 TO 34.9

35.0 TO 49.9

50.0 AND OVER

Figure 18. Per Cent Increase in Rural Population by States: 1940 to 1950. (Source: U. S. Bureau of the Census.)

195

the territory covered by a city could become larger. They made possible, too, the growth of smaller urban places not included in the network of steam transportation.

The Location of Urban Communities

In addition to promoting the growth of cities, transportation has been a leading factor in determining their location. While many forces operate to place cities, probably no single factor has been of more importance than transportation. The relation between transportation and city location and development was set forth by R. D. McKenzie. The thesis advanced by McKenzie was that the pattern of urban settlement reflects the influence of three types of transportation. Each stage in the development of transportation was accompanied by definite trends in the growth and location of American cities.[2]

The first period was the era of water transportation, which lasted to about 1850. During this period population centers were located along the seacoast, lakes, navigable rivers, and canals. The Hudson River, Erie Canal, and Great Lakes formed one important water-highway system, with Albany, Buffalo, Detroit, Cleveland, and Toledo as the principal cities. At the head of this route was New York City. The other chief system consisted of the Mississippi, Ohio, and Missouri Rivers. The leading cities were Cincinnati, Pittsburgh, Louisville, St. Louis, and Nashville, with New Orleans at the head. Other cities of the period such as Philadelphia and Baltimore were also dependent on waterways. Thus while the population of the country as a whole remained largely rural, a pattern of urban growth emerged.

By the time of the advent of railroads, the outlines of settlement along and east of the Mississippi were established. In the Far West, Los Angeles, San Francisco, Portland, and Seattle were going centers before they were connected with the East by railroads. The railroad map of the United States took form between 1850

---

[2] R. D. McKenzie, *The Metropolitan Community*, New York, McGraw-Hill, 1933, pp. 129–143.

and 1890. The first railroads were built to augment the waterway system. Soon, however, rail transportation began to compete with water. The flow of Middle Western traffic was diverted from a north-south direction to east-west. Railroads were rapidly extended westward across the continent.

The effect of the railroad was to modify the original pattern of settlement. The power of nature to dictate the distribution of urban people was weakened. Along the railroads villages and towns appeared. New centers developed at points of intersection. The growth of these new cities was hastened by the construction of lines connecting them with neighboring cities. Towns and cities that owed their location to waterways owed their rapid expansion to railroads. Chicago is a notable example. Like the spokes of a wheel, railroads converged on the great Middle Western hub. From a town of a little over 4,000 people in 1840, Chicago grew into a city with a population of over 1 million by 1890.

After the railroad came the motor vehicle and further modification of urban settlement. Motor transportation has not been responsible for the creation of new large cities, but it has changed the patterns in local areas. Avenues of mobility have been opened between the main arteries of transportation. This development has occurred everywhere, but it is especially evident in the vicinity of towns and cities. The spaces between the spokes of the wheel have been filled in with a supporting network. The automobile has made possible the extensive growth of towns and cities surrounding big cities. In the last two decades the function of motor highways in linking distant places has become increasingly important. Along these motor "main lines" are strung businesses that are rural in location but urban in character.

TYPES OF TOWNS AND CITIES

Why do men live in towns and cities? Why do they not live scattered and evenly distributed throughout the land? Is it because strong gregarious motives inevitably cause some men to come together to live? The growth of towns and cities is not merely the result of a desire to live near other people. Apart from any gregarious preference that individuals may have, cities exist because of the functions they perform. They are necessary in order to maintain the type of social organizations required if certain benefits and services are to be provided. They are vitally related to the social and economic organization of the surrounding territory and of the country as a whole. Thus the functions of cities are primary factors in their growth.

A Functional Classification

More than thirty years ago a classification of towns and cities according to their functions was made by Marcel Aurousseau.[3] He named at least twenty-eight types of towns and cities under six main classes. (1) Capital cities and (2) revenue cities exist for the purpose of *administration*. (3) Fortress towns, (4) garrison towns, and (5) naval bases have the duty of *defense*. (6) University towns, (7) cathedral towns, and centers of (8) art, (9) religion, and (10) pilgrimage serve the main purpose of *culture*. (11) Manufacturing and (12) craft cities are concerned with *production*. Towns and cities acting as *communication* links may be divided into three major groups: *collection, transfer,* and *distribution*. In the collection group are (13) depot towns, (14) mining towns, (15) fishing towns, and (16) forest towns; in the transfer group are (17) market towns, (18) fall-line towns, (19) break-of-bulk towns, (20) bridgehead towns, (21) towns at the tidal limit, and (22) towns at the head of navigation; in the distribution group are (23) export and (24) import towns, and (25) supply towns. The sixth functional class, *recreation* centers, includes (26) health, (27) tourist, and (28) holiday resorts. This comprehensive classification serves to suggest the many essential activities for which cities are focal points. It will be recognized, as Aurousseau pointed out, that many cities discharge more than one major function.

[3] Marcel Aurousseau, "The Distribution of Population: A Constructive Problem," *Geographical Review*, vol. 11, October, 1921, pp. 569–572.

Cities in the United States

A functional classification of cities in the United States has been made by Chauncy D. Harris.[4] The study includes 605 urban units, involving 988 cities. The classification is based on the activity of greatest importance in each city as indicated by employment and occupation figures. Nine principal types of cities are identified, the first three listed being the most numerous.

1. *Manufacturing cities.* Most of the manufacturing cities are located in an area east of the Mississippi and north of the Ohio, with extensions into the Southeast along the Piedmont and the Great Valley in the Appalachians. Some of the cities in this class started as trading centers but have shifted to a dominance of manufacturing.

2. *Retail centers.* Most of the retail centers are smaller cities outside the manufacturing area. Almost half of the cities of this type lie near the eastern margin of the Great Plains.

3. *Diversified cities.* In cities in this class trade and manufacturing are both important, but neither is dominant. Diversified cities are widely distributed, but they are especially numerous in the territory between the manufacturing area and the retail belt. Many of the larger cities are diversified.

4. *Wholesale centers.* There are two types of wholesale centers: small cities engaged in assembly and large cities engaged in distribution. The chief enterprises of small wholesaling centers are associated with assembling, packing, and marketing agricultural products. The distribution centers are usually the largest cities in a wide region. The two most important wholesale distribution centers, New York and Chicago, do not fall in this class since wholesaling is only one of the many activities of these large diversified cities.

5. *Transportation centers.* Among the cities of more than 25,000 population, 32 are classified as transportation centers. Of these, 18 are railroad centers and 14 are ports. The largest transporta-

---

[4] Chauncy D. Harris, "A Functional Classification of Cities in the United States," *Geographical Review*, vol. 33, January, 1943, pp. 85–99.

tion city is New Orleans. In the large cities in this class growth may be attributed to other factors in addition to transportation. Within the manufacturing area railroad cities are often important for their manufacturing. Outside the manufacturing area railroad cities tend to be diversified. In port cities wholesaling is usually more important than manufacturing.

6. *Mining towns.* Mining is the dominant activity in only fourteen urban areas of more than 10,000 population. Coal mining is usually carried on in small places not included in this study. Larger centers in mine districts frequently have only a small proportion of their workers employed in mining. Commercial, manufacturing, and transportation occupations generally are in the lead in larger cities within mining districts.

7. *University towns.* Most of the seventeen places classified as university towns are relatively small centers in the Middle West dominated by large state universities. In addition there are numerous smaller college-centered towns not included in this classification.

8. *Resort and retirement towns.* Most of the resort cities are either summer or winter resorts. Only a few are important throughout the year as residential and retirement centers.

9. *Other types of cities.* Harris notes that his classification might further be expanded. He points out that such cities as regional capitals, political capitals, army bases, naval bases, professional centers, and financial centers have not been differentiated statistically. Fishing towns, logging camps, and farming towns usually have less than 10,000 population and therefore are not classified.

Washington, D.C., provided the best example of a city dominated by political activity. Also the political function is clearly dominant in sixteen state capitals, and probably dominant in twenty others.

A Tributary-area Classification

Using a different approach, Harris and Ullman have reduced the types of cities to three. Every city provides services for and in turn is supported by its tributary area. Cities may be classified according to their function in relation to the territory from which their support is received. On this basis the three general categories in which cities may be placed are (1) cities as central places performing comprehensive services for a surrounding area, (2) cities as transport focuses and break-of-bulk points, and (3) cities as concentration points for specialized services.[5]

As *central places*, cities perform comprehensive services for a tributary area. They tend to be evenly spaced where resources are evenly distributed, and unevenly spaced where resources are unevenly distributed. In size, they range from very small to the largest metropolises. Though found in all regions, they are typified best by the trade centers of the Middle West, Southwest, and West.

The area of support of a *transport city* may be geographically near or remote. Such cities develop at focuses of transportation or at points where there are breaks in transportation. A break in transportation encourages the development of services such as repackaging, storing, and sorting. Inasmuch as transportation facilities are unevenly distributed, these centers are unevenly and irregularly located.

A *specialized city* performs a specialized function for its tributary area. This supporting territory may cover a large area and may include the tributary areas of many other cities. Thus specialized mining, manufacturing, and recreation centers receive their support from a wide area.

THE STRUCTURE OF CITIES

The growth of most American cities has been unplanned. Sometimes slowly, sometimes rapidly, they have expanded—more industries, more stores, more transportation facilities, more houses, and more people. At first glance the result seems to be a haphazard hodgepodge of people and buildings without reason or design. But

[5] Chauncy D. Harris and Edward L. Ullman, "The Nature of Cities," *The Annals*, vol. 242, November, 1945, pp. 7–12.

closer observation reveals that the sprawling masses of matter which are our cities are not so irregular and disorderly as they at first appear. The distribution of buildings is found to be functionally related to the activities and relationships within the city. In the seemingly chaotic conglomerate, regularities of organization and structure can be discovered. Further, certain uniformities of organization and structure occur from one city to another. Although largely unplanned, the internal growth of cities has tended to follow discernable patterns.

The first sociologists to turn attention to the study of patterns of city growth were the social ecologists. *Social ecology* is the study of spatial distribution of human beings and their activities. Applied to cities, it is concerned with the structure of cities, and with the relationship between the structure of cities and the people and culture of cities. Many of the first important urban ecological studies were made in and around Chicago. As a growing city, Chicago provided an excellent laboratory for research. It was in this setting that the concentric-zone theory of city growth was developed.[6]

Concentric-zone Theory

According to the concentric-zone theory, as the city grows it forms a pattern of five concentric zones, as follows:

1. *The central business district.* This is the life center of the city. Commerce, entertainment, civic life, and transportation focus here. It is the downtown district of stores, offices, theaters, banks, hotels, restaurants, clubs, and organization headquarters. Land values are high. Except for those inhabiting hotels, residents are few.

2. *The zone in transition.* Encircling the central zone is an area of a mixed character. Here are wholesale houses, warehouses, railroad yards, light manufacturing, rooming houses, tenements, and deteriorated residences. It is called the zone in transition because

[6] R. E. Park, E. W. Burgess, and R. D. McKenzie, *The City*, Chicago, University of Chicago Press, 1925, pp. 47–62.

of the steady encroachment of business and industry on the residential areas. As the city expands at the center, the pressure is first felt in this zone. Much of the land is owned by persons who hope to profit from the increase of land values as business and industry move in. Little attention is given to maintenance of residential buildings. Rents are low. Maximum returns are gained by dividing residences into small units. Living conditions are crowded. Sanitary facilities are inadequate or nonexistent. In this area live unattached individuals, members of the lowest-income groups, poor migrants from the country, and colonies of immigrants. The stresses and strains and the tensions and conflicts of city growth are experienced more painfully in this zone than in any other area.

3. *The zone of workingmen's homes.* This belt of the city is inhabited by workers who have escaped from or avoided the slums. The residences are multiple dwellings, but not tenements. They are in better repair than those in the area of deterioration. Rents, although higher than nearer the center, are still relatively low. The population is more stable; there are more skilled workers; there are fewer foreign-born; and incomes are higher. Many of the inhabitants are just one generation removed from the slum zone.

4. *The zone of better residences.* This is an area of single, detached dwellings and of apartment buildings. Incomes and rents are higher, and facilities are better than nearer the center. There are more space and more lawns and gardens. Some restricted residential districts and exclusive apartments are found in this zone. The residents include persons of the middle and the privileged classes; members of the clerical, managerial, business, and professional groups.

5. *The commuters' zone.* In this zone, occupational and service dependence on the city proper is considerable. Many of the residents travel daily to the city. It is chiefly a residential area, but its make-up is diversified. It includes high- and low-class residential settlements, scattered estates, golf courses, industries, satellite towns, and farm land.

The concentric-zone theory is helpful in giving an over-all view of cities. In a broad and general way it applies to a great many American cities. But the usefulness of the theory is conditioned by the realization that the scheme set forth is highly generalized. It is an ideal construct. Probably no city conforms to the design in every detail; and numerous cities manifest major deviations from the general plan. The pattern may be modified or distorted by elevations in the land; by rivers, lakes, and the location of highways; and by the paths of railroads cutting through the city. Chicago itself, to which the theory was first specifically applied, does not conform to the ideal-typical scheme. There are a number of obvious deviations, the most conspicuous being that in Chicago the circular pattern is cut almost exactly in half by Lake Michigan.

The concentric-zone theory is not usually presented in precisely the same form as it was originally, and it will probably require further modification. It must be remembered that the construct was first set forth as a theory of city growth and that the city on which it was based was a large and rapidly growing city. Therefore the description of the zones assumes large and rapidly expanding urban centers. But what of smaller cities, and what of cities characterized by stability rather than by growth? And what, too, of the cities which, though continuing to grow, are less influenced by the force of expansion from within than by external growth. The concentric-zone theory was advanced early in the 1920's, before the automobile had in a significant way altered the patterns of city growth. The advantages of decentralization within urban areas had not become evident. What happens to the zone in transition when pressure from the center zone becomes less? Who are the inhabitants of the area and how is their culture characterized when immigration is markedly reduced? Further, the theory assumes that the movement outward from the center is related to income. That is, as families can afford to do so, they move into more desirable areas. Thus workmen live in the third zone and higher-income groups live in the fourth zone. But there have been important economic changes which have raised the income levels of workmen. There are workmen who can afford to live in the fourth zone quite as well as can members of the former middle-income occupational groups. Thus if the assumed relation between income and place of residence is valid, the line between zones three and four becomes less distinct. Our purpose is not to discount the general usefulness of the concentric-zone theory, but to suggest that the make-up of the various zones should not become stereotyped. They are not necessarily fixed, and modification of the plan is required accordingly.

Sector Theory [7]

The sector theory is based on an earlier theory of axial development, according to which city growth occurs along main transportation routes or along the lines of least resistance, thus forming a star-shaped city. Using this approach, Homer Hoyt has developed a theory in which the entire city is viewed as a circle with sectors radiating out from the central business area. Within each sector the type of land use tends to be the same from the center to the periphery. New growth on the arc of a sector takes on the character of the earlier growth of that sector. Thus if a sector of a city first develops as a low-rent residential area, low-quality housing will extend in the same direction to the outer edge of the city. Likewise, as a high-rent residential area moves outward it tends to remain within its sector.

Hoyt summarizes the principles relating to the growth of better residential areas as follows: [8]

"1. Growth tends to proceed, from given points of origin, along established lines of travel or toward another existing nucleus of buildings or trading centers.

"2. The zone of settlement tends to progress toward high ground

[7] Homer Hoyt, "City Growth and Mortgage Risk," *Insured Mortgage Portfolio*, vol. 1, nos. 6–10, December, 1936–April, 1937; and Homer Hoyt, *The Structure and Growth of Residential Neighborhoods in American Cities*, Federal Housing Administration, 1939.

[8] Hoyt, "City Growth and Mortgage Risk," *Insured Mortgage Portfolio*, vol. 1, no. 6, December, 1936, p. 9.

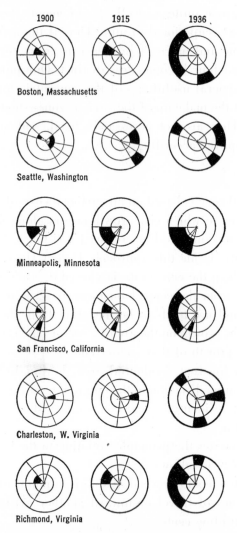

Figure 19. Changes in the Location of Fashionable Residential Areas. The fashionable areas are those in solid black. The changes indicated here occurred between 1900 and 1936. In each case the location of fashionable residences shifted outward from the center of the city. (From Homer Hoyt, *The Structure and Growth of Residential Neighborhoods in American Cities*, Federal Housing Administration, 1939, p. 115.)

which is free from the risk of floods and which has greater scenic beauty and a more pleasant atmosphere.

"3. Residential districts tend to grow toward the section of the city which has free, open country beyond its edges and away from 'dead-end' sections which are limited by natural or artificial barriers to expansion.

"4. The higher-priced residential areas tend to grow toward the homes of the leaders of the community.

"5. Trends of movement of office buildings, banks, and stores, where the higher-income groups work, tend to throw the trend of movement of the higher-priced residential areas in the same general direction.

"6. These residential areas tend to develop along the fastest existing transportation lines.

"7. Their growth tends to continue in the same direction for a long period of time."

The sector theory does not give equal attention to all aspects of the structure of cities. It has been applied particularly to the growth of residential areas and in this connection corrects certain of the conclusions of the concentric-zone theory. Like the concentric-zone theory, the sector theory is highly generalized. No two cities manifest the sector aspect in exactly the same form. Topography and transportation again are factors which cause deviation from the ideal pattern.

Multiple Nuclei [9]

Students of the city have repeatedly noted the tendency for subcenters to develop within cities. This observation has been refined in the theory of multiple nuclei. In most cities there is a central core around which the land-use pattern is arranged; but in many cities the total structure includes not one, but a number of centers. Harris and Ullman identify at least six types of districts which have developed around nuclei in most large cities in the United States.

[9] Harris and Ullman, *op. cit.*, pp. 14–17.

The *central business district* is described in much the same way as in the concentric-zone theory. It is observed, however, that in

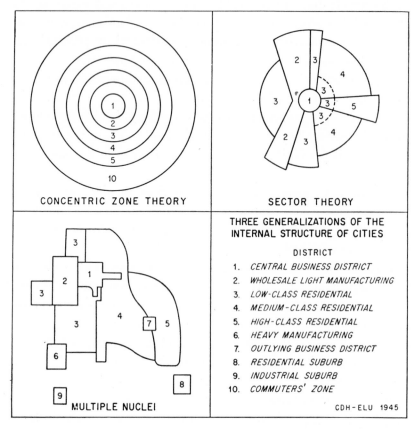

Figure 20. Generalizations of Internal Structure of Cities. The concentric-zone theory is a generalization for all cities. The arrangement of the sectors in the sector theory varies from city to city. The diagram for multiple nuclei represents one possible pattern among innumerable variations. (From C. D. Harris and E. L. Ullman, "The Nature of Cities," *The Annals*, vol. 242, November, 1945, p. 13.)

most large cities this district is not actually in the areal center, but is usually near one edge. Also, in most large cities the retail and the financial areas of the business district, although near to each other, are separate. The concentration of customers causes a gravitation of stores toward one area; convenience in carrying on business causes a clustering of office and financial buildings in another area. In small cities retail shops and financial buildings and offices are intermingled.

The *wholesale and light-manufacturing district* is located near the focus of transportation facilities which connect the city with outside regions. Wholesale houses require the services of railroads and trucks. Their usual location is along the railroads and near the business district. Light manufacturing is attracted to areas of this type by transportation, storage space, and marketing advantages.

The location of the *heavy industrial district* is influenced by the need for transportation, the requirement of space, and the desirability of segregation because of noise, odors, and waste-disposal problems. It therefore is located along rail or water transportation on the edge of the city, or in an area which at one time was on the outer edge.

Residential districts are specialized. Better residential areas are often away from railroads, smoke, noises, and odors on well-drained, high land. Poor housing tends to be near factories and railroads, wherever they are located in the city.

Included in the *minor nuclei* are cultural centers, parks, outlying business districts, and small industrial centers. Outlying business districts may be potential major centers.

Suburbs and satellites constitute the sixth type of district.

These separate nuclei have sometimes been part of the original pattern of the city, but frequently they emerge as the city grows. Their development may be attributed to the need for specialized facilities, the conveniences and profits deriving from proximity, the detrimental consequences of the close association of unlike activities, and the selective and segregating effect of rents and land values. The multiple-nuclei theory emphasizes rents and land values less than does the concentric-zone theory. This is not because they are unimportant in influencing the pattern of the city, but rather because they are seen in relation to other significant factors.

A Comprehensive View

The theories of city structure which have been presented are not to be regarded as mutually contradictory. Despite their discrepancies they may be regarded as supplementing each other. Taken separately, none of the schemes gives a complete picture, but when they are considered together the structure of the city stands out in clearer detail. The concentric-zone theory provided a general basis for the study of the pattern of the city and remains useful. The sector theory and the multiple-nuclei theory, each using a different approach, serve to correct, refine, and add to the earlier theory.

SUMMARY

In 1950 the census counted as urban all places of 2,500 or more. Urban growth in the United States has been rapid. In contrast to 1790, when one out of twenty persons lived in an urban area, in 1950 about three out of five persons were living in urban areas. In 1790 there was no city of 50,000 in the United States. In 1950 five cities had populations of more than 1 million. Continuing rapid urban growth is indicated by population increases between 1940 and 1950. The extraordinary growth of urban communities has resulted from migration rather than from rapid growth from within cities. Important factors involved in the growth are methods of agriculture which decrease the demand for people on farms and expanding occupational and economic opportunities in urban places.

Further, cities have grown rapidly because they perform necessary functions in our type of society. Almost every city in the United States can be classified on the basis of its major functions. Most cities can be classified in one of three general categories: places performing comprehensive services, transport focuses and break-of-bulk points, or concentration points for specialized services.

The internal growth of cities, though largely unplanned, is not

without pattern and order. The study of the relationship between
the structure of cities and the people and culture of cities is the
work of social ecologists. The concentric-zone theory is a significant contribution to urban ecology. According to the theory, as a
city grows it comes to be divided into five concentric zones each
having distinctive characteristics. The five zones are the central
business district, the zone in transition, the zone of workingmen's
homes, the zone of better residences, and the commuters' zone. The
theory is useful when critically evaluated.

Other theories of city growth are the sector theory and the
theory of multiple nuclei. According to the sector theory, within
each sector of a city the type of land use tends to be the same from
the center to the outer edge. The multiple-nuclei theory takes into
account the tendency of subcenters to develop within cities.

SELECTED REFERENCES

Alihan, Milla A.: *Social Ecology*, New York, Columbia University Press, 1938.

Gist, Noel P., and L. A. Halbert: *Urban Society*, New York, Crowell, 1948.

Hatt, Paul, and Albert J. Reiss: *Reader in Urban Sociology*, Glencoe, Ill., Free
Press, 1951.

Hoyt, Homer: *The Structure and Growth of Residential Neighborhoods in
American Cities*, Washington, GPO, 1939.

Mitchell, Robert B., ed.: "Building the Future City," *The Annals*, vol. 242,
November, 1945.

Mumford, Lewis: *City Development*, New York, Harcourt, Brace, 1945.

National Resources Committee: *Our Cities: Their Role in the National Economy*, 1937.

Park, R. E., E. W. Burgess, and R. D. McKenzie: *The City*, Chicago, University of Chicago Press, 1925.

Quinn, James A.: *Human Ecology*, New York, Prentice-Hall, 1950.

Schlesinger, Arthur M.: *The Rise of the City*, New York, Macmillan, 1933.

Smith, T. Lynn, and C. A. McMahan: *The Sociology of Urban Life*, New York,
Dryden, 1951.

Taylor, Griffith: *Urban Geography*, New York, Dutton, 1946.

CHAPTER TEN

The Urban Way of Life

It is commonly recognized that the way of life of the city is different from that of the country. Also, it has many times been observed that the influence of the city is increasing and spreading. The term *urbanization* is used in connection with this extension of city influence. But what does urbanization imply? Does it mean that cities are expanding in number and in size and that as they grow they extend into areas which at one time were rural farm territory? Or does it mean that there is an increase in the proportion of our total population living in urban areas? Urbanization means these things and more. A diffusion of the pattern of life of the city is taking place. Not only are more people moving to the city and new areas being included within the bounds of cities; the urban way of life is reaching out beyond the city. This is what is suggested by the seemingly contradictory but substantially correct phrase, *the urbanization of rural society*.

If it is held that the urban way of life is spreading, then it should be possible to delineate the distinctive nature of urban social life. This is not a simple matter. An analysis of life in the city reveals that not all the elements of the culture of cities are being diffused to areas outside the city. Some features of city life are born of the unique social and physical environment of the city, and apart from that environment they do not exist. There is an urbanism of towns and there is an urbanism of cities; they have much in common, but they cannot always be equated. It is proposed in this chapter to consider a number of the characteristic manifestations of the urban way of life as practiced in larger cities.

212

In so doing, we are probably dealing with *maximum urbanism* rather than with *typical urbanism*.

BASIC FEATURES OF CITY LIFE

Much of the distinctiveness of the way of life of the city derives from its density of population, diversity of groups, and physical environment. Within a relatively small area a great number of people work, play, raise families, and seek satisfaction for their physical and psychological needs. Innumerable diverse groups are involved in the ongoing social and economic life of the city. Separately and yet together they pursue their ends. This they do in a particular type of physical environment. It is in this combination of circumstances that the distinctive way of life of the city has its source.

Population Density

Density of population is an urban characteristic. In 1950 in the United States as a whole there were 50.7 persons per square mile. In the 157 areas which the Bureau of the Census defined as *urbanized areas* in 1950, the population per square mile was 5,438. The density of *central cities* in urbanized areas was 7,788; the density in *urban fringe areas* in urbanized areas was 3,200. The density of central cities varied from 1,414 for the Duluth-Superior urbanized area to 24,537 for New York, Newark, and Jersey City, the three central cities of the New York–northeastern New Jersey urbanized area.

Density of population influences both the number and the nature of social contacts. The inhabitant of the city is daily near a great number of people. There is ever-present opportunity to make new acquaintances. Measured merely in terms of the number of people around him, possibilities for social contact are almost unlimited. The multiplicity of relationships affords a stimulating social environment for the urbanite.

It is obvious, however, that there is a limit to the number of

Triborough Bridge and Tunnel Authority

Air View of Part of New York City. On Manhattan Island in the heart of New York, urban centralization and population density reach their peak in this country.

people who can be known to one individual. Inevitably the inhabitant of a densely populated urban area is surrounded by myriads of persons who are unknown to him. Indeed, he is acquainted with only an exceedingly small proportion of the people whom he sees. Most of the people are strangers to him, as he is to them. We shall consider later the significance of this urban phenomenon of proximity without acquaintance.

Density of population may be both stimulating and requiring. The greater the number of people who live in a small area, the greater the number of adjustments the individual must make. In the course of one downtown trip, hundreds of adjustments are made to other people. For some persons the physical, emotional, and mental wear and tear of these countless contacts is tremendous. Others move through the maze of urban social relations without stress or strain. But whether the result is tension and fatigue, composure and placidity, or numbness and indifference, some type of adjustment must be made to the vast number of people encountered. These adjustments help to mold the urban personality.

Another aspect of the density of urban population is its relation to living quarters. Not only are more persons found per square mile in the city, but household living conditions are more crowded. Families are less isolated from each other and have less privacy. Around single, detached houses yard space is small. A high percentage of dwellings are double houses, row houses, apartment houses, tenement houses, and rooming houses. In the most densely populated areas residential units are often small, and under the most crowded conditions families of more than average size live in one room.

In summarizing the relationship between urbanity and density of population, Sorokin, Zimmerman, and Galpin observe that "the density of population, measured either by the number of individuals per unit territory, by the number of families per one dwelling or building, or by the number of families or individuals per one structurally separated dwelling is positively correlated with urbanity and with size of urban community and negatively with rurality and the smallness in size of the community." [1]

Social Differentiation

The city has always been the home of a heterogeneous population. People of many races, nationalities, occupations, religions, interests, and classes live together within a relatively small area. In this regard American cities are no exception, unless it be that their inhabitants are exceptionally varied in culture. The Urbanism Committee of the National Resources Committee wrote: [2]

[1] P. A. Sorokin, C. C. Zimmerman, and C. J. Galpin, *A Systematic Source Book in Rural Sociology*, Minneapolis, University of Minnesota Press, 1930, vol. 1, pp. 201–202.

[2] National Resources Committee, *Our Cities: Their Role in the National Economy*, 1937, p. 10.

"Never before in the history of the world have great groups of people so diverse in social backgrounds been thrown together into such close contacts as in the cities of America. The typical American city, therefore, does not consist of a homogeneous body of citizens, but of human beings with the most diverse cultural backgrounds, often speaking different languages, following a great variety of customs, habituated to different modes and standards of living, and sharing only in varying degrees the tastes, the beliefs, and the ideals of their native fellow city dwellers. In short, far from presenting a picture of a single unified body of human beings, the American city is a motley of peoples and cultures forming a mosaic of little worlds which in part blend with one another, but, in part and for a time, remain segregated or come into conflict with one another."

In the United States the foreign-born and their children are concentrated in cities. When the foreign-born white population was at its peak, in 1930, about 80 per cent of the total lived in cities. The proportion of foreign-born has been highest in the largest cities. Since immigration has been restricted, the percentage of the urban population born outside the United States has declined. But although the proportion of foreign-born in cities continues to decrease, ethnic diversity will not soon disappear. Variations in culture which have their source in differences of national origins may be expected to persist for many years.

The cityward migration of the Negro has also contributed to the ethnic heterogeneity of American cities. In the South the major shift in Negro population has been in the direction of the city. Negroes who have moved from the South to the North have become concentrated in the larger urban centers.

Not all the cultural complexity of American cities has its origin in racial and nationality differences. Many of the "outsiders" who live in cities are native Caucasians. Migrants from country to city take with them attitudes, customs, and values that are rooted in the rural way of life. A "cultural shock" is experienced by many rural migrants when they feel the initial impact of the urban environment. The shock comes to persons of rural background whether they are immigrants or natives. Their rural customs and ideas are jolted and modified by the urban way of life, and in numerous cases an adequate adjustment is never made. Rural migrants, in turn, leave their mark on the city. They add still more elements to the admixture which is the culture of cities.

In contrast to rural areas, occupational differentiation in cities is extremely manifold. Most rural residents have some understanding of the work activities of the people around them. Since a high proportion of country people are engaged in agriculture, they have much common occupational knowledge. They can also have some familiarity with the limited number of nonfarming occupations. In the city the situation is vastly different. The urban dweller is surrounded by thousands of people who, when they are at their work, engage in activities about which he knows nothing at all. They speak occupational languages which he does not understand. They have work habits and customs that are strange to him. In short, they live in different occupational worlds. A complex division of labor and the resultant occupational specialization and social differentiation are significant factors in limiting communication and interaction among the inhabitants of cities.

The social differentiation which characterizes the urban way of life extends to religious groups. In rural America as a whole are found a profusion of religious denominations and sects, but the variety of religious groups in most cities far outnumbers that of any one rural community. Although Catholicism is well established in some rural areas, many rural communities are almost exclusively Protestant. In most cities there are churches representing at least the three major religious groups: Protestants, Catholics, and Jews. In addition there may be Mohammedans, Buddhists, Confucianists, Hindus, and others. The many immigrants who located in cities contributed greatly to religious differentiation. There are certain groups, such as the Greek Orthodox and the Jewish, which are found in cities but which only rarely are among the religious groups in rural areas. Other groups which are chiefly urban are the Salvation Army, Christian Scientists, and Unitarians. The city has given birth to sects and denominations such as Four Square Gospel, Theosophy, and spiritualism, which, in the main, have continued to be urban.

In a description of the many groups into which the population of a city is divided, interest groups and voluntary associations must be included. These are the groups formed in order that the members may follow a particular interest. It would be impossible to list all the thousands of such groups that might be found in one city. They include, to name only a few types, political clubs, service groups, fraternal societies, veterans' organizations, business associations, professional societies, alumni associations, women's clubs, civic associations, educational organizations, and a countless variety of recreational groups. Almost every conceivable interest is represented by a formal or an informal group.

In addition to providing a channel for the expression of specialized interests, these groups are a means by which status is established. The city dweller takes his place in the urban community by participation in voluntary associations and interest groups. If he "is someone" outside his home and away from his work, it is usually within one or several of these groups. Only a relatively small number of city residents receive general recognition throughout the city as a whole.

In view of the existence of a great number of interest groups, it must not be assumed that all persons join such groups to the same extent. Actually many persons have only the slightest association with groups of this type. The reasons for limited participation are many. Some persons are excluded from activities because of cost. Others have not the leisure time to engage in many group activities. Some, of course, have time but their interests seem not to go beyond the necessity of earning a living. There are still others who have the interest and the inclination, but who lack facility in making the contacts which would take them into voluntary associations. This nonparticipation in interest groups is significant because in a sense it, too, is indicative of the segmentation of urban society. Without choice every individual falls into some type of group, but the families and individuals having almost no contact with interest groups form the minutest segments of urban society. They are isolated units within the city.

The division of city people into multifarious groups is evident in the numbers of social classes. There are many social and economic groups, and each group has its rank in the status and prestige structure of the city. The reason for the greater number of social-class groups in urban society than in rural society is that in every other way there is more differentiation in cities. There are more racial and nationality groups, more religious groups, more interest groups, and more occupational groups. Thus there is more basis for making distinctions. Between the president of a big corporation and the unskilled laborer performing the most menial tasks there are many different types of work, each rated as being above or below other types of work. The economic rewards offered in the city also vary widely. Although both country and city have had much poverty, in modern times great wealth has been concentrated in the city. It is there that the difference between the highest and the lowest incomes is most extreme. Wealth and income differences are important factors in producing the complex class structure of urban society.

Finally, social differentiation within cities is territorial. Every city is divided into many residential sections. In large cities there are hundreds of these areas. The part of the city in which an individual or a family locates is determined by the combined influence of all the other differentiating factors of race, nationality, occupation, religion, interests, and class. In some instances, one factor is of primary importance. For example, income-group membership is frequently a leading factor in determining the residential distribution of the population. Thus families of the same general income level may live in the same area even though they are of different nationalities, occupations, and religions. In certain areas race and nationality are primary factors in selecting the population composition. *Chinatowns, Little Italies, Deutschlands,* and *black belts* are such sections. Within areas of this type there is often a further division according to income levels. Areas of a city which are predominantly Catholic or predominantly Jewish are examples of separation strongly influenced by religion.

The effect of the division of cities into many territorial parts varies from family to family and from area to area. Residence in one part of a city may mean a great deal more than having a place to live. It can also mean exposure to a particular set of customs, attitudes, values, and beliefs. This is especially true in areas in which race, nationality, or religion are important in selecting the population. Racial, national, and religious segregation produce cultural isolation. A specialized culture is transmitted to Negroes in Negro areas, to Italians in Italian areas, to Protestants in Protestant areas, and to middle-class families in a middle-income residential area.

Cultural isolation within the city is most pronounced when the regular orbit of activities is confined to one section of the city. Despite the mobility of city dwellers, a strictly circumscribed mode of life, while not characteristic, is not uncommon. In large cities there are persons who almost never leave their section of the city. Others who go on more frequent excursions to other parts have only the most impersonal contacts on such occasions. This is one manifestation of urban provincialism. Having interests which are limited to the locality is usually associated with rural society, but it is found in the city as well.

Isolation within one area, however, is not the rule in the city. Attachment to a locality has never been as great in the city as in the country. There is evidence that local areas in cities are becoming even less important as places in which social contacts are concentrated. Friends and acquaintances, centers of activity, and places of employment are scattered over a wide area. But the dispersion of social contacts does not eliminate differentiation by race, nationality, occupation, religion, interests, and class. Indeed, even when contacts and activities are distributed over a large area, territorial bounds are not removed. The urban individual does not regularly go to all parts of the city. He may travel through almost all parts of the city, but except when he attends large public events, he usually goes only where members of his own groups live, work, and play. Mobility may create the illusion of knowledge of all parts of the city, but social differentiation functions to limit the city dweller's firsthand knowledge to certain groups and areas. It is an understatement to say of city people that "one half doesn't know how the other half lives."

Physical Environment

The way of life of the urbanite is profoundly influenced by the physical and material environment in which he moves. Repeatedly and regularly he is exposed to sets of stimuli which are peculiar to the physical environment of the city. What the individual sees, hears, smells, feels, and thinks is determined by the physical stimuli about him. To these stimuli some kind of response must be made. A process of conditioning is constantly going on. Habits of response are formed which may be considered as characteristic of the urban way of life. What, then, is the nature of the physical environment to which the residents of cities become habituated?

Characteristically the urban environment is congested. The congestion is greatest at the center of the city but is by no means limited to the center. It is evident on every hand. Space is at a premium. In downtown areas there is the day-long crowding of people on foot. On sidewalks and in stores and other places of business the milling of people goes on throughout the day, reaching peaks of intensity in the morning, noon, and evening "rush hours," and often reviving later during the entertainment hours. Transportation is correspondingly congested. During some periods of the day all available space on public transportation facilities is utilized. To reduce crowding by increasing the number of transportation units would be to increase costs and reduce profits. Automobile traffic is likewise heavy and at times moves bumper to bumper and two or more abreast. Parking is a major problem.

Chicago Park District

Grant Park in Chicago Adjoining the Central Business District. Despite the intensity of urban land use for commercial and residential purposes, many American cities maintain sizable park areas. Even so, in most cities there is need for many more areas of this type.

Experienced but nonurban drivers are sometimes fear-struck at the prospect of becoming involved in city motor traffic.

Competition for space and consequent crowding is conspicuously evident in the living conditions. In slum areas an inordinate number of people are compressed into a small compartment. In newer low-rent residential areas crowding is somewhat less marked; nevertheless real-estate values encourage the maximum utilization of space. In higher-income districts, too, the meaning of "privacy" is rather relative. Even in exclusive "town houses" and apartments, residents often have only as much seclusion as is afforded by the separation provided by alleys, courts, and window draperies.

A further characteristic of the physical environment of the city is disorder. In blighted areas there is the disorder of deterioration: shattered steps, broken walls, decaying posts, and dismantled doors. Streets are cluttered with garbage cans waiting to be relieved of their contents, and the air is strung with cross-court clotheslines. In areas where the new is replacing the old, the process proceeds haphazardly. Tall buildings are attached to short ones; red brick joins with orange brick; wide streets suddenly become narrow; and service stations are built beside churches. Attractive houses are seen against the backdrop of factories, smokestacks, and water tanks standing boldly exposed. Everywhere there are signs—hanging, protruding, and elevated—bidding for attention. And, as though somehow tying all the incongruous pieces together, wires crossing wires, bridges over bridges, and railroads elevated over surface roads add their contribution to the disorder.

The city is also a center of noise. The concentration of noise was measured some years ago in Chicago.[3] One hundred per cent was made to represent noise that would drive one to distraction if continued over an extended period. Rural areas had from 8 to 10 per cent noise; suburbs had 15 per cent; residential areas had 25 per cent; commercial areas had 30 per cent; industrial areas had 35 per cent; and the central commercial area had from 40 to 43 per cent. At a distance of three blocks the noise of a streetcar was 15 per cent. Twenty feet overhead, the noise of an elevated train was 90 per cent. Tests made in a Bronx zoo showed that if a lion were to stand on a busy New York street corner and roar he could not be heard more than twenty or thirty feet away.

This description of the physical environment of the city is not a commentary on the desirability or the undesirability of such surroundings. The point is that adjustment to their distinctive type of environment is a component of the way of life of city people. Many who live in the city become well acclimated to the stimuli surrounding them. In fact they feel maladjusted when they are too long removed from the setting to which they are accustomed. Some urbanites find rural quiet and seclusion intolerable except for brief periods. It is not at all uncommon for apartment dwellers to consider their mode of life decidedly preferable to all others. The author recalls a conversation with a woman belonging to the upper-

---

[3] *Chicago's Health*, vol. 23, no. 11, Mar. 19, 1929, pp. 74–75.

middle-income group who was horrified at the very thought of not living in a row house.

There is another but rather different way in which the physical environment of the city influences mode of life. In order to draw the contrast, let us look at the physical setting of the countryman. He lives near the soil, plants, and animal life. This natural environment he tends, cultivates, and domesticates. He is not independent, for he counts on the efforts of other people; but if necessity should require, by utilizing the provisions of nature he could survive. The inhabitants of cities, on the other hand, live amidst an environment of buildings, streets, factories, bridges, and vehicles. This is an environment of their own making upon which they are all dependent. Together they maintain what they have created. Independently only a few could survive, for their material environment does not provide the resources for independent existence. The interdependence of city dwellers is therefore almost absolute.

DERIVATIVE FEATURES OF CITY LIFE

The foregoing characteristics of city life may be regarded as basic in the sense that other important characteristics derive from them. Population density, social differentiation, and physical environment condition the nature of social interaction, social solidarity, and social problems in the city.

Social Interaction

As suggested earlier, one inevitable result of the size and density of city populations is that it is impossible for an individual to know more than a small proportion of the people whom he sees. With thousands of people he never has any direct social contact. They walk the same streets, ride the same buses and trains, attend the same theaters and athletic events, and shop in the same stores; but they do not speak nor even recognize each other. There is, to be sure, a type of interaction between an individual and the countless unknown around him, but it is entirely impersonal. They are merely "other people," without identity as persons. The absence of direct social contact is taken for granted. The person who, without an acceptable reason, violates the assumption of noncommunication is regarded as an oddity. The urbanite does not move in his daily orbit without any direct contact with people whom he does not know. There is reason for interaction with clerks, newsboys, ticket takers, policemen, taxi drivers, waitresses, doormen, shoe shiners, and many others. Such contacts are usually brief, superficial, and, again, impersonal. Their very brevity is one reason for their impersonality. The interacting parties meet only in passing; there is no time for more than superficial relations.

There are other reasons for impersonality. To behave in a more personal manner might require additional effort. Sustaining a personal level of interaction in all situations would for many people be an exhausting ordeal. Impersonality is less demanding. Furthermore, the introduction of the personal element involves a risk. There is little basis for predicting how the unknown person would react to more personal social contact. Impersonal behavior seems to be more predictable. The more impersonality is practiced, the more it is expected.

The tendency to respond impersonally is not limited to those contacts which occur only once or very infrequently. Similar behavior is observed in contacts repeated regularly. An individual may patronize the same barber or buy from the same druggist year after year and never learn much about them. Conventional forms of friendliness are practiced, but relationships are not intimate. The same is often true of other relationships such as those of employers and employees, members of the same church, or persons living in the same block. The person who is accustomed to more intimate and personal contacts considers this lack of intimacy to be an indication of the unfriendliness of city people.

The concept of *social distance* has been developed to denote the degree of social separation between individuals and between groups. In the city spatial distance and social distance are often unrelated. The chances that an individual in a city crowd will talk to certain people near enough for him to touch are hardly greater than if they were miles away. People whose homes are within hearing distance of each other may be socially further apart than if they lived in different towns. If such people do meet and speak, social distance may still exist. There are many barriers to intimacy other than the barrier of space.

All the factors that cause social differentiation are involved in the maintenance of social distance. Persons of different racial, nationality, occupational, and class groups generally are more distant, socially, than are the members of any one of these groups. The degree of intimacy possible between persons who fall in the same group is greater than between persons of different groups. In part this is because members of the same group have similar customs, attitudes, interests, values, and ways of thinking. They have, therefore, more basis for interaction. They "have more in common"; they can communicate more readily; and they can better interpret each other's responses. Social distance between members of different groups is also greater because standards of acceptable degrees of intimacy come to be socially defined. Social distance between groups tends to gain the support of custom. This is particularly true where there are differences of status. In general, social distance increases as the difference in status increases.

Impersonality and social distance are characteristic of a large proportion of the contacts of city people, but to discuss urban social interaction wholly in these terms would be a distortion. Urbanites like ruralites have intimate social contacts. Many of the religious, special-interest, and occupational relationships are of a personal nature. As primary groups the family, the play group, and the neighborhood provide intimate response. In the case of the neighborhood, however, there is evidence that as interests and activities have come to be more widely dispersed throughout the city, social distance within the neighborhood has increased. It is not actually the lack of personal relationships which characterizes life in the city; it is rather the ever presence, in addition to personal relationships, of an enormous number of impersonal relationships.

City patterns of social interaction have varying effects on urban personalities. Many city residents make an adequate personal adjustment in accord with the impersonality which surrounds them. They practice and accept impersonality. They expect social distance in many of their relationships. For some, impersonality and social distance are quite painless because their need for intimate response is satisfied in primary groups and because they feel that their status is established in groups which are important to them. But there are others who are maladjusted. Of these, some are migrants from communities having less impersonality who interpret the new type of interaction in terms of what it would mean in the places from which they came. Others are individuals, separated from family and primary groups, whose need for intimate response is not satisfied. Still others are persons who become increasingly isolated as they lose status and become disassociated from groups to which they once belonged.

Social Solidarity

It appears to be a major marvel that the inhabitants of cities can survive at all. Without resources from within the city, thousands of people, most of whom are unknown to each other, manage daily to satisfy their needs. Food and clothing are distributed, services are provided, activities are organized, and behavior is regulated. As one massive, complex whole, life in the city functions to achieve individual and collective ends. Viewed in this way, it is evident that the city is not the scene of uncontrolled social chaos. It is a center of integrated and unified social activity. What, then, is the basis of integration and what are the forces that effect social solidarity within the city?

The cohesion which is characteristic of the city can best be seen in contrast. In certain types of solidarity cities are weak; in other types they are strong. There are a number of factors working against urban unity. Membership in a vast social aggregate is not conducive to the development of a strong sense of belonging. One can truly feel that he belongs to a family, to a church, or to a

Triborough Bridge and Tunnel Authority

The Triborough Bridge, New York City, with Randall's Island Interchange in the Foreground. Elaborate networks of motor thoroughfares and rail lines are required to facilitate the daily massive movement of people into and within metropolitan areas.

neighborhood; but one is unlikely to have a deeply rooted feeling of identification with the entire population of a city. The individual does not in any meaningful way consider fellow inhabitants of the city to be "his people." He cannot think of them all as "his kind of people." Urban social differentiation produces just the opposite effect. Awareness of difference is greater than awareness of likeness. There is, therefore, throughout the population of a city as a whole, very little solidarity arising from what F. H. Giddings called *consciousness of kind,* that is, unity based on common traits, like attitudes, and similarity of experience.

The impersonality and the social distance of urban life are separating rather than uniting influences. An individual feels no strong kinship with people who give him only superficial attention, nor is he inclined to assume much personal responsibility for those who stay some social distance from him. The city has often been represented as a place of tolerance, when in fact what passes as tolerance may be only indifference. The urban dweller gives little attention to the behavior of other people if it does not touch his activities, privileges, and groups. When his interests are involved, his attitude may be decidedly different. There are so many people, events, and circumstances about which the city person has no interest and no concern simply because he seems uninvolved. Voluntary assumption of responsibility for other individuals, therefore, is minimal.

For similar reasons the informal social controls of gossip and social approval and disapproval are weak. In the anonymity of the city it is possible to mingle with people who disregard all sorts of behavior as long as they are not affected. And if there are disapproving groups, nearly always there can be found other groups that will give approval. Under these circumstances, what other people think and say does not regulate behavior to the degree that it does in places in which relationships are more personal and more all-embracing.

The city is the scene of change, and social change is often a disruptive rather than a stabilizing and unifying force. Relationships shift frequently, events occur in rapid succession; and circumstances are quickly altered. The clash of ideas, attitudes, and values acts as a catalyst to change in customs. The old is constantly challenged by the new and different. In American cities the type of social solidarity that arises from commonly held and long-established traditions is weak.

It is apparent that the social solidarity of the city does not have its source in homogeneity, personal relationships, unchanging customs, and strong consensus. But the city does have its own character-istic type of unity and control. It is a unity that arises from inter-dependence. Life in the city is maintained by a complex social organization. No city dweller is self-sufficient. An individual can exist only because thousands of other individuals perform their assigned tasks. In every area of urban activity there is a division of labor. Each individual who contributes to the ongoing life of the city accepts certain specialized responsibilities. The integration that results from this division of responsibility is to a degree self-enforc-ing, for the individual who does not perform his part is penalized through the rewards and recognition which he receives. The right of an individual to occupy a position depends upon the adequacy with which he carries out his obligations. The worker is responsible to his employer; the manufacturer is under obligation to his custom-ers; the president of an organization has duties to perform for the membership. The individual is under pressure to meet his commit-ments or to forfeit his position and its rewards. The social cohesion of the city does not come into being because people do the same things, but because they do different things and in so doing place themselves in contract relationships with each other.

Informal social controls such as custom, social approval and dis-approval, and gossip function to regulate behavior in cities, but to a less complete degree than in more homogeneous communities. In complex heterogeneous communities the area in which informal control is effective is limited. Within a family, or a neighborhood, or a church, informal controls may operate effectively to regulate behavior. Also social expectation regulates behavior within class groups and in a society as a whole. Social pressure produces a con-siderable amount of conformity among all the members of a society. But in a complex society, after social pressure has done all that it can, there are still many areas of activity that are left uncontrolled. For example, how effective would traffic regulations, tax require-ments, and legal contracts be if only informal social controls were relied upon to enforce them? It is at this point that the need for formal agencies of control becomes apparent. Policemen, courts, restrictions, laws, codes, regulating commissions, contracts, and investigators are associated with the urban way of life. They represent the high degree of formal social control within cities.

Specialization and formal control are reflected in the social services of the city. Poor, deviant, and distressed persons may be aided by unorganized efforts and individual generosity, but to a large extent the urban population counts on specialized agencies to provide social services. Social workers, clinics, organized recreation, legal-aid services, reform groups, and many others are part of the urban program to give assistance to persons who are in need. Through organized social services city communities attempt to give help which in less complex communities is provided on a more informal and personal basis. It is, of course, a huge task to try to give aid in a large city, and it is certain that many persons are neglected.

Problems of the City

An enumeration of all the problems of urban life would result in a long list. Only a few of the more important continuing problems have been selected for inclusion here. Certain of these problems are not peculiar to the city; they are found also in rural areas. However, the manifestations, the consequences, and the methods of dealing with problems are not always the same in rural areas as in urban areas. The urban way of life is reflected in the form that social problems take in the city.

How to maintain the health of millions of people who live together in cities is a major problem. It is not a problem that is ever "solved"; it requires constant and continuous attention. The available data indicate that, in spite of the health progress that urban areas have made, on the whole it is still healthier to live in the country than in the city. Death rates appear to be slightly higher in urban areas than in rural areas. Urban death rates, however, are not higher for all diseases.

At the same time, the city has been the center of health and medical advances. Doctors, nurses, and dentists practice there in greatest numbers. Hospital facilities are largely concentrated in cities. Health organizations promote sanitation, control of communicable diseases, research, and education. More money is spent for public health services than in rural areas.

The fact is, however, that the full extent of the city health problem is not demonstrated either by making rural-urban comparisons

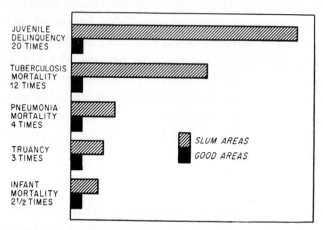

Figure 21. A Contrast of Four Slum Areas and Four "Good" Areas in Chicago. (Adapted from *Children and Youth at the Midcentury—A Chart Book*, prepared by the Midcentury White House Conference on Children and Youth, Raleigh, Health Publications Institute, 1951, p. 28.)

or by calling attention to the advanced health and medical facilities of the city. The urban health record in certain respects is better than rural-urban comparisons reveal. On the other hand, health facilities in the city are much less extensive than at first glance they appear to be. Whatever the complete health record of the city may be, large segments of the urban population suffer from deficient diets and from unhygienic living conditions. Likewise, the benefits of medical and hospital services are not equally available to all groups. Thus the high disease and death rates found in some groups in cities present a major health problem. The differences between urban and rural death rates are less than the variations within cities.

Housing is another major urban problem. A survey of sixty-four

Buffalo Municipal Housing Authority

Housing in a Slum Area. These houses in Buffalo were demolished to make way for a new public housing development.

cities made in 1934 by the Department of Commerce and the Civil Works Administration showed that more than one-sixth of 1,500,-000 residential dwellings were substandard. That was in the midst of a great depression during which building activity slowed down. The Second World War practically halted home building. A building boom followed the Second World War, but most of the home construction was in the outlying areas. Meanwhile within cities miles and miles of deteriorated and obsolete homes remain. The rebuilding has begun in some cities, but it is usually extremely incomplete and always very slow.

Looking to the future, just after the end of the Second World War, the Comptroller of the City of New York suggested some of the implications of bad housing as seen from the point of view of municipal administration: [4]

[4] Joseph D. McGoldrick, "City Building and Renewal," *The Annals*, vol. 242, November, 1945, p. 100.

"There is no greater opportunity [for productive activity] or challenge than that presented by the need to rebuild huge areas of our cities. A recent survey of New York City by the Consolidated Edison Company revealed that 40 per cent of all dwelling units in Manhattan are more than 40 years old and that half of these lack bathrooms. There are very sizable areas in Manhattan and the old sections of Brooklyn where the average age of the dwellings is not 40 years, but 50, 60, and 70 years. Public capital will have all it can do to provide for the lowest income group and provide the schools and hospitals, the parks and playgrounds, and the sewers and disposal plants which a modern community needs. In fact, it will have a hard time doing even this, if it permits these interior areas to continue to rot. Such obsolete areas have many public facilities for which the city debt is as yet unamortized. Municipal services in these cost more than in average areas, and this cost usually is far in excess of the taxes which such areas yield. But the push of population into new areas is constantly forcing cities to extend water, sewage, transportation, and other services, and provide new schools, parks, and playgrounds.

"If a way or a variety of ways can be found to permit these areas to be rebuilt, a wide field for useful postwar employment can be opened and the areas put back into a sound, self-supporting status. All of this points to the need for broadened concepts of city planning; because without sound and realistic planning, such efforts will bear little fruit. Most cities cannot longer afford to neglect this problem, because it goes to the roots of so many other separate municipal problems."

The urban recreation problem is seen most obviously in the lack of play space and recreation facilities for children. American cities have been built with a minimum of planning; as a consequence after areas are thickly covered with buildings it is difficult to open parks, playgrounds, or other play areas. The problem is all the more real because the city child has a great deal of free time. As a rule he has few fixed duties. An attempt is made to provide programs of recreation, but the proportion of children who participate in organized recreation is small.

Adults as well as children are influenced by limitations of space. Outdoor activities such as gardening, hunting, and fishing are not near at hand. Furthermore, shorter working hours and the use of home appliances have given more leisure time. As a result of this increase of leisure time there has been a tremendous expansion of commercial amusement and entertainment. Other than commercial recreation, the radio and television have become the chief means of passing time in some groups. In the upper middle and upper classes especially commercial entertainment is supplemented by a a private schedule of "social activities." It appears that active participation in games, sports, and hobbies is growing, but for the present the vast majority of urbanites are making a passive and spectator adjustment to the new leisure.

Crime as an urban problem has been widely publicized. Exact data for making comparisons are not available; however, on the basis of existing evidence, crime rates are believed to be higher in urban areas than in rural areas. It appears that, in general, crime rates increase with population density. Rates are highest near the center of the city and tend to decline gradually from the center outward to the rural hinterland. In larger cities crime rates are higher than in smaller cities. Three types of crime seem to flourish notoriously well in the urban environment: crimes against property, organized and commercialized crime, and juvenile delinquency. Rates for crimes against persons, such as homicide and rape, are not higher in urban areas than in rural areas.

The higher urban rate for crimes against property, such as robbery, burglary, and larceny, may in part be attributed to actual need coupled with the seeming accessibility of the things desired. More important, however, is the reflection in crimes against property of the urban preoccupation with things and money. It is difficult to say where "needs" end and where "wants" begin. Certainly a high proportion of those who attempt to acquire money and things by illegal means do not do so because they lack the essentials for existence. But in a society of impersonal and secondary contacts, money is far more than a means of subsistence. Money and the things that money buys are symbols of prestige. The deprivation that motivates crimes against property is often psychological rather than physical. The struggle is for status and not merely for survival.

Some of the reasons why organized and commercialized crime operates in the city are fairly obvious. The greatest market for the things in which the racketeer deals—gambling, sex, liquors, dope, and "protection"—is in the city. The protective anonymity of the city reduces the risk of detection. Equally important is the fact that social control is often weak. Racketeering cannot thrive without either the active or the passive cooperation of law-enforcement agencies.

This touches on the general problem of social control in cities. We have already observed that when social relations are primary and personal, informal controls such as approval and disapproval are effective. When social relations are secondary and impersonal, informal control is supplemented by the formal control of legal agencies. But in a secondary-group society, who controls the agencies of formal control? In other words, how are the police to be made to carry out their functions when they are not inclined to do so? Or how are the agencies responsible for improving housing, health, and recreation to be made to function for the maximum benefit of all? It is evident that in many cities the control of the people over those who are supposed to protect and promote their welfare is weak. Thus improvement of the urban way of life presents problems of control as well as of planning and organization.

SUMMARY

The urban way of life is different from that of rural areas. Much of the distinctiveness of the way of life of the city derives from its density of population, diversity of groups, and physical environment. Urban population density influences both the number and the nature of social contacts. Social interaction in an urban environment is stimulating and at the same time demanding. The many responses that must be made help to mold the urban personality.

City populations are heterogeneous. People of many different characteristics and cultures live together within a relatively small area. Immigrants, Negroes, and rural whites have contributed to urban cultural diversity. All varieties of religious groups may be found in cities. Occupational and class differentiation is complex. Also the city is divided into many territorial segments.

The way of life of the city dweller is influenced by the material environment in which he lives. The urban environment is congested. In physical movement other people must be taken into account. Competition for space is marked. Privacy is limited. Cities are places of physical disorder and of noise. Adjustment to this distinctive physical environment is part of the urban way of life.

Population density, social differentiation, and physical environment condition the nature of social interaction, social solidarity, and social problems in the city. As a result of the size and density of city populations many social contacts are impersonal. In certain situations social intimacy is precluded by definitions of social distance.

The social solidarity of the city is distinctive. Urban population size and density, heterogeneity, and impersonality do not foster strong feelings of unity. The informal controls of social approval and disapproval are often weak. Nevertheless the city does have social unity—a unity that arises from interdependence. No urban dweller is self-sufficient. He is dependent on other people. The social unity of the city arises not because people do the same things, but because they do different things. In so doing they are placed in obligation to each other.

The urban way of life is reflected in the form that social problems take in the city. Among the outstanding social problems of the city are those of health, housing, recreation, crime, and social control. These problems are not peculiar to the city, but they have some characteristically urban manifestations.

SELECTED REFERENCES

Bernard, Jessie: *American Community Behavior*, New York, Dryden, 1949.

Faris, Robert E. L., and H. Warren Dunham: *Mental Disorders in Urban Areas*, Chicago, University of Chicago Press, 1939.

Gist, Noel P., and L. A. Halbert: *Urban Society*, New York, Crowell, 1948.

Lynd, Robert S., and Helen M. Lynd: *Middletown in Transition*, New York, Harcourt, Brace, 1937.

Mumford, Lewis: *The Culture of Cities*, New York, Harcourt, Brace, 1938.

National Resources Committee: *Our Cities: Their Role in the National Economy*, 1937.

Shaw, Clifford R., and Henry McKay: *Juvenile Delinquency and Urban Areas*, Chicago, University of Chicago Press, 1942.

Smith, T. Lynn, and C. A. McMahan: *The Sociology of Urban Life*, New York, Dryden, 1951.

Whyte, W. F.: *Street Corner Society; the Social Structure of an Italian Slum*, Chicago, University of Chicago Press, 1943.

Zorbaugh, Harvey W.: *The Gold Coast and the Slum*, Chicago, University of Chicago Press, 1929.

CHAPTER ELEVEN

Metropolitan Communities

The concept of the metropolitan community is made necessary by the trends which urban development has taken in the present century. The population of the United States has increasingly come to be concentrated in urban places. But the big city delimited by political boundaries is not a satisfactory unit for the analysis of urban concentration. Cities have grown so that often they extend far beyond their political limits. Outside the political city, but within the area of urban concentration, are new settlements and towns that represent the growth of the city around its edges, and older settlements that have been surrounded by the expanding city. In almost every way except politically, the areas of urban concentration constitute integrated units. Socially and economically each area with its many districts, sections, settlements, and suburbs is a functioning whole. The political city is inadequate, therefore, as a unit both for the analysis of urban population concentration and for the study of the extended urban community.

At the same time that cities have expanded geographically, their social and economic influence has grown wider. When, then, the area of urban concentration is satisfactorily circumscribed, the territory of definite urban dominance still is not defined. The transportation, communication, markets, financial services, occupations, manners, and customs of the city extend into the region which surrounds the large population center. The old concept of the city as a discrete entity has lost much of its meaning. It is not necessary to live within the city limits, or even in a population center, in order to come under the continuing influence of the city. In turn the central city is involved in the web of social and economic life of the region around it. The concept of the metropolitan community is used to designate a territory characterized by significant social and economic interdependence and by the dominance of a sizable population center.

CENSUS DEFINITIONS AND DATA

In 1950 the Bureau of the Census gathered data which are relevant for our purposes on two types of areas: *urbanized areas* and *standard metropolitan areas.*

Urbanized Areas

Urbanized areas were defined for the first time in the 1950 census. The purpose was to separate rural and urban population in the vicinity of larger cities in a more satisfactory way than had been done in the past. (This definition is not to be confused with the rural-urban distinction referred to earlier.) As a result of the use of the urbanized-area concept, 6,203,596 persons were counted as urban who under earlier definitions would have been regarded as rural. Below is the census definition of an urbanized area: [1]

"An urbanized area is an area that includes at least one city with 50,000 inhabitants or more in 1940 or later according to a special census taken prior to 1950 and also the surrounding closely settled incorporated places and unincorporated areas that meet the criteria listed below. Since the urbanized area outside of incorporated places was defined on the basis of housing or population density or of land use, its boundaries for the most part are not political but follow such features as roads, streets, railroads, streams, and other clearly defined lines which may be easily identified by census enumerators in the field. The urbanized area boundaries were selected after careful examination of all avail-

[1] U.S. Bureau of the Census, *U.S. Census of Population: 1950*, vol. 1, *Number of Inhabitants*, 1952, p. xxvii.

able maps, aerial photographs, and other sources of information, and then were checked in detail in the field by trained investigators to insure that the criteria were followed and that the boundaries were identifiable. . . .

"The urban fringe of an urbanized area is that part which is outside the central city or cities. The following types of areas are embraced if they are contiguous to the central city or cities or if they are contiguous to any area already included in the urban fringe:

"1. Incorporated places with 2,500 inhabitants or more in 1940 or at a subsequent special census conducted prior to 1950.

"2. Incorporated places with fewer than 2,500 inhabitants containing an area with a concentration of 100 dwelling units or more with a density in this concentration of 500 units or more per square mile. This density represents approximately 2,000 persons per square mile and normally is the minimum found associated with a closely spaced street pattern.

"3. Unincorporated territory with at least 500 dwelling units per square mile.

"4. Territory devoted to commercial, industrial, transportational, recreational, and other purposes functionally related to the central city.

"Also included are outlying noncontiguous areas with the required dwelling unit density located within $1\frac{1}{2}$ miles of the main contiguous urbanized part, measured along the shortest connecting highway, and other outlying areas within one-half mile of such noncontiguous areas which meet the minimum residential density rule.

"Although an urbanized area may contain more than one city of 50,000 or more, not all cities of this size are necessarily central cities. The largest city of an area is always a central city. In addition, the second and third most populous cities in the area may qualify as central cities provided they have a population of at least one-third of that of the largest city in the area and a minimum of 25,000 inhabitants."

In 1950 a total of 157 urbanized areas were identified. Somewhat less than one-half of the total population was living in these areas. More than seven-tenths of the urban population was in such areas. This reveals the degree to which urban population is concentrated in larger cities and their environs. Of the 69,249,148 persons in urbanized areas, 48,377,240 lived in the 172 central cities and 20,871,908 were in urban fringe areas. In urban fringe areas 12,949,890 persons were living in 859 incorporated places of 2,500 population or more, 577,992 in 457 incorporated places of under 2,500 population, and 7,344,026 in unincorporated territory. In size of population urbanized areas ranged from 56,046 in the Fort Smith urbanized area in Arkansas to 12,296,117 in the New York–northeastern New Jersey urbanized area.

Standard Metropolitan Areas

The *metropolitan-district* concept has been employed by the Bureau of the Census, with varying definitions, since 1910. In 1940 metropolitan districts were delimited for every city of 50,000 population or more, some districts having two or more such cities. Metropolitan districts included, "in addition to the central city or cities, all adjacent and contiguous minor civil divisions or incorporated places having a population density of 150 or more per square mile." On the basis of this definition 140 metropolitan districts were identified in 1940.

In 1950 *metropolitan districts* were replaced by *standard metropolitan areas*. The new definition was adopted in order to facilitate comparison of data with those gathered by other agencies. Counties replaced minor civil divisions as the basic component of the areas. The definition in 1950 was: [2]

"Except in New England, a standard metropolitan area is a county or group of contiguous counties which contains at least one city of 50,000 inhabitants or more. In addition to the county, or counties, containing such a city, or cities, contiguous counties are included in a standard metropolitan area if according to certain

[2] *Ibid.,* p. xxxiii.

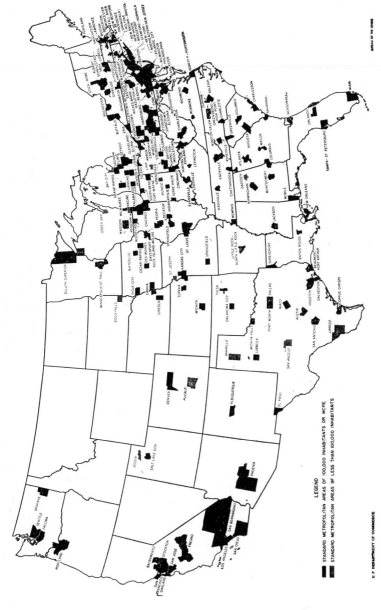

Figure 22. Standard Metropolitan Areas: 1950. (Source: U.S. Bureau of the Census.)

criteria they are essentially metropolitan in character and socially and economically integrated with the central city.

"The criteria of metropolitan character relate primarily to the character of the county as a place of work or as a home for concentrations of nonagricultural workers and their dependents. . . .

"[In New England] towns and cities were the units used in defining standard metropolitan areas. . . .

"Although there may be several cities of 50,000 or more in a standard metropolitan area, not all are necessarily central cities. The largest city in a standard metropolitan area is the principal central city. Any other city of 25,000 or more within a standard metropolitan area, and having a population amounting to one-third or more of the population of the principal city, is also a central city."

In continental United States in 1950 there were 168 standard metropolitan areas. Their total population was 84,500,680. This was 56.1 per cent of the total population, whereas they covered only 7 per cent of the total land area of the United States. The 14 standard metropolitan areas with a population of 1 million or more had a total population of 44,440,496. The 17 areas with a population of less than 100,000 had a total population of 1,430,-076. More than two-thirds of the standard metropolitan areas had populations ranging between 100,000 and 500,000. Of the total population of standard metropolitan areas, 58.5 per cent lived in central cities. Forty standard metropolitan areas had less than half their total population in their central cities. Of the 84,500,680 persons living in standard metropolitan areas, 68,989,014 were in urbanized areas. Only 260,134 persons in urbanized areas were outside of standard metropolitan areas.

METROPOLITAN EXPANSION

The definition of urbanized areas, metropolitan districts, and standard metropolitan areas represents the effort of the Bureau of the Census to take cognizance of the trends of urban enlargement.

Two processes have operated concurrently. It is clear that the city-ward movement of people has resulted in the concentration of population in and around larger cities. At the same time there has been a dispersion of people outward from city centers. The definition of urbanized areas provides a new measure of the expanded physical city. The description of metropolitan districts and of standard metropolitan areas takes into account the unity which extends beyond the physical city. At this point we are interested in the development of metropolitan expansion as it has been brought about by the simultaneous processes of urban concentration and urban dispersion.

Metropolitan Concentration

The same factors that were considered as causes of general urban growth have contributed to metropolitan concentration. In agriculture and the extractive industries the proportion of workers required to till the soil and to obtain raw materials became less; while the demand for labor to process, manufacture, and distribute goods became greater. Improved transportation facilitated the free flow of raw materials and goods to and from city centers. A territorial concentration of service functions was made possible. Transportation encouraged the cityward movement of people, and it increased the ease of mobility within cities. Better water and sanitary systems made practicable the maintenance of life for larger city populations.

These factors help to account for the expansion of the physical city, but we are left with the need to explain the gravitation toward larger cities. Why is the urban population not more evenly distributed among urban centers?

The commercial functions of cities have always been a leading cause of their growth. Many larger American cities began chiefly as commercial centers and their commercial importance has not diminished. In fact the commercial advantages provided by the large city tend to be cumulative. The more commercial services a city offers, the more attractive it becomes for the location of new commercial services. The capacity of certain services to function depends on the prior existence of other commercial activities. Also many large cities have from the beginning enjoyed the commercial benefits which derive from a favorable geographical location. These natural advantages make it difficult for other cities to compete for commerce and for the people who follow commerce. The ten largest urbanized areas in the United States—New York–northeastern New Jersey, Chicago, Los Angeles, Philadelphia, Detroit, Boston, San Francisco–Oakland, Pittsburgh, St. Louis, and Cleveland—all owe much of their growth to the commercial advantages deriving from geographical location.

The accelerated growth of large cities may also be attributed to their attractiveness as places for manufacturing. The cumulative effect of commerce is further evidenced here. Manufacturers have found it desirable to locate where materials and goods are readily bought and sold. In some types of manufacturing the immediate accessibility of materials and markets is important. In many cases, however, it is the availability of commercial services necessary for buying, selling, transportation, and distribution that manufacturers have valued in larger cities.

In the location of manufacturing industries the availability of power is an essential consideration. In the past the larger urban centers have been the chief producers of power. The use of steam for industrial purposes had a concentrative effect, for in order to be produced cheaply steam had to be made in large quantities. With the discovery and application of electric energy, the concentrative influence of power became still greater. The first electric generating plants were located in large city centers, which promised the largest potential markets to power producers. Generating units were small. The distance that electricity could be carried from generating centers was definitely limited. Even after great generators were built and after vast transmission networks were developed, the use of electric power for industrial purposes continued to be somewhat concentrated, for the cost of electricity was influenced by the quantity in which it was produced. Inasmuch as consumption of electric energy was greatest in larger centers, industries were attracted by lower power prices.

As has been pointed out, the services provided by cities are primary causes of their growth. At the same time the size of a city helps to determine the number and variety of services that it can offer. There are some services that only large cities can give because out of a total population only a limited number of persons require these services. In smaller communities the demand is not great enough to support specialized services, whereas in large cities there are enough customers to make such services possible. The more services a city provides, the more personnel it requires. The larger the personnel it supports, the more services a city can and must provide. Thus size contributes to size.

There is perhaps another way in which size is a cause of size. For some persons the big city is attractive because it is big. They find a fascination in the variety of activities, the number of people, and even in the physical proportions of large cities. The people and the events of larger metropolitan centers receive a great amount of publicity. The big city appears to be "the place where things happen." It may be that since the definite separation of rural life and urban life has broken down, the lure of the big city, as such, has diminished. But in the past, at least, the very size and complexity of large cities pulled many people to them.

Metropolitan Dispersion

Many ancient and medieval cities were walled cities. In the most literal sense the inhabitants lived "within cities." In modern societies, walled cities have disappeared, but until the present century the advantages, activities, and areas of cities were circumscribed. In the twentieth century the city lost its limits. In referring to the effect on the physical city, Lewis Mumford calls it "shapeless giantism." Residentially, commercially, industrially, and recreationally cities have come to be spread over large and indefinite areas. This dispersion of people, buildings, institutions, and services is probably the most characteristic feature of metropolitan expansion.

Growth at the periphery of the city is, of course, not new. A growing city, unless it is to increase only in population density, must expand at its borders. Furthermore, the suburban trend did not wait for the automobile. Before the invention of the automobile suburbanization was well started as a result of railway commuter service. It is not newness, but rather it is the vast extent and the modified pattern that lends importance to the peripheral growth of cities in recent decades. Earlier the expansion of a city at its perimeter was less rapid, and it usually occurred in areas immediately adjacent to the city. In the present century the process has been accelerated and the spread is over a wider territory. Many outlying residential sections have appeared which are not directly contiguous to the city. Moreover the location and the growth of suburbs is no longer determined by rail transportation. The spoke-like distribution of suburbs along railway lines is not necessary. Suburbs now flourish in areas lying between the older arteries of transportation.

Suburbs are characterized by dependence upon the central city. Queen and Carpenter have given a classification of types of urban communities that are or that have been suburbs. The main concern in the classification is with the degree of dependence upon or absorption into the metropolis. (1) The first type of community is relatively isolated from the rest of the metropolitan area. It functions with a minimum of dependence upon the central city. (2) The difference between the first and the second type is one of degree. In some ways it is independent of the city, but its relationship with the metropolis is stronger than that of the first type. (3) The suburb of the third class is in the process of losing its geographical separation from the city. As both the city and the suburb expand they grow into each other. (4) Overflow residential suburbs are primarily places to live. The inhabitants of such areas are definitely dependent upon the city for employment and for most

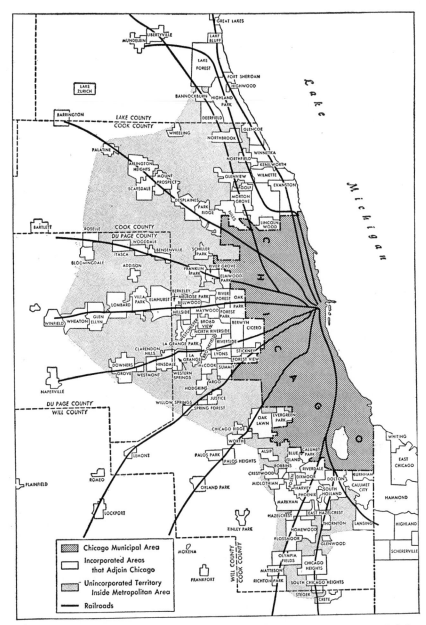

Figure 23. Map of Chicago and Surrounding Area Showing Location of Suburbs along Railroad Lines. (From *Chicago Daily Tribune*, May 17, 1948.)

249

services. (5) Industrial suburbs frequently are larger than other suburbs and also possess more self-sufficiency with regard to services. The residents are less directly dependent upon the central city, but indirectly they receive benefits from the city through the economic and financial services essential for the operation of their industries. (6) The partially absorbed community is one that has been surrounded by or annexed by the central city. Local community life slowly declines, and the area tends to lose its identity. (7) The completely absorbed community is one that no longer has any separate identity; the area has become merely a segment of the big city.[3]

In describing the communities that surround large cities, the terms *satellite suburb, satellite town,* and *satellite city* are often employed. These terms are used with various meanings, and we are not here concerned with the finer distinctions that are made. In general, satellite communities are characterized by geographic separation from the central city and by a fair degree of independence and self-sufficiency. Some of the suburbs in the foregoing classification in Queen and Carpenter would fall into the satellite category. There are other satellite communities, towns, and cities, which because of their distance from the metropolis and because of their high degree of self-sufficiency cannot be classified as suburbs. Nevertheless they are within the orbit of the larger city and their life is influenced by it.

Metropolitan expansion is not merely residential. It is marked also by industrial decentralization. The movement has not been so great nor so extensive as was anticipated a number of decades ago. Large industries with huge plants and investments have been slow to move. There has been, however, a significant relocation of industries, and many new plants, both large and small, have found it desirable to locate away from the central city. But industrial decentralization has remained largely within metropolitan areas. There is little indication of a dispersion of industry away from metropolitan regions.

[3] S. A. Queen and D. B. Carpenter, *The American City,* New York, McGraw-Hill, 1953, pp. 121–130.

The decentralization of services is notably evidenced by the establishment of shopping centers and branch stores in suburban areas. Suburbs have usually provided some trading services, but recent years have seen an increase in the number and variety of stores. Some large department stores have given up expansion within the city in favor of annex stores in the suburbs, thus minimizing problems of transportation and parking for their customers in outlying sections. Promoters of housing districts are taking the initiative in locating clusters of stores and shops within easy reach of new residential areas. Also service establishments are distributed ribbonlike along the main roads leading to the city. Highway service stations, tourist courts, taverns, and restaurants are components of the expanded metropolis.

The environs of the large city include the *rural residue*. In the quest for space and seclusion, people who are dependent upon the city move out of the city and out of the suburbs and into the country. In the vicinity of cities persons of many different types and economic levels live in a semiurban-semirural manner. They include the residents of large estates and of small country homes; gardeners and farmers; "gentlemen farmers" and "dirt farmers"; professionals, businessmen, and laborers who are also part-time agriculturalists. Among them, too, are full-time dairymen, truckers, fruit growers, and poultrymen who rely heavily upon metropolitan markets. All these fringe residents are not equally urban-oriented, and the admixture makes the bounds of the extended metropolis all the more indefinite.

The trend of urban expansion into metropolitan areas was summarized in the report of the Urbanism Committee to the National Resources Committee as follows: [4]

"The central cities contain a declining proportion of the total population of the metropolitan districts, indicating that metropolitan growth is in even larger degree than formerly a suburban trend. But what might at first glance appear to be a decentralization of population, therefore, is revealed upon closer inspection to be

[4] National Resources Committee, *Our Cities*, 1937, p. 35.

merely a redistribution of the urban population within metropolitan regions or a dispersion from the central city into the adjacent suburban periphery. It is not a general devolution of cities or a flight from the city. What is actually happening is, rather, that the urbanite is steadily being transformed into the suburbanite. While the movement of the last 100 years toward the centralization of population apparently continues, actually satellite cities and satellite rural areas are increasing so rapidly as to evidence a powerful dispersive force within urban regions. This dispersion has not yet become a definite centrifugal movement, but might well develop into one.

"Far from being on the decline, the city thus gives evidence mainly of a new phase of its growth by emptying at the center and spilling over its own corporate boundaries. The basis of this centrifugal tendency is to be sought in the urge on the part of those who have the means to escape the congestion, the disadvantageous family life, the undesirable and expensive housing and living conditions, and the high taxation which urban life so frequently involves. The hegira from the city is motivated by the ease of commutation and communication giving ready access to urban technical and cultural facilities combined with the lower taxes and land values, the better housing, more desirable family and community life, and more healthful conditions of existence prevailing in the suburbs. The intraregional dispersion of industry follows in the main from the same factors. Sometimes it precedes and stimulates and at other times it follows and accentuates the centrifugal movement of population.

"The redistribution of the urban population into the peripheries of metropolitan regions involves the close and constant dependence of the suburban communities upon the economic and technical functions and cultural opportunities which the metropolis provides. The model suburb, whether it is industrial or residential, however superior, aloof, and detached it may believe itself to be, has its basis of existence and draws much of its sustenance from the noisy, grimy city of which economically and culturally it is an integral part, but from which it has managed to remain independent politically.

"It has been said that the suburbanite shuttles back and forth from a place where he would rather not live to a place where he would rather not work. In his daily or periodical pendular movement, of which the clock and the time schedule are symbolic, the suburban commuter exhibits the peculiar segmentalization between working and living so characteristic of modern urban society. The bedrooms of American cities are increasingly to be found in the dormitory colonies of the suburbs. The suburbanite, who in his daily routine oscillates between his vocation involving the humdrum, high-speed, technical work of business, industry, and the professions in the heart of the metropolis, and his avocation, which may range from amateur gardening and similar pastoral activities to suburban politics, is not an exception to the urban type of personality but is merely a variety of it. The motives leading to this type of existence are to be sought in the urge to escape the obnoxious aspects of urban life without at the same time losing access to its economic and cultural advantages. In the process, the form and the functions of the city are being revolutionized."

THE METROPOLITAN COMMUNITY

According to the definition adopted in an earlier chapter, a community exists when the people of a locality are served by the same institutions and services. On the basis of this definition an extensive metropolitan region may be regarded as a community, for the inhabitants of a large geographical area are dependent upon some common institutions and services. To be sure, all their services and institutions are not the same, but they do share a common reliance upon basic financial, industrial, marketing, transportation, education, recreation, regulatory, and other services. There is a necessary division of labor and interdependence within the territory. Although a metropolitan area may be vast in size, a true community may exist within it.

Metropolitan expansion has created interest in the mapping of
metropolitan communities. The interest is utilitarian as well as
academic. Almost every larger city has attempted to mark off the
territory which falls within its sphere of influence. Commercial
and advertising organizations want to know from how wide an

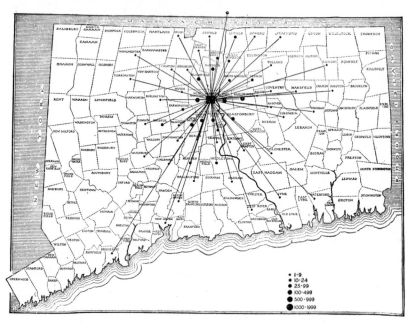

Figure 24. Map of Connecticut Showing Residences of Workers Employed in
a Hartford Department Store in 1948. The number of workers living in Hartford is not shown. (From Walter C. McKain, Jr., and Nathan L. Whetten,
"Occupational and Industrial Diversity in Rural Connecticut," Bulletin 263,
University of Connecticut Agricultural Experiment Station, November, 1949,
p. 49.)

area they can expect to attract customers. Service and utility agencies find it desirable to view the metropolitan community as a
whole in order to plan their services. Demographers want to follow
population trends. Sociologists are interested in the organization,
social relationships, and culture of metropolitan communities.

How far do the boundaries of metropolitan communities extend?
The census definitions of urbanized areas and of standard metropolitan areas are inadequate as definitions of the metropolitan

community. The urbanized area defines the territory in which the
urban population is concentrated, but it does not include the wider
area of dependence on the metropolis. The standard metropolitan
area covers a larger territory and encompasses outlying places.
However, its limits, following county lines, are arbitrary. It may

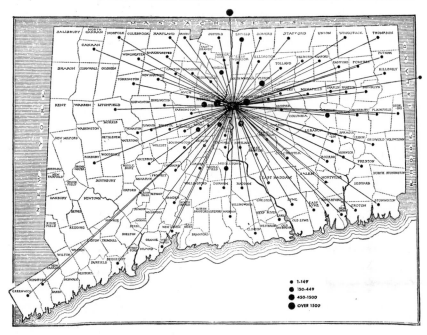

Figure 25. Map of Connecticut Showing Residences of Workers Employed in
an Aircraft Manufacturing Concern in East Hartford in 1948. The number of
workers living in East Hartford is not shown. (From Walter C. McKain, Jr.,
and Nathan L. Whetten, "Occupational and Industrial Diversity in Rural
Connecticut," Bulletin 263, University of Connecticut Agricultural Experiment
Station, November, 1949, p. 37.)

therefore include territory that is not served by the metropolis,
and it may exclude areas that are dependent upon the metropolis.

Whatever the measure employed, the limits of the metropolitan
community cannot be definite. The bounds are to be thought of not
as fixed lines, but as zones of influence. Outward from the central
city, metropolitan influence declines gradually as the circumfer-
ence of the zones widens. Three areas of influence may be consid-

ered: the utility area, the work-commutation area, and the trade area.

The utility area is the territory in which the inhabitants have common water, light, sanitation, and power problems. Community within this territory does not derive solely from these services, but they provide a convenient means of designating the area. Social and economic interdependence is pervasive throughout the area. Occupational reliance on the metropolis is extensive, and trading contacts with the central city are frequent. The people who live within this area to a full degree belong to the metropolitan community.

The second area of influence reaches as far as people commute daily to the city to work. Within this zone nonoccupational contacts with the city are also maintained, though with somewhat less frequency than in the first zone. Trips to the central city are for more specialized purposes. Service dependence on the metropolitan center is not so direct. There is much variation in the distances commuters travel to work. The number of commuters declines significantly beyond fifteen miles from the center of the city; but some cities have numerous daily commuters who live from twenty-five to fifty miles from the metropolitan center, and others considerably farther. As work-commutation distances increase, nonoccupational contacts with the city decrease.

The third sphere of influence extends beyond the work-commutation area. It includes the tributary area for which the metropolis is the marketing and financial center. It is the territory for which the big city is the wholesale center, the area in which chain stores receive merchandise from metropolitan warehouses, and the area from which customers make occasional shopping excursions to the city. The outer rim of the trade zone may be regarded as the widest limits of the metropolitan community.

SUMMARY

The concept of the metropolitan community is made necessary by the trends of urban development. Increasingly the population of the United States is concentrated in urban places, but the concentration extends beyond the political city. Moreover the influence of the metropolis reaches far into the region that surrounds the population center.

The Bureau of the Census has taken into account these trends by defining urbanized areas and standard metropolitan areas. A large part of the total population of the United States is living within such areas.

Metropolitan expansion has been brought about by the simultaneous processes of concentration and dispersion. As the population has moved urbanward, the trend has been in the direction of the larger cities. Gravitation toward the larger cities may be explained by such factors as their commercial advantages, their attractiveness as places of manufacturing, the variety of services they offer, and the psychological pull of bigness.

As a result of urban dispersion the city has lost its limits. Residentially, commercially, industrially, and recreationally cities have come to be spread over large and indefinite territories. The area within which the advantages of the metropolis may be had is greatly enlarged. Employment and services have been decentralized within metropolitan areas. Outside the larger city are many satellite centers. The environs of the large city include a heterogeneous population living in the country but dependent upon the city.

The people who live in an extensive metropolitan region may be regarded as belonging to one large community. They are dependent upon the same institutions and services, although to varying degrees. The bounds of a metropolitan community cannot be drawn definitely. Outward from the central city, metropolitan influence declines gradually.

SELECTED REFERENCES

Bogue, Donald J.: *The Structure of the Metropolitan Community*, Ann Arbor, Mich., University of Michigan, School of Graduate Studies, 1949.

Creamer, Daniel B.: *Is Industry Decentralizing?* Philadelphia, University of Pennsylvania Press, 1935.

Hatt, Paul, and Albert J. Reiss: *Reader in Urban Sociology*, Glencoe, Ill., Free Press, 1951.

McKenzie, R. D.: *The Metropolitan Community*, New York, McGraw-Hill, 1933.

Mitchell, Robert B., ed.: "Building the Future City," *The Annals*, vol. 242, November, 1945.

Mumford, Lewis: *The Culture of Cities*, New York, Harcourt, Brace, 1938.

National Resources Committee: *Our Cities: Their Role in the National Economy*, 1937.

Odum, Howard, and Harry E. Moore: *American Regionalism*, New York, Holt, 1938.

Quinn, James A.: *Human Ecology*, New York, Prentice-Hall, 1950.

Sanders, S. A., and A. J. Rabuck: *New City Patterns*, New York, Reinhold, 1946.

Schmid, Calvin F.: *Social Trends in Seattle*, Seattle, University of Washington Press, 1944.

Thompson, Warren S.: *The Growth of Metropolitan Districts in the United States, 1900–1940*, Washington, GPO, 1948.

PART THREE: Classes

CHAPTER TWELVE

Social Stratification

The American people are divided into many nationality, racial, religious, occupational, and age groups. They are divided also into locality and territorial groups such as those constituted by the populations of neighborhoods, towns, cities, metropolitan areas, states, and regions. These groups are not too difficult to discover. There is a rather definite basis for identifying the members of each group. With a fair degree of accuracy the number of people belonging to the various groups can be counted.

Our population is divided into groups of another type, more difficult to identify and to count. These are the social class groups. The popular use of the terms "lower class," "middle class," and "upper class" indicates a general awareness of the existence of class differentiation. But a vague awareness of class groups is quite different from the identification of discrete segments of the population. The difficulty in identifying class groups arises because there is not one single criterion, such as race, religion, or place of residence, by which membership is recognized. Instead, a combination of interrelated factors determines the class group into which an individual falls. Unlike the members of occupational, age, territorial, and other groups, class-group members often do not know to which class they belong. Indeed they may object to the very idea that they are associated with a particular class. But although classes are not easily delineated, and although class members frequently do not consciously identify themselves with a particular class, the existence of class groups is very real. The study of a society is incomplete without an analysis of its class structure.

Because the concept of social classes involves the ranking of individuals as being "higher" or "lower," sociologists have found it convenient to think of classes in terms of *social stratification*. Stratification suggests a division into levels or layers. Social stratification implies a division into social levels or layers. A social class consists of those individuals or groups having somewhat similar social status; that is, they occupy the same level in the prestige structure of their society.

In this chapter we shall deal with the questions: What determines the status of an individual or of a group? What are the major social classes in the United States? To what degree are Americans aware of their class membership?

STATUS STANDARDS

What determines the class position of an individual or of a group in American society? Why is one person rated as lower middle class and another as lower upper class? Or to put it in another way: if an individual rated as "upper lower" wanted to be rated as "upper middle," what would he need to do? What is it that confers status?

To approach status determination with these questions is not to suggest that individuals generally go about consciously classifying each other. They do not. They may use the terms "lower," "middle," and "upper," but rarely with any degree of precision or consistency. What individuals do from day to day is to invest each other with more or less prestige, and that often rather unconsciously. In their attitudes and behavior toward each other they reflect the values of their society. They are influenced by what is commonly held to be of importance and confer status accordingly.

Furthermore the desire for higher status is not equally great in all individuals. The author remembers well the vigorous objection of a student who protested that the impression was being created that everyone is struggling to climb into the upper class. She said that she felt no such urge. The objection is well taken, for there is much variation in the prestige motives of individuals. There is considerable acceptance of present status on the part of many. Others are involved in a struggle for higher status without being very conscious of their motives. Still others are deliberate and conscious "social climbers." But whether present status is accepted or whether one is motivated to achieve higher status, there are identifiable factors which determine the existing status of the individual or the group.

Research on social stratification has not resulted in unanimity on what are the most significant status-conferring factors in American society; however, the importance of certain criteria is widely recognized. The primary determiners of status are wealth and income, occupation, power, birth, and personal qualities.

Wealth and Income

In the thinking of many people, economic status and social status are so closely related that they mean practically the same thing. When asked, "What gives social position?" they answer, "Money." We shall later see that money is not usually the sole standard for conferring status; nevertheless, the judgment that money gives prestige is well founded. Wealth and income is an important status-conferring factor in American society. The fact that economic position and social position are so frequently equated is telling evidence of the prominence of wealth and income in our prestige system.

The acceptance of money as a status standard is seen in the tendency to associate income with achievement. It is assumed that the man whose income is low has achieved little; whereas the man whose income is high is assumed to have achieved much. Even ability is measured in part by income. Thus when an individual moves from one job to another his new salary in many cases is not determined by his ability alone, but also by his previous salary. Earning power is regarded as an index of capabilities.

The acceptance of the income-achievement-ability standard was carried to its most logical end in the case of a Protestant minister who received $15,000 a year, a salary well beyond the average for his profession. The individual involved said that he saw no reason why he should receive such a salary, while his colleagues earned much less. He explained, however, that in order to hold the respect of the men in his church he had to earn at least $15,000; by their standards he had to be able to command this salary or he would not be considered worth employing at all. The measure of the man was his income.

In considering money as a status-conferring factor, it must be observed that it is not merely the possession of money but also its use that gives prestige. Hoarded money does not appreciably affect the class status of an individual. The significance of the use of money was analyzed by Thorstein Veblen in *The Theory of the Leisure Class*, in which he applied the term *conspicuous consumption* to money spent as a means of displaying wealth and income. Veblen wrote especially about conspicuous consumption as it is evident in the upper classes, but it is found on every level. In the upper classes it may take the form of a costly debut. In the middle class it may take a different form. Suppose, for example, that a middle-class woman shows her new coat to her friends. The coat, it is obvious, will both keep her warm and increase her attractiveness. Before the conversation ends, however, the purchaser may inject one final detail—how much she paid. Or she may casually call attention to the label. In terms of standards of utility and attractiveness the comments on cost are irrelevant, but in terms of conspicuous consumption they are meaningful. In lower-income groups conspicuous consumption may show itself in unsuccessful attempts to imitate the buying patterns of the classes above, such as the purchase of cheap but gaudy dresses or large but thirdhand automobiles. The effort to buy the symbols of status is seen on all levels, but it is especially prevalent among those who are desirous of gaining higher status and among those who have recently achieved higher status.

Each socioeconomic group develops a set of money-spending patterns. Even when there is no conscious conspicuous consumption there is a tendency to conform to the standards of the group with which one prefers to be associated. The test of the importance of spending patterns in the status structure is not whether one is actively trying to buy the symbols of status, but rather the test is whether one could maintain a particular status if he did not conform to the money-use habits of his class. There are some persons who do not conform to the patterns of their group and who nevertheless maintain their status for other reasons, but the majority of people tend to conform.

Occupation

Historically there has been a close relationship between occupation and class membership. Terms such as "peasants," "artisans," "soldiers," "merchants," and "rulers" have carried both occupational and class connotations. Likewise in modern times the occupational designations "laborers," "skilled workers," "white-collar workers," "businessmen," and "professional people" have class meanings. The connection between occupation and class position is so marked that some students of stratification have treated occupation as a reliable index of class. While this procedure is subject to error, it is clear that social status is closely related to the type of work that one does.

One reason why occupation is an important criterion of status is that the type of work done often determines income. But if income status and occupational status always varied together there would be little justification for treating them separately. It is necessary to consider them separately for two reasons: first, because some types of work give prestige which is out of proportion to income received; and second, because some occupations that bring high monetary returns have low or even negative prestige value. For example, in occupation-evaluation studies the position of United States senator is rated near the top even though, relative to their status, senators are not high-salaried. On the other hand, a racketeer may acquire great wealth without raising his social status proportionately. His money notwithstanding, public knowledge of his activities may prevent him from achieving the same status as other persons of comparable wealth.

Many attempts have been made to discover how Americans rank the various occupations. There is a high degree of agreement in the results of these studies. North and Hatt have analyzed a nation-wide job-prestige survey made by the National Opinion Research Center.[1] The persons interviewed were asked to evaluate ninety different jobs. A procedure was devised to translate the ratings on each of the jobs into a single score. When the occupations were classified by groups they ranked as shown in the accompanying table.

Classification	Number of occupations	Average score
Government officials *	8	90.8
Professional and semiprofessional workers	30	80.6
Proprietors, managers, and officials (except farm)	11	74.9
Clerical, sales, and kindred workers	6	68.2
Craftsmen, foremen, and kindred workers	7	68.0
Farmers and farm managers	3	61.3
Protective-service workers	3	58.0
Operatives and kindred workers	8	52.8
Farm laborers	1	50.0
Service workers (except domestic and protective)	7	46.7
Laborers (except farm workers)	6	45.8

* The census classifies some of these officials as professional and others as managerial.

The status that accrues from occupation is a product both of the general rank of the occupation and of individual rank within the occupation. Intraoccupational status is determined by ability, by influence and control over other people, and by the somewhat indefinite attributes of "success," "front," and "reputation." The position of an individual within his occupation is a factor in fixing his class status, but usually to a limited degree. It is unlikely that the status of a most capable construction foreman in charge

[1] Cecil C. North and Paul K. Hatt, "Jobs and Occupations: A Popular Evaluation," *Opinion News*, Sept. 1, 1945, pp. 3–13.

of a large group of men will be as high as that of a mediocre judge.

Power

In considering power as a criterion of status we have in mind the capacity to influence and control other people. Such control has prestige value. Power may be associated with occupational position. To speak of a fellow townsman as being "in charge of ten men," or as having "fifty men working under him" is to indicate something about his status. Prestige-giving power may also be political or governmental. Both the elected official and the political boss are ranked, in part, in terms of their power. The status of corporation officials and of union leaders is influenced by their economic power and by their authority over large groups of people. The prestige of army officers is related to their authority position.

The prestige of power demonstrates the interrelatedness of the criteria of status. Control over other people usually does not stand in isolation; it is often associated with wealth and with occupation. Money and job may contribute to power. And yet when power has been achieved it may operate as a prestige factor somewhat independent of wealth or of occupation. Or power may come first and thereafter be used to achieve economic and occupational status.

Birth

The importance of birth as a determinant of social status may be seen in at least three ways: first, in the initial ranking of individuals according to family status; second, in the control of birth over opportunities to acquire the symbols of new status; third, in the tendency of family status to adhere for some time after the symbols of new status have been acquired.

The child is born into the social class of his parents. Every community has its "leading families" and its "ne'er-do-wells," with a number of other categories falling between. Children are appraised according to family status. In the ranking process a family is treated as a unit. Although individual family members have varying prestige, to a large degree it is the ranking of families, rather than individual family members, that results in the formation of social classes. Thus family affiliation is the first status-conferring factor.

Birth determines the initial status of an individual, but in our society it does not permanently control status. Beyond the years of childhood, status may be achieved through the means already discussed—income, occupation, and power. Nonetheless birth continues to be involved, for even the achievement of new status may be influenced by family membership. All persons do not have the same opportunities to acquire the symbols of new status. How much money the family can afford for education, whom the parents associate with and know, how much political power or professional influence the parents have are all matters that may be related to the opportunities of family members.

On the whole, when an adult individual in American society acquires the symbols of new status he is accorded that status with a minimum of regard for the status of his parents and relatives. However, to a degree the kinship factor persists even when the marks of new status have been achieved. This is particularly true in the upper classes. It appears that the class importance attached to kinship increases from the lower to the upper classes. Thus it has many times happened that persons of lowly birth who have achieved great wealth and power have not been accepted in the "upper upper" class. Their children and grandchildren, however, may gain acceptance.

Undue importance must not be attached to birth as a determinant of status. The relative importance of birth in relation to other status-conferring factors is one of the most significant features of any system of social stratification. We shall reserve for the next chapter the discussion of this aspect of stratification in America.

Personal Qualities

Anything that marks individuals as being different from each other may be used as a basis for rating. Personal qualities and characteristics, therefore, are a further status-conferring factor. An individual is evaluated by many characteristics: sex, age, height, beauty, strength, intelligence, wit, speech, posture, manners, attitudes, interests, and many others. Some of these traits are entirely beyond the control of the individual; others he may achieve.

Personal qualities are both cause and effect of class membership. Personal qualities influence class membership, and class membership influences some personal qualities. The individual who acquires the necessary personal characteristics gains prestige. On the other hand, personal qualities are frequently the product of association in the groups into which an individual is placed by birth. Differences in habits, tastes, interests, manners, speech, and many other qualities result from *differential association*. Thus, the possibility of acquiring prestige-giving personal qualities is greater in the higher-status groups than in the lower-status groups.

There are limits to the status that can be achieved by personal qualities alone. Although personal qualities may enhance one's position and although certain minimum qualities may be required in order to maintain a status, prestige-giving personal characteristics must be found in combination with other factors in order to confer high status. Personal qualities supplement income, occupation, power, and birth.

SOCIAL CLASSES IN THE UNITED STATES

When the status standards of wealth and income, occupation, power, birth, and personal qualities are applied to the population of the United States, six major social classes are discovered. It is possible that on the basis of these same criteria, some or all of the six classes could be further subdivided. Also it is evident that the six-class structure does not exist in every community. The following is a generalized description for the country as a whole.

At the bottom of the stratification structure is the *lower lower class*. Many of the members of this class live on the poverty level. They have almost no possessions. Employment is often irregular. Many families are on relief. Each new job, payday, or relief check gives a temporary lift; in the intervals between they merely exist. Occupationally the members of this class are unskilled. They perform the most undesirable tasks. In rural areas they include migratory workers. They are people without power or influence, usually unknown or avoided by the "right people." The level of education is extremely low. They do almost no reading and belong to no clubs or organizations. Fighting, drinking, and sex are the chief diversions from a dull state of survival. These people are not involved in a struggle to "get somewhere" and to "be somebody." While the members of the lower lower class may feel that they "never had a chance," by the middle and upper classes they are regarded as irresponsible and "shiftless."

On the next level is the *upper lower class*. Under normal circumstances these people are regularly employed and self-supporting. They include both unskilled and skilled workers. Their incomes are low, and acquiring the necessities of life requires most of their time and energy. Children often leave school as soon as possible and go to work. The members of the upper lower class work for other people, and they usually take rather than give directions. There is more concern about respectability than in the lower lower class. Standards of respectability are uncomplicated and involve chiefly the avoidance of behavior attributed to the lowest class. Public drunkenness and fighting, acceptance of relief, and sex scandal are matters of concern in the upper lower class. Although desirous of acquiring certain material possessions, the members of this class in the main are unaware of the distinctions in taste made by the classes above them. Motivation is greater than in the lower lower class, but to get ahead financially is extremely difficult.

The next class is perhaps the most heterogeneous. The *lower middle class* includes a wide variety of occupational groups. There are highly skilled laborers, foremen, farmers, protective-service

		Upper	Upper Middle	Lower Middle	Upper Lower	Lower Lower
I	Monday Club	50%	50%			
I	Rotary	16.7%	80.6%		2.7%	
II	D. A. R.	57.1%	4.3%	28.6%		
II	Hospital Aid	51.6%	32.8%	15.6%		
II	Country Club	29.9%	27.8%	42.3%		
III	Masons	14.7%	19%	65.3%		
III	Lions	4.8%	23.8%	71.4%		
IV	Odd Fellows	2.2%	20%	42.2%	35.6%	
IV	American Legion Auxiliary	1.6%	11.1%	63.5%	22.2%	1.6%
IV	Eastern Star		8.3%	91.7%		
IV	Girl Scout Mothers		9.3%	50%	35.2%	5.5%
V	Royal Neighbors			69%	28.2%	2.8%
VI	Polish National Alliance			8.3%	83.4%	8.3%
VII	Free Methodists				100%	
VII	Gospel Tabernacle				87.5%	12.5%

(Size of membership in each class is represented by the shaded areas.)

Figure 26. Class Distribution of Selected Associations and Churches. The class status of an individual is indicated only in part and within limits by the associations to which he belongs, since associations may include individuals from more than one social class. But the associations and churches have differential status in the community, as shown in the above chart of the tentative class distribution of several organizations in a Middle Western city. In other communities some of these organizations may have a different social rating. (From W. Lloyd Warner, Marchia Meeker, and Kenneth Eells, *Social Class in America*, Chicago, Science Research Associates, 1949, p. 95.)

workers, lower government employees, small businessmen, and clerical and sales workers. These people live simply but without economic hardship. Homes are small but usually well kept. The members of this class belong to some organizations and participate in community activities, including political affairs. They read newspapers and popular magazines. They encourage their children to go as far in school as they can afford. Emphasis is placed on the virtues of work, thrift, and cleanliness. Women take pride in their domestic skills. This class appears to be relatively secure psychologically. There are rather definite standards of employment, material gain, respectability, and morality to be maintained. But living is not dominated by the struggle to achieve higher social status. The members of the lower middle class are removed from the lower classes, and they are not pulled by the possibility of moving into the upper classes. Their ambitions for higher position are expressed through their children. They want their children to have all the opportunities and advantages possible, including those which they themselves did not have.

The *upper middle class* includes successful businessmen, managers, professionals, and higher-level government administrators. Most of these people are not wealthy, but they live quite comfortably. Their homes are in the better residential areas and are well furnished. Their regular expenditures include entertaining, books, music, and travel. Their children go to college. Many have help in caring for their homes. If they are uncomfortable it is because their goals exceed their present achievements, for the upper middle class is probably the most aspiring class. More than any other group it is dominated by the desire to get ahead. High value is placed on the status that accompanies being "successful." The symbols as well as the comforts of "gracious living" are important. Thus certain forms of entertainment and "culture" may be pursued as much for their symbolic value as for the pleasure they give. A college education is essential for the children of upper-middle-class families, not merely as a means of acquiring knowledge and skills, but as a means of gaining prestige and "making contacts." Upper-middle-class members usually belong to numerous social and civic organizations. Much of the community leadership comes from this group. In many communities this is the highest social class.

Above the four classes already named are the relatively small upper classes. The *lower upper class* is made up of wealthy businessmen, industrialists, and a few professionals. They practice a way of life quite remote from the experience of the classes below them. The clubs to which they belong, the schools that they attend,

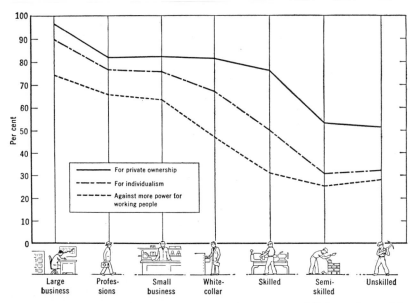

Figure 27. Attitudes of Urban Occupational Groups toward Private Ownership, Individualism, and More Power for Working People. This chart is based on responses to questions put to a representative sample of the adult white population. It indicates that people who occupy different occupational levels have different attitudes toward some issues. (From Richard Centers, *Psychology of Social Classes*, Princeton, Princeton University Press, 1949, p. 63.)

and the activities in which they engage keep them at some distance from persons not in their class. The lower upper class, in the main, is composed of families that do not have a long background of upper-class membership. Nonetheless most of these families are secure in their status. They feel no need for striving, for they have arrived. The comforts and the symbols of success are important to them, but the display is less competitive. They may support worthy causes, but membership in community organizations has no significant prestige value.

Upper-upper-class families are distinguished from those of the lower upper class by having a longer background of upper-class membership. They attempt to maintain their identity as a group apart. They are reluctant to recognize as belonging to their group any except families which have been upper class for several generations. They consider themselves as being far beyond the need for ostentation. They call attention with scorn to the competitive ostentation of the "new rich." Actually the manner of living of the two upper classes is often very similar. Judged by purely objective criteria the distinction between the two classes is difficult to make. In fact the justification for regarding one of these classes as higher than the other diminishes when it is observed that the lower upper class appears unconcerned about imitating the upper upper class. Nonacceptance into the upper upper class is the ultimate barrier between the two upper classes, but to this nonacceptance the families of wealth and power who constitute the lower upper class seem to be somewhat indifferent.

VARIATIONS IN STRATIFICATION

The analysis of social stratification in the United States as a whole is necessarily generalized. We have considered five standards of status; we have described six social classes. Other and overlapping status standards might be added, and the number of social classes in particular communities might be more or less. Nevertheless for our purposes generalization is required. The usefulness of a generalized analysis rests upon recognizing that it is just that—a general analysis. It is useful also to the degree that deviation from the typical is understood. We shall consider briefly two outstanding possibilities of variation in stratification.

Status Standards

The order in which individuals and families are ranked depends upon the bases of evaluation. Usually the prestige factors of income, occupation, power, birth, and personal qualities function together to determine status. They are often intimately interrelated. But equal emphasis is not placed on each factor in all groups nor in every community. The criteria of status vary. For example, in some rural areas social stratification is influenced less by occupational differentiation than by other factors. If nearly everyone is engaged in farming and if most of the farmers in the community perform manual labor the importance of occupation in giving prestige is reduced to a minimum. Also in some rural communities there is little concentration of power. Prestige under these circumstances derives not from occupation and power, but from wealth, appearance of farms, "family," and personal qualities. By way of contrast, Washington, D.C., is a community in which occupation and power are prestige factors of considerable importance. Among persons receiving pay from the Federal government there is occupational differentiation—government workers, professionals, officials, military officers, representatives, senators, diplomats, cabinet members, Vice-President, and President. Here the relationship between occupational position and power position is marked. Thus in the status system of the Washington community, men of little wealth and lowly family origins often enjoy the highest prestige. On the other hand, in the prestige values of the Philadelphia "Main Line" wealth and birth are emphasized more than occupation or political power. In some educational centers knowledge gives more prestige than in other communities. The whole matter of value variation is further complicated by traditional rural and urban value differences, and by religious, nationality, and ethnic differences.

Class Structure

A second type of variation in stratification is in the structure of social classes. It is immediately evident that the six-class arrangement which we have described cannot be applied to every community in the United States. It is a generalized structure for American society as a whole. In many communities the system of stratification is not so complex; that is, there are fewer than six classes.

This is true especially in rural and in small urban communities. The procedure of naming six classes involves the identification of classes in communities in which the structure is complex. It

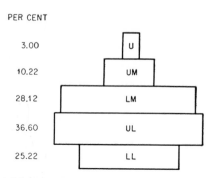

PER CENT

3.00 — U
10.22 — UM
28.12 — LM
36.60 — UL
25.22 — LL

Figure 28. Class Structure of "Yankee City." (From W. Lloyd Warner and Paul S. Lunt, *The Social Life of a Modern Community*, New Haven, Yale University Press, 1941, p. 88.)

must then be discovered what positions individuals and groups in simple-structure communities occupy with reference to the more complex system.

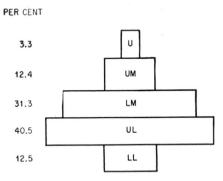

PER CENT

3.3 — U
12.4 — UM
31.3 — LM
40.5 — UL
12.5 — LL

Figure 29. Class Structure of "Jonesville." (Computed from W. Lloyd Warner et al., *Democracy in Jonesville*, New York, Harper, 1949, p. 219.)

The relative position of an individual is not necessarily the same in the six-class structure as in his own community. He may rank near the middle in the former and near the top in the latter. Thus groups regarded as upper class in certain communities are upper middle in the six-class structure. In some communities there are no persons who fall into either the lower lower or the upper upper classes. Obviously it follows that the proportion of the population in each class varies from community to community.

In a diagrammatic representation of social stratification, lines are drawn to indicate status levels. In reality class lines in the United States are not clear-cut. Rather than being sharply divided,

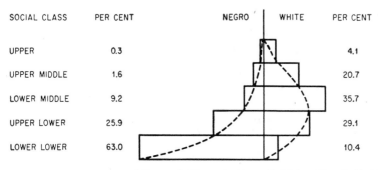

SOCIAL CLASS	PER CENT	NEGRO	WHITE	PER CENT
UPPER	0.3			4.1
UPPER MIDDLE	1.6			20.7
LOWER MIDDLE	9.2			35.7
UPPER LOWER	25.9			29.1
LOWER LOWER	63.0			10.4

Figure 30. Class Structure of Biracial "Georgia Town." (From Mozell C. Hill and Bevode C. McCall, "Social Stratification in Georgia Town," *American Sociological Review*, vol. 15, December, 1950, p. 725.)

the classes merge into each other. In this regard, too, stratification varies from place to place. In some communities the marks of division are distinct. Groups are clearly set apart by possessions, customs, manners, and privileges. Elsewhere, although strata exist, the lines of separation are blurred or extremely vague.

AWARENESS OF CLASS MEMBERSHIP

According to one definition of social class,[2] "the concept of class loses its sociological significance if it is *defined* by any purely objective criterion, such as income level or occupational function. Class does not unite people and separate them from others unless they *feel* their unity or separation. Unless class-consciousness is present, then no matter what criterion we take, we have not a social class but a mere logical category or type. If 'white-collar' workers

[2] R. M. MacIver, *Society*, New York, Rinehart, 1937, p. 167.

do not regard themselves as belonging to the same class as artisans, then they do not together form one social class." It is questionable whether this definition is applicable to the six classes that have been delineated for the United States. Identification with one's class group is a recognized aspect of social stratification, but in the United States such identification is indefinite.

Attempts have been made to discover the extent to which Americans are aware of class membership. The American Institute of Public Opinion asked individuals to classify themselves as upper class, middle class, or lower class. The results of the survey were as follows: [3]

Upper class	5%
Middle class	87%
Lower class	8%

Richard Centers reports a similar survey of a national cross section of white males.[4] The results were:

Upper class	3%
Middle class	43%
Working class	51%
Lower class	1%
Don't know	1%
"Don't believe in classes"	1%

The first survey is widely used to show that most Americans regard themselves as middle class and therefore are not very conscious of class membership. Centers used the second study as proof that Americans are class-conscious. Probably neither conclusion is entirely justified. The striking difference between these surveys is the effect of giving respondents an opportunity to classify themselves as "working class" rather than as "lower class" in the Centers study. The percentage of persons who identified themselves as working class indicates a reluctance to be called lower class but nonetheless a willingness to be considered something other than

[3] George Gallup and Saul F. Rae, *The Pulse of Democracy*, New York, Simon and Schuster, 1940, p. 169.

[4] Richard Centers, *The Psychology of Social Classes*, Princeton, N.J., Princeton University Press, 1949, p. 77.

middle class. The assertion that most Americans think of themselves as middle class is probably an overstatement. On the other hand, there is little evidence in the study by Centers that the respondents did much more than classify themselves occupationally.[5] The degree to which they "feel their unity or separation" is not known.

Indefinite class identification and the absence of strong class cohesion exist on every level. Persons occupying the very lowest position may be acutely aware of their low status without feeling a bond between themselves and others of similar low status. Indeed because of their aspirations or because of the achievements of their children they may think of themselves as belonging to a class higher than their actual status warrants. Middle-class identification is particularly vague. Persons both of high and of low status associate themselves with the middle group. Many parents do not occupy the same status level as their adult offspring; but parents and children may nevertheless feel that they are middle class. Among persons of upper-middle status there is little evidence of sensitivity to a unity which separates them from persons of lower-middle status. Class consciousness is strongest on the upper levels, but here too unity is lacking. High-status groups sometimes have conflicting standards of superiority.

In the main the feeling of unity and separation to which MacIver refers in defining social classes appears to be weak in the six social classes that cut across the United States. When such a feeling of unity and separation exists it is usually within local communities. It is on the local level that differences in wealth, power, privileges, rank, and association are most evident. Sensitivity to the differences helps to create class consciousness. But even in local communities many individuals have little awareness of belonging to a self-conscious social class. An individual may be aware of his own status and the status of people about him without being strongly class-conscious. In the United States competition for individual prestige and status has been great. Americans are aware of their

[5] *Ibid.* (especially Chap. 6).

status relative to that of the people with whom they come into social contact. But this consciousness of individual prestige and status is not to be equated with class consciousness.

UPPER UPPER CLASS		LOWER UPPER CLASS
"Old aristocracy"	UU	"Old aristocracy"
"Aristocracy," but not "old"	LU	"Aristocracy," but not "old"
"Nice, respectable people"	UM	"Nice, respectable people"
"Good people, but 'nobody'"	LM	"Good people, but 'nobody'"
	UL	
"Po' whites"	LL	"Po' whites"

UPPER MIDDLE CLASS		LOWER MIDDLE CLASS	
"Society" {"Old families"	UU	"Old aristocracy" (older)	"Broken-down aristocracy" (younger)
"Society" but not "old families"	LU		
"People who should be upper class"	UM	"People who think they are somebody"	
"People who don't have much money"	LM	"We poor folk"	
"No 'count lot"	UL	"People poorer than us"	
	LL	"No 'count lot"	

UPPER LOWER CLASS		LOWER LOWER CLASS
	UU	
"Society" or the "folks with money"	LU	"Society" or the "folks with money"
	UM	
"People who are up because they have a little money"	LM	"Way-high-ups," but not "Society"
"Poor but honest folk"	UL	"Snobs trying to push up"
"Shiftless people"	LL	"People just as good as anybody"

Figure 31. The Social Perspectives of the Social Classes in "Old City." How each class looks upon its own members and the members of other classes. (From Allison Davis, Burleigh B. Gardner, and Mary R. Gardner, *Deep South*, Chicago, University of Chicago Press, 1941, p. 65.)

SUMMARY

Social stratification refers to a division into social levels or layers. A social class is made up of those individuals or groups occupying the same level in the prestige structure of their society. The class position of an individual or of a family is determined not by one, but rather by a combination of factors. In American society the primary determiners of class position are wealth and income, occupation, power, birth, and personal qualities.

When these status standards are applied to the population of the United States, six major social classes are discovered. The six classes may be identified as lower lower, upper lower, lower middle, upper middle, lower upper, and upper upper. Although in some respects the classes share a common culture, each class has a somewhat distinctive culture. Each class has characteristic economic, family, recreational, value, and belief patterns.

An analysis of social classes is necessarily generalized. There are numerous deviations from the typical. Equal emphasis is not placed on each status-conferring factor in every group nor in every community. Also in some communities there are more and in other communities fewer than six social classes. In some communities class lines are rather definite; in others the lines of separation are extremely blurred.

A number of attempts have been made to discover the extent to which Americans are aware of class membership. The evidence is not conclusive, but it appears that the feeling of unity within classes is weak. Although class identification is more definite in some groups than in others, the absence of strong class cohesion exists on every level. When a marked feeling of class unity exists it is usually within local communities rather than nationwide.

SELECTED REFERENCES

Bendix, Reinhard, and Seymour M. Lipset: *Class, Status, and Power*, Glencoe, Ill., Free Press, 1953.

Centers, Richard: *The Psychology of Social Classes*, Princeton, N.J., Princeton University Press, 1949.

Dollard, John: *Caste and Class in a Southern Town*, New Haven, Conn., Yale University Press, 1937.

Hollingshead, August B.: *Elmtown's Youth*, New York, Wiley, 1949.

Mills, C. Wright: *White Collar: The American Middle Classes*, New York, Oxford University Press, 1951.

Veblen, T. B.: *The Theory of the Leisure Class*, New York, Huebsch, 1919.

Warner, W. Lloyd, and Paul S. Lunt: *The Social Life of a Modern Community*, New Haven, Conn., Yale University Press, 1941.

—— and Leo Srole: *The Social Systems of American Ethnic Groups*, New Haven, Conn., Yale University Press, 1945.

——, Marchia Meeker, and Kenneth Eells: *Social Class in America*, Chicago, Science Research, 1949.

West, James: *Plainville, U.S.A.*, New York, Columbia University Press, 1945.

Zorbaugh, Harvey W.: *The Gold Coast and the Slum*, Chicago, University of Chicago Press, 1929.

CHAPTER THIRTEEN

Social Mobility

Systems of social stratification differ in status standards, in the complexity of their organization, and in the degree of class consciousness. They differ, too, in the amount and kind of *social mobility* permitted. Social mobility includes movement within a class and movement from one class to another. Movement from one group to another on the same class level is referred to as *horizontal mobility*. Movement from one class level to another is called *vertical mobility*. This chapter deals primarily with vertical mobility.

TYPES OF CLASS SYSTEMS

The social definitions of how much freedom an individual or a family has to move out of one class and into another are essential elements of every system of stratification. In this regard the two chief contrasting types of stratification are *caste* systems and *open-class* systems.

Caste

A caste system of stratification is one in which birth is the definitive and final criterion of status. With but few exceptions the child inherits the class position of his parents. He is born into a social class in which he remains throughout his life. There is no reason for him to aspire to reach a higher level, for the avenues of mobility are closed. The acquisition of possessions, power, or personal qualities cannot change his class membership. In fact, the income, occupational, and power possibilities open to him are largely controlled by his socially inherited class position.

283

Caste systems are characterized by definitely prescribed privileges and prohibitions. Where a member of a particular caste may live, whom he may marry, with whom he is permitted to eat, and how he is to behave toward members of other castes are often regulated in detail. For example, barbers serving one class may be prevented from serving certain other classes; or some castes may be prohibited the use of public facilities such as roads or schools. Usually an individual must marry within his caste. In the most rigid kind of caste system the occupation of the father is inherited by the son, and the members of a caste have a common occupation.

Control of behavior is from within as well as from without the caste. The traditions and customs of a caste are pervasive regulatory forces. Both the prohibitions and the privileges of membership are accepted. They are transmitted from one generation to the next as part of the total culture. Caste control is interrelated with other strong forms of control. A caste may be united by a common religion, and caste conduct may be enforced by religious sanctions.

We have been dealing with the caste idea. Any system of stratification that may be called a caste system tends toward the type that has been described. In actual practice class position is not entirely hereditary under any system. Even under the rigid system of India some persons have married outside their caste and some have changed from one caste to another. At least to a degree vertical social mobility appears to be inevitable. Conversely caste is present in every system of stratification, for fixed hereditary status is found in every society.

Open Class

In contrast to the caste type of stratification, an open-class system is characterized by vertical social movement. The term *open class* is used because, while classes exist, avenues of mobility out of one class and into another are open. The movement may be either to a higher or to a lower social level. In order for stratification to be open-class it is not necessary that every individual and every family be mobile. Such a situation is hypothetical, and it is hardly conceivable that a class structure could exist at all under this condition. Distinctive class characteristics and modes of living could scarcely develop if there were a constant and complete interchange of class members. Even in an open-class system there are many practical difficulties hindering vertical movement. The essential feature, however, is that mobility is possible. There are no society-wide beliefs or legal prohibitions to prevent changes in class membership.

Open-class stratification is based on competitive acquisition of the symbols of status. An individual is free to acquire as much wealth as possible, buy whatever he can pay for, work at any job he can get, acquire as much education as he is capable of, achieve as much power as he can practice, and cultivate the personal qualities that he prefers. Inasmuch as the material symbols of status are most conspicuous, competition for them becomes particularly intense in an open-class society. Education, power, and personal qualities can be acquired, but they cannot be displayed so easily as material possessions. This accounts in part for the emphasis placed on material marks of status in open-class societies.

Because of the relative freedom in the acquisition and display of the symbols of status, open classes are more difficult to identify than are castes. Open-class behavior is not so definitely prescribed as is caste behavior. An individual need not dress in a designated way, or live in an assigned place, or observe a given set of customs. Thus the dress of members of different classes may appear quite similar. A family may develop some tastes and interests typical of the upper middle class and other tastes and interests typical of the lower middle class. An individual of limited means may associate with the lower upper class largely on the basis of his personal qualities. A wide range of traits may appear in an individual or in a family. This range of traits results in significant overlapping of open classes and contributes to the difficulty of classification.

THE AMERICAN IDEAL

Prevailing American beliefs and values support open-class stratification. "Getting ahead" has been a national virtue. Parents want
their children to "go beyond" them; they want them to get more
education, earn more money, and receive more recognition. "Everyone has the same chance" is an open-class slogan. Every area of
achievement has its symbols of mobility. From office boy to president of the corporation is a symbol of economic mobility. From
one-room school to college presidency is a symbol of educational
mobility. From log cabin to White House is a symbol of political
mobility. Generations of young Americans have been challenged
to follow the lead of the outstanding examples of achievement
from lowly beginnings. They have been advised to aim high if they
hope to gain success. The theme of movement upward has been
prominent in much American lore.

It is assumed that material and prestige rewards will not be
equally distributed. Despite a certain reluctance to speak of "social
classes," it is taken for granted that different groups occupy different prestige positions. At the same time it is believed that ideally
the rewards that a society has to offer should be distributed on the
basis of individual merit. The circumstances should be such that
every individual can get as much education, money, recognition,
and power as he deserves. The ideal does not require equality of
rewards but rather equality of opportunity.

This does not mean that it is universally believed that all "successful" persons are deserving. There may be considerable feeling
that the advantages held by some individuals are undeserved. But
the existence of unmerited position does not destroy the basic belief
that other people can get ahead, too. By working hard, by giving
proper attention to "connections," and with "a few breaks" an individual can enhance his position. Advantages that are achieved
by hard work are unquestionably deserved. Advantages that are

gained by "connections" and by "breaks" are regarded with mixed attitudes. "Getting something for nothing" is not in full keeping with the ideal of rewards based on equality of opportunity and on individual effort. And yet the capacity to create convenient "connections" and the ability to "take advantage of the breaks" are regarded as constituting a type of merit.

It is necessary to distinguish between equality of opportunity as a social ideal and as a social reality. As an ideal equality of opportunity is a condition to be aspired for and to be approximated as nearly as possible. As a social reality it is a condition already achieved. In common usage the ideal and the real are often confused.

There is a logical corollary to the belief that equality of opportunity is an actuality. If opportunity is the same for all persons, and if achievement depends on merit, then it follows that everyone gets what he deserves. It further follows that those who do not get ahead receive what is their due. The ultimate of this logic was expressed by the mother who wrote to her daughter in college, "Do not become unduly concerned about the circumstances of other people. Remember that there are no poor people who are undeserving of their poverty."

Probably there are only a limited number of persons who hold this extreme view of the meaning of equality of opportunity, for it is evident that in practice the ideal of an equal chance is not fulfilled. Taken literally and interpreted statistically it obviously is not true that "anyone can become President of the United States." Moreover, the chances of becoming president of anything—corporation, college, or country—are not the same for all persons. Where an individual is born, how he learns to speak and dress, the kind of training that he gets, the people whom he meets, and the attitudes that he acquires are not factors over which he has full control. These, however, are factors that may have an important relation to chances for vertical mobility.

The democratic ideal, then, seems to call for two essential conditions. First, the circumstances and opportunities over which the individual has little control shall be made as nearly equal as possible; and second, effort and ability shall be the chief factors determining the distribution of rewards.

FACTORS RELATED TO MOBILITY

The American ideal of mobility is a product of the practice of mobility. The practice in turn has been supported by the ideal. Historically Americans have believed in getting ahead not merely because it was something they wanted but also because it was something they had either observed or experienced. A number of factors have combined to promote upward mobility and to nurture the ideal.

Frontier Culture

Social mobility was fostered by the conditions under which the North American Continent was settled. For more than 250 years Americans pushed from the east coast westward. For each new generation there were new territories to be conquered, new lands to be cultivated, new forests to be cut, new mineral deposits to be mined, and new towns to be built. Opportunity awaited those who were impelled to seize it. The look was toward the future. Men on the frontier planned and worked not merely to survive today, but because they believed that they could be better off tomorrow. The ambitions of many were fully justified. Men who had very little to start with acquired property, started businesses, and achieved economic security; and some became wealthy.

These circumstances were conducive to the development of attitudes upholding an open-class system. First, frontier society was individualistic. Rewards were to be gained by those who placed confidence in their own capacities. Although there were cooperative patterns of living, there was also impatience with impeding commitments. The frontier was a proving ground for individual effort, unrestrained by too firmly established group patterns. The measure of a man was his own achievement rather than the status of his group. A corollary to this standard of individual worth was a manifest disdain for aristocratic values. Frontier society had its symbols of status, but they were not the symbols of inherited position. On the contrary traditional standards of high status were held suspect. People who themselves were struggling to get ahead were reluctant to recognize a class established by custom. They preferred to regard the roads to security and success as wide open. Their attitude concerning entrenched aristocracy was not the embittered animosity of the hopeless; it was the proud protestation of the expectant. The ordinary man had reason to believe in the possibility of economic achievement; he believed because he saw it happen.

The influence of the frontier must not be too narrowly conceived. There were many frontiers. For several hundred years the settlement of new territory went on in many different places. After the original settlement followed the development of resources and the organization of production. Throughout large areas there was the mood of getting somewhere by starting things new. The mood did not quickly subside. The attitudes of the frontier survived long in many communities.

Rural Culture

The United States has been a predominantly rural nation throughout most of its history. Rural culture in this country has been in the main an influence in favor of open classes. In many respects the influence of rural culture is similar to that of frontier culture. Our interest here, however, is in the somewhat distinctive contribution of rural society, particularly of rural agricultural society, to open-class thinking and behavior.

In many areas of the country rural patterns of association have tended to prevent the development of rigid barriers between social classes. Within rural communities families, irrespective of wealth, have often been associated in common activities. Rural schools have served all children in the community. Rural churches have not been divided into "fashionable" and "poor" churches to the same degree as urban churches. Rural recreational activities have frequently included all groups. In brief, rural people have shared a common world of experience.

Until recent decades, occupational differentiation in agricultural communities was minimal. Farming is the chief rural occupation, and in the past most persons engaged in agricultural pursuits actually worked on the land. Many farms were operated as family enterprises with nearly all family members performing farm labor. When there was nonfamily assistance, owners, tenants, and hired hands planted and harvested together. The social distance between the various types of agricultural workers was not great. This is in marked contrast to urban society with its innumerable and rather definite occupational distinctions.

Differentiation based on wealth also has been less prominent in rural than in urban areas. There has always been rural poverty, but in the past the extremes of poverty and wealth have not been conspicuous. Great concentrations of wealth have not been characteristic of the rural economy. The older family type of farm supported the family and the hired hands, but it did not allow accumulation of great wealth. Frequently there was no marked difference in the standards of living of farm tenants and of farm owners. Furthermore the agricultural way of life did not produce a leisure class, distinguished by exclusive patterns of entertainment and recreation.

It must be understood that we are looking for the sources of the open-class system in the United States. The analysis above applies to traditional agricultural society. Clearly it does not apply to the same degree to rural society today. Moreover the situation was not alike in all sections of the country. Associational, occupational, and economic differentiation were more evident under plantation and large-scale agriculture than under the smaller family-farm system. Still the over-all influence of the traditional rural way of life was strongly on the side of minimal differentiation and weak social barriers between classes.

Industrialization

The general economic and urban growth caused by industrialization increased social stratification; it also provided new opportunities for social mobility. The rapid expansion of industry resulted in the accumulation of vast fortunes. The new financial and industrial leaders were not usually men who started with great wealth. They were men of limited means who were carried upward by the surge of an expanding economy. The poor boy who grew rich became a familiar figure on the American scene. Mobility was not peculiar to the new rich. On all levels occupational opportunities increased. The new enterprises created innumerable new types of jobs, each ranked high or low in relation to other jobs. Personnel for the higher positions was drawn from the ranks below. Someone was always being moved up, and that rather rapidly. A good job was one that led to a better one. Occupational expansion extended beyond industry. The growing urban communities created by industrial development required multiplied services. Vocational opportunities offered by commercial, recreational, educational, personal, and professional services made the city the place to go to get ahead.

One study of the effects of technological change on the occupational structure showed that in 1870 the professional, business, and clerical occupations included only little more than 10 per cent of the nation's workers, whereas in 1930 they included about 30 per cent. During the same period the proportion of workers engaged in farming dropped from 48 to 21 per cent. If the occupational distribution had remained the same as in 1870, some 9 million persons would have been in manual labor in 1930 instead of in white-collar work. An average of 150,000 workers per year moved from blue-collar to white-collar jobs.[1]

[1] Elbridge Sibley, "Some Demographic Clues to Stratification," *American Sociological Review*, vol. 7, June, 1942, pp. 322–330.

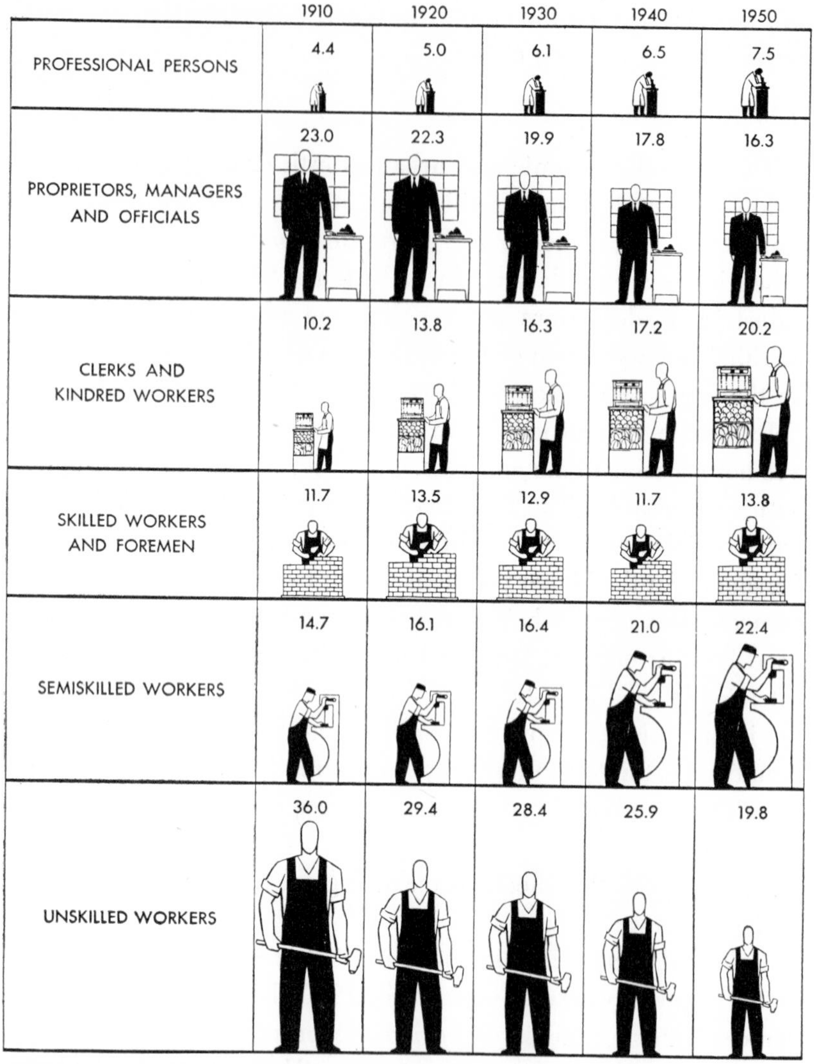

	1910	1920	1930	1940	1950
PROFESSIONAL PERSONS	4.4	5.0	6.1	6.5	7.5
PROPRIETORS, MANAGERS AND OFFICIALS	23.0	22.3	19.9	17.8	16.3
CLERKS AND KINDRED WORKERS	10.2	13.8	16.3	17.2	20.2
SKILLED WORKERS AND FOREMEN	11.7	13.5	12.9	11.7	13.8
SEMISKILLED WORKERS	14.7	16.1	16.4	21.0	22.4
UNSKILLED WORKERS	36.0	29.4	28.4	25.9	19.8

Figure 32. Changes in the Composition of the Labor Force in the United States between 1910 and 1950. The decline in the proportion of unskilled workers is one manifestation of mass mobility. Because of the inclusion of farm owners and managers in the category of "proprietors, managers, and officials," the above percentages in this category are considerably higher than those reported in some other labor-force studies. This also accounts for the percentage decline in proprietors, managers, and officials indicated here. (From Ewan Clague, "Labor Force," *Scientific American*, September, 1951, p. 41.)

Population Trends

Vertical mobility in the United States would have been less if the higher occupational and income groups had reproduced themselves. As it was, fertility rates in these groups declined markedly. There was approximately an inverse relationship between high occupational status and family size. Since high-level positions could not be filled by replacements from within the class, recruits were drawn from lower levels. Fertility rates being higher among the lower occupational groups, workers could be spared for advancement to higher positions.

Immigration was another population factor contributing to mobility. In an earlier chapter we gave an account of the influx of millions of immigrants. We observed that the great majority of immigrants began life in the New World in lowly occupations. For this reason their coming measurably affected the occupational status of persons already living in the United States. In an economy in which the manpower demand was unabated, the steady arrival of laborers who could be recruited for low occupations permitted the upgrading of other workers. Native Americans were the first to be moved up by the tide of immigration. But as one wave of immigrants followed another the immigrants too were carried upward; new arrivals replaced earlier immigrants on the lowest levels. Clearly the same degree of vertical mobility would not have been possible without immigration nor if immigrants had been distributed proportionately in all occupations.

Mass Mobility

In using the term *mass mobility* we do not have in mind changes in relative status, that is, individual movement out of one class into a higher class. We are dealing, rather, with an elevation of the general level of living of large segments of the population, without reference to shifts in status. The occupational shifts referred to above in a sense represent this type of mobility. Technological change resulted in a massive movement of workers out of

agricultural jobs into industrial jobs and out of blue-collar occupations into white-collar occupations. To be sure, the advantages
gained from these shifts were not the same for all individuals.
Some individuals benefited much more than others from the opportunities that opened. Nevertheless many of the occupational changes

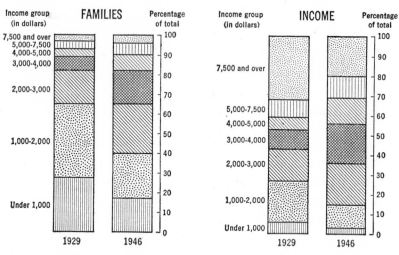

Figure 33. The Rising Levels of Income among the Masses. Percentage of families in major income groups and percentage of income received. Since the
1920's there has been a great upthrust of families to successively higher levels
of income. The proportion of moderate-income families ($2,000–$5,000) nearly
doubled between 1929 and 1946. The price level was approximately the same.
(From Harold G. Moulton, *Controlling Factors in Economic Development*,
Washington, The Brookings Institution, 1949, p. 286.)

that accompanied technological development may be viewed as a
large-scale transfer to work that was considered more desirable.
It is conceivable that a transfer of this type could occur without
greatly affecting the relative status of many of the individuals
involved.

Mass mobility is evident in other areas. The general trend of
wages has been upward. Purchasing power has been redistributed.
On the whole, the people who fall into the middle- and the lower-
income groups have more money to buy more things. When the
wage worker who remains a wage worker compares his mode of

living with that of wage workers of several generations ago, he recognizes that his level of living is higher. At the same time modern inventions have modified the way of life of almost every group. The individual who is in the same social class as his great-grandparents enjoys comforts and conveniences that they could not have. Further, the contrast between past and present is manifest in education. Children from every class stay in school longer. Educational opportunities for nearly all segments of the population have steadily increased.

The purpose here is not to minimize individual mobility. It is rather to show that the feeling of getting ahead has been fostered by social change even when the relative change of status was little. Mass mobility has bolstered open-class ideology.

SPECIAL LIMITATIONS ON MOBILITY

In the American class system, as in all others, there have always been limitations on mobility. While strong forces have favored vertical mobility, other factors have functioned to check movement upward on the social scale. Later we shall discuss the present importance of such checks on mobility in our society. However, in addition to the restrictions that apply to the society as a whole, there are special restrictions that have applied to particular groups. For these groups the class system has not been open to the degree that it has been for others. Their practice of mobility has been more limited.

The chief case in point is that of the Negro. The Negro group is set apart from the white population. Indeed the separation has been so great that the position of the Negro is sometimes described as a caste status. In a number of respects the description seems appropriate, for the status of the Negro resembles a caste position. Of first importance, intermarriage of Negroes and whites is forbidden by custom and, in many states, by law. This is an essential prohibition for the preservation of caste lines. Further, there are strong taboos concerning physical intimacy. In some communities Negroes and whites may not sit beside each other, eat together, drink from the same fountain, or touch each other under certain circumstances. It is significant that the prohibitions do not include all forms of physical intimacy. Care of children, preparation of food, and sex relations initiated by white males have not been regarded as violating caste barriers. It is not intimacy itself but intimacy that implies equality that is tabooed. In addition, the occupational status of the Negro shows some semblance of caste. Job opportunities for Negroes are limited; they are prevented from entering some types of work; and certain menial tasks are defined as "Negro work."

However, despite these castelike features, the term *caste* does not accurately denote Negro status. Under a caste system each group accepts its inherited position. But most American Negroes no longer accept the traditional definition of their status. They are convinced of their right to move higher, and many are hopeful of doing so. Under a caste system the total configuration of values gives support to the rigid and inflexible system of stratification. But fixed inferior status and inequality of opportunity for a particular group is a contradiction of dominant American values. A large number of whites reject the idea that Negroes as a group should have inferior status. In a caste system there is no change of class position. But Negroes are mobile within their own group and some are recognized as having high status in American society as a whole.

TRENDS IN VERTICAL MOBILITY

The measurement of vertical mobility presents a complex and difficult problem, and any attempt to indicate trends must be made with caution. However, at least a few tentative conclusions seem to be justified by observable social trends and by available studies.

Social Trends

A review of the historical factors that fostered mobility shows that there are counterdevelopments that may check mobility. This is true of the influence of the frontier. The geographic frontier is gone, and with it went some of the opportunities for acquiring land and other wealth when one had very little to start with. In many areas frontier ideas carry over, but the circumstances in which they are applied are different. Communities that once boasted of a dislike of aristocracy have created their own aristocratic classes.

The change from a rural society to a predominantly urban society has placed a larger proportion of the population in a more definitely stratified type of social organization. Furthermore the class structure in rural communities has increased in complexity. Urban class values influence the standards of rural areas. Rural patterns of association on a community-wide basis have diminished. Occupational distinctions in agriculture are greater. Large-farm owners, farm managers, tenants, hired workers, and migratory laborers cannot be grouped together in one occupational class. Agriculture now has its own class of big businessmen, men of wealth and power who have little in common with small, family-farm operators. The development of a more definitely stratified rural society is not in itself an indication either of more or of less mobility, but it is a change that must be recognized in the measurement of mobility.

The industrialization of our society provided two types of opportunities for advancement. One was to work for yourself by starting a new business or by opening up a new line of production. The other type of opportunity was to work for other people in new jobs that were being created. Both types of opportunities remain. Small businesses are constantly being started, but much of the growth of our modern economy is absorbed by the expansion of established organizations. Thus for an increasing number of people, getting ahead is by advancement in an existing organization rather than by starting a new business.

Opportunities for advancement in a hierarchical organization are limited. If the organization does not grow, advancements can be made only to fill positions vacated by resignations or by retirements. The chances for any one person on the lowest level to be moved up are small. If the organization does grow, job expansion is not proportional on all levels, especially on the top level. A corporation may double the number of its workers without proportionately increasing the number of top executives. Furthermore the pattern of starting at the bottom and working to the top is less common. Persons are brought into the organization to do the type of work for which they have been trained. A laborer may become a foreman, but the chance that he will become an executive is very remote.

The influence of immigration on upward mobility diminished rapidly following the restrictive legislation of the 1920's. Americans no longer are pushed upward by a mass of foreign-born workers ready to take the lowest jobs. Movement from the bottom level is now more competitive.

While differential fertility has promoted vertical mobility, the resultant number of opportunities must not be overestimated. In 1944, when differential fertility was more marked than at present, the effect was summarized as follows: [2]

"The students of population have discovered that people in the professional and managerial classes fall short by 20 per cent of reproducing their numbers. That is, every five such people in one generation will produce only four in the following generation. If we should assume that all the children of upper and upper-middle class parents manage to retain or to better these positions (an assumption which is, of course, not true), there will still be opportunity for people from below to rise and fill one in five of the upper and upper-middle class positions. This is a rather limited opportunity, since one-fifth of the upper and upper-middle positions is

[2] W. Lloyd Warner et al., *Who Shall Be Educated?* New York, Harper, 1944, pp. 153–154.

only 2 or 3 per cent of the total number of positions in our society and all of the lower and lower-middle classes, some 85 or 90 per cent of the population, may be candidates for these few higher positions."

Selected Studies

In the 1920's Sorokin made a study of the economic starting point of American millionaires. He compared the living generation of millionaires with those deceased. The percentage of millionaires who started their careers poor was twice as high in the deceased as in the living group. Also the percentage of millionaires who started their careers rich was almost twice as high in the living as in the deceased group. Thus the data indicated an increase in the hereditary transmission of economic status within the group studied.[3]

After a review of the studies of occupational transmission Sorokin concluded that [4] "in the majority of cases the sons enter the occupation of the fathers in a greater proportion than any other one; . . . that each of the occupations is recruited principally from the sons of the fathers who have such an occupation.

". . . children of common laborers enter principally occupations of unskilled and skilled labor. Only a relatively small part of them succeed in entering the higher professional occupations, becoming managers and owners of big business enterprises. On the other hand, the children of the professionals and successful business men, in a great majority, enter the professional and business and privileged occupations."

In a study of American business leaders Taussig and Joslyn found that higher business positions are filled mainly by persons whose fathers were business leaders. A sampling of 7,371 showed that although business and professional men constituted only about 10 per cent of the working population they produced about 70

[3] Pitirim Sorokin, *Social Mobility*, New York, Harper, 1927, pp. 464–465.
[4] *Ibid.*, pp. 438–439.

per cent of the business leaders. Around 110 times as many business leaders came from the business group as from the unskilled and skilled groups together.[5]

In their second study of Middletown, made in the 1930's, the Lynds reported: [6]

"When one brings together all of the above trends as to the likelihood of becoming one's own boss in the Middletown of the 1920's, the central point that emerges is that in every major field of work the share of the population employed was growing more rapidly than the share of the population self-employed or employing others. . . . The situation in Middletown's industries roughly epitomizes the general situation in all occupations. What one seems to be witnessing here is a fundamental alteration in the vaunted American ladder of opportunity by which one has traditionally been supposed to 'go up in the world,' 'get ahead,' 'improve oneself,' 'arrive.'

". . . Andrew Carnegie's advice to enterprising young men to begin at the bottom appears no longer to be sound advice. Men of his type are advising young men today to get a toe hold in one of the managerial or technical departments halfway up the ladder. What appears increasingly in Middletown industries is not one unbroken ladder but two: the one becoming shorter, harder to climb, and leading nowhere in particular; the other a long and repaying one but beginning a long jump above the plant floor. Middletown's industries consist more than ever before of a large, crowded floor of little differentiated 'hands,' and a different class of individuals (businessmen and engineers) doing all the 'going up' in a world of their own largely beyond the reach of the working class."

A significant finding comes from a study by Anderson and Davidson. Their sample included 7 per cent of the gainfully employed in San Jose, California. They found that there may have been

[5] F. W. Taussig and C. S. Joslyn, *American Business Leaders*, New York, Macmillan, 1932.

[6] Robert S. Lynd and Helen Merrell Lynd, *Middletown in Transition*, New York, Harcourt, Brace, 1937, pp. 70–72.

an increase in specific occupational changes between father and son. These shifts, however, may occur without changing the general social-economic level of the son.[7]

On the other hand, it is also significant that Davidson and Anderson found that 20 per cent of professional men and 20 per cent of proprietors had come from the homes of skilled, semiskilled, or unskilled laborers. Of the white-collar clerical workers, 18 per cent had semiskilled or unskilled fathers; and of the skilled artisans, 10 per cent had unskilled laboring fathers.[8]

Conclusion

The above studies were selected because they are representative of numerous other studies. When historical changes and the various mobility studies are taken together they provide some basis for a very tentative summary of vertical mobility trends. Some of the factors that in earlier periods fostered indefinite stratification and rapid mobility have diminished in importance. Movement from manual-labor occupations to white-collar occupations has declined. There is still significant movement from manual labor and lower-white-collar occupations into own-businesses, especially the smaller types of own-businesses. Much modern mobility is of the bureaucratic variety, that is, movement upward in the white-collar ranks of larger organizations. White-collar workers usually begin their careers as white-collar workers. A high proportion of white-collar workers are advanced from one position to another without ever moving out of their original occupational class. Specialization has made education an important factor both in determining at what level an individual enters the occupational ranks and in qualifying him for advancement to higher positions. The educationally qualified sons of manual-worker and lower-white-collar fathers are placed in high-level positions, but a high proportion of such positions are filled from within the higher classes.

Patterns of mobility in the near future may be greatly influenced

---

[7] Percy E. Davidson and H. Dewey Anderson, *Occupational Mobility in an American Community*, Stanford, Calif., Stanford University Press, 1937.

[8] *Ibid.*

by trends in education. There is considerable evidence indicating that when workers enter some occupations their opportunities for mobility are limited. But what about their children? Education helps to determine at which level a young person will begin his work career. How equal are educational opportunities and how equal will they become? Is the economic status of the parents becoming more or less important in determining the educational opportunities of their children, particularly opportunities for advanced education? What will be the effect of providing a college education for a much higher proportion of American youth? How important will education be in selecting persons to fill positions which offer advancement to high levels? Vertical mobility in the United States will be influenced by the way in which these questions are answered.

We may repeat that the measurement of mobility presents a complex problem. Available data indicate rather definite changes in patterns of mobility. There are suggestions of the effect of these changes on the amount of mobility, but as yet the actual effect on the amount of mobility is not well known.

SUMMARY

Movement from one class to another is called vertical mobility. With regard to the amount of vertical mobility permitted, the two contrasting types of stratification are caste systems and open-class systems. In a caste system status is defined by birth, and rigid barriers prevent movement from one class to another. An open-class system, on the other hand, is characterized by vertical mobility. There are barriers, but the avenues of movement out of one class and into another are open. Open-class stratification is based on the competitive acquisition of the symbols of status.

American beliefs and values support open-class stratification. The theme of movement upward has been prominent in the national ideology. It is assumed that rewards will not be equally distributed, but that they will be distributed on the basis of merit. Effort and ability shall be the chief factors determining the distribution of rewards. The ideal is not one of equality of rewards but of equality of opportunity.

A number of factors have combined to promote upward mobility and to nurture the ideal. Life on the American frontier was marked by the struggle to get ahead, and traditional standards of high status were held suspect. In the main, rural culture, too, has been an influence in favor of open class. Under industrialization new opportunities for social mobility were provided. Differential birth rates and immigration have facilitated movement between classes. Elevation of the general level of living of large segments of the population has bolstered open-class ideology.

There have always been some society-wide checks on mobility. In addition there are special limitations that apply to particular groups. Limitations on Negro mobility have been so great that the position of the Negro has sometimes been referred to as a caste status. But although the position of the Negro is castelike, it is not in reality a caste position.

Research and social changes provide some basis for very tentative conclusions concerning trends in mobility. The measurement of vertical mobility is complex and much remains unknown.

SELECTED REFERENCES

Anderson, H. Dewey, and Percy E. Davidson: *Ballots and the Democratic Class Struggle*, Stanford, Calif., Stanford University Press, 1943.

Bernard, Jessie: *American Community Behavior*, New York, Dryden, 1949.

Davidson, Percy E., and Dewey H. Anderson: *Occupational Mobility in an American Community*, Stanford, Calif., Stanford University Press, 1937.

Linton, Ralph: *The Study of Man*, New York, Appleton-Century, 1936.

Lynd, Robert S., and Helen M. Lynd: *Middletown in Transition*, New York, Harcourt, Brace, 1937.

Myrdal, Gunnar, et al.: *An American Dilemma*, New York, Harper, 1944.

Sorokin, Pitirim: *Social Mobility*, New York, Harper, 1927.

————: *Society, Culture, and Personality*, New York, Harper, 1947.

Taussig, F. W., and C. S. Joslyn: *American Business Leaders*, New York, Macmillan, 1932.

Warner, W. Lloyd, Robert J. Havighurst, and Martin B. Loeb: *Who Shall Be Educated?* New York, Harper, 1944.

PART FOUR: Institutions

CHAPTER FOURTEEN

Family Institutions

When society is viewed in its institutional aspect attention is focused on the beliefs, the rules, and the expected ways of behaving that control the activities and relationships of society. Institutions are a primary factor in giving order to society. Their ultimate function is to regulate behavior so that society can be maintained and so that the needs of the members of society can be met.

In observing the nature of social regulation it is discovered that beliefs, rules, and expected behaviors are not to be regarded as so many separate and unrelated elements. Rather they are intricately interrelated. They influence, check, and support each other. When their relatedness is analyzed institutions emerge in clusters. At least five major types of activity are found in nearly every society: family life, economic activity, government, education, and religion. The institutions that develop in connection with each type of activity function together. They regulate behavior so that particular ends can be achieved. In complex societies like our own, the institutions relating to each major type of activity constitute rather discrete regulatory systems. At the same time, the major insitutional systems are all interrelated.

It must be understood that most institutional systems are not fully integrated. The expectations and rules may in fact conflict with each other. For example, a parent may encounter the expectation that in training his child he will on some occasions use corporal punishment, and he may encounter the conflicting expectation that he will never use corporal punishment. Similarly the major institutional systems, though interrelated, are never fully integrated. Thus some religious institutions may conflict with some economic institutions. The lack of institutional integration is covered by the concept of *social disorganization.* To a degree almost every society is disorganized. But if the functional needs of society are to be met, organization must have ascendancy over disorganization.

The brief treatment of American institutions in the following chapters is necessarily limited. It is incomplete in many ways. Among other things, we do not give attention to the detailed expectations and rules which are essential components of the institutional system. Also we touch very little on the varying institutional subsystems in communities, classes, and ethnic groups. In dealing with institutions we are guided by two chief purposes: to identify some of the over-all expectations, beliefs, and values that control American society; and to show the development of these with particular emphasis upon change and the factors that have been related to change.

Probably as much as any the institutions of the family have been involved in and influenced by social change. The modern family performs many of the functions that it performed earlier. In significant respects, however, it is different from the family system from which it developed. We shall treat selected aspects of this change. In order to emphasize the contrast between past and present we begin with the early American family.

THE EARLY AMERICAN FAMILY

In characterizing the American family during the colonial period, it cannot be assumed that all families were similar. There was considerable variation. Family life in New England differed in certain respects from that in the Southern colonies, and family patterns in both of these regions contrasted to those on the Western frontier. There were also differences between rural and urban families. Even within local communities family customs varied. Nevertheless, after due allowance has been made for differences, it is still possible to discover a number of attitudes, roles, practices, and functions which were fairly typical of the early American family.

Attitudes toward Marriage

Much may be learned about a family system by observing the way in which marriage is regarded. In colonial America great importance was attached to marriage. It was expected that everyone who could would marry. By marrying and establishing a family the individual took his place as a responsible member of his community. The position of the unmarried person was unenviable. He was an extra in someone else's household. The unmarried person who could show no good reason for his unmarried state was particularly unpopular. Attitudes toward the unmarried found expression in ordinances requiring them to pay special taxes and forbidding them to live alone. In some localities single persons could live only with families licensed by a magistrate.

Marriage at an early age was encouraged by custom and by circumstances. Financial and occupational obstacles to early marriage were few. It was said of Connecticut youth in 1704: "They generally marry very young, the males oftener, as I am told, under twenty years than above." The marriage of girls at sixteen was not uncommon. One observer tells of grandmothers who were 27 and 30 years of age. Many women were grandmothers at 40.

In marriage it was assumed that there would be children, an unlimited number of children. The Biblical advice to "be fruitful and multiply and replenish the earth" was heeded quite literally. Many families had twelve children and some had twice that many. Cotton Mather, referring to one of his contemporaries, wrote: [1]

"He was twice married. By his first wife, the vertuous daughter of parents therein resembled by her, he had six children. But his next wife was a young gentlewoman whom he chose from under the guardianship and with the countenance of Edward Hopkins Esq., the excellent governor of Connecticut. . . . By the daughter

---

[1] Quoted in A. W. Calhoun, *A Social History of the American Family*, Cleveland, Ohio, Clark, 1917, vol. I, p. 88.

of that Mr. Launce, who is yet living among us, Mr. Sherman had no less than twenty children added unto the number of six which he had before. . . . One woman [in New England] has had not less than twenty-two children: whereof she buried fourteen sons and six daughters. Another woman has had no less than twenty-three children by one husband; whereof nineteen lived unto men's and women's estate. A third was mother to seven-and-twenty children: and she that was mother to Sir William Phips, the late governor of New England, had no less than twenty-five children besides him; she had one and twenty sons and five daughters. Now unto the catalog of such 'fruitful vines by the side of the house' is this gentlewoman Mrs. Sherman to be enumerated. Behold thus was our Sherman, that eminent fearer of the Lord, blessed of him."

Although the birth rate was high, its effect on family size was somewhat counteracted by a high death rate. It may be noted in the above quotation that in one case only two out of twenty-two children survived. This was not a typical family in terms of number of births or number of deaths; but it was typical in that, despite the circumstances, reproduction was unchecked. It is reported that a Plymouth gravestone carries the significant inscription: "Here lies _____ _____ with twenty small children." Often when families did become extremely large the children were not all born to one wife, but to a succession of wives. Childbearing was a frequent cause of female deaths, and remarriage was common.

Sex relations before or outside of marriage were strongly condemned. Those who violated the code were sometimes fined, imprisoned, whipped, place in stocks, made to wear the scarlet letter, or forced to confess publicly. It appears that there was with regard to sex a degree of ambivalence; much secrecy was associated with the subject of sex, and yet extravagant publicity often was given to sex offenses. It is doubtful how successful publicity and punishment were in reducing sex irregularity. The records of one New England church show that out of 200 members, 66 confessed to premarital sex relations. Illegitimacy was common. There was more tolerance of premarital intimacy when marriage was intended than otherwise. In the South departure from the conventional standard often resulted in miscegenation. The double standard of morality was more prevalent in the South than in other parts of the country.

Status of Family Members

In theory and in practice the father was the head of the colonial family. He was granted full power over his household. He was chief disciplinarian and the final source of authority. He expected obedience and respect from his children and from his wife. His success as a father was judged by his ability to control his own family. To be sure, there must have been variation in the degree to which men were suited for this dominant role, but the prerogatives of weak men and of strong men were protected by the ideology of male supremacy.

The position of the wife was that of a subordinate. By religion, custom, and law the colonists had been trained to believe in the inferiority of women. Willing obedience to her husband was a measure of the devotion and loyalty of a wife. Subordination of women was not necessarily against their will, for they, as well as men, accepted the inevitability of their position. Both men and women treated the Biblical injunction, "Wives be in subjection to your husbands," as proof of the desirability of the existing situation.

The ideal woman was a good mother and homemaker. Her own household was the sphere of her activity. Here she achieved success or failure. She was not supposed to concern herself with the affairs of men. Education for women was believed to be unnecessary, and consequently educational opportunities for them were extremely limited.

English law provided the basis on which the legal status of women was defined in America. The following statement by Blackstone was acceptable to Puritans and to Cavaliers alike: [2]

2 William Blackstone, *Commentaries on the Laws of England*, 15th ed., vol. 1, pp. 441 *ff.*

"By marriage the husband and wife are one person in law: that is, the very being or legal existence of the woman is suspended during the marriage, or at least is incorporated and consolidated into that of the husband: under whose wing, protection, and *cover,* she performs everything; . . . . Upon this principle, of an union of person in husband and wife, depend most of the legal rights, duties, and disabilities, that either of them acquire by the marriage. . . . For this reason a man cannot grant anything to his wife, or enter into covenant with her, for the grant would be to suppose her separate existence: and to covenant with her would be only to covenant with himself: and therefore it is also generally true that all compacts made between husband and wife, when single, are voided by the intermarriage. . . ."

Subordinate though she was, the wife was not without opportunities to achieve recognition and influence in the family. In a society in which so much importance was attached to childbearing and to homemaking, it was natural that the successful homemaker and mother would gain respect. There is evidence also that then, as now, the wife was often able to exercise strong control over the household of which her husband was master.

The child was regarded more as a miniature adult than as a child. That is, he was judged by and expected to conform to adult standards. Childhood was a period to be passed through as quickly as possible. When children were incapable of fitting into the way of life of their elders, they were at least not supposed to interfere with adult activities. The rule that children were to be seen but not heard in the company of adults, although probably repeatedly violated, was characteristic of parental attitudes. The inability of children to conform to adult patterns of behavior was taken as evidence of natural stubbornness. By the theologically minded it was interpreted as a manifestation of the inborn wickedness of man. Said one colonial divine: [3]

"Surely there is in all children (tho not alike) a stubbernes and stoutnes of minde arising from naturall pride which must in

[3] Quoted in *ibid.,* p. 112.

the first place be broken and beaten down that so the foundation of their education being layd in humilitie and tractableness other virtues may in their time be built thereon." Strict discipline and religious training were combined to break the will of the child and to prepare him for a proper life as an adult.

The extent to which the conduct of children was prescribed is illustrated by a choice excerpt from a book of etiquette widely circulated in colonial days: [4]

"Never sit down at the table till asked, and after the blessing. Ask for nothing; tarry till it be offered thee. Speak not. . . . Look not earnestly at any other that is eating. When moderately satisfied leave the table. Sing not, hum not, wriggle not. Spit nowhere in the room but in the corner. . . . When any speak to thee, stand up. Say not I have heard it before. Never endeavor to help him out if he tell it not right. Snigger not; never question the truth of it."

Family Unity and Solidarity

The colonial family posssesed a high degree of unity and solidarity. Family members shared a common life, and ties that bound them together were strong. This characteristic of the early American family has been subject to romanticism, but it is not necessary to romanticize traditional family solidarity in order to recognize it. Family unity was evidenced in many ways. There was, for example, little tendency for children to "leave home" to move to other communities. After marriage the young person continued to be in close association with his family, living near his father's home, or not infrequently remaining in the father's household. Thus the type of family known as the *great family* was perpetuated. The individual did not belong to a family made up only of father, mother, and children; he was part of a larger kinship group consisting of father, mother, children, grandparents, uncles, aunts, cousins, and others. The members of this larger family group were not merely people who happened to be related by blood. They

[4] Alice Morse Earle, *Child Life in Colonial Days*, New York, Macmillan, 1899, pp. 215–217.

constituted a meaningful social unit. There was a significant sense of belonging to the great family. Solidarity showed itself in the control that the family was able to exercise over its members. Courtship, marriage, religion, occupational decisions, and financial matters all were subject to strong family influence. Family approval or disapproval was not treated with indifference. The permanency of marital ties was another indication of family unity. Marriages were expected to last. Condemnation of divorced persons was severe. Divorces were granted, and slightly more liberally in some places than in others, but everywhere divorce was a serious affront to the family and to the community.

To a large degree the strongly united family system was brought to America from Europe. The emphasis placed on the family certainly did not have its origin in this country. As James Truslow Adams writes: [5]

"The dominant note in this social life was that of domesticity. In the somewhat romantic atmosphere with which Americans clothe this early period, it is perhaps the peace, simplicity, and unity of family life which contributes the elements of greatest charm. . . . It is noteworthy that although American cultural life was woven of many ethnic strands, all of those which at the end of the seventeenth century were most effective—English, Dutch, French, and German—were of races in which the solidarity of the family was strongly ingrained."

And yet the American family was not a replica of the European family. In certain respects family sentiment, as such, was weaker than in Europe. In many ways family unity in the colonies was a practical matter. Under some circumstances it was a necessity. In its own way the new setting contributed to the cohesion of the kinship group. Returning to James Truslow Adams: [6]

"To this home-making instinct, rooted in the inheritance of the settlers, was added the influence of environment. Under the con-

---

[5] James Truslow Adams, *Provincial Society*, New York, Macmillan, 1927, pp. 10–11.
[6] *Ibid.*

ditions of a frontier existence the family tended to become greatly strengthened as a social, economic and even military unit."

Making a living on the new continent demanded the participation of everyone, young and old. There was work for all. The family was the basic economic unit, and each family was responsible for its own welfare. Under these conditions little allowance could be made for the individual who would not cooperate. The entire family had to pursue common economic ends. The well-being of each member was directly related to the success with which the goal of family self-sufficiency was attained.

Family self-reliance extended to nearly all areas of living. The family provided its own supply of food and made its own clothing. The manufacture of candles, utensils, and furniture were common household tasks. In addition the family was largely responsible for the education of children. Worship and religious training were conducted in the home. The family had to depend on its own resources for recreation, and usually recreational activities were family affairs. In times of illness family adequacy was put to a test. Thus the family was in reality an economic, educational, religious, recreational, and social welfare unit.

When a family was geographically and socially isolated, the situation described above was all the more extreme. Early frontier families were almost entirely on their own. It is not surprising that in circumstances of isolation the demand for family cooperation was strictly enforced. Nor is it strange that where social contacts were limited the associational value of the family helped to cultivate a marked clannishness.

THE FAMILY IN A CHANGING SOCIETY

The characteristics of the eighteenth-century American family may be summarized as follows: The married state was highly favored for all. Marriage at an early age was encouraged and unwillingness to marry met with severe disapproval. The sex code was strict but nevertheless violated. Since unlimited procreation was taken for granted, families were large. The family system was patriarchal. Male domination was accepted, and the subordination of women and children was expected. Strict and unquestioning obedience to parental authority was the rule for children. The family was a strongly knit unit and included a larger kinship group than father, mother, and children. Breaking up the family by divorce was strongly opposed. Family unity was supported by practical necessity as well as by sentiment and tradition.

After the opening of the nineteenth century the traditional family system was exposed to social forces which were destined to affect it profoundly. Family change was inseparably related to other social changes.

The Growth of Democracy

American democracy was not complete at the time of the founding of the national government. Family life was not then democratic, nor was education, nor was economic life. Even government was not truly democratic. The founding fathers provided the basis on which political democracy could be constructed, but time and change were required to grant the right of political participation to the entire adult population. Just as political democracy did not immediately appear, democratic beliefs and practices in general did not spring forth full grown. The emergence of democracy was by a process of change and growth. This was no less true in the family than in other groups.

Historians have repeatedly stressed the influence of the frontier on American democracy. The frontier way of life fostered a carelessness about the distinctions of social rank. Ax and rifle "made all men equally tall." Individuals were accepted for their performance, not for their past. There was little time to be concerned about whether all the details of social convention were being observed. The effect on the family was marked. Family control over marriage weakened. Class distinctions and pecuniary considerations did not stand in the way of persons who wanted to marry. Many women abandoned the exclusively domestic role. With much work to be done, men could ill afford to insist that women engage only in traditional home duties. The westward movement disrupted the large family of relatives in the East. Clans were broken up as young men with individualistic ambitions left their home communities in conquest of new territories.

It was almost inevitable that the general expansion of democratic ideas would modify family relationships. The obvious contradiction between the preachments of democracy and the practices of the patriarchal family could not escape attention. Authoritarianism, subordination of children, and the social and legal inferiority of women were inconsistent with the democratic spirit. The transition was slow, and it was not until the second half of the nineteenth century that women had much opportunity to assert their emancipation. To a great extent the ideology of democracy had to wait for an assist from new conditions of living to bring about the practice of democracy in the family.

The New Economy

During the nineteenth century the family became less self-sufficient economically. The trend was toward specialization and factory production. Raising and processing food for home consumption decreased in importance as family activities. Factory-made clothing replaced the homemade, and the manufacture of other goods was taken away from the home. On the farm the change came more slowly and was less complete; the ideal of self-sufficiency lingered longer. However, the farmer too came to depend more on "store-bought" goods; he was less concerned about raising all his own food. He found it convenient to raise cash crops to make the money to buy what he needed. All in all the family was dislodged from its paramount place as an economic producing unit. With the departure of many of its economic functions went much of the family unity which previously had been so essential.

Industrialization provided new opportunities for employment away from home. From the beginning women and children formed a large proportion of the labor force in factories. It has been estimated that in the first half of the nineteenth century from two-thirds to three-fourths of the factory workers were women. They were preferred over men because their services could be bought more cheaply. From the country came the daughters of agriculture to earn their own wages. Improved methods of farming likewise released from the soil a substantial number of young men who found their way into urban occupations. The economic hold of the family on its members grew weaker, and the individual ambitions of young people grew stronger. Paternal discipline was robbed of some of its sanctions when children could declare their financial independence.

Probably the most pronounced effect was on the role and status of women. Young women, spinsters, and widows were freed from a dependent position. Without the aid of male relatives, they were capable of supporting themselves. Furthermore, the longer men were exposed to this possibility, the more they favored it. As men came to expect it, female self-support gained respectability. But there were results which the male mind may not have anticipated. Employment of women outside the home defined for them a new nondomestic role and later contributed measurably to the definition of new status. The economic emancipation of women opened the way for their general emancipation and for the dissolution of their subordinate position.

The Trend toward the City

The movement of people toward the city was more than a population shift; it involved a shift in ways of living and thinking. In the urban environment decentralization of the interests of family members was fostered from many quarters. Opportunities abounded to engage in activities away from home. Necessary pursuits, to say nothing of special interests, sent family members in different directions. In the city individual capacities could be cultivated; recreation, education, and a variety of occupations were available. Success was individual rather than familial.

Family adjustment to the city was not a painless process. For lower-income groups, housing presented a piteous problem. Writings on housing are replete with statistics on crowded living quarters: three to five persons in a one-bedroom apartment, seven people in four rooms, thirty-one people in fourteen rooms. These conditions were extreme, but they were found in almost every city. Although middle-income families did not experience hardships of this sort, they also had to accommodate to space limitations.

In the city the traditional family entered a losing struggle for the survival of its standards. The clash of attitudes and of ideas in a heterogeneous society made it difficult to transmit a fixed set of customs from one generation to the next. Every family could not successfully perpetuate its own kind of culture. The rapid influx of immigrants added to the cultural confusion. In a sense it is paradoxical that the coming of European immigrants helped to cause the disintegration of traditional family patterns, for they brought with them family systems which had many of the characteristics of the early American family. Nevertheless, in the conflict of cultures, family influences were weakened.

The impersonality and anonymity of the city afforded a setting in which personal inclinations and desires could be fulfilled with a minimum of restraint. Without the active support of social approval or disapproval, older family standards lost their power to control behavior; eventually the standards were modified. Tolerance of or indifference to the repudiation of traditional rules of conduct was in itself a new standard.

War and the Family

Wars are disruptive events, and as such they cause the breakdown of established ways of living. Some of the changes produced by war are relatively temporary; others are permanent. Even the seemingly short-term adjustments frequently have lasting consequences. In the case of the family one of the effects of war has been the acceleration of changes already in process.

War has contributed to the impermanency of marriage. In part this is because of the circumstances under which many marriages are entered in time of war. When war becomes imminent the demand for marriage licenses soars. Normal considerations of courtship diminish in significance. The desire to avoid military service, the wish to "have someone to come back to," and the impulse to have "one last fling" result in the marriage of persons not well prepared for matrimony and not well suited for each other. When the discovery is made, the divorce rate goes up.

Even marriages that appear to be successful are susceptible to disintegration in wartime. During the extended period of separation husband and wife live very different lives. They are forced to get along without each other and therefore may find it difficult to get along with each other. The wife may have grown accustomed to a new role and to making independent decisions. Because of her own experience her husband may appear inadequate for his responsibilities. The husband may have difficulty in returning to his prewar family position. He may feel unneeded, or he may find home obligations irksome after life in the army. Thus there follows an increase in the number of broken homes.

Sex codes have been influenced by war. The soldier is removed from his family, neighborhood, church, and old friends. He enters a new group in which the expectations of persons back home seem remote. Restraints on sexual behavior are weak. At the same time the situation of women is altered. A scarcity of men increases competition among women. In the competition for the companionship of available males personal sex codes may be relaxed. Lonely wives as well as unmarried girls may modify their standards under these circumstances.

The rise in the status of women is one of the most conspicuous effects of war on the family. It was observed after the Civil War, especially in the South. In the absence of men, women took over the management of plantations. Having learned to like their new status they were not inclined quickly to retire to subservience upon the return of their husbands. The pattern was repeated in the First and Second World Wars. At home the wife was head of the family. She was both mother and father to "her" children. Outside the home women took their places beside men in almost every type of occupation. In the Second World War, the military organization itself created a place for women through the formation of women's auxiliary corps.

Diversity and Experimentation

Although from the beginning American families varied, they usually possessed certain common characteristics. It is in this typical sense that we have treated the family. There have been groups, however, in which a notable lack of conformity to typical family patterns has existed. The influence of these nontypical family practices should not be overemphasized, and yet they must not be ignored. Diversity and experimentation were involved in American family change, even though, as compared with other factors, their effect was not outstanding.

The history of the Negro in the United States has been such as to produce family practices different from those of the white majority. During slavery the Negro had little opportunity to develop normal family life. The transitory relationships of men, women, and children only remotely resembled families as we know them. The chief control over Negro families was the economic and sexual control exercised by white masters. After the Civil War the social life of the Negro changed only slowly. As under slavery, families tended to be mother-centered, and male irresponsibility continued. Migration of Negroes from country to city and from South to North led to the emergence of groups of Negroes who were motivated to imitate the conduct of whites. Mulattoes, who had achieved a more advantaged position even before the end of slavery, became a channel through which the customs of the majority group were transmitted to Negroes. Although in general sex behavior remained rather free, there developed a Negro middle class which emulated monogamous standards. These so-called "black puritans" are found both in rural and in urban areas. Very slowly in some groups and more rapidly in others, the Negro family has tended toward white practices.

Slavery left its mark on the Southern white family as well as on the Negro family. Accessibility of women slaves for sex purposes fostered a double standard of morality. The presence of slave labor made almost every type of work unacceptable for a large class of Southern women. Training of children also was often in other hands. Together the double standard of morality and female economic unimportance helped to place the women of the old South in a subordinate position. After slavery family life was one of the areas in which reconstruction was needed.

The immigrant family in the United States presents another example of diversity. At the same time that numerous social forces were interacting to remake the American family, millions of immigrants, bringing with them traditional family values, were arriving from Europe. But the immigrant family could withstand the pressures on its old forms no better than the native family. Solidarity in the foreign family was briefly strengthened by the threat of hostile forces from the strange outside world, yet in the end it too succumbed. The presence of the foreign-born contributed to the clash of values, but in the final analysis the immigrant family influenced the forces that played upon it less than it was influenced by those forces.

Occasionally groups decidedly divergent in their family practices have appeared. The Mormon adoption of polygamy was an extreme case. After having been practiced by certain leaders for about twelve years, the desirability of polygamy was publicly announced in Utah in 1852. The practice was encouraged by the church, although actually less than one family in ten was polyg- amous. By 1890 polygamy was outlawed. Another experiment in unorthodox family life was made in Oneida, New York, under the leadership of John Humphrey Noyes. Here a community of religious perfectionists practiced group marriage for a number of decades. In 1879, under strong criticism, the community became monogamous. It is significant that the past century produced these deviations; it is equally significant that they were not permitted to survive.

THE MODERN AMERICAN FAMILY

In viewing the modern family there is no reason for supposing that a fixed or final stage has been reached. Rather we are probably observing phases of a continuing process of change. In the following pages the contrast between past and present should become evident.

The Making of Marriages

Modern marriage is usually regarded as an arrangement between two individuals rather than between two families. Family approval and disapproval are involved; families take part in weddings; but who is to marry whom is considered to be a matter of personal preference. This point of view is generally shared by parents as well as by their courting children. If parents do not approve of a marriage they nonetheless are likely to think that they should not interfere. When there are parental objections young people may feel that this is regrettable but that such objections do not necessarily constitute an obstacle to marriage.

Although marriage in the United States has never been so strongly controlled by the family as in some countries, the present individualization of marriage is in striking contrast to earlier attitudes and practices. It may be accounted for in part by the circumstances under which young people today meet each other. In older communities family participation in the selection of a marriage partner was made possible by the common associations of all members of a family. Parents and children moved in the same circle of acquaintances, and thus mate selection was an outgrowth of the selection of family friends. In modern society, with its variety of educational, recreational, occupational, and other contacts, the choice of friends slips out of the control of the family.

Moreover present-day thinking about the choice of a marriage partner is in keeping with the general emphasis on individualism. Ideas stressing individual rights and privileges are applied to courtship and marriage. When these attitudes are coupled with a degree of economic independence from the family the assertion of freedom of marital choice becomes unallayable. Belief in this freedom is now so deeply ingrained that its practice does not always depend on economic adequacy. Financial aid may be forthcoming from parents, but the prospective bride and groom will probably feel that this in no way should influence their choice of each other.

The belief that marriage is an individual matter is given substantial support by the romantic ideal of marriage. With the aid of novels and of movies, this concept has gained wide acceptance. The essence of the belief is that romantic love is sufficient basis for marriage. Romantic love begins upon the meeting of two persons who discover a natural affinity for each other. They know that they belong to each other, and all other considerations vanish into insignificance. Common backgrounds and the approval of family and friends become matters of the least concern. They are in love, and unless the spell of romance is broken they feel that nothing should interfere with their marriage. Such an approach to marriage would have been unthinkable to most Americans prior to the nineteenth century. Then, as now, men and women fell in love, but the idea that one should give affection without regard for economic, educational, religious, and other cultural factors had little place in their thinking.

Nevertheless, despite the individualization of marriage and notwithstanding the romantic ideal, most persons do not have the whole world to choose from in finding a marriage partner. In practice both love and freedom operate within limits. The tendency is for persons of similar educational and economic backgrounds to marry each other. Even now, direct control of marriage sometimes occurs, especially in families in which there is a sizable amount of wealth to be distributed.

Toward Egalitarianism

We do not yet have an equalitarian family system. Many families, particularly in rural areas, are still essentially patriarchal. But we have moved a long way in the direction of greater equality in the relationships of men and women and of parents and children. The enhanced position of women is manifest in rights granted by law, in education, in political participation, and in opportunities for gainful employment. It is reflected in the right of women to decide when and under what conditions they will enter marriage. Studies show that most women still desire marriage, but it is their privilege, without social ostracism, to remain unmarried if they choose. In marriage the wife shares in disciplining children and in money management. Her interests are considered to be of equal importance with those of her husband.

It has been suggested by some observers that in many families in the United States the wife has taken over the dominant role. While the husband occupies himself with his work, striving to give financial support and social status to his family, the wife administers the household, directs the expenditure of funds, and becomes the chief source of authority in the training of children.

Egalitarianism is nowhere more evident than in the attitudes of modern parents toward their children. The child is granted rights which are uniquely his own. He is permitted much time for play. He may express his desires and feelings. He may question the opinions of his parents. Parents may, in spite of themselves or because of ignorance, require their children to fit into adult patterns, but this is not in keeping with their parental code. In some families not only do parents refrain from requiring their children to conform to the adult order of things, but most of the activities are organized around the children. This is known as the *child-centered family*. In some instances regard for the feelings, desires, and inclinations of children exists to such a degree that the term *child-dominated family* might be appropriate. As one father confessed, "There are times when I find it necessary to remind myself that parents also have rights." Such a statement serves to illustrate how far the family has moved away from the patriarchal system.

Size of Families

Modern families are smaller than their predecessors in two ways: the size of the meaningful kinship group is smaller, and the number of children in a family is smaller.

The great family, although not extinct, has become rare in the United States. Extended kinship groups never were exceedingly closely knit in this country, but urbanization and mobility have reduced whatever unity they once had. The bonds that bind relatives to each other are feeble. Members of kinship groups tend to be scattered, and they have infrequent opportunities for association. There are survivals of the larger kinship unit, notably in the upper classes, where the perpetuation of the great family is related to the function of the family in controlling wealth and in transmitting social status.

Most Americans identify themselves with the *simple* or *conjugal family* composed of father, mother, and children. Relatives are occasionally attached to the family, but by tenuous ties. The simple family does not need the great family. In pursuing its goals, the family must be free to move about and to make its own way unhampered by the wishes of relatives. The larger kinship group does not assume responsibility for the economic welfare of conjugal families, nor can it usually confer lasting status upon them. Hence the usefulness of the great family has declined.

The size of the conjugal family itself has been reduced. It is not a simple matter to discover the exact average size of families because of the definition employed by the United States census. The census family includes all persons in the household related to the head of the family by blood, marriage, or adoption. Nonmembers of the two-generation conjugal family are included, and therefore for our purposes the figures are distorted. However, on this basis, in 1790, 50.8 per cent of families had six or more members as compared to 32.8 per cent in 1900, 20.1 per cent in 1930, and 12.1 per cent in 1948. In 1790 the per cent of families having two or three members was only 20.2 as compared to 34.3 in 1900, 48.0 in 1930, and 56.9 in 1948. It must be stated that these statistics are not altogether comparable, since the figures for 1790 and 1900 include lodgers, servants, and other unrelated persons.[7] The reasons for this trend are discussed in Chapter 6.

Functions of the Family

Much has been written about the loss of the historical functions of the family, and with good reason, for many of the older functions have either declined or disappeared. Activities that were carried on in the home have been transferred elsewhere. The family is no longer an economic producing unit, this function having been taken over by specialized producing establishments. Responsibility for the formal education of children has shifted from the home to the school. The child spends an increasing amount of time in school. He starts school younger, remains in school until he is older, and attends school more months of the year. Religious training for children, once almost exclusively given by the family, is now provided by Sunday school and other church activities for the young. The recreational interests of family members are widely dispersed. For every family assemblage to take in favorite radio or television programs, there are countless occasions on which the members go their separate ways.

Even so, awareness of these declining activities must not obscure the continuing and increasing functions of the family. The modern family does a number of highly important things for its members, among which are its economic, educational, and affectional functions.

Although today the family is not an economic producing unit, it remains a consuming unit. In most families how much is consumed is determined by the earning power of the father. In some

[7] Ernest W. Burgess and Harvey J. Locke, *The Family*, New York, American Book, 1950, p. 496.

cases husband and wife cooperate in supporting their family. Between 1890 and 1948 the proportion of married women working outside the home increased from 4.6 to 22 per cent. Children may contribute to the family fund in small amounts, but they almost never earn enough to cover their full support. Up to a certain age, therefore, the economic dependence of children is just as real as it was when the family produced for its own consumption.

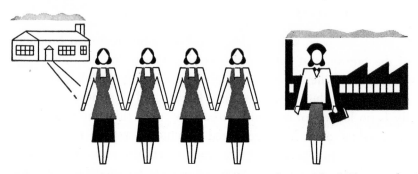

Figure 34. Working Mothers. One out of five mothers with children under eighteen years of age works outside the home. (From *Children and Youth at the Midcentury—A Chart Book*, prepared by the Midcentury White House Conference on Children and Youth, Raleigh, Health Publications Institute, 1951, p. 12.)

Closely related to the economic function of the family is its importance as a conferrer of status. To the extent that social status is associated with economic position in our society, the family confers status, either high or low, upon its members. The position of the wife is usually determined by that of her husband. The status of children is related to the position of their parents. In later years children may achieve status on their own, but during years of dependence economic status is transmitted through the family.

The educational function of the family is no longer that of assuming responsibility for the formal education of children. This task is being performed by the school. Nevertheless the family plays a primary part in the training of children. In view of the role of the school the place of the family has sometimes been discounted. There are parents who are inclined to turn over almost all child training to the school. There is, however, a type of training which cannot be delegated to the formal agencies of education. Willingly or unwillingly, consciously or unconsciously, there is an education that is transmitted through the family by the mere fact of association. For parents to attempt to leave the teaching and training of children to the school does not exclude them from participation in education. The growing child is constantly exposed to the customs, beliefs, and attitudes of his parents. Whether or not parents try to teach their children to accept these practices and ideas, children learn them or in some way are molded by them. In the early formative years, when the child is in most intimate contact with his family, he is extremely impressionable. Either in a positive or in a negative sense he continues to be influenced by his family throughout his youth. It is impossible for parents to escape some responsibility for the acceptance or the rejection of their culture by their children.

The primacy of parents in the transmission of attitudes to children was indicated in a study made by Hartshorne and May.[8] They assumed that the relative influence of the child's associates on his thinking could be measured by finding the degree of correspondence between the child's thinking and that of the people with whom he had regular contact. Children's ideas of right and wrong correlated with those of their associates as follows:

Child and his parents	0.545
Child and his friends	0.353
Child and his club leaders	0.137
Child and his day-school teachers	0.028
Child and his Sunday-school teachers	0.002

A perfect positive correlation would be 1.000; a perfect negative correlation would be −1.000.

What the school itself can achieve is dependent upon what the family does. Attitudes, manners, skills, and language are all part of the informal education of the child, and the family is one of the chief agencies for their transmission. A home-acquired atti-

8 "Testing the Knowledge of Right and Wrong," Religious Education Association, Monograph 1, 1927, pp. 47–48.

tude toward learning may condition the response of the child at school. Manners may have bearing on the social adjustment of the child, which in turn may be related to his academic success or failure. Minor skills learned at home can give the child an advantage in school. Language, which is basic in learning, derives from family training and usage. There appears to be a growing awareness of the importance of the family in complementing formal education and as an educational agency in its own right.

Family patterns of association have changed, but social contacts within the intimate family group are still meaningful in the psychological experiences of the individual. In some ways the affectional function of the family is made more significant by our type of society. A large proportion of our social contacts are of an impersonal nature. But there remains a need for association which affords intimacy and emotional security. There is need for a group in which the individual can be truly himself and accepted for what he is. This need can be met by the family.

It is evident that the family does not always fulfill this need. Emotional rejection of children by their parents is a common occurrence. Psychological divorce is one of the results of separation of the interests of husbands and wives. Yet the need for intimacy and for emotional security is still present. The unfulfilled need is likely to show itself in the personality of the individual and in his relationships with other persons. Hence the affectional function is important both because of what the family does and because of what it does not do. In a unique way the family can starve its members emotionally or it can nourish normal and healthy personality growth.

Family Stability

Measured in terms of the frequency of divorce, the family is less stable now than in the past. The annual number of divorces in the United States increased from about 33,000 in 1890 to a high of over 600,000 in 1946. In 1950 divorces numbered around 385,-000. In 1950 the population was less than two and a half times greater than in 1890, but the number of divorces was almost twelve times greater. The marriage rate was 9.0 per 1,000 population in 1890; 10.3 in 1910; 10.1 in 1929; 7.9 in 1932; 12.1 in 1940; 16.4 in 1946; and 11.1 in 1950. The divorce rate for the same years was 0.5 per 1,000 population in 1890; 0.9 in 1910; 1.7 in 1929; 1.3 in 1932; 2.0 in 1940; 4.3 in 1946; and 2.6 in 1950.

Any explanation of divorce is open to criticism. Each divorce has its own unique causes. It seems clear, however, that the long trend toward higher divorce rates is closely related to other social changes that have affected the family. The solidarity of the family which derived from the need for economic self-sufficiency has diminished. From an economic point of view a man can get along without a wife, and a woman can get along without a husband. Impersonal community relationships exercise less direct control over behavior than did the more intimate contacts of times past. The possible sources of culture and personality conflict have multiplied. Also it is doubtful whether the "equal but separate" roles of many husbands and wives give enduring satisfaction to marriage. Thus, while new sources of marital dissatisfaction and conflict have emerged, the social and economic forces that helped to hold marriages together have weakened. Affection then is left as a primary tie binding partners in matrimony.

An analysis of this sort gives great importance to affection in modern marriage. This will be regarded by many as an outstanding gain. It is certainly true that there is nothing loftily ethical about a relationship that lasts only because of economic necessity and social pressure. On the other hand, affection does not thrive in a vacuum. Common culture and cooperative activities seem to be helpful elements in the growth of lasting affection. Modern society has not been highly successful in supplying these elements or in finding substitutes for them.

Statistics and discussions on divorce frequently give a distorted view of the family. The family has changed; it is involved in the stresses and strains of culture change; family relationships contribute to personality problems; and some marriages end in divorce. Nevertheless in many respects the family is a stable institution; it continues to perform essential social functions; family relationships are of surpassing significance to family members; and most marriages do not end in divorce. Further family change may be expected, but it is also to be expected that the established importance of the family will continue.

SUMMARY

In early America great importance was attached to marriage, and everyone who could was expected to marry. Marriage at an early age was encouraged. Procreation was unlimited. In the family the father was the recognized head. The wife occupied a subordinate position and was expected to restrict her activities to the domestic sphere. Children were required to fit into adult patterns and were pressed into adulthood as rapidly as possible. Family unity was strong, and the meaningful kinship group extended beyond the simple family of father, mother, and children. Self-sufficiency was a family ideal.

The American family system has been exposed to strong social forces which altered it radically. The family has been influenced by the growth and spread of democratic ideals. Authoritarianism, subordination of children, and the inferior position of women were recognized as being inconsistent with the democratic mood. Further, economic changes affected family ideas and patterns of behavior. The family became less self-sufficient. Many of the economic functions of the family declined. New employment opportunities weakened family discipline. The status of women was raised by greater economic freedom. Ways of thinking were influenced by the trend toward the city. In the city success was individual rather than familial, and the freedom of the city weakened the control of traditional standards. Wars too have promoted the breakdown of established family ways.

The modern family stands in contrast to the traditional family system. Modern marriage is highly individualistic; it is usually regarded as an arrangement between two individuals rather than between two families. Thus in the making of marriages emphasis is placed on freedom of choice on the part of marriageable persons. In the selection of a marriage partner the importance of economic, educational, religious, and other cultural factors has been superseded by romantic love.

The modern family is more equalitarian. Women have more nearly equal rights with men. Women have departed from the solely domestic role, and their interests are regarded as being as important as those of men. Children have gained conspicuous new rights and privileges.

Modern families are smaller. The large kinship group, known as the great family, has almost disappeared. The meaningful kinship group is the conjugal family, and the size of the conjugal family itself is smaller.

Many of the traditional functions of the family have declined or disappeared. Nevertheless the family continues to have important functions. It is still an important economic unit. Family members are strongly dependent upon the family for support. The family is also a leading educational group. Much of the informal training of children is acquired in the family. The success of formal education depends in part on family efforts. The affectional function of the family is as important as ever, and in some respects more important.

Social change has disrupted family patterns. Marriage relationships have been affected. The number of broken marriages indicates that the family has declined in stability. Even so the family system, although subject to change, continues to serve individual and social needs.

SELECTED REFERENCES

American Journal of Sociology, vol. 53, May, 1948.
Baber, Ray E.: *Marriage and the Family*, New York, McGraw-Hill, 1953.

Burgess, E. W., and L. S. Cottrell: *Predicting Success or Failure in Marriage,* New York, Prentice-Hall, 1939.

—— and H. J. Locke, *The Family,* New York, American Book, 1953.

Calhoun, Arthur W.: *A Social History of the American Family,* Cleveland, Ohio, Clark, 1917–1919, 3 vols.; republished by Barnes & Noble, New York, 1945.

Frazier, E. Franklin: *The Negro Family in the United States,* Chicago, University of Chicago Press, 1939.

Goodsell, Willystine: *A History of Marriage and the Family,* New York, Macmillan, 1935.

Hagood, Margaret Jarman: *Mothers of the South,* Chapel Hill, N.C., University of North Carolina Press, 1939.

Kinsey, A. C., et al.: *Sexual Behavior in the Human Female,* Philadelphia, Saunders, 1953.

——: *Sexual Behavior in the Human Male,* Philadelphia, Saunders, 1948.

Landis, Judson T., and Mary G. Landis: *Readings in Marriage and the Family,* New York, Prentice-Hall, 1952.

Lichtenberger, J. P.: *Divorce,* New York, McGraw-Hill, 1931.

Nimkoff, Meyer F.: *Marriage and the Family,* Boston, Houghton Mifflin, 1947.

Terman, Lewis, et al.: *Psychological Factors in Marital Happiness,* New York, McGraw-Hill, 1938.

Waller, Willard, and Reuben Hill: *The Family,* New York, Dryden, 1951.

CHAPTER FIFTEEN

Economic Institutions

The development of economic institutions in the United States demonstrates well that institutional change is a result of many and complex factors. Institutions are not altered merely by the passing of time, but by the interaction of social forces. The necessities of subsistence, material equipment and inventions, conflict and accommodation among groups, the force of conflicting institutions—these and more are involved in molding and modifying economic institutions.

EARLY CAPITALISM

To understand the present economic organization of the United States it is necessary to see the background out of which it came. The economic practices and ideas of today are the result of a long process of adjustment and change.

The Rise of Capitalism

The beginning goes back to thirteenth-century Europe. At that time the economy of Europe was largely agricultural. By far the greater portion of the population lived in rural areas, where their lives were controlled by firmly fixed traditions and by the power of feudal lords. They lived in small settlements called vills or manors. Land was owned by the king, the nobility, or the church, but these overlords were guided by well-established customs with regard to the use of land. Villagers worked part of the time on the land of the lord and the rest of the time on plots assigned to them. They could not move from place to place at will; thus families worked the same land for generations. A small group of villagers sold their services as craftsmen. What was produced on the manor was consumed there, and each community was self-sufficient to a large degree.

A relatively small number of persons lived in towns and cities. Some of the inhabitants of towns cultivated nearby fields or had plots of their own. Others depended on handicrafts or on trading and commerce for a living. Apprentices and journeymen worked in the small shops of master craftsmen. For the most part master craftsmen sold their products directly to consumers. In addition to buying and selling in small shops trading was carried on at weekly or semiweekly town markets and at fairs held twice a year near the larger towns. Associations of craftsmen and traders, called guilds, rigidly regulated economic activities in towns and cities. A minimum of exchange took place between towns, although there was trading between towns and surrounding country districts. Foreign trade, which was on a small scale, was regulated by government-recognized associations of traders.

The changes which led to the emergence of capitalism did not occur rapidly, nor did they take place in all European countries at the same time. The transition from the old to the new economy was in the initial stages in the fourteenth and fifteenth centuries. Several centuries after the discovery of America were required, however, before capitalism took the form which became the basis of American economic life.

The advent of capitalism was marked by the decline of the local subsistence economy of the medieval manor and by the rise of an economy of trading and commerce. The change showed itself first in the northern Italian cities of Venice, Genoa, and Florence. Here manufacturers began to join together to accumulate enough capital to make possible trading between cities. After commerce with the East was promoted by the Crusades goods were distributed through Italian cities to the countries of western Europe. Along trade routes towns and cities appeared. The desire of western European merchants to gain some of the profits that Italians were enjoying from trading with the East brought about a search for new trade routes. With the consequent discovery of America, the attention of traders was diverted from the East to the New World, and the center of commerce shifted from the Mediterranean region to western Europe.

The new foreign commerce enterprises required capital, more capital than individuals and small groups could provide. To meet this need large trading companies were formed. Because they believed that national welfare and power were involved, the governments of the various countries of Europe took much interest in the affairs of trading companies. In Spain most trading was directly controlled and supported by the Government. In England private capital was used, but the government granted rights and gave protection and encouragement.

At the same time manufacturing and domestic trading were stimulated. Local marketing and producing units, however, continued to be small. The expansion was in the number of units, not in their size. As more producers entered the field, regulation by guilds diminished. New industries developed which could not be controlled by guilds. Merchants struggled to get out from under guild control of the conditions under which trading could be carried on. New methods of financing the growing enterprises were devised. Merchants had been an early source of borrowed money. Goldsmiths, with whom money was deposited for safekeeping, began to lend money from these deposits. As it became acceptable to charge interest for money lent, the moneylending business became quite profitable. Banking as such, however, was not established for some time. The first bank, the Bank of England, was chartered in 1694.

The developments outlined above occurred over a period of almost 500 years, beginning in the thirteenth century and extending into the eighteenth century. The changes most directly associated with the rise of capitalism came more rapidly after 1500 than before. By the time of the rebellion of the American colonies the new economy had taken rather definite form.

The Creed of Capitalism

Early capitalism could be identified by its precepts as well as by its practices. It consisted of more than a set of ways of carrying on economic life. It had produced a set of beliefs about these ways of doing things. Along with capitalistic practices a capitalistic creed developed. The chief ideas and beliefs of capitalism were related to (1) private property, (2) the profit motive, (3) freedom of enterprise, and (4) the price system.

1. Property is the legal right to acquire, to use, and to dispose of wealth. The right of individuals to use and control wealth has not always and everywhere existed. The possessions of primitive man were few. Property rights were first recognized with respect to clothing, tools, household untensils, and weapons. Under feudalism, the right to use and control land, the most important agent of production, was regulated as much by custom as by law. The whole system was based on an accepted arrangement of rights, duties, and privileges, in relation to which legal property rights were a minor consideration. But when feudalism disintegrated and the economy came to be dominated by buying and selling, by profit making, by transportation of goods to and from distant places, then a man's possessions acquired new significance. He transferred rights to others in exchange for rights transferred to him. For this economy of exchange, tradition and custom were inadequate. Law was required to define property rights. Moreover the new capitalists wanted to be free to manipulate their possessions unhampered by custom and tradition, or even by law. Thus developed the belief that it is a function of law to grant the rights of private property, but that law should control the use of wealth only to the least possible degree.

2. Under the new economy, money-making achieved respectability. This was the most striking reversal of attitudes that accompanied the rise of capitalism. In the precapitalistic period, seeking financial gain was regarded as a tainted activity. To sell a commodity for more than it cost was frowned upon. The church taught

that it was unethical to ask interest for money lent. Civil laws helped to enforce the church's prohibitions against charging interest. There was a small money-making group, but it was not highly respected. But when, under the new system, more persons realized financial gain, it became acceptable to do so. The profit motive was then defended as inevitable and desirable. Pecuniary self-interest was believed to be essential for the economic welfare of all. It was held that without profit-seeking the economy would have no driving force. Religion gave its support to the idea by regarding the acquisition of wealth as a mark of industry and of virtue. The money-making group was elevated from a low to a high position.

3. Briefly stated, the idea of freedom of enterprise is that every individual knows best what will serve his economic well-being; that by enhancing his own economic position the individual best promotes the welfare of all; and that therefore the individual must be granted all possible freedom to work out his own economic destiny. The origin of this belief is not to be found in objections to modern economic controls. On the contrary, in its origin the freedom-of-enterprise ideology was a protest against traditional group control over economic activity. It has already been noted that, bound by powerful customs, the overlords supervised economic activities in feudal communities. In towns and cities all phases of economic life were regulated by guilds. When foreign commerce became profitable the national governments of Europe, under a system known as mercantilism, used their power to control commerce in order that state ends might be served. All these, or any other types of regulation, proved irksome to profit-seeking artisans, traders, and financiers. They wanted to be free to exploit the market fully, without interference by custom or law. Practical men of the market place were supported by economic theorists who taught that when individuals pursue pecuniary advantages for themselves they thereby promote the welfare of their fellows; therefore group control of economic affairs is unnecessary and undesirable.

Applied to government, freedom of enterprise meant nonparticipation by government in business. This is the doctrine of *laissez faire*. It was built on the predication that government and business have separate spheres in which to operate, and that the functions of government have little to do with economic activities. According to the doctrine, government should be almost, but not entirely, divorced from business. Allowance was made for a few protective functions. Government should ensure the rights of private property, enforce contracts, and referee competition when necessary. But on the whole it was believed that in economic matters "that government is best that governs least."

4. It was not held that when government remains aloof from business the economy is left unregulated. The ever-functioning regulator is the market. It is supply and demand on the market that maintains order in the economy. This is known as the *price system*. Everything that is exchanged on the market has its price. This is true of land, capital, and services, as well as commodities. Those who engage in exchange have equal bargaining power. When supply is great in relation to demand, the price goes down; when supply is scarce in relation to demand, the price goes up. In this way rents, interest, wages, and the cost of goods are automatically regulated and kept in balance. Because of the automatic control from within, regulation from without, particularly by government, produces disorder instead of order. The economy functions best when the private-property right of every individual to use his possessions as he chooses is protected, when every individual gives full expression to the desire to gain profit, and when the free market is not interfered with in any way. This was the interpretation of the price system.

EXPANSION AND CHANGE IN AMERICA

In 1776 the case for capitalism was set forth by the Scottish philosopher-economist, Adam Smith, in his influential work, *An Inquiry into the Nature and Causes of the Wealth of Nations*. By this time, too, economic life in Europe and in America was entering a new era. Already changes were taking place which were to modify tremendously the operation of the economy. Up to the latter part of the eighteenth century the character of capitalism was determined chiefly by trading; it was *commercial capitalism.* At the opening of the nineteenth century early capitalism was on the verge of being revolutionized by expansion of production and by new methods of finance.

Industry

Colonial America was predominantly agricultural. Industrial production was limited. Clothing, soap, candles, shoes, tools, and furniture were manufactured at home for use there. There was also some household manufacture for the outside market. The production of such things as nails, shingles, casks, pottery, and tools sometimes expanded into small shops. Most of the work was done by hand. At the end of the colonial period the factory system was unknown. Only in a few of the larger towns were several weaving machines to be found in the same shop.

Then followed two fundamental changes in methods of manufacture: (1) handicraft was replaced by machine production, and (2) manufacture was taken out of homes and into factories. These innovations and the changes that accompanied them are referred to as the *Industrial Revolution.* The transition in methods of manufacture began in England and spread to the United States. In this country the change was under way, at least to a minor extent, at the end of the eighteenth century.

Early industrial expansion was gradual. Adoption of machine production and the factory system was not rapid. Factories in which the spinning jenny was used were opened in Philadelphia and in Beverly, Massachusetts, in 1787. In a factory founded in 1814 in Waltham, Massachusetts, spinning and weaving were for the first time carried on at the same place by mechanical means. The textile industry led all others in the adoption of the factory system, in the number of persons employed, and in the amount of

Factory Organization in the Shoe Industry. The factory system involves the bringing together of workers to one place to carry on related activities. The organization of workers results in a detailed division of labor. An attempt is made to gear each operation to all others.

capital involved. Growth in cotton textiles was most rapid. Woolen machinery was introduced later than cotton machinery, and household manufacture of wool was prolonged. Growth in the woolen industry was speeded up after 1840. Iron production was another of the important early industries. American industry has always been heavily dependent upon iron and steel. The factory system required the manufacture of a steadily increasing number of machines. The demand for larger quantities of iron was expanded still further by the use of the steam engine for transportation. By 1850 processing food outside the home was on the increase. Flour milling; factory meat packing; manufacture of by-products from hoofs, hair, and fats; and production of beverages were growing industries around the middle of the century.

Notwithstanding the considerable industrial growth in the United States up to 1850, it must be pointed out that most manufacturing

Machine Production in the Textile Industry. The function of the worker in many factory processes is to act as overseer to a machine. In almost every type of manufacturing reliance is placed on machines to do rapid and laborsaving work.

was still carried on at home or in small shops. Furthermore the economy was still essentially agricultural. But after 1850 American economic life was increasingly influenced by two factors: (1) the rapid expansion of industrialization, and (2) large-scale production.

The years between 1850 and 1860 marked the opening of a period of phenomenal industrial expansion. In that decade textile and iron industries increased by two-thirds. By 1890 manufacturing exceeded agriculture as the chief source of wealth. At the turn of the century the value of manufactured products was more than twice that of agricultural products. Already in 1894 the United States had become the leading manufacturing nation in the world. The value of manufactured goods increased eighteenfold from

1859 to 1914, and thirty-threefold from 1859 to 1919. The value of manufactured products increased from \$23 billion in 1914 to \$60 billion in 1919 to \$140 billion in 1945. The increase of manufacturing has involved the growth of old industries and the appear-

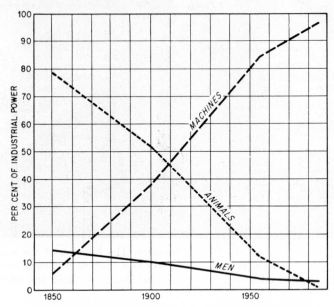

Figure 35. Sources of Power in Industry. Since 1850 the sources of power have changed radically. Men and animals have contributed a smaller and smaller percentage of the power; machines have contributed a larger and larger percentage. Estimates carry the curve beyond 1980. (From Karl T. Compton, "Engineers," *Scientific American*, September, 1951, p. 66.)

ance of many new. Outstanding among the industries that have come to the fore in the present century are the petroleum, automobile, electrical, chemical, rubber, and machinery industries.

The expansion of manufacturing has been accompanied by a trend toward large-scale production and industrial concentration. In some fields of manufacturing a few large industries came to dominate. The concentration was first evident particularly in the iron and steel, cotton-textiles, and leather industries. To a lesser degree it existed in the farm-implements, carpet, glass, boot and

Ford Motor Company

Air View of the Ford Rouge Plant, Dearborn, Michigan. Here concentrated large-scale industrial organization reaches enormous proportions. On 1,212 acres are located ore docks, coke ovens, blast furnaces, steel mills, a glass factory, a paper mill, and automotive plants. The power plant could supply all the homes in Boston with electric power. As much water is used as in Detroit, Washington, and Cincinnati combined. There are 22 diesel locomotives, 110 miles of railroad tracks, 81 miles of conveyers, and four bus lines. Almost 60,000 people are employed, and the daily payroll is approximately $1 million.

shoe, paper, tobacco, meat-packing, and shipbuilding industries. The trend did not show itself in industries that were essentially local. Industrial concentration is now characteristic of most of the leading fields of manufacturing. In recent decades in the steel and automobile industries three or four major corporations have been responsible for more than one-half the production. In 1929, of the total number of manufacturing establishments of all types, 6 per cent had an output valued at $1 million or more, but this 6

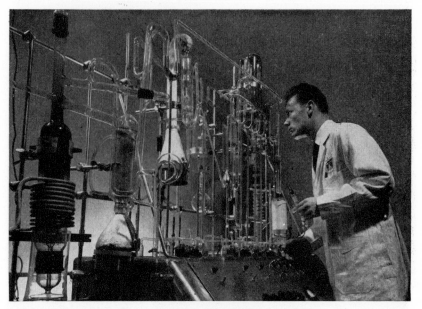

Systematic Research Helps to Guide Much Modern Production.

per cent employed nearly 60 per cent of the wage earners. In 1945 the 250 largest manufacturing corporations owned 66.5 per cent of the total manufacturing capacity of the nation.

Agriculture

At the same time that manufacturing methods were being revolutionized, a similar transformation was occurring in agriculture. Before 1825 the farmer had to depend on hoes, shovels, forks, rakes, harrows, and wooden plows, frequently homemade and crude. Then appeared a number of improvements. The metal plow came into general use after 1825. In the 1830's mowing and reaping machines were built. The threshing machine took the place of older methods. Horse hayrakes, seed drills, rollers, and cultivators helped to increase the number of acres that one man could farm. Greater attention was given to crop rotation, and the importance of fertilizer was recognized. Thus it became possible for the farmer to raise more than could be consumed by his family, and special-

TVA

Generators at Fontana Dam, North Carolina—Symbols of the Vast Power Production Required in the United States.

ized and commercial agriculture tended to replace self-sufficient farming.

These advances occurred before 1860, but it would hardly be correct to say that agriculture was revolutionized by that time. The real revolution in American agriculture came after 1860. The first farm machines were rapidly improved, and new inventions were added. Sulky plows, sulky harrows, improved seeders, and straddle-row cultivators speeded up the planting process. Haying was facilitated by the sulky rake and by loading, stacking, and baling equipment. Hand shelling and later hand cutting of corn were made unnecessary. The combine was created to perform the reaping and threshing operations at the same time. The tractor was introduced around 1905. Although at first its adoption was

Picking Corn in Pennsylvania. The use of farm machinery has increased the production per man, and it has also helped to increase production per acre.

slow, it has made the horse practically extinct as a work animal in large sections of the country. It is estimated that farm use of power increased eight times between 1900 and 1935. Scientific farming moved ahead after 1890, when the supply of land was less abundant, and American farmers became interested in the yield per acre as well as in the yield per man.

The mechanization of agriculture produced significant results in addition to making farming less laborious. It changed the character of agricultural operations, and it has changed the economic position of the farmer. Today one farmer can cultivate far more land than could be cultivated by one man in the premachinery days. It is estimated that, compared to horse farming, mechanization has trebled the acreage that one man can cultivate. This greater productivity of farm labor has brought about an increase in the size of farms.

Insomuch as the economic position of the farmer is concerned,

Mechanical Cotton Picker. Although cotton farming long resisted mechanization, the use of machinery is gradually increasing.

one of the results of the revolution in agriculture was to make the
farmer more dependent on money. Now his economic well-being
is not determined by his ability to produce those things needed by
his family; it is determined rather by his ability to acquire enough
money to buy what is needed. The modern farmer has become
much involved in buying and selling. Thus his economic welfare
is intimately related to the economic welfare of the country as a
whole.

Of equal importance to the nonagricultural population is the
meaning of the rising productivity of farm labor. In brief it means
that an increasing proportion of nonfarmers are dependent on a
decreasing proportion of farmers. In 1790 it was necessary for 95
out of every 100 persons to be engaged in farming in order to
provide food and agricultural raw materials for the nation; now

USDA

Combining Wheat in Kansas. Wheat farming is the most highly mechanized type of agriculture. Also it is in big-scale wheat production that the largest farm machines are used.

fewer than 25 out of 100 persons must be so employed. This has the effect of heightening the economic dependence of a greater proportion of the population. What the farmer does and does not do has far-reaching consequences.

Transportation and Communication

Transportation and communication have been primary factors in shaping the economy of the United States. They have facilitated expansion. Without adequate transportation and communication a national economy would have been impossible and American economic life would have remained essentially local in nature.

Already at the opening of the nineteenth century there was awareness of the inadequacy of existing means of transportation. Inland waterways were utilized as much as possible, but overland transportation was avoided because of the prohibitive cost. Construction of turnpikes was one of the steps taken to correct this situation. The achievements of turnpikes were limited because local needs were given first consideration, and therefore construction of through routes was retarded. In the building of canals more attention was given to other than local needs. One of the objectives of canal promoters was to obtain waterways to the states further west. After the War of 1812 canal construction proceeded with some enthusiasm for about twenty-five years.

The breakdown of a local type of economy was aided by the advent of the steamboat. Although others had built steamboats before him, it was Robert Fulton who made a success of the invention when he sailed the *Clermont* from New York to Albany and back in 1807. In 1809 one steamboat was in use on Lake Champlain, one on the Raritan, and one on the Delaware. Two years later the steamboat was introduced in the West on the Ohio. Probably no part of the country benefited as much from the early use of steamboats as the West. In the region of the Mississippi and its tributaries, the river boat became the link between local and distant markets. Steamboats appeared on the Great Lakes around 1817, but their adoption for lake transport was less rapid than on rivers. The regular use of steam-powered vessels for trans-Atlantic trade occurred around 1840.

The most important innovation in transportation was the railroad. It is hardly possible to overemphasize the effect of railroads on the American economy. The first railroad of any consequence, the Baltimore and Ohio, was opened for traffic in 1830. At that time the country had about twenty-three miles of railroad. The first transcontinental railroad was completed in 1869. By the time of the First World War a network of railroads covered the entire country.

In recent decades other means of transportation have gained in importance. The automobile has changed the working habits of millions of Americans; it influences both where they work and often the kind of work they do. The improvement of highways has resulted in a rapid increase in the number of motor trucks. These trucks are now giving serious competition to railroads for freight traffic. It is estimated that motor trucks carry almost 25 per cent of all traffic moved on land. The most spectacular transportation invention was the airplane. The extensive use of air transportation for commercial purposes is relatively recent.

Only brief mention can be made of developments in the field of communication. The telegraph and the telephone have facilitated commercial contacts. The postal service, including rural free delivery, began in 1896; the parcel-post system was introduced in 1912. These provided a new means of economic exchange. As one of the mass media the press provides a ready source of business news and is one of the chief means of advertising. Radio and television are also leading channels of advertising.

The economic significance of changes in the fields of transportation and communication has already been suggested. They were instrumental in bringing about the decline of a local type of economy. Markets were widened. Local and regional specialization developed. Easy contact throughout the country between persons having business to transact was made possible. In short a national economy emerged. Furthermore, as similar changes occurred in other countries and as commerce between countries expanded, a world economy was established.

Finance

The economic expansion which has taken place in this country during the last 150 years has involved notable results in the field of finance. Capital accumulated, production increased, and trading was extended. At the same time saving was promoted, credit was needed, and facilities for carrying on financial transactions became an essential part of the economy. It is not necessary here to discuss all the financial developments, but attention may be called to three of the more important: banking, corporate finance, and security markets.

Banks deal in money and credit. They provide a place where funds may be deposited, and they make loans to persons who need to borrow. Usually they lend their credit rather than their funds. The part played by banks in extending credit may be seen by observing that in 1929 the bank capital in the United States was about $5,500,000,000, on the basis of which banks had lent about $50,000,000,000.

The first real bank in this country, the Bank of North America, was founded in Philadelphia in 1781. Early banks were located in seaport towns and commercial centers, but the need for credit in other places soon led to the opening of banks serving smaller local communities. The number of banks increased from 28 to more than 1,600 between 1800 and the beginning of the Civil War. By 1920 there were nearly 30,000 banks. In addition banking functions are performed by organizations such as trust companies, finance companies, loan companies, and credit unions.

One of the principal instruments of modern business organization and finance is the corporation. A business corporation is a legally constituted association of individuals joined together to carry on a common enterprise. It is, above all else, a device for raising capital. In a modern economy in which large-scale operations are possible, it is often impossible for single individuals or small groups of individuals to provide the capital necessary to carry through the enterprises which they are able to envisage. Corporate enterprise is the result. The directors of a corporation are legally authorized to secure funds. Persons who lend their money are the "owners" of the business. Ownership is expressed in shares of stock. Shares of stock are transferable from one individual to another, and ownership may be highly concentrated or widely distributed.

When the Constitution became effective in 1789, there were only 21 business corporations in the United States, and almost none of these were manufacturing companies. As business developed on a large scale the number of corporations grew, so that by 1904 there were at least 51,094 manufacturing corporations in this country, and by 1932 there were 91,849. In recent decades the trend has been for corporations to increase in size rather than in

number. Despite the large number of corporations, their importance in our economy cannot be measured by counting how many
corporations there are. Most manufacturing establishments in
this country are not corporations; nevertheless about nine-tenths
of all manufactured products are made by corporations.

As business ownership came increasingly to be expressed in
terms of stocks and bonds, centers appeared in which stocks and
bonds, referred to as *securities,* could be bought and sold. Markets
in which securities are sold when they are first issued are called
new-issues markets. Markets in which "old"securities are bought
and sold are called *stock exchanges.* New-issues markets tend to
be widely scattered; stock exchanges are concentrated in the largest commercial centers, especially in New York City. It is the function of security markets to facilitate the transfer not of goods and
commodities but of capital.

Labor

As the American economy has expanded and changed, the position of labor has been greatly altered. Indeed, before the invention of power machines and the rise of the factory system, only a
small class of people worked regularly for wages. In the colonial
period workers in agriculture and domestic manufacture tended
to be self-employed. But in the nineteenth century mechanization
and the reorganization of industry resulted in a large class of wage
earners. In the new economy the division into employer and employee groups became definite. Some persons promoted, financed,
and managed the new and expanding enterprises, and large groups
of other persons came to them to work for wages.

For many years workers were largely, but not entirely, unorganized. The movement to organize wage earners developed slowly.
A number of local craft organizations were formed before 1800.
Workers in factories began to organize in the 1820's. The date for
the beginning of a real labor movement is often given as 1827.
In that year the Philadelphia carpenters were joined by other
building trades in a strike for a ten-hour day. This action led to

the formation of the Philadelphia Mechanics' Union of Trade Associations. Similar associations were organized in other cities. A number of trades established national organizations. A national meeting of labor representatives was convened for the first time in 1834.

Many of the purposes of early labor organizations were not unlike those of labor unions today. They wanted to protect their wages and increase them if possible. Attempts were made to shorten working hours, to improve working conditions, and to gain various kinds of other benefits. It is significant that one of the chief demands of the first labor party, formed in 1827 and called the *Working Man's Party*, was for universal, free, public education. Apparently some of the early leaders of labor foresaw that education could be a most important avenue of occupational and economic mobility for the children of wage workers.

After the 1830's the fortunes of trade-unions fluctuated for some time. Union membership and activity declined following the panic of 1837. Many of the early organizations disintegrated. A recovery was made in the 1850's and new trade unions were formed. The pattern of union growth during periods of prosperity and union decline during economic depressions was repeated several times. At the close of the 1860's about thirty-two national trade-unions were in existence. It is estimated that in 1886 the total membership of all labor unions was almost one million.

A most important development in the labor movement in the latter part of the nineteenth century was the trend toward cooperation among unions of different trades and industries. The precursors of this trend were the National Labor Union and the Knights of Labor. Each enjoyed a brief period of power and then disappeared. In 1881 several groups called a convention which led to the formation of the American Federation of Labor in 1886. As the name suggests, the purpose of the new organization was not to replace but to federate the separate unions in order to make possible the achievement of common goals.

From the 1880's to the 1930's the American Federation of Labor

(AFL) occupied the ascendant position in organized labor. Even so, until 1898 the growth of the federation was slow. Thereafter its growth was more rapid. Between 1898 and 1904 membership increased from 278,000 to over 1,600,000. The membership of the federation in 1904 included about 81 per cent of the membership of all unions. A second burst of growth came during the First World War. Membership increased from 2 million to 4 million between 1914 and 1920. Most of the unions in the federation were craft unions, but several industry-wide unions were also affiliated. Not all the major unions joined the federation; a number of important groups steadfastly maintained their independence.

Until the 1930's the majority of unionized workers belonged to trade-unions rather than to industrial unions. A trade-union is made up of workers in the same craft. Unions of bricklayers, painters, or plumbers are examples of this type. An industrial union is constituted of workers in the same industry and includes persons in different kinds of work, both skilled and unskilled. The organization of the Knights of Labor was of the industrial-union type. The Industrial Workers of the World, formed in 1905, was militant in promoting industrial unions. The United Mine Workers of America and the International Longshoremen's Association were among the larger industrial unions. It was not until the 1930's, however, that industrial unionism flourished. At that time the AFL itself organized many unions of the industrial type, but some groups within the AFL did not consider the efforts sufficiently aggressive. As a result in 1935 the Committee for Industrial Organization was formed. This group broke with the AFL and established a new organization committed to the promotion of industrial unionism. In 1938 the name was changed to the Congress of Industrial Organizations (CIO).

This review of the background of the American labor movement should not create a false impression. Organized labor has a long history in this country, but it did not achieve major importance until recent decades. The turning point came in the 1930's. A favorable climate in government and impetus within the movement combined to effect the change. Both in membership and in power organized labor surged ahead. Between 1935 and 1945 the total number of union members increased from around 3,400,000 to approximately 13,600,000. In 1953 the AFL reported 8,500,000 members, the CIO reported 5,000,000 members, and independent unions reported 2,500,000 members.

Today organized labor is economically and politically powerful. Labor unions are a force to be reckoned with in the councils of industry and in the decisions of government. Many of the early objectives concerning hours, wages, and working conditions have been achieved to a large degree. To the first objectives have been added new and broader goals. Labor unions have an established role in representing workers in a wide variety of matters affecting their present well-being and their future security. Union organization has become an integral part of the industrial structure. To a degree it has also become part of the nonofficial political structure.

As labor unions have expanded in size they have tended to become increasingly bureaucratic in organization. They have developed systematic and standard administrative procedures. Many situations involving union members are regulated by impersonal rules. Hierarchical definitions require local unions to accept the decisions of the larger organization, and subordinate officials are expected to execute policies and programs determined at higher levels. Although procedures are employed by which union members vote approval or disapproval of policies and officials, policy making is largely the function of top officials. Membership in the policy-making group comes after a long process of struggle, performance, and selection.

Modern labor unions, then, are not directed by amateurs. In most respects the individual worker has no more control over the specific conditions of his employment than he did before unions were formed. Instead the individual worker gives his support to professional labor representatives who bargain with employers in fixing the terms of employment. The bargaining power of labor representatives derives, of course, from the willingness of workers collectively to withhold their services when the conditions of employment are defined as unsatisfactory. Labor-contract patterns are usually set in negotiations involving top union officials and officials of large corporations or associations of corporations.

ECONOMIC PROBLEMS

It has been seen that as the economy of the United States expanded it underwent great change. The expansion and change in turn brought new problems to the fore. Some of the problems were actually new; others were merely old problems in a different or more extreme form. Six major problem areas of our economy will be considered here: economic instability, income and economic insecurity, agricultural problems, monopolies, industrial conflict, and international economic problems.

Economic Instability

Our economy is characterized by fluctuations in production and business activity. There are periods of intense activity and expansion followed by periods of diminished activity and contraction. These periods of heightened and diminished activity vary in length. Sometimes the expansion or the contraction lasts less than two years; at other times it may continue for more than a decade. Because of the wavelike pattern of the successive rising and falling movements they are called *business cycles.*

Throughout the history of the United States the economy has passed through many periods of depression, albeit not all of equal severity. There was a financial crash in 1837, when banks that overextended their credit demanded repayment of loans. Banks were much involved again in 1857 when another boom ended and a depression began. In part because of reckless railroad finance, the country was thrust into a four-year depression in 1873. The panic of 1893, precipitated by railroad bankruptcies, was followed by a depression of three and a half years. There was a brief but sharp financial crisis in 1907 and again in 1914. After the First

World War the wartime prosperity was followed by a reaction which started in 1920.

The most recent and most severe depression in our history was the one that followed the stock-market crash of 1929. With one unsuspected stroke the economy was sent reeling into a recession from which recovery was slow. The depression of the 1930's was one of unprecedented proportions. Wholesale prices declined 38 per cent from the 1929 peak. The price of farm products dropped almost 60 per cent. In 1932 industrial production was 46 per cent below 1929. Between 1929 and 1933 national income fell 44 per cent. It is estimated that the number of unemployed reached 15 million.

Minor fluctuations in business may perhaps be considered irritating but inevitable. It is difficult to take the same attitude toward major depressions. The economic welfare of many persons is involved. Life savings may be wiped out, investments and businesses are destroyed, and endowments are swallowed up. Millions of persons are deprived of the opportunity to earn a living. Variations in economic activity are not new, but the consequences are intensified and extended in a highly industrialized, money-dependent economy, in which economic security derives not from the capacity to produce for oneself, but rather from the opportunity to earn a wage or a salary. The seriousness of depressions is all the greater inasmuch as various segments of economic life are intricately related.

Income and Economic Insecurity

In the final analysis one of the best ways to provide higher levels of living and greater economic security is to maintain a stable and highly productive economy. But the plane of living that an individual or a family can sustain does not depend merely on the total national production of goods; it depends also on the way in which goods are distributed. In our society the distribution of goods is determined largely by the distribution of income, and for most persons income depends upon the opportunity regularly to sell their services for a satisfactory wage or salary. Anything that decreases this opportunity, whether it be depressions, inadequate wages, accidents, sickness, or old age, lowers the level of living and causes economic insecurity.

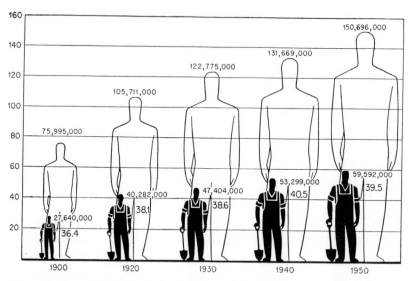

Figure 36. Size of the Labor Force as Compared to the Total Population, United States, 1900–1950. The numbers at the left side of this diagram are millions of people. The large figures represent the total population; the smaller figures in black, the labor force. Beside each of the figures is the number of people that it symbolizes. Beneath each of these numbers for the labor force is the percentage of the total population that it represents. (From Ewan Clague, "Labor Force," *Scientific American*, September, 1951, p. 38.)

It is one of the contradictions of modern life that even in times of prosperity there are persons who subsist on the meagerest of incomes. The prosperity is not enjoyed by all. In 1947, of the total spending units—individuals and families—14 per cent received less than $1,000 of money income. All together this 14 per cent of the spending units received only 2 per cent of the aggregate money income of the United States. In the long run it appears that the whole economy suffers from such inequity. The prosperity of the 1920's was not well distributed and the consequences were dire for all. As well-known economists have put it: [1] "Although the United States had increased production, it had not proportionately or simultaneously expanded distribution. Truly it is an uncertain or ill-digested prosperity that is unable to consume its own huge output because of a maldistribution of purchasing power among the masses of people and because of instability of income over periods of time."

Insufficient income during periods of employment is only one of the causes of economic insecurity; another is the threat of unemployment. This is a problem which to some extent is a product of modern life, for the problem is particularly acute in an economy of industrialization and specialization. Rewards in earlier agricultural economies were limited, but men who tilled the soil never lacked employment and the means for gaining sustenance. In our society there are a variety of sources of unemployment. The types of unemployment may be classified according to their causes. Cyclical unemployment is that which is a result of the depression phase of the business cycle. Seasonal unemployment is found in those industries in which there is a decline or a cessation of activity at certain times during the year. Technological unemployment is due to the displacement of men by machines in particular industries. So-called casual unemployment results from daily and weekly fluctuations in the amount of work to be done. Other hazards to economic security are accidents, sickness, and old age. It is obvious that much unemployment is brought about by circumstances over which the individuals who are victims have little control.

Agricultural Problems

The problems of agriculture clearly demonstrate the relatedness of the various segments of our economy. The farmer's problems are not exclusively his problems; they are the problems of the entire population. It is doubtful whether national prosperity can long

[1] S. Howard Patterson and Karl W. H. Scholz, *Economic Problems in Modern Life*, New York, McGraw-Hill, 1948, p. 534.

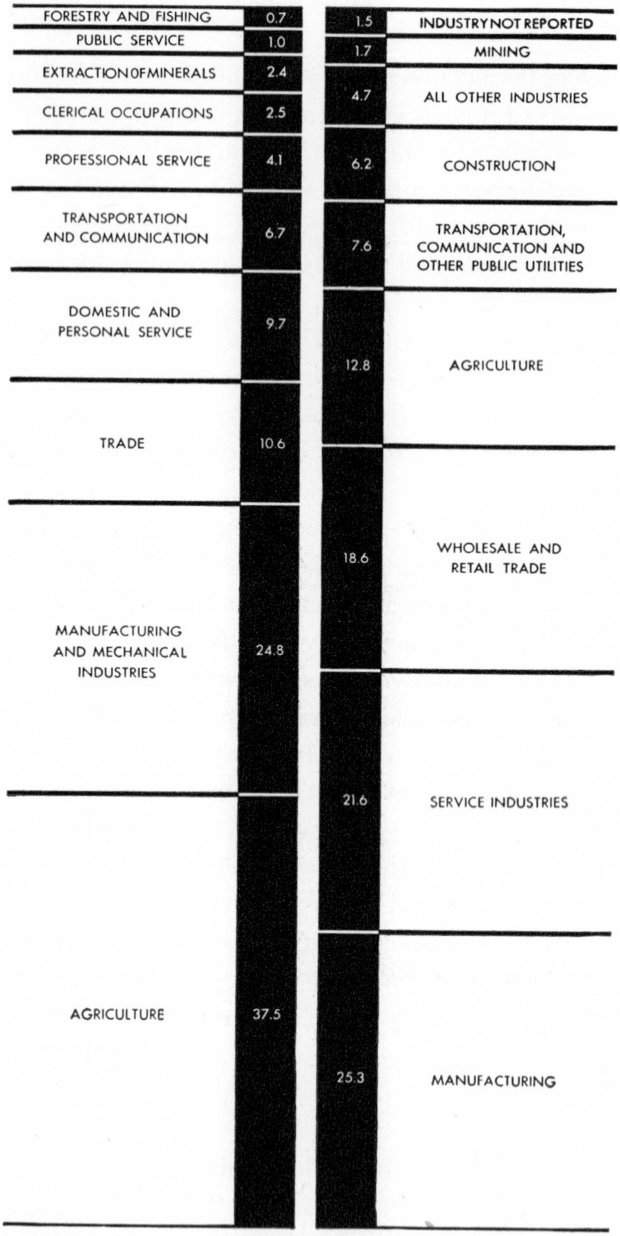

	1900 (left)	1950 (right)	
FORESTRY AND FISHING	0.7	1.5	INDUSTRY NOT REPORTED
PUBLIC SERVICE	1.0	1.7	MINING
EXTRACTION OF MINERALS	2.4		
		4.7	ALL OTHER INDUSTRIES
CLERICAL OCCUPATIONS	2.5		
PROFESSIONAL SERVICE	4.1	6.2	CONSTRUCTION
TRANSPORTATION AND COMMUNICATION	6.7	7.6	TRANSPORTATION, COMMUNICATION AND OTHER PUBLIC UTILITIES
DOMESTIC AND PERSONAL SERVICE	9.7	12.8	AGRICULTURE
TRADE	10.6		
		18.6	WHOLESALE AND RETAIL TRADE
MANUFACTURING AND MECHANICAL INDUSTRIES	24.8		
		21.6	SERVICE INDUSTRIES
AGRICULTURE	37.5		
		25.3	MANUFACTURING

Figure 37. Kinds of Work Occupying the Labor Force, United States, 1900 (left) and 1950 (right). The percentage of the labor force in each kind of work is indicated in the black columns. The categories of 1900 and 1950 are not directly comparable. They do show, however, significant changes in certain types of work. (From Ewan Clague, "Labor Force," *Scientific American*, September, 1951, p. 40.)

survive unless the farmer shares in that prosperity. The farmer is thought of primarily as a producer, but he is also a consumer. When he is prosperous, he buys clothing, machinery, and luxuries in large quantities; and urban manufacturing benefits thereby. On the other hand, to those who consume the products of agriculture it may appear that the prosperity of the farmer comes at a high price.

The "farm problem" is not simple; it has many facets. But how to increase agricultural production and at the same time maintain farm incomes is a major problem, and a perennial one. When the price of farm products declines the tendency is for the individual farmer to try to ensure his own income by producing more, selling more, and thus profiting more. But when the same thing is done by many farmers, the greater supply of farm products only further lowers prices, and the farmer gets nothing but more work for his efforts. It would seem, therefore, that the farmer could save his energy and gain more income by producing less and forcing the price of his products up. Such a solution has its difficulties. Among other things, farmers have not always been well organized to control production systematically in order to raise prices. Farming has been competitive and individualistic; each farmer has attempted to serve his own interests. Nor has agricultural production been very sensitive to supply and demand. Farms go on producing even when prices go down. Business failure on the farm does not necessarily end production; it may merely bring about a change of ownership. Moreover serious questions may be raised about the desirability of discouraging agricultural production as long as there are persons who do not have enough food and clothing. Even in this country in which the population as a whole is relatively well fed and well clothed, agriculture has not produced more than could be consumed if prices permitted. The products of the farm are needed, but the problem has been to maintain and increase the supply without undermining the economic security of the farmer.

The situation has been complicated by the disparity between

farm prices and other prices. The farmer's prosperity is determined not only by the price he receives for his products, but also by the price he pays for nonagricultural products. The relationship between agricultural and nonagricultural prices has frequently been unfavorable to the farmer. For example, in 1933 the price of farm commodities had declined to about 50 per cent of their level before the First World War, while the prices the farmer paid were slightly higher than they were from 1909 to 1914. Between 1929 and 1933 the price of farm products dropped 63 per cent, but the price of farm implements declined only 6 per cent. The effect on the purchasing power of the farmer is easily seen.

Monopolies

In an economy in which competition exists in buying and selling, prices tend to be sensitive to supply and demand. But when competition in buying and selling does not exist, prices may be controlled and may be unrelated either to production costs or to supply and demand. This absence of competition is called *monopoly*. Although complete monopoly, which is complete lack of competition, almost never exists, monopoly is found in varying degrees in our economy. How to prevent monopolistic control of production and prices presents a continuing problem.

Monopolies may arise in a number of ways. In some instances there is little opportunity for competitors to enter the field because of the natural scarcity of a particular good. In certain businesses, especially in those in which a large amount of capital is required and in which overhead costs are high, competition may be unprofitable. Frequently monopoly is achieved by the creation of business combinations. There are buying as well as selling monopolies. At one time, the "big five" meat packers of Chicago were able to exert great influence on the price paid for cattle because of their concentrated buying power.

Our interest here is primarily in monopolies that arise through business combinations. Such combinations may be extremely loose and informal or they may be altogether formal and integrated.

The pool or cartel is an informal type of combination in which the participants maintain their organizational independence. They enter into agreements without becoming actual business combinations. These agreements may affect quantity of production, division of territory, patent rights, and prices. In practice pools have been unstable, since the "gentlemen's agreements" entered into by members cannot be enforced. Nevertheless pools have been successful in their purpose to reduce competition and manipulate prices.

One of the formal types of business combinations is the security-owning corporation or holding company. The term *holding company* is usually applied to a corporation which owns a controlling interest in the stock of other corporations, although any corporation which holds the stock of another corporation might be called a holding company. When a holding company owns a controlling interest in the stock of other corporations it may actively direct the business of these subsidiary companies. This leads to concentration of control, and it may also serve as a disguise for the existence of a monopoly.

The most complete integration of separate companies is achieved by the formation of a giant corporation. Smaller companies are absorbed into a larger company, or two or more companies unite to form a new corporation. Again the result is concentration of control.

It must be pointed out that business combinations do not necessarily create monopoly situations. However, the concentration of control which they make possible may be extremely effective in reducing competition.

Industrial Conflict

The story of the struggle of labor for rewards, recognition, and power is filled with episodes of conflict. Strikes, boycotts, and riots were countered with violent strikebreaking, arbitrary police action, and punitive release from employment. Labor unions were matched by employers' associations. In the propaganda battle vilification and distortion were practiced on both sides. Even though conflict was intermittent rather than constant the sides remained formed. Moreover open conflict was not peculiar to the early period. The years following the Second World War were among the most turbulent in American industrial history.

At this date there is little point in asking how much of the industrial conflict of the past was necessary. Given the attitudes and beliefs on both sides, a considerable amount of conflict was inevitable. A large proportion of employers were schooled in the idea that labor is a commodity to be purchased as cheaply as possible. Workers who wanted to improve their lot could see no alternative to conflict in realizing their goals. The action of labor was regarded by employers as a threat to their profits and to their control. And indeed labor intended that its power should be a threat to employer control as traditionally defined. One segment of labor held that the conflict between workers and employers could not come to an end until the capitalist class was abolished and all the machinery of production placed under the control of the working class.

But the latter point of view has been held only by a minority. The great majority of American workers have never regarded the contest between workers and employers as one in which the opposition would finally have to be destroyed. In the main they have assumed the continuation of an economic organization in which there would be investors, managers, workers, distributors, and consumers. They have advocated some regulation of the economy by government; they have wanted to be politically powerful; but they have not anticipated the domination of government by labor. They have expected that many groups would wield power through government in matters affecting economic life.

In this situation there is reason for asking what degree of industrial conflict will be necessary in the future. Bitter conflict probably was unavoidable during the rise of the labor movement, and indefinite conflict would be demanded if capitalism were to be destroyed. But in a system which includes capitalists, managers, workers, distributors, and consumers the satisfactory functioning

of the economy is the concern of all. The interests of one group
are not wholly separate from the interests of other groups. In an
organization of interdependent groups malevolent conflict can be
costly to everyone.

This is not to suggest that economic relations can be regulated
by sweet reasonableness. The gain of one group may be the loss of
another, and economic interests often are antithetical. In the struggle for rewards and power there will be conflict. Nonetheless ours
is an extremely interdependent economy demanding a high degree
of industrial cooperation if it is to give maximum benefits to all
groups.

International Economic Problems

Only a few decades ago the economic and political attitudes of
many Americans were strongly nationalistic and isolationist. The
ideal of national economic self-sufficiency was widely accepted. It
was believed that the United States could produce for its own needs
without dependence on other countries. The slogan "Buy American" was a reflection of this attitude. But isolationist thinking notwithstanding, the United States is not now economically self-sufficient, nor has it ever been. In early years this country depended
heavily upon Europe for manufactured goods. Later, American
manufacturers came to depend on all parts of the world for raw
materials. Supplies of materials such as rubber, tin, silk, platinum,
nickel, and asbestos have come almost entirely from other countries. American products, both raw materials and manufactured
goods, have been marketed in every part of the world.

It may be that the implications of international economic relations are not yet fully recognized, but a world-wide depression and
two world wars have modified our thinking. There is much awareness that we are part of a world economy. There is awareness, too,
that no nation can indefinitely enjoy prosperity regardless of economic conditions in other countries. Problems of economic stability and security are international in scope.

The importance of world economic relationships becomes all the greater in view of their close connection with world politics. International disputes over the conditions under which world trade should be carried on have been bitter and bloody. Prolonged military campaigns have been carried on in order to gain access to raw materials distributed throughout the world. National governments do not remain indifferent to the economic interests of their citizens who have investments abroad. Much attention is given to the economic strength of allies in international political struggles. In short, economic conditions have given rise to many international conflicts, and economic power has been an important factor in determining the results of international conflicts. Although it would be an extreme oversimplification to say that an end to economic problems would mean an end to international political problems, it is certainly true that the character of future international relationships will depend to a great degree upon the way in which international economic problems are dealt with.

MODIFIED CAPITALISM

Capitalism had its origin in a relatively simple economy of self-employment, handicraft, and small producing units. Under these conditions the ideology of a market-regulated economy developed. It was believed that each individual should give full rein to pecuniary self-interest; that individuals should have the right to use and control wealth; that there should be freedom in the exchange of property rights; that land, capital, services, and goods were all to be regarded as marketable commodities; that a free competitive market would automatically serve to regulate the functioning of the economy; and that, except in a policing capacity, government should remain aloof from economic affairs.

Then came expansion and change. Handicraft gave way to the machine; self-employment declined and employment for wages increased; the size of producing units was tremendously enlarged; finance was reorganized. The new economy created new problems. Insomuch as the expanding economy was controlled by social rules, it was by means of the dominant expectation that all things economic would be satisfactorily regulated by the market. But although the overruling market ideology remained in control, the conditions under which the market operated were greatly altered. In the latter part of the nineteenth century and throughout the twentieth century, the organization of economic life came to resemble less and less the economic models of simple capitalism.

Property

Traditional capitalism made several basic assumptions concerning wealth and the use of wealth. (1) It was believed that the right to acquire, use, and dispose of wealth should be largely individual rather than collective or public. (2) It was assumed that the right to acquire, use, and dispose of wealth was one and the same as the actual control of wealth. When an individual applied his wealth to production it was taken for granted that he would exercise control over that production. Ownership was accompanied by responsibility for policies and decisions concerning prices, wages, working hours, and the quantity and quality of goods. Modern capitalism has departed from these traditional assumptions in a number of important ways.

The corporation is an outstanding deviation from the doctrines of private property and individual enterprise. A corporation is a collective rather than an individual enterprise. A number of persons cooperate for business purposes. In large corporations thousands of persons are joined in economic efforts. Individuals who invest through a corporation continue to have certain private property rights over the wealth that they make available to the corporation. At the same time the corporation is treated legally as an individual. The corporation is granted property rights; it acquires, uses, and disposes of wealth. Individuals do not have private rights over corporate property. Even though the shareholders change, the rights of the corporation continue.

The modern corporation is also a departure from the traditional assumption that ownership and control go together. The "owners" of the corporation are the shareholding investors. There are a few large corporations in which control is in the hands of families or groups of individuals who own at least a majority of the shares. But most shareholders have no control over the corporations through which they invest capital. In some cases financial and policy control is maintained by minority blocs of shareholders. In other cases stock ownership is so widely dispersed that there is almost no relationship between ownership and control.

The effective control of the large corporation is vested in the board of directors and the officers of the corporation employed by the directors. The directors derive their authority from the stockholders. The votes of most stockholders are cast by proxy by the directors themselves. In this manner actions concerning the present operation of the corporation are taken, and by this method new directors are elected. To a large degree the board of directors is autonomous and self-perpetuating. Thus the directors, although frequently having only a small share of ownership, control the corporation.

Government has been much involved in the deflection of capitalism from its traditional precepts of private property. According to eighteenth-century capitalism the chief function of government with regard to property was the protection of private-property rights. In the United States government has been a strong sustainer of private property and in many instances has defended it as a natural and inalienable right. On the other hand, there probably never was a time in this country when all property rights were unlimited by government. In a sense the very fact that property rights are granted by government implies the power of restriction by government. But beyond its protective and permissive functions, government has increasingly become involved in defining the rights of property. The effect of many of the definitions has been to weaken or limit private rights.

Governmental restrictions of the property rights of individuals are numerous; a few may be named for illustrative purposes. The basic right of government to collect taxes places a limitation on the private use of wealth. The individual does not have the right freely to use and dispose of that part of the wealth which he is required to turn over to the state. Taxation has steadily been extended, and the extension entails a limitation of private-property rights. Some tax funds are used to defray the expenses of government; others are applied to assistance, subsidies, and services. In this respect government becomes a redistributor of property rights. Govern-ment limits the rights of property in many cases in which the welfare of the general public is involved. For example, a druggist is not free to sell whatever he wants to, nor may a food-processing company package anything it chooses. Property rights are checked by the welfare of consumers as written into pure food and drug laws. Companies that provide such services as communication, transportation, and power come under strong governmental regulation. Property rights in these public utilities are defined as being "clothed with public interest" and are controlled accordingly. In urban areas what an individual does with the land that he owns depends in part upon what other people want to do with the land that they own. Land use is regulated by zoning and building ordinances.

In the final analysis property rights are what government defines them to be. The courts have defended private property and at the same time they have helped to create the modern corporation and have upheld the regulation of public utilities. Thus whatever the beliefs concerning *natural* property rights, in practice property rights have been *granted* rights.

Price System

Traditional capitalism held that nothing should regulate prices but supply and demand. The prices paid for land, goods, services, and money were to be determined solely by the worth they acquired as scarce commodities. And there was to be no organized control of supply and demand. The price system assumed a free competitive market. In this regard, also, capitalism has deviated in many ways from its original form. In our modern economy competition is often incomplete and sometimes entirely absent, and prices are not determined by supply and demand alone.

The size of many modern business organizations has become so great that the economics of the free market does not apply to the things they buy and sell. If a corporation expands until it becomes the only buyer or the only seller of a particular product, it then has full control over the market of that product. This is a perfect monopoly. However, it is not necessary for a corporation to have a complete monopoly in order to control prices. A corporation that expands until it becomes the chief buyer of a product gains some control over the price of the product. Similarly if a corporation becomes the chief producer of a good, it can manipulate its price. The same result may be achieved by a group of producers who operate with the tacit understanding that they will not enter into price competition. Price leadership among such a group of producers may be given by a dominant corporation or it may shift from one firm to another. In any case the corporations involved follow the leader and price competition is eliminated. There may be competition to improve the quality of products and to sell them through advertising even though there is almost no price competition. This, for example, is the kind of competition found in the tobacco industry and in the automobile industry, in which there is very little price competition. The sale of cigarettes and automobiles in modern Pittsburgh, Atlanta, and Denver is not comparable economically to the sale of tobacco and carriages in colonial Lancaster, Baltimore, and Providence. It should be pointed out that size alone does not give corporations control over prices; nevertheless the expanded size of business organizations has greatly facilitated price manipulation.

The price system has been further significantly modified by the organization of labor. Early capitalism assumed that the price of services, like the price of goods, would be controlled by the market. Each individual worker was looked upon as having bargaining power equal to that of his employers. He traded services for wages on a free market. But in reality the bargaining power of workers was limited. Workers could not withhold their services at will; they could not move easily from one locality to another whenever wages were unsatisfactory; outside workers were frequently brought into a community for the purpose of keeping wages low. Instead of having equal bargaining power with employers, many workers were insecure victims of the job market.

It seems inevitable that workers would do something together to try to protect themselves against the insecurities of the job market and to gain a greater share of the economic rewards offered by the new industrialism. But tradition was against it. Workers were often as individualistic as their employers. They preferred to regard themselves as independent agents. Moreover many workers did not permanently identify themselves with an insecure and low-income position. They hoped to move to a higher and more secure level. But despite bitter opposition both within and without the ranks of labor, organizations of workers were formed.

The point of major importance here is that the principle of collective bargaining is now established in the American economy. It is understood by workers and employers alike that wages are not determined on a free labor market. Collectively workers bargain with their employers, and together workers and employers control wages. We have been referring chiefly to industrial workers. Many workers, including industrial workers, are not union members. But the wages of union members and of nonmembers are influenced by the activities of organized labor.

The trend away from freely determined market prices has not occurred without the participation of government. Groups from all sides have worked through government to establish prices favorable to themselves. Under the parity system farmers are guaranteed a price level below which farm commodities are not to fall. By means of government subsidies an effort is made to maintain a somewhat stable relationship between the prices farmers pay for goods and services and the prices they receive for their own products. By means of labor legislation the right of workers to bargain collectively is protected and minimum wages are fixed below which the services of workers are not to be bought. By means of *fair-trade laws* manufacturers have curtailed price competition by requiring retailers to charge the prices fixed by manufacturers. The interest price of money is regulated in part by Federal Reserve banks. The interest charged by the member banks of the Federal Reserve System tends to be high or low depending upon the interest they are charged by central Federal Reserve banks. The Federal Reserve Board also attempts to influence over-all price levels by making available or by withholding government bonds. The purpose in so doing is to control the amount of money available for other things. In times of emergencies such as war direct governmental price controls are used. The rates charged by public utilities are set by agencies of government. These are some of the ways in which government is involved in the decline of the free-market economy.

Laissez Faire

Ours is not a laissez-faire economy. Economic affairs and government are inseparably joined. It is doubtful that they ever were entirely separate in the United States. Certainly the alliance was formed early. Protection of manufacturing by means of tariffs was a political issue from the beginning. As the American economy expanded, the association of business and government became stronger and more complex. In the middle of the nineteenth century the trend toward higher protective tariffs gave aid to new industries. Also in the middle of the last century when economic growth was in its prime the development of railroads was encouraged by land grants and government subsidies. The previously mentioned role of government in the creation of the corporation, the definition and redefinition of property rights, the regulation of wages and prices, and the control of interest rates are all indications of the close relationship between business and government.

Although the association of economic activities and government is not new, there have been major innovations since the great depression of the 1930's. Government has come to be more definitely defined as an instrument for the maintenance of economic stability and for the promotion of the welfare of all economic groups. To serve these ends agencies such as the Reconstruction Finance Corporation, Public Works Administration, Federal Housing Administration, Tennessee Valley Authority, and many others were created in the 1930's. During the Second World War the total economy was regulated by the Federal government to support the war effort. After the end of the war the machinery of government was used to guard against a postwar economic decline and to try to check inflation. These events have made the laissez-faire concept meaningless in the United States. The separation of government from economic life in our society is impossible. Moreover the people have come to expect and demand governmental regulation of some phases of the economy.

Economic Beliefs

What are the prevailing economic beliefs of the present? We have been talking chiefly about what has been happening in practice rather than about what Americans think about their economy. To discover what are now the dominant economic beliefs would require long and careful analysis, for there are many different beliefs. A few general observations must suffice here. It is apparent that there is a wide discrepancy between economic reality and the ideas of many people. Notwithstanding the many changes that have taken place economic life is viewed in the frame of reference of simple capitalism. A free competitive market is assumed, and all participation of government in economic affairs is regarded as an unnecessary intrusion. Farmers who receive subsidies and workers who engage in collective bargaining hold to laissez-faire beliefs, businessmen who received loans from the Reconstruction Finance Corporation talk about individual enterprise and free competition, and corporation officers emphasize the inviolability of private property. On the other hand, a marked alteration of beliefs has accompanied changes in economic organization and practice. It is widely recognized that the modern market system is far different from the original market system. Further, for many persons government economic regulation as such is not an issue. The question is not whether government should be involved in economic matters, but how and under what circumstances. On the whole, economic beliefs have become more humanitarian. Ethical considerations are regarded as having some relevancy. The profit motive, once regarded as the principle and essential driving force, has been modified. Only a small proportion of the population lives by profit making. Most people receive wages and salaries, and their economic well-being is dependent upon general economic stability and upon the continuing operation of the organizations in which they work. Profits are often sacrificed in favor of financial stability. Eighteenth-century capitalists, whose beliefs were represented by Adam Smith, would hear with amazement the talk of modern businessmen about "service" and "social responsibility." A few years ago a business leader who left the presidency of one of the largest corporations to join the President's Cabinet stated: [2]

"It is increasingly clear that our large industrial corporations are not merely economic institutions but that they have social responsibilities as well—that business decisions must be made and adopted not only in the light of short and long-term economic factors but also with due recognition of pertinent social values and possible social reactions."

SUMMARY

The rise of capitalism was marked by the decline of the local subsistence economy of the medieval manor and by the appearance of an economy of trading and commerce. Early capitalism could be identified by its precepts as well as by its practices. Much importance was attached to private-property rights. The profit motive was believed to be inevitable and essential. The desirability of granting the individual all possible freedom to determine his own economic destiny was strongly defended. Except in a policing

[2] From a statement by Charles Erwin Wilson, quoted in *The Knoxville News-Sentinel*, Jan. 8, 1953.

capacity, government was to remain apart from economic affairs. The market, it was held, would automatically regulate the economy.

After 1800 the economy of the United States underwent enormous change. Handicraft was replaced by machine production and manufacturing was taken out of homes and into factories. Industrial production was greatly expanded, and in time large-scale production was established. Before the opening of the twentieth century the United States had become the leading manufacturing nation in the world. At the same time a similar transformation was taking place in agriculture. When farm machinery made it possible for the farmer to produce more than could be consumed by his family, self-sufficient farming tended to be replaced by specialized and commercial agriculture. Improved transportation and communication facilitated economic expansion and were instrumental in bringing about the decline of a local type of economy. A national economy emerged. Economic expansion resulted in new methods of finance. Banking, corporations, and security markets came into prominence. Organized labor achieved a position of industrial and political power.

Economic expansion created problems. Fluctuations in production and business activity have serious consequences in a highly industrialized, money-dependent economy in which economic security derives from the opportunity to earn a wage or a salary. Furthermore, even in times of prosperity there are persons who cannot regularly sell their services for a satisfactory wage or salary. Unemployment and the threat of unemployment are ever present. How to increase agricultural production and at the same time maintain farm incomes is another major problem. The welfare of the farmer is intimately related to the functioning of the entire economy. In an economy of large business units the prevention of monopolistic control of production and prices requires constant attention. Industrial conflict can harm the economic welfare of many groups. Finally, problems of economic stability and security are now international in scope.

Capitalism in the United States has been significantly modified. The modern corporation represents a deviation from the ideas of private property and individual enterprise. It has also resulted in the separation of ownership and control. Government has increasingly become involved in defining property rights, and governmental restrictions of the property rights of individuals are numerous. Whereas early capitalism assumed a free competitive market, in our economy competition frequently is incomplete and prices are not determined by supply and demand alone. Then too, the separation of economic affairs and government as advocated traditionally is not a reality in the American economy.

SELECTED REFERENCES

Arnold, Thurman W.: *The Folklore of Capitalism*, New Haven, Conn., Yale University Press, 1937.

Berle, A. A., Jr., and G. C. Means: *The Modern Corporation and Private Property*, New York, Macmillan, 1934.

Bining, Arthur Cecil: *The Rise of American Economic Life*, New York, Scribner, 1943.

Dulles, Foster Rhea: *Labor in American Life*, New York, Crowell, 1949.

Kaplan, A. D. H.: *Small Business: Its Place and Problems*, New York, McGraw-Hill, 1948.

Knauth, Oswald: *Managerial Enterprise*, New York, Norton, 1948.

Lilienthal, David E.: *Big Business—A New Era*, New York, Harper, 1953.

Lynch, David: *The Concentration of Economic Power*, New York, Columbia University Press, 1946.

Mills, C. Wright: *The New Men of Power*, New York, Harcourt, Brace, 1948.

Patterson, S. Howard, and Karl W. H. Scholz: *Economic Problems in Modern Life*, New York, McGraw-Hill, 1948.

Veblen, Thorstein: *The Theory of Business Enterprise*, New York, Huebsch, 1923.

Warner, W. Lloyd: *The Social System of the Modern Factory*, New Haven, Conn., Yale University Press, 1947.

Whyte, William Foote: *Industry and Society*, New York, McGraw-Hill, 1946.

CHAPTER SIXTEEN

Governmental Institutions

The governing of men has been by might, by divine right, or by the authority of the people who are governed. It is sometimes said that in the final analysis all government is by the consent of the governed in the sense that no military dictator or king can rule under conditions of constant open rebellion among his subjects. However that may be, it is clear that merely permitting rulers to exercise control is far different from organized participation in government.

The genius of American government has been the organized participation of the citizenry. The participation, to be sure, differs both in kind and in degree. For some the power to govern derives from public office. The official rulers are Presidents, governors, legislators, Cabinet members, judges, mayors, policemen, and other public administrators and officials. For others the power to govern derives from control over the political positions of other men. Political bosses, party leaders, and pressure-group spokesmen constitute an "invisible government." For still others the power to govern derives from economic position. Financiers, corporation presidents, union leaders, and men of private wealth exert strong governmental power both by their manipulation of politicians and through their influence on economic conditions. For the great majority of citizens the power to govern is exercised through approval and disapproval, by acceptance and rejection of public officials and their policies. Even this form of sharing in government is not equally practiced by all, but nonparticipation is usually a result of lack of inclination rather than lack of opportunity.

379

When we say that American government is characterized by organized participation of the citizenry we do not refer merely to the legally instituted organization of government. The formal machinery of government is indispensable, but so also is the whole extralegal configuration of values, beliefs, customs, rituals, and practices which are part of government. Without the latter the machinery of democratic government probably could not be maintained.

Although established ideas and practices are essential for the continuation of a democratic state, government must not be viewed as fixed and immutable. It is rather dynamic and changing. To be sure, the Constitution is only rarely modified, many slogans persist generation after generation, and certain procedures change but little and then almost imperceptibly. But beneath the thin and transparent façade of sameness there is flux and alteration. Both the formal and the informal components of government change. Laws, machinery, and roles are modified, as are also values, ideas, customs, and extralegal practices.

TRADITIONAL FEATURES OF AMERICAN GOVERNMENT

The basic ideology of American government is set forth in the Constitution. It is a relatively brief document, but it embodies the fundamental principles believed to be essential for the establishment and development of governmental order in a free society.

Popular Sovereignty

Sovereignty refers to the highest right to control others. The central idea of American government has been that the right to control others shall be given or withheld by popular consent. Men who command other men shall not rise to power by inheritance, nor by military might; they shall be brought to power by the approval of the people according to pre-established procedures. The Constitution does not detail or even assert the principle of popular sovereignty, but it is clearly assumed and implied. The preamble states that it is "the people of the United States" who ordain and establish the Constitution; and the type of government established could not function without the consent of the people.

Because the Constitution does not elaborate on the practice of popular sovereignty, the actual extent of popular government has varied with place and with time. The people do not share in granting authority unless they have the right to vote. Eligibility for voting originally was left for the states to define, and standards were not everywhere the same. In general the unenfranchised groups were noncitizens, persons under twenty-one years of age, Negroes, and women. Many states also maintained property qualifications for voting. We shall later observe the suffrage changes that have occurred since the early years of the Republic.

Federalism

The government of the United States might have been organized on a centralized basis, or as a confederation, or as a federal union. A centralized government would have exercised full administrative control over state and local governments. It would have had the power to create and to abolish state and local governments and to confer and to withdraw their functions. But the possibility of establishing a centralized system was precluded by the existence of states that were unwilling to relinquish all their authority. A confederation, on the other hand, would have been an association of the states in which the power of the central government would have been weak and the autonomy of the states would have been largely unaffected. Such a union was considered too feeble to achieve the common objectives of the people of the states. The plan forged by the constitutional founders provides for a federal system in which the states are preserved as self-governing units and in which strong power is vested in the Federal government to deal with matters affecting the nation as a whole. Authority is divided between state governments and the Federal government, and the range of each is constitutionally defined.

In the division of power between the Union and the states, specific functions are assigned to the Federal government. Among these functions are the control of military affairs; the conduct of foreign relations; the regulation of interstate and foreign commerce; the coinage and regulation of money; adjudication in interstate cases at law; and control of patents, copyrights, bankruptcies, and naturalization. The Federal government further is granted the right to make all laws "necessary and proper for carrying into execution" the powers vested in it.

Whereas the powers of the United States are enumerated, the powers of the states are not. To the states are left all powers consistent with the Constitution which are not assigned to the United States and which are not specifically denied to the states. It is evident that by not listing the powers of the states it was the intent of the framers of the Constitution to leave to the states a large share of the functions of government. In the Tenth Amendment the division of power as it affects the states is made explicit: "The powers not delegated to the United States by the Constitution, nor prohibited by it to the States, are reserved to the States respectively, or to the people."

Separation of Powers

The powers of the Federal government are divided between the legislative, the executive, and the judicial branches. The same principle is applied to state governments. The Constitution does not state that the powers shall be separate, but the powers of the three branches are set forth in three different articles, and the opening sentences of these articles imply that the powers of the three branches are separate. Article I begins: "All legislative powers herein granted shall be vested in a Congress. . . ." Article II begins: "The executive power shall be vested in a President. . . ." Article III begins: "The judicial power . . . shall be vested in one Supreme Court, and in such inferior courts as the Congress may from time to time ordain and establish."

The creation of branches of government each having a defined sphere of power was more than a convenient organizational arrangement. It reflects a characteristic distrust of concentration of power. The founders were in rebellion against the tyranny of concentrated power as it had been experienced in Europe, and some of them had absorbed the ideas of the Englishman Locke and the Frenchman Montesquieu, who had advocated separation of power. The system had been practiced in the colonies. The purpose was to disperse power in order to limit it. Inasmuch as the branches of government are functionally interrelated, in the exercise of its own powers each branch acts as a restraint on the others. Moreover procedures are specified by which the three divisions of government serve to check each other.

Separation of powers is by no means complete. The very practice of checking breaks down the separation. When the President vetoes a legislative measure the executive department becomes involved in the legislative process. Similarly, through control of appropriations the legislative branch becomes involved in administration. When the Supreme Court declares a law unconstitutional or when it disallows an executive action it influences legislation and administration. Further, in many positive ways quite apart from checking procedures the powers of the three branches are related. For example, the President presents a legislative program to Congress; the President appoints judges of the Supreme Court; the Senate shares the appointing power of the President; the jurisdiction of the courts is to a large degree determined by the action of legislative bodies; the decisions of the judiciary are ineffective unless carried out by executive agencies. Thus the powers of government are coordinate as well as separate.

Limited Government

How to limit government while at the same time granting enough power to achieve desired ends has been a continuing concern of Americans. Recognition of the need for strong government has been mixed with fear of the coercive and restraining potentialities of strong government. The concern found expression in the Constitution in many ways. The purpose was to establish a strong government with limited powers. The framing of a written constitution was itself intended as a safeguard against arbitrary governmental action. The separation of executive, legislative, and judicial functions and the system of checks and balances were regarded as means of assuring limitation of power. In addition there are numerous provisions restricting and denying specific powers.

Constitutional defense of individual liberty is explicit. Definite restrictions are placed on the Federal government and on the states. The first ten amendments, commonly referred to as the Bill of Rights, were quickly added as a bloc in order to prevent encroachment on the rights of persons. A number of later amendments deal with the same issue. Limitations are fixed to safeguard freedom of religion, freedom of the press, and freedom of speech, and to protect personal liberty against arbitrary arrest, trial, and punishment. There are provisions regarding the rights of citizenship and the rights of aliens. Private-property rights are protected by clauses covering the manner in which property may be taxed, regulated, or taken for public use. A most important defense against infringement of individual rights by the states is included in the Fourteenth Amendment. According to the first section of that Amendment: "No state shall make or enforce any law which shall abridge the privileges or immunities of citizens of the United States; nor shall any State deprive any person of life, liberty, or property, without due process of law; nor deny to any person within its jurisdiction the equal protection of the laws."

Civilian Control over the Military

Fear of military government is a concomitant of fear of unlimited government. Military authority in the United States is limited through its control by civilian authority. The English contributed in at least two ways to the establishment of civilian supremacy in the new nation. They provided a precedent in their own system. Civilian control over the military was deeply rooted in the English tradition and was therefore taken for granted by the framers of the American Constitution. On the other hand the colonies had been subjected to considerable arbitrary military regulation by the British. The action of British troops in the colonies served to strengthen American aversion of military control.

Civilian supremacy is established in numerous ways. In operation the military is under the executive branch of the government, but both the executive and the legislative branches exercise control over it. The President, a civilian, is Commander in Chief of the Armed Forces. By tradition the secretaries of the branches of the Armed Forces are civilians. Nominally military officers are commissioned by the President. Money for military purposes must be appropriated by Congress and cannot be appropriated for more than two years at one time. War can be declared only by Congress. Strict limitation is placed upon the suspension of habeas corpus, and guarantees are provided for the maintenance of judicial rights. Soldiers may be quartered in a house in peacetime only with the consent of the owner, and in wartime only as prescribed by law. The people are granted the right to keep and bear arms, and the right of the states to maintain militia is recognized. The military organizations of the states are likewise under civilian control.

Expectation of Change

It is amply evident that while the people who founded our Republic purposed to establish a lasting basis for political order based on law created by the people, they expected that government and the constitutional basis for government would change. The supreme law was instituted by the authority of the people, and by their authority it was anticipated that it would be altered. The matter was put with poignancy by Jefferson: [1]

"Some men look at constitutions with sanctimonious reverence and deem them like the ark of the covenant, too sacred to be touched. . . . But the laws and institutions must go hand in hand with the progress of the human mind. . . . We might as

[1] Quoted in Saul K. Padover, *Thomas Jefferson on Democracy*, New York, New American Library of World Literature, 1949, p. 67.

well require a man to wear still the coat which fitted him when a boy as civilized society to remain ever under the regimen of their barbarous ancestors. . . . Each generation . . . has a right to choose for itself the form of government it believes most promotive of its own happiness. . . ."

The method of amending the written Constitution is set forth in Article V. Amendments may be proposed by Congress and must be ratified by three-fourths of the states. The states may take the initiative in the amending process, for on the application of the legislatures of three-fourths of the states, Congress must call a convention to propose amendments. In all, twenty-one amendments have been added to the Constitution.

But the modification of government is not only by constitutional amendment. The practice of government is based on custom, interpretation, and usage. Even when written law is unaltered its application changes. While remaining within the constitutional frame of reference, American government has been changed more by social events and by usage than by amendment of the written Constitution.

THE STRUCTURE OF AMERICAN GOVERNMENT

In a significant sense we have been analyzing part of the structure of government in the preceding section, for the beliefs, values, and standards explicit in the Constitution and implicit in practice constitute an important component of government structure. We turn, then, to a consideration of the machinery by which the ends of government are achieved.

Political Parties

The prominence of political parties in our government strikingly illustrates that government is established by practice as well as by constitution. The Constitution says nothing about political parties. Along with numerous other matters delegated for local regulation, the determination of electoral methods was left to the states.

Indeed a large proportion of the practices governing elections developed apart from the official operation of government. Nevertheless political parties, which are essentially associations organized for the purpose of placing people in public office, have a secure place in the structure of government.

The appearance of political parties seems now to have been inevitable. Some kind of organization is necessary in order to project the will of the people in the articulation of issues and in the choice of candidates. The purpose in placing men in public office is thereby to exercise power. Parties thus provide an effectual link between the people and their government. They were, in the beginning, officially unauthorized, though not illegal, groups of persons banded together to influence government along lines toward which they were disposed. To the present, parties continue to function in an unofficial capacity, but as their activities increasingly have come under legislative regulation they have acquired a somewhat quasi-official character.

Political parties are not inventions of modern government nor are they exclusively democratic devices. Ancient cliques of soldiers, priests, aristocrats, or merchants effectively manipulated government to suit their desires. Even in a state under the sway of a dictator are found dissenting factions plotting to come to power. But it is precisely in this regard that parties in a democracy differ from parties in nondemocratic states. Party organization to gain power in a democracy is not a conspiracy against the established government; it is an open effort to secure power within the established government. Power is achieved not by violence but by persuasion. Power goes to the party that wins the contest for popular consent. Because political groups in a democracy contend for popular approval, their objectives may not be too narrowly defined. Popular consent would hardly be given to a party coveting power only to serve the interests of soldiers, or of priests, or of aristocrats, or of merchants. In a democracy the appeal for political support must be broader than the interests of any particular group.

There is another important aspect of the difference between

democratic and nondemocratic party power. Political power is usually relative, and its practice even by a dictator is modified by the intrigues and threats of contenders for power. Nevertheless the power of a dictator and his supporting party is unshared by other parties. But in a democracy party power is never complete; it is always shared. Legislators representing various parties

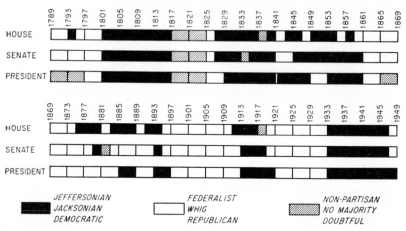

Figure 38. Party Composition of the Political Parts of the United States Government: 1789–1949. (From James C. Charlesworth, "Is Our Two-party System 'Natural'?" *The Annals*, vol. 259, September, 1948, p. 4.)

are placed in office. Further, under the American system of separation of powers it is possible for the majority of the legislators to be of one party while the top officials of the executive department are of a different party. Also under the federal system party influence varies from state to state and between state governments and the Federal government.

A two-party system has developed in the United States. Third and fourth parties have met with little success in electing candidates and have only occasionally influenced the balance of power between the leading parties. Control is shared by the major parties, but the absence of other influential parties gives to the party in power more control than it could have if consideration had to be given to third and fourth parties. Under a multiparty system the majority party must solicit minority support in order to protect its program from defeat by coalitions of minorities. In the two-party system of the United States, although the majority party shares power with the minority, it can carry out a program effectively when it can control its own members in public office.

American political parties frequently have difficulty in controlling their own members. This is in part because they are not single-interest groups, but rather coalitions of many interest groups. Diverse territorial, economic, religious, ethnic, educational, and class groups are found within the same party. Party members have one common purpose: to elect their candidates. To this end differences within the party are reconciled, compromised, and suppressed. But as public officials respond to pressure from their constituents and from groups to whom they are politically indebted, differences of interest and even contradictions within the party are apparent. The campaign commitments made by Republican Congressmen from rural farm areas may be in conflict with those made by Republicans from urban centers. Similarly Southern Democrats and Northern Democrats find themselves at odds. Moreover, when there is a difference between the program of the party and the interests of groups of constituents, public officials tend to be responsive to their constituents. Such lack of party regularity frequently has about the same effect that a multiparty system might have in preventing the decisive exercise of power by the party nominally in control.

Congress

The function of embodying the wishes of the people in national legislation is assigned to Congress. Much importance has been attached to the role of the legislature as an instrument for keeping control in the hands of the people. The authors of the Constitution of the United States and of state constitutions were particularly fervent in their desire to establish strong legislative bodies. While great power was vested in the executive branch, the ideal was a government by law rather than by executive decree. Ideas for laws come from many sources—legislators, private individuals, special-interest groups, and the executive department—but ultimate responsibility for lawmaking belongs to Congress. And among the laws that Congress is directed and permitted to make are numerous laws affecting the operation of the executive and the judicial branches.

Congress is a bicameral body consisting of the Senate and the House of Representatives. Each state has two members in the Senate. Membership in the House of Representatives is apportioned among the states according to population as determined by a census taken every ten years. In theory Senators are representatives of their states as such, whereas Members of the House of Representatives speak for the people of the country without reference to their states. Until the adoption of the Seventeenth Amendment in 1913 members of the Senate were elected by state legislatures; since that time Senators have been elected by popular vote. Prior to the Seventeenth Amendment the Senate was inclined to be the more conservative body and acted as a check on the less moderate House of Representatives. With the election of Senators by popular vote the difference between the types of legislation approved by the two bodies tended to decrease. Inasmuch as measures must be passed by both bodies, each functions as a check on the other.

Congress is organized on a partisan basis. A Speaker, the presiding officer, is elected by the House of Representatives and is always a member of the majority party. The Vice President of the United States is President of the Senate. A member of the majority party is elected President pro tempore; he presides over the Senate in the absence of the President. A floor leader who is chief spokesman and strategist is selected by both parties in the House and in the Senate. Committee chairmanships go to the majority party in each chamber. On both House and Senate committees each party is represented in proportion to its strength. Party authority in Congress derives from the party caucus or conference. In the Senate and in the House members of the same party meet to select their leaders, to make committee appointments, to define the party program, and to determine the party position on specific issues as they arise.

A Member of Congress is elected by the people living in a given geographical area, thus suggesting that his representation is territorial. But the people living in any voting area do not make up a unified group. The interests of workers, employers, farmers, shippers, builders, merchants, housewives, and others are different, and the things they want in government are frequently different. Along with electoral approval of some general campaign proposals the legislator brings to Congress the requests and demands of a great variety of groups. He is on occasion reminded of his general campaign commitments, but the specific demands of interest groups are more persistent. A legislator is not sent to Congress with an over-all mandate to use his discretion in voicing the will of his constituents on all issues that may arise. Instead he is always a focus of political pressure and is repeatedly informed of the wishes of particular groups on specific issues.

The exertion of political pressure by special-interest groups has received considerable criticism. But political pressure is a democratic necessity. The legislator acting on his own judgment without reference to the particular groups involved could hardly represent his constituents. The wishes of people are specific, not general. Through the legislative process the common and the conflicting demands of groups of people are refined and compromised. Every individual cannot get everything he wants, but it is the function of the legislature to see to it that every individual and every group can realize as many objectives as possible without violating the rights of others.

The Presidency

As titular head of the state and as chief executive of the government, the President occupies the most important position of national leadership. Yet in many respects his powers and responsibilities are not well defined by the Constitution. Some duties are assigned him, certain limitations are placed upon him, but in many areas he acts under the general provision that "the executive power shall be vested in a President of the United States." Thus Presidents have interpreted their duties variously. The exercise of presidential leadership and power has been determined by the circumstances of the times and by the characteristics of the man.

Though there has been much variation in the spirit and the manner in which it is carried out, the role of the President as national leader has acquired rather definite form. The President is head of a Cabinet appointed by him consisting of the heads of the Federal administrative departments. Cabinet members conduct the affairs of their respective departments, but responsibility rests with the President. It is his duty to execute laws and treaties, and to enforce the Constitution and the decisions of Federal courts. His control over the entire executive branch is strengthened by his power of appointment and removal. He chooses or nominates many administrative officials. Purely executive officials he may remove at will; officials having semijudicial powers he can remove only as provided by law. In the conduct of foreign affairs the President has first responsibility. The Senate may approve or disapprove treaties and diplomatic appointments, Congress controls the funds for representation to other countries, but the conduct of formal relations with foreign countries is left with the President. As Commander in Chief of the Armed Forces, the President has great power over the military in peacetime and in war. He can make appointments and determine major policy, and some Presidents have given considerable attention to detail, particularly in wartime. The President has an important judicial function; he has the power to grant pardons and reprieves.

The President helps to make as well as to execute law. Congress is the lawmaking body, but its legislative power is shared with the President. Without his signature a bill does not become law unless it is repassed by a two-thirds vote of Congress. The President shares in lawmaking by formulating the policies of his administration and by calling upon Congress to write these policies into legislation. Further, the executive branch helps to make law when Congress writes laws in general terms and gives to executive agencies the power to fill in the details required for execution.

The President is both a national leader and a party leader. A presidential candidate is a party candidate, and his success is the success of the party. It is expected that the President and his administrators will place party members in most of the positions under their control. The manner in which the President conducts his administration reflects on the party as a whole, including legislators who hold office under the party banner. It is important, therefore, that the President and the members of his party in Congress work together to assure the success of their legislative and administrative program. Again in this regard Presidents have differed greatly. Some have been in strong control of their party; others have found themselves practically without a party.

Administrative Agencies

Administration of the Federal government is carried on by a vast force of employees some of whom work in Washington and many of whom are scattered throughout the country. Their activities are organized under the ten major administrative departments and under numerous other agencies variously known as commissions, boards, corporations, authorities, and administrations. Organization is on the basis of functions performed, although there are many exceptions. Some of the executive departments are given assignments which are only remotely related to their central function. In the main the commissions and boards provide a single service. As the administrative operation has expanded in function and in size, there has been increasing duplication, overlapping, and indefinite delineation of duties.

Efficient administration of the complex accumulation of executive agencies is a herculean task. A few agencies are directly responsible to Congress; some agencies are more closely related to Congress than are others; but for the conduct of most executive agencies the President is finally responsible. In such a massive operation presidential direction can be given only through a hierarchical organization with the President at the top and with satisfactory channels of control extending downward throughout the system. Even at best the task is extremely difficult and in many instances practically impossible.

When analyzed in relation to the principle of popular control of government the role of executive agencies acquires additional significance. The defined function of Congress is to determine policy; the defined function of administrative agencies is to execute policy. But in reality the policy-making function is shared by executive agencies. This is done through requests for legislation which are made by administrative groups. Probably more suggestions for important legislation come from administrators of government than from any other single source. Also policy decisions are frequently involved in the execution of law. A statute does not have the effect of law until it is carried into execution. In practice many of the policies set forth by Congress through legislation allow for considerable latitude in administration. Thus a second set of important policy decisions is required in the executive area. At this point there is extensive opportunity both for the reflection and for the deflection of the wishes of the people.

The Military

Military power is divided between Congress and the President. Congress is empowered to raise and support armed forces, to make rules for their regulation, and to declare war. The President is Commander in Chief. Congress and the President have at times contended for control over the military, but in operation the Armed Forces are a division of the executive branch.

The National Security Act of 1947 as amended in 1949 joined the Armed Forces under one huge administration, the Department of Defense. The Secretary of Defense, a civilian, is a member of the President's Cabinet. Under the Department of Defense are three subordinate military departments, the Army, the Navy, and the Air Force, each having a civilian Secretary. Because of the long-established separation of the branches of the Armed Forces, their formal unification was not accomplished without difficulty, and the achievement of actual functional unity has been even more hard fought.

The military power of Congress and the President has few limitations. The declaration of war may be for defensive or for aggressive purposes. Full use may be made of manpower, money, and property in support of armed forces. Traditionally the influence of the military on the state has been greatly restricted. Peacetime forces have been maintained, but there has been strong public demand that the forces be kept as small as possible without jeopardizing national security. Public sentiment has favored forces made up of citizen-soldiers expanded as required by the exigencies of war. In recent decades, however, the influence of the military has markedly increased. A high proportion of the appropriations made by Congress are for military purposes. The large-scale nature of modern wars, the potential range and destructiveness of newly developed weapons, and relatively unrelieved international tension have resulted in the maintenance of a large military organization.

The Judiciary

Under the United States Federal system, the Federal government enforces its laws and the states are left to enforce the laws that they make. Federal courts have jurisdiction when Federal laws, treaties, and constitutional issues are involved.

At the peak of the Federal judicial hierarchy is the United States Supreme Court. It has broad authority to call up, review, and rule on cases that have been in the lower courts. The Court is free to decide which cases shall come before it. In cases involving constitutional questions the ultimate objective is to carry the matter to the Supreme Court for final decision. When a case reaches the Supreme Court it has come to the end of the judicial process. The Supreme Court has therefore acquired a somewhat sacred character as the highest guardian of the whole American system.

Below the Supreme Court are the United States circuit courts of appeals; and below the circuit courts are the United States district courts. Most cases originally are brought to trial in district courts. Circuit courts have little original jurisdiction, their work being largely appellate. Cases that have been decided by Federal district courts, legislative courts, and quasi-judicial commissions may be appealed to circuit courts. Some cases cannot be appealed beyond the circuit courts; others may be passed on to the Supreme Court.

The Supreme Court, circuit courts of appeals, and district courts are the regular courts of the Federal judicial system. In addition there are special courts created to aid in the administration of laws. Among these courts are the Court of Claims, Customs Court, Court of Customs and Patent Appeals, Territorial Courts, Tax Court of the United States, Court of Military Appeals, and Emergency Court of Appeals. It is significant that notwithstanding the separation of powers, judicial and administrative functions are combined in such tribunals.

The principal function of courts is to interpret law and to support its enforcement. In so doing courts help to make law. They do not legislate, but they do share in the making of enforceable rules. When in specific matters the mandate of a statute is not definite, and when there exists no clear legal precedent, a court is nevertheless called upon to render a decision. Thus the court makes law. The decision that is handed down becomes part of the body of precedents to which the courts will later refer. Like the joining of judicial and administrative functions in some courts, the part that the courts play in making law is indicative of the unitary nature of government.

State and Local Government

State governments are empowered to perform those functions which are not assigned to the Federal government. They may exercise whatever powers are not denied them explicitly or implicitly by the Constitution of the United States. State governments have functions and responsibilities which are defined by their own constitutions. They are not administrative units of the Federal government, and governors and other state officers cannot be directed by the President or by Congress. So long as they are not in violation of the Constitution of the United States, the states are free to conduct their own affairs.

State governments have a great variety of functions. Along with numerous other activities they maintain peace and order; punish crime; define personal and property rights; establish courts to settle disputes and protect rights; regulate private economic enterprise; promote education, health, sanitation, conservation, and recreation; construct buildings, bridges, and roads; enforce standards for professions and trades; care for dependent persons; grant licenses; keep statistics and records; and do those things necessary for the operation and maintenance of government.

State governments have tended to be legislatively centralized and administratively decentralized. The state legislature makes law for the entire state. On the other hand, in administration the principle of local self-government has usually been followed. In keeping with the local-government tradition thousands of administrative officials come to office through local election rather than by state appointment.

The plan is not everywhere the same, but in most states there are four levels of administration. The central state government is at the top. It includes the governor and department heads. Next are the counties. Their officers include boards of commissioners or supervisors, treasurer, auditor, recorder, and others. On the next level are cities, villages, towns, boroughs, and townships. At the bottom level are various types of districts and precincts which are usually organized for specific purposes.

Although the political subdivisions of the states have delegated rather than self-determined responsibilities, they are ordinarily

permitted a maximum of local authority. Counties and municipalities are created by the state and are allowed relative freedom
of administration. The independence granted to municipalities is
in fact so great that functionally municipalities must be regarded
as more than mere subdivisions of the state.

In the main the states have not been very successful in combining efficient administration with local control. Amidst the sprawling assortment of political units, locally controlled offices, and
variously defined functions, state administrations have great difficulty in carrying out effective programs. Numerous states have
attempted some type of administrative reorganization on the top
level. However, the states still fall short in coordinating activities
on top levels with those on levels below.

GOVERNMENTAL INSTITUTIONS AND SOCIAL CHANGE

The problem of making necessary changes while at the same
time maintaining stability is of singular importance as it applies
to government. The central principle of government by the consent of the people is unchanged in the United States. Most of the
fundamental concepts remain. Yet as the practice of government
has changed, so also has the interpretation of basic concepts. The
continuity of our national government has never been interrupted,
and only once, in the Civil War, was it seriously threatened. But
stability and continuity notwithstanding, government has undergone significant changes both in practice and in theory.

Constitutional Government

The United States Constitution is a written document which has
only infrequently been amended. But it has proved to be a flexible
and adaptable guide for government. This is because the constitutional basis for government is not to be found in the written
document alone. The basis for our government is in the written
document, adapted by interpretation, elaborated by custom, and
advanced by usage. The Constitution is not something that was

made finally; it is always being made. An inflexible written constitution would have been inadequate at a number of critical points. At least some of the present characteristics of government could not have developed strictly within the confines of the written Constitution.

The leading sources of constitutional change may be listed briefly. Federal courts help to bring about changes when they modify earlier interpretations. New problems, new circumstances, and new judges bring new meanings and new opinions. Courts, including the Supreme Court, sometimes reverse their own decisions. Because all other courts are bound by its decisions, the Supreme Court is the final authority on constitutional interpretation. However, inasmuch as all cases are not carried to the Supreme Court, the lower courts share in interpretation and thereby contribute to change. The Constitution is also interpreted by Congress. In many respects the Constitution is what Congress says it is. The Supreme Court has committed itself to the principle that acts passed by Congress shall be regarded as valid unless violation of the Constitution is "proved beyond all reasonable doubt." Many innovations introduced by Congress are never questioned in the courts. When Congress by its legislative action places new meaning on general phrases in the Constitution, and when these meanings are accepted, the effect is often the same as if formal amendments had been made. The President too interprets the Constitution. By his orders and his actions he helps to define the powers and responsibilities of his office. Presidents have frequently taken powers which are not specified in the Constitution. The action of the President is rarely challenged in any court, and the powers of one President are assumed by later Presidents. Finally, the Constitution is elaborated by custom. Many of the fundamental features of our government are established by long usage. Political parties, the President's Cabinet, and legislative committees all derive their authority from custom. They are not provided for in the written Constitution, but they are as firmly established as any amendments.

Popular Government

Popular government has increased through the extension of suffrage. Originally the definition of voting rights was left entirely to the states, and most states restricted suffrage to certain classes of property-owning, white males. Property restrictions have been largely removed by the states themselves, although they have not completely disappeared. Otherwise extension of voting rights has been brought about chiefly by action of the Federal government. The Fourteenth Amendment provides for a reduction of congressional representation for any state if the right to vote is denied to any male citizen over twenty-one in an election to fill a Federal office. This penalty has never been enforced. The Fifteenth Amendment provides that no citizen shall be denied the right to vote because of "race, color, or previous condition of servitude." The Nineteenth Amendment provides that no citizen shall be denied the right to vote because of sex. Thus by law suffrage has been extended to include practically all adult citizens.

Nevertheless in practice some groups are prevented from voting. In a number of states citizens are required to pay a poll tax or to pass a literacy or education test before voting. These requirements are not illegal, but they are not applied in the same way in all places or for all groups. Local officials decide when the requirements for voting have been met. Abuse of the requirements by discriminatory application is an effective method of disenfranchisement. However, the preponderance of court decisions and the weight of public opinion are against the discriminatory use of voting restrictions. While abuse of requirements continues in some localities, the trend is toward the impartial administration of electoral machinery.

It is worth noting that while voting rights have been increasing, participation in voting by eligible citizens has been decreasing. One report of the percentages of eligible voters who voted in selected years showed 83 per cent in 1896, 72 per cent in 1916,

57 per cent in 1936, and 51 per cent in 1948.[2] After due allowance has been made for possible inaccuracies, these percentages indicate a trend. Is the trend to be attributed to the feeling that one vote does not matter, or to the remoteness of citizens from their government, or to ignorance of candidates and issues, or to the belief that it makes little difference who is elected? Whatever the reasons, it is evident that popular participation in government involves more than extension of suffrage.

Governmental Functions

From the beginning the government of the United States was not a strictly minimal government. Such a government would have been given power only to preserve law and order. Despite traditional American suspicion of too much government, the responsibilities originally defined were not merely negative. It was anticipated that the Federal government would act in the interest of the nation in those areas in which the states could not act. Congress was empowered to collect taxes to "provide for the . . . general Welfare of the United States." Nevertheless, in view of what was left to the states it is clear that the founders intended to establish a Federal government having limited functions. Moreover, whatever they may have had in mind in writing the "general welfare" clause, they could not, under relatively simple conditions of life, have anticipated the complex functions of the modern state.

From a largely agricultural nation, with relatively self-sufficient communities, and predominantly local problems, the United States grew into a gigantic rural-urban, agricultural-industrial, interdependent nation. Problems of prosperity, poverty, communication, employment, credit, resources, health, and education became nationwide in scope. Economic conditions in one part of the country or in one segment of the economy affected conditions

---

[2] Compiled by Jennings Randolph, reported by Joseph R. Bryson, *Congressional Record*, vol. 95, part 13, Mar. 21, 1949, p. A1604.

TVA

Tennessee Valley Authority Wheeler Dam in Alabama. The program of conservation, flood control, and power production promoted by the Federal government through the Tennessee Valley Authority is one of many evidences of the expansion of governmental functions.

elsewhere. Furthermore, as national unity became stronger the democratic ideology demanded that well-being should be general throughout the land. At the same time the United States emerged as a major international power involved in world-wide economic and political problems.

Under these conditions expansion of governmental functions was inevitable. Regulation of business, agriculture, and conditions of labor; promotion of relief and old-age benefits; supervision of conservation; regulation of transportation and communication; promotion of commerce; control of credit; aid to education—these and others are the domain of government. Suspicion of government as promoter of the general welfare persists, yet any government that refused to perform these functions would be regarded as deficient. A candidate may campaign on a platform of less government, but if his program does not provide for the accustomed services he loses support.

The growing functions of the Federal government have helped to create a consciousness of centralized power. Individual citizens encounter government more frequently as government engages in more different kinds of activity. Also, as compared with earlier responsibilities, the functions of the Federal government have increased more than those of the states. Therefore although centralization is real it has been magnified by contrast. It must be observed that in spite of increased government functions vital areas of individualism and freedom are undiminished by these services. American society remains relatively unregimented. Moreover centralization has not resulted in the overthrow of local and dispersed centers of power. Where there is dispersed power centralized government can be prevented from becoming a device for domination and can be used as an effective instrument for orderly and coordinated advancement.

Federal and State Cooperation

The principle that the states are free to conduct their own affairs does not prevent a high degree of cooperation between the Federal government and the states. As interdependence throughout the country has increased it has become desirable and necessary to coordinate state and Federal efforts in many fields. It has fallen to the Federal government to encourage the development of state programs in certain areas. There is cooperation in a great variety of fields including education, conservation, health, social security, agricultural problems, banking, housing, labor problems, taxation, and transportation. Congress is giving more attention to the creation of machinery whereby Federal and state officials can work together. Numerous state agencies are federally subsidized and are required to maintain federally prescribed standards in order to continue receiving support.

The states are not administrative units of the Federal government; on the other hand they are not independent political bodies. They have not been independent bodies since the founding of the Republic. They are subject to the restrictions imposed by the Federal Constitution. Where there is conflict between state and Federal law the authority of the latter is superior. The constitutionality of Federal law is judged by Federal courts and not by the states.

The constitutionally subordinate position of the states as established by practice along with the national importance of many major problems have tended to reduce the degree of state independence. The drift has been toward greater national unity. Nevertheless the states continue to perform important functions of local government. And, probably of equal significance, they serve as forceful centers of dispersed political power within the national unity.

Big Government

Expansion in the size of government was made necessary by the population and territorial growth of the United States. But these factors alone could not account for the dimensions of modern government. Growth in the size of government must also be attributed to the extension of government functions and the resultant increase in areas of government participation.

The expansion of government is indicated by the increase in the number of persons employed in government. In 1900 the total number of civilian employees in Federal, state, and local governments was approximately 1.3 million. The number of persons similarly employed in 1950 was 6.4 million; one out of every nine or ten civilian workers was a government employee. In 1950, of the total number of civilian government workers, 2,080,500 were Federal employees.

In the Federal government growth in the executive branch has been outstanding. The organization overseen by early Presidents was minute indeed as compared to the present executive operation. The relative simplicity of government management in the

FEDERAL GOVERNMENT—
A BUSINESS
GIANT

CAPITAL ASSETS*

MILITARY	**$146,000,000,000**
NAVY	71,000,000,000
ARMY	41,000,000,000
AIR FORCE	34,000,000.000
CIVILIAN	**$35,447,000,000**
ELECTRIC-POWER FACILITIES	4,300,000,000
ATOMIC-ENERGY DEVELOPMENTS	5,000,000,000
MERCHANT SHIPS (War Reserve)	6,000,000,000
ARMAMENT FACTORIES (War Reserve)	500,000,000
STRATEGIC-MATERIALS STOCKPILE	3,500,000,000
HOUSING, COMMUNITY FACILITIES	1,000,000,000
SURPLUS FARM PRODUCTS	3,000,000,000
NATIONAL PARKS, MONUMENTS	3,547,000,000
PUBLIC LANDS, NATIONAL FORESTS	3,500,000,000
FEDERAL BUILDINGS, INCLUDING POST OFFICES	5,100,000,000
TOTAL	**$181,447,000,000**

*Current replacement value of military assets, ships, armament factories, parks, public lands, buildings, acquisition cost of other items

LOAN INVESTMENTS

LOANS TO FOREIGN GOVERNMENTS	**$11,000,000,000**
FARM LOANS	**4,200,000,000**
HOUSING LOANS	**600,000,000**
RURAL-ELECTRIFICATION LOANS	**2,200,000,000**
OUTSTANDING RFC LOANS	**500,000,000**
TOTAL	**$18,500,000,000**

LIABILITIES UNDER INSURANCE PROGRAMS

INSURED BANK DEPOSITS	**$122,000,000,000**
HOME-MORTGAGE GUARANTEES	**27,000,000,000**
VETERANS' LIFE INSURANCE	**43,100,000,000**
TOTAL	**$192,100,000,000**

Figure 39. (Reprinted from *U.S. News & World Report*, an independent weekly news magazine published at Washington. Copyright 1954. United States News Publishing Corporation, July 23, 1954.)

early period was characterized by an incident which occurred during the administration of the fifth President: [3]

"James Monroe was President of the United States. William Wirt was his Attorney General. On the occasion of this incident, the President was meeting with the members of his Cabinet. Up to this time Mr. Wirt and his predecessors in office had not presented much of an administrative problem to the Chief Executive. The Attorney General had no office except his private law office, and no clerks or secretaries. He received only the modest remuneration of $3,000 a year. But when the Cabinet met on this particular day, Mr. Wirt presented the President with a number of requests. He wanted a raise in salary, an office, and a clerk, and he proposed that the President so recommend to Congress. After some consideration, the President decided that he should first assess the situation in the other departments of the government and then make a recommendation which would cover them all in an equitable manner."

In 1953 the Justice Department headed by the Attorney General had more than 30,000 employees and spent $171,579,000. Whereas the first President supervised nine agencies, today there are at least seventy agencies requiring presidential supervision. The Federal executive branch employed approximately 600,000 civilians in 1930; 1,000,000 in 1940; 1,966,000 in 1950; and 2,486,000 in 1953.

In addition to population growth and the extension of governmental functions, the rise of big government has been notably influenced by war and national defense. At the peak of their strength in the Second World War the Armed Forces of the United States numbered over 12 million. In 1953 the military force was approximately 3.5 million. In addition, of the total number of civilians employed by the Federal executive branch in 1953, approximately one-half, or 1,257,000, were under the Department of Defense. In recent years more than 80 per cent of Federal expenditures have been for past and present military programs.

[3] From an address by Harold D. Smith before the American Political Science Association, Dec. 29, 1940.

As government has increased in size, its costs have multiplied. For the period between 1789 and 1800 Federal expenditures averaged $5,717,000 annually. Between 1901 and 1905 the annual average was $535,559,000. The figure for 1930 was $3,440,000,-

THE BUDGET DOLLAR

WHERE IT COMES FROM...

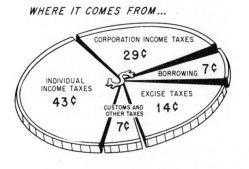

WHERE IT WILL GO............

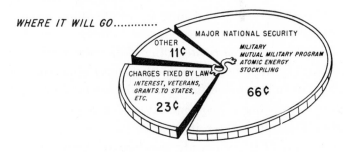

ESTIMATE FOR FISCAL YEAR 1955

Figure 40. (Source: U.S. Bureau of the Budget.)

000. During the Second World War a high of $98,702,000,000 was reached in 1945. In 1953 Federal expenditures were $74,-607,000,000.

Unitary Government

In June, 1953, almost a year before the Federal Supreme Court handed down its decision declaring segregation in public education to be unconstitutional, a national periodical reported: [4]

[4] *Time*, vol. 61, June 22, 1953, p. 26.

"After six months of study and discussion, the U.S. Supreme Court could still not make up its mind about the legality of racial segregation in public schools. . . . In an unusual procedure, the court last week asked counsel for both sides . . . to reargue the pending cases next October. Further, the court invited the U.S. Attorney General to take part and listed specific questions which need more research and discussion. Among them:

". . . 'If segregation is unconstitutional, what kind of court decisions could effect an orderly change in existing segregated school systems?' "

Why, if the legislative branch makes law, and the executive branch administers law, and the judicial branch interprets law, should the Supreme Court be concerned with anything but the interpretation of law? Why, if the powers of government are separate, should the Supreme Court raise questions that have to do with the execution of law before rendering a judgment? This case demonstrates again that in operation the branches of government function together. In many respects their powers might better be described as *coordinate* rather than *separate*. This does not mean that they do not check each other, but to function effectively they must be in agreement far more than they are in disagreement.

While the practice of coordinate government developed throughout the nineteenth century it was not until the twentieth century that the concept gained wide acceptance. In a practical way President Theodore Roosevelt was touching on this matter in a letter that he wrote in 1902 to Senator Henry Cabot Lodge in which he explained some of the considerations that controlled him in appointing a judge to the Supreme Court: [5]

"In the ordinary and low sense which we attach to the words 'partisan' and 'politician' a judge of the Supreme Court can be neither. But in the highest sense, in the proper sense, he is not in my judgment fitted for the position unless he is a party man, a constructive statesman, constantly keeping in mind his adherence to the principles and policies under which this nation has been

[5] Quoted in Charles A. Beard, *American Government and Politics*, New York, Macmillan, 1944, p. 54.

built up and in accordance with which it must go on; and keeping in mind also his relations with his fellow statesmen who in other branches of the government are striving in cooperation with him to advance the ends of government. . . . The Supreme Court of the sixties was good exactly in so far as its members fitly represented the spirit of Lincoln. . . . The majority of the present Court who have, although without satisfactory unanimity, upheld the policies of President McKinley and the Republican party in Congress, have rendered a great service to mankind and to this nation."

Woodrow Wilson, before he was President, recognized the unitary nature of government. Although many men in public life would not have thought in these terms and certainly some would have disagreed, Wilson was stating an important change in the theory of government when he wrote: [6]

"It is difficult to describe any single part of a great governmental system without describing the whole of it. Governments are living things and operate as organic wholes. Moreover, governments have their natural evolution and are one thing in one age, another in another. The makers of the Constitution constructed the federal government upon a theory of checks and balances which was meant to limit the operation of each part and allow to no single part or organ of it a dominating force; but no government can be successfully conducted upon so mechanical a theory. Leadership and control must be lodged somewhere; and the whole art of statesmanship is the art of bringing the several parts of government into effective cooperation for the accomplishment of particular common objects. . . ."

SUMMARY

The basic ideology of American government is set forth in the Constitution. The right to control others shall be given or withheld by popular consent. Under a federal system authority is di-

[6] Woodrow Wilson, *Constitutional Government in the United States*, New York, Columbia University Press, 1908, p. 54.

vided between state governments and the Federal government. The powers of the Federal government are divided between the legislative, the executive, and the judicial branches. The powers of government are constitutionally limited. Civilian supremacy over the military is established. Government, including the constitutional basis of government, is subject to change.

The structure of American government includes political parties, Congress, the Presidency, administrative agencies, the military, the judiciary, and state and local governments. Although the Constitution says nothing about political parties they have become essential in providing a link between the people and their government. The function of embodying the wishes of the people in national legislation is assigned to Congress. The President is titular head of the state, chief executive of the government, and leader of his party. He is responsible for most executive agencies. Military power is divided between Congress and the President. Federal courts have jurisdiction when Federal laws, treaties, and constitutional issues are involved. State governments are empowered to perform those functions which are not assigned to the Federal government.

While most of the fundamental concepts of American government remain, the practice of government and the interpretation of concepts have changed. The Constitution has proved to be an adaptable guide for government. It has been modified by amendment, interpretation, and usage. Popular government has been advanced by the extension of suffrage, but participation in voting by eligible citizens has decreased. As the nation has grown and as social life has become more complex, the functions of government have increased. Although suspicion of big government persists, it is expected that a long array of functions will be performed. Cooperation between the Federal government and the states has grown. Although legislative, judicial, and executive powers are defined as separate, in operation the branches of government function together. In the present century the concept of coordinate government has gained wide acceptance.

SELECTED REFERENCES

Appleby, Paul H.: *Big Democracy*, New York, Knopf, 1945.
Arnold, Thurman W.: *The Symbols of Government*, New Haven, Conn., Yale University Press, 1935.
Chase, Stuart: *Democracy under Pressure*, New York, Twentieth Century Fund, 1945.
Gallup, George H., and Saul F. Rae: *The Pulse of Democracy*, New York, Simon and Schuster, 1940.
Hyneman, Charles S. *Bureaucracy in a Democracy*, New York, Harper, 1950.
Key, V. O.: *Politics, Parties, and Pressure Groups*, New York, Crowell, 1942.
Laswell, Harold D.: *Politics: Who Gets What, When, How*, New York, McGraw-Hill, 1936.
Lazarsfeld, Paul F.: *The People's Choice*, New York, Columbia University Press, 1948.
MacIver, Robert M.: *The Web of Government*, New York, Macmillan, 1947.
Merriam, Charles E.: *Public and Private Government*, New Haven, Conn., Yale University Press, 1944.
Swisher, Carl: *The Growth of Constitutional Power in the United States*, Chicago, University of Chicago Press, 1946.
Truman, David B.: *The Governmental Process*, New York, Knopf, 1951.

CHAPTER SEVENTEEN

Educational Institutions

Every society has some means of transmitting its culture to the next generation. In the broadest sense this is education. Most individuals and groups are thus involved in education. In addition many societies assign the transmission of some parts of the culture such as specific attitudes, knowledge, and skills to designated educational groups. It is this more formal aspect of American education with which we are concerned here.

THE DEVELOPMENT OF EDUCATION IN THE UNITED STATES

Like all American social institutions, the institutions of education have been gradually transformed. In this section we see the present educational organization of the United States in the making.

The Background

The prevailing educational philosophy in early America was religious and aristocratic. Education in the colonies had its beginning as a result of religious motivation. Religious materials were used for instruction, and teachers were required to be theologically sound. Lessons in reading were at the same time lessons in religion. Because education had its origin in religion, it was looked upon as a responsibility of the church or of the family rather than the state. The idea of public schools open to all was foreign to the thinking of the day. Education was for those children whose

412

parents could afford to hire tutors or to send them to small local schools.

A more universal type of education had only the slightest beginnings during this period. The practice of apprenticing poor and neglected children, brought to this country from England, was given legal support in a number of colonies after 1641. In addition to training in a trade or occupation, guardians were required to provide for some further education. There was considerable variation in the amount of education received, but teaching in reading was regarded as the minimum. Some apprentices received the same education as the guardian's children. This public responsibility assumed for the training of poor and dependent children was not a democratic departure from aristocratic ideas about education. The main purpose was to train needed skilled workers and to prevent poor children from becoming public charges.

In several New England colonies an attempt was made to establish schools on a systematic basis, but with little success. The legislative efforts of Massachusetts, Connecticut, and New Hampshire were frequently disregarded in practice. Most of the colonial legislatures demonstrated no interest in education. Parochial schools supported entirely by the church or jointly by local church and civil authorities were common in New York, Pennsylvania, and New Jersey. In the South, as elsewhere, education generally grew out of local community interest.

Attendance at school was a strict and serious matter and was held to be more appropriate for boys than for girls. Little education other than reading and writing was considered necessary for girls. They were usually taught at home, although at times they were admitted to town schools. Educational discipline was severe. The rod was not spared as a means of encouraging learning and as an instrument to counteract the power of the devil over the lives of children. The whipping post was a common piece of pedagogical equipment.

All higher education in the colonies was private. In 1769 there were nine colleges in the colonies, all philanthropically supported. Of the nine, all but one were established under the auspices of religion. The College of Philadelphia, now the University of Pennsylvania, was founded by Benjamin Franklin with liberal, non-theological aims.

Free Public Education

The theory and practice of free public education developed slowly in the new Republic. The belief that education is a function of the church and the family was well established, and the idea that it should be a function of the state was not readily accepted. One of the strongest advocates of state-supported education was Thomas Jefferson. He believed that in the new democracy the public welfare depended upon the education of people without regard to "wealth, birth, or other accidental conditions or circumstances." Men like John Adams, Tom Paine, and Benjamin Rush spoke in similar terms, but the immediate results were small. "Public school" continued to have a meaning quite different from today. The term was applied to schools that were free as well as to those supported almost entirely by tuition. Even in those places in which tax support was permitted, schools financed by public funds often were not attended by the upper classes.

The appearance of free public education was paralleled by the emergence of a new social and political order in a way that can hardly be considered coincidental. The old order was one of distrust of the common man. Leadership and training for it were privileges bestowed by birth. Education for all merely resulted in dissatisfaction among persons born to inferior positions. The new order, symbolized politically by Jacksonian democracy, was less impressed by inherited status. Opportunity should be open to everyone. The spirit was one of dissatisfaction with the *status quo*. It was in this setting that Horace Mann, Henry Barnard, and their colleagues promoted universal education. The type of education they advocated was in accord with the trend of the times.

The speed with which public education became a reality differed from state to state and from community to community within the various states. After the desirability of universal education was accepted, the problem was to gain tax support. The belief that tuition and philanthropy could and should pay the bill was given up reluctantly. Some states passed through a period of permissive legislation before making tax support mandatory. Under this plan communities were permitted to collect school taxes if they chose to do so. Progress from the first mild legislation to the final compulsory taxation was slow and covered twenty-five years or more in many states. In 1835, after a bitter battle over a law passed in 1834, Pennsylvania led the way in accepting the principle of tax-supported schools. During the fifty years following most of the states took similar action.

State responsibility for education means more than public support of schools. State control of education is also a feature of public education. To this end the various states have established some form of administrative control over the schools. New York, in 1812, was the first state to create a central office of education. By 1850 thirty-one states had established such offices. Today each of the states exercises control over its schools through a state office of education.

Extending Education Upward

The oldest type of secondary school in the colonies was the Latin grammar school. It was a traditional classical school and always held to the primary purpose of preparation for college. Although it survived into the nineteenth century it was by that time well on the way to extinction.

The Latin grammar school was displaced by the academy, which flourished in the period between the middle of the eighteenth and nineteenth centuries. Like other schools, many of the first academies were organized and controlled by religious groups. Gradually they became less sectarian. They were in general private institutions subject to no outside supervision. They appealed especially to the middle class. The popularity of these schools was attested by their rapid growth in all parts of the country. By 1850 there were more than 6,000 with 260,000 pupils. But the academies were privately controlled tuition schools and as such were destined to decline.

The upward extension of public education was inevitable. There was a growing demand for secondary education for persons who could not attend the tuition-charging academies. The public high school was the answer. The demand, of course, was not unanimous. The same arguments that had been used against public elementary education were used again. Taxation was not popular. In the early stages growth was slow. However, the ultimate acceptance of the high school was assured. In 1827 Massachusetts passed a law requiring a tax-supported high school in all cities, towns, or districts of 500 families or more. This was the real beginning of the public-high-school movement, although several high schools had been established in Massachusetts, Maine, and New York prior to that date. In 1860 there were about 100 high schools in the United States; by 1880 there were about 800; and in 1900 there were more than 6,000. In the present century the growth of the high school has been tremendous.

After 1830 higher education also realized an extraordinary expansion. Approximately 170 colleges were founded between 1830 and 1860, almost three times as many as during all of the preceding years. By 1900 there were nearly 500 schools on the collegiate level. This multiplication of colleges was brought about largely by intense denominational activity. Most of the colleges were supported by student fees, gifts, and denominational funds. Competition from denominational schools and opposition to taxation checked the early growth of state schools of higher education. The first state university, the University of North Carolina, was opened in 1795. At the outbreak of the Civil War there were only seventeen state schools. Accelerated growth of state schools of higher education did not occur until the present century. In 1890 the total public support of universities and colleges was only $1,383,000 as compared with more than $33,000,000 in 1918.

Among the schools of higher education that appeared during

the nineteenth century were those offering specialized and professional training. The expansion of education created the need for teacher-training schools. Private schools for teachers were opened in the 1820's, and in 1839 and thereafter state teacher-training schools, called *normal schools,* were established. The first technical school, Rensselaer Polytechnic Institute at Troy, New York, was founded in 1824. Professional schools of religion, medicine, and law were organized in the 1700's, but their development, particularly the latter two, was retarded until well into the 1800's. The first school of pharmacy was established in Philadelphia in 1822, and the first school of dentistry in Baltimore in 1839. The first graduate school, The Johns Hopkins University, was opened in 1876.

Toward Equalization and Popularization

As education has expanded in the United States there has been a trend toward greater equality of educational opportunity. Education for women is one example. Until the rise of academies, girls had few advantages other than a very limited elementary education. Many academies opened their doors to girls. It was some time, however, before seminaries and colleges for women were established. Troy Seminary was founded in 1821, and Mount Holyoke was founded in 1837. By 1860 there were some sixty seminaries and colleges for women. Oberlin was established as the first coeducational college in 1833. Nearly all the state universities founded after 1850 were coeducational or became so rather quickly. Between 1890 and 1910 the number of men in colleges and universities increased about 214 per cent, while the number of women increased 348 per cent in women's colleges and 438 per cent in coeducational institutions.

The establishment of public schools and the growth of schools of higher education did not, in and of themselves, achieve the popularization and democratization of education. Direct benefits received from the schools varied markedly. As late as 1890 only 44 per cent of the five-to-seventeen age group was in regular attendance at school. By 1930 this figure had increased to 67 per cent. In the public secondary schools, between 1890 and 1930 enrollment increased at least 100 per cent in each decade except one. In 1890 only 3 per cent of the eighteen-to-twenty-one age

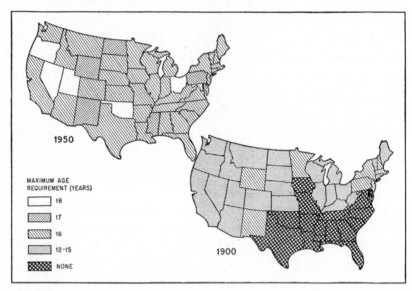

Figure 41. All States Now Require School Attendance. The 1950 map at the top shows that all states require school attendance at least up to sixteen years of age. The lower map, 1900, shows that very few states had as much as a sixteen-year requirement—one-third had no school attendance requirement at all. (From *Children and Youth at the Midcentury—A Chart Book*, prepared by the Midcentury White House Conference on Children and Youth, Raleigh, Health Publications Institute, 1951, p. 65.)

group was in attendance in schools of higher education, as compared to about 14 per cent in 1938.

There are still significant regional, class, and racial differences in educational opportunities and in the extent to which existing opportunities are utilized, as will be seen later.

What and How to Teach?

The question of what to teach has for many years been a live and controversial issue in American education. That much of our education is state-supported, that it includes all groups in the population, and that our economy and social structure have undergone phenomenal changes are all factors which have complicated the matter. The search for an answer has resulted in much experimentation, a full quota of fads, and, all in all, appreciable change in the content and methods of education.

On the elementary level the aim of education at the time of the Civil War was to teach the child to read and write the English language, use the number system, and accept prevailing beliefs and values. Between 1865 and the end of the century the curriculum was expanded to include elementary science, geography, history, civics, and literature. In some of the more progressive schools music, art, manual arts, and domestic arts—called *expression subjects*—were introduced. On the whole, education during this period was rigidly formal. The desire to conform to the newly developed graded system produced a preoccupation with classifying students according to their mastery of specific subjects and skills.

The revolt against formalism has been one of the most prominent features of American education in the twentieth century. The preceding century had its advocates of a new type of education, but the practitioners paid them little heed. Near the turn of the century the influence of psychology made its way into courses for teachers and thence into the schools. New theories of learning were advanced, and new methods of teaching followed.

Traditional education was organized around the objective of transmitting knowledge and a few skills from one generation to the next. Much emphasis was placed on drill, memorization, and the accumulation of facts. This old system, the reformers of education held, was attempting to teach the wrong things and doing it in the wrong way. They insisted that education must be fitted to the child, not the child to education. Children are different in their abilities, needs, and motives; therefore education must be adjusted to these individual differences. Furthermore they argued that drill and the storing up of facts which may some day be useful are poor ways of learning. The true basis of learning is experience which has present meaning. The child learns best by doing and when learning is related to other experiences of the present and to experiences of the future which can be anticipated. This general philosophy of education has come to be known as *progressive education*. No single individual was responsible for the trend that ensued, but the writings of John Dewey were the main source of inspiration for the movement.

The prestige of this philosophy in American schools has been great. By no means have all schools become "progressive schools," but many of the ideas have gained wide acceptance. In elementary schools the influence is reflected in an emphasis on self-expression, child initiative, and personality adjustment, and in the planning of projects and units of work based on the experience of the child and developed around central activities of social life. There are evidences of the sway of progressive education on all levels, but particularly in the elementary and secondary schools.

Alteration of secondary education went hand in hand with revision of elementary schooling. Between 1865 and 1900 the content of secondary education was modified by the introduction of new subjects. Of the new subjects, the sciences were introduced first and in greatest number. Other subjects added were in the social studies, industrial and manual arts, homemaking, and occupational guidance. As subjects became more numerous than one student could take, courses of study were organized. Some schools offered only one course; others offered as many as seven from which the student might choose. The addition of new subjects usually stayed within certain bounds. Offerings were for the most part confined to English, ancient and modern foreign languages, mathematics, natural science, history, geography, and some additional subjects intended for persons planning to enter trade and commerce.

After 1900 it became increasingly evident that the academic nature of the curriculum was not well suited for all of the many students who were coming to the high schools in ever greater numbers. Schoolmen therefore attempted to develop a curriculum that would provide general education for all, vocational training for some, and preparation for higher education for others. The outcome was a rapid increase in the number and variety of courses offered.

In higher education the changes in content may in many ways be interpreted as a practical response to the advent of modern science and to momentous social and economic changes. Educational theory had its influence, but that influence was minimized by other forces. The prominent place that the sciences have in higher education is related to the high prestige that science has in our society as a means of discovering, inventing, and getting things done. The demand for education that prepares students to "do something" has led to the expansion of courses in engineering, commerce and business administration, military science, physical education, home economics, public administration, social service, and agriculture. The trend in higher education has been toward scientific, vocational, and professional training.

The Structure of Education

In colonial America there were elementary schools of various types, Latin grammar schools, academies, and colleges; but these schools were entirely unintegrated, and there was very little comparableness. Because of the college-preparatory function of Latin grammar schools, there was an informal connection between these schools and the colleges. With this possible exception, the general practice was for each school to operate independently without being regulated by what was happening in other schools. There was no "educational system." The transition from this haphazard situation to a graduated, standardized, and integrated system of education was a significant phase of the development of education.

The reorganization of ungraded elementary schools into graded schools was proceeding rapidly by 1880. The period of elementary education was being defined; a degree of uniformity was appearing in the curriculums; and teaching in secondary subjects had been transferred to secondary schools. The high school took its place as a school of terminal education and as a connecting link between elementary school and college. The independent position of the colleges was maintained longer than that of the lower schools. But as the college population increased, junction between the secondary schools and the schools of higher education became more definite. Thus by the end of the nineteenth century the schools of this country had achieved a fair degree of integration. In the present century the junior high school and the junior college have become established parts of the system.

Even after the educational structure had taken form, the quality and level of instruction varied from school to school and from one section of the country to another. Educational standards were inadequate. An organized effort to set standards was necessary. Uniformity and standardization as they now exist were brought about by state offices of education, accrediting organizations, regional and national education associations, and by give and take within the education profession.

EDUCATION IN THE UNITED STATES TODAY

Education in the United States is a vast enterprise. A large segment of our population is regularly occupied in giving or in getting an education. Billions of dollars are invested in school property, and more billions are spent each year for operation. We shall briefly survey the huge undertaking of organized education as it functions today.

Statistical Summary [1]

In 1950 there were in the United States a total of 138,600 elementary schools. Of this number 10,375 were nonpublic schools and 128,225 were public schools. Of the public elementary schools 59,652 were one-teacher schools. There were a total of 27,873

---

[1] *Biennial Survey of Education in the United States, 1948–50*, Chap. 1, "Statistical Summary of Education, 1949–50," Washington, GPO, 1953.

secondary schools, of which 24,873 were public and 3,331 were nonpublic. In the same year there were a total of 1,851 colleges, universities, and professional schools; 641 publicly controlled and 1,210 privately controlled. In addition there were 1,065 schools of nursing not affiliated with colleges and universities, and an unknown number of private vocational and trade schools and non–degree-granting schools of art, music, dancing, dramatics, and Bible.

Total enrollment in 1949–1950 in public and private full-time day schools from kindergarten through college was 31,402,051.

Enrollments in elementary public and nonpublic day schools reached a peak of 23,717,796 in 1929–1930. There was a gradual decrease to 19,891,631 in 1943–1944, followed by an increase to 22,201,505 in 1949–1950.

Between 1929–1930 and 1939–1940 enrollments in secondary schools increased from 4,804,255 to 7,123,009, an increase of about 48 per cent. During the Second World War there was a decrease of about 1,100,000, but by 1949–1950 almost 400,000 of this number had been regained. The enrollment in 1949–1950 was 6,427,042. Of the fourteen-to-seventeen age group, the proportion attending high school increased from 7 per cent in 1889–1890 to 77 per cent in 1949–1950.

Before the Second World War, in 1939–1940, the total enrollment of college students in the regular session was 1,494,203. After the war, in 1947–1948, this group reached 2,616,262. In 1949–1950 enrollment in higher education was 2,659,021 of which 1,354,902 were in publicly controlled schools and 1,304,119 were in privately controlled schools.

Since 1919–1920 there has been a rapid growth in junior-college enrollments. At that time there were 52 junior colleges with a total enrollment of 8,102. In 1949–1950 there was a total enrollment of 242,740 in 483 junior colleges, 256 publicly controlled and 227 privately controlled. Nearly half of the enrollment in public junior colleges is in California.

The following figures help to indicate the proportions of the edu-

cational enterprise in the United States and the extent to which
education is public and free. The total income for all organized
education in 1949–1950 was $8,213,342,000. Of this amount 80
per cent was received from Federal, state, and local appropriations
and taxes; 5 per cent from student fees; 1 per cent from private
subsidies, gifts, and grants; and 13 per cent from other sources.
The total expenditure for education in 1949–1950 was $8,795,-
635,000, of which 80 per cent was for publicly controlled education and 20 per cent was for privately controlled education.

The Educational Ladder

At one time there were only three levels of education in the
United States: elementary, secondary, and higher education. These
remain as the chief divisions of education, but the structure is no
longer so simple. The steps in the present ladder of education
appear to be as follows: (1) nursery school, (2) kindergarten, (3)
six years of elementary school, (4) junior high school, (5) senior
high school, (6) two years of junior college or four years of college, and (7) specialized or professional schools. To these might
be added an eighth, adult education, which is entered upon after
the termination of more formal education at any level.

This structure of education is not uniform for all groups or in
all localities. Only a limited number of children attend kindergarten, and an even smaller number attend nursery school. There
are many eight-year elementary schools, especially in rural areas.
Junior high schools include grades seven and eight in some communities and seven through nine in others, with the majority in
the latter category. High schools vary between three- and four-year
schools in the same manner. Although the junior college has gained
greatly in popularity, the number of such schools in most parts of
the country is still relatively small.

There are educators who predict and hope for a further reorganization of education. A new arrangement frequently advocated is the 6-4-4 plan: six years of elementary school, four years
of high school, including grades seven through ten, and four years

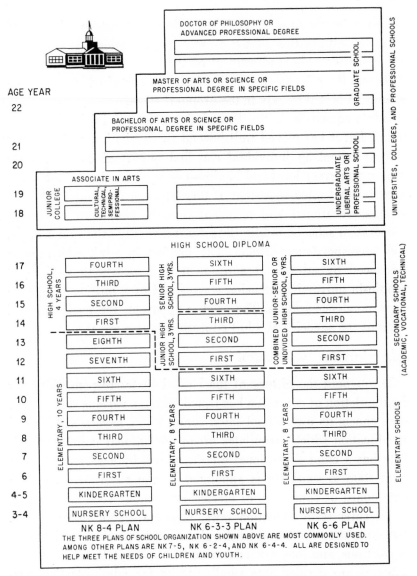

Figure 42. Organization of Education in the United States. (Source: U.S. Department of Health, Education, and Welfare.)

of college made up of grades eleven through fourteen. This would mean the elimination of the present junior college. It would require considerable readjustment on the level of higher education. Although the plan has been tried in a number of widely scattered schools, it is still largely in the proposal stage.

Adult education in the United States is still in the formative phase, but it has moved well beyond the beginning period. After leaving school an individual can find opportunities for further training on every level and in almost every field. Among the many agencies that offer education of this type are free public evening schools, vocational and technical schools, continuation schools, cooperative schools, public libraries, university-extension schools, and correspondence schools. The interest in adult education is evidenced by an annual enrollment of approximately 175,000 people in university-extension classes and of 2 million in private correspondence schools. The need is apparent; the inadequacy of some of the agencies of adult education is also apparent.

Administration and Control

Throughout the history of the United States responsibility for the regulation of education has rested with the various states. Each state enacts its own school laws. Many states have a state board of education which formulates broad educational policies. Every state has a chief educational officer, known by a variety of titles from state to state. He is appointed by the governor, or by the state board of education, or elected by popular vote. His work is to interpret state education laws, promote school improvement, distribute state funds and teachers' certificates, make appointments to positions, and integrate education within the state.

States are divided into smaller units for administrative purposes. The county, district, township, or town are the usual subdivisions. The most common policy is to have an intermediate *school district* between the state organization and the local schools. In some states the county organization is the connecting link between the state and the local units. Cities of specified sizes usually constitute school districts which deal directly with the state. In some states local communities acting in accordance with state laws are practically autonomous in administering their schools. The town, township, or small district has its own board of education. School taxes are locally determined. Thus schools in close proximity may differ markedly in the manner of their administration and in the funds provided for their support.

Private elementary and secondary schools are regulated by the laws of the state and are subject to state supervision in the same manner as public schools.

The right of schools of higher education to confer degrees is authorized by the states. State-supported schools of higher education operate under powers granted to them by the states.

The U.S. Office of Education is a service and advisory agency rather than a control organization. It collects statistics and other education information; conducts studies and surveys; formulates recommendations regarding educational standards, objectives, and methods; provides a consultative service; and administers grants-in-aid. Such control as has been exercised has been chiefly through conditions attached to grants-in-aid. In general, however, the tradition of state and local control of education has kept the Office sensitive to the charge of Federal control.

Educational Inequalities

Equality of educational opportunity is a symbol of democracy in the United States. The right to an education has probably been one of the least disputed of all rights. Yet notwithstanding the idealized and the actual part that education has played in the promotion of democracy, great differences of educational opportunity exist in this country. While there may be uncertainty as to just what constitutes equality or inequality of opportunity, there are some contrasts which are so conspicuous that their meaning can scarcely be missed.

Money comparisons provide one index of lack of equality. The range in expenditure per pupil in state school systems in 1949–

1950 was from $80 for the lowest state to $295 for the highest state. In city school systems expenditure per pupil ranged from $76 to $385. In 1949–1950 average salaries for public school-teachers ranged from below $2,000 in five states to above $3,500 in seven states. The lowest-salary state paid an average of $1,416.

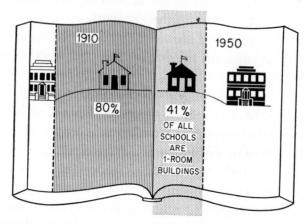

Figure 43. One-room Schools Still Abound. (From *Children and Youth at the Midcentury—A Chart Book*, prepared by the Midcentury White House Conference on Children and Youth, Raleigh, Health Publications Institute, 1951, p. 72.)

Attendance and enrollments in 1949–1950 varied as follows. The average length of term was 177.9 days. In Illinois the average term length was 186.6 days as compared to 165.1 in Kansas and 152.5 in Mississippi. Also in 1949–1950, the national average percentage of the total school enrollment that was enrolled in high school was 22.7. However, twelve states had less than 20 per cent of their total school population enrolled in high school.

These public-school contrasts represent rural-urban, income-group, and race differences in educational opportunity. In some rural communities opposition and inertia have prevented progress in the schools. Financial support has remained meager. But in many respects the inequality has economic sources. The ability of localities and of individual families to bear the costs of education remains an important factor in determining the distribution

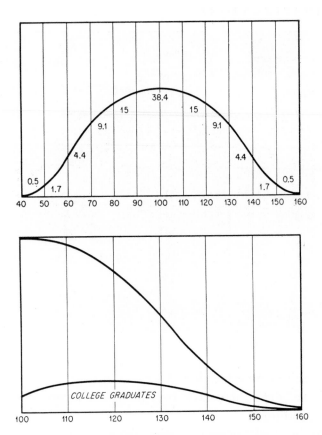

Fig. 44. The top diagram shows the distribution of intelligence in the United States population. Distribution of intelligence in the population is shown by a curve based on the scores compiled by those who took the Army General Classification Test. The numbers at the bottom of this diagram represent the scores of the test; the numbers closer to the curve show the percentage of people who made a score in that range. The bottom diagram shows the intelligence of college graduates as compared to the intelligence of the total United States population. Distribution of college graduates on the AGCT scale is shown by the curve near the bottom of this diagram. The curve that begins at the upper left is a section of that in the top diagram. The area between the two curves approximates the proportion of people of better-than-average intelligence who do not go to college. (From Dael Wolfle, "Intellectual Resources," *Scientific American*, September, 1951, p. 45.)

429

The One-room School—Still a Landmark.

of opportunities for education. Added to this is the fact that some groups have very little control over their schools and over educational expenditures.

On the level of higher education the economic factor is even more important than in the lower schools. College costs are out of the reach of some groups. Motivation to continue in school may help to account for the differences, but it does not discount basic inequalities. Inadequate preparation for college might be another factor causing the differences, but this is only further evidence of inequality of opportunity.

School and Community

A growing interest in school and community relationships has been displayed in recent decades. In a sense it is strange that this should be a matter requiring attention, for to a large degree schools have been community activities; and community customs and values frequently are transmitted through the schools. Even so, the

Primary School, Deerfield, Illinois; Perkins & Will, architects-engineers

A Modern Setting for Education. Despite huge expenditures for new schools, construction of schools has not kept up with consolidation, expansion, and replacement needs.

emphasis on school and community relationships is not without justification. Although schools are community agencies it is altogether possible for them to operate somewhat apart from other phases of community life. That the school-community emphasis originated with educators themselves seems to indicate awareness of some separation on their part. Such separation has come to be defined as undesirable both for schools and for communities.

Educators stress the advantages of close school and community relationships. The school needs the influence of life in the community to keep its program in accord with the realities of living. To be sure, any education worthy of the name lifts the individual out of his locality and gives him familiarity with wide human experience in other times and places. Still it is in communities that people live, and meaningful education must be guided by the demands of community living. Also the school is not to be seen as an isolated agency. There are other community agencies having common ends with those of the school. Both the school and other organizations of the community can gain from cooperative and coordinated efforts. The school thus can draw from community resources and can provide resources. The contribution of the school must not be too narrowly defined. In addition to fulfilling formal educational functions it can serve in broader and less formal ways. Further, an educational program can be set up to include all age groups. These are a few of the ways in which professional educators think of the school and community relationship.

CURRENT ISSUES IN EDUCATION

Controversy is as characteristic of education today as it has ever been. Educational thinking is in a constant state of flux. On some issues the differences of opinion are between professional educators and laymen. On other matters the professionals battle with each other. Consideration will be given to some of the broad issues that confront modern education.

General Education

Modern schools have expansive curriculums. This is particularly true of secondary schools and colleges. An almost unlimited number of subjects are taught. To the impressive array of curricular offerings are added the extracurricular activities. Amidst this multiplicity the student moves with considerable freedom, but frequently with the feeling that he is being directed by a conspiracy of circumstances which he cannot combat.

The present inflated condition of school curriculums may be attributed to three developments in the field of education. The first was the adoption of the elective system. Until late in the nineteenth century the curriculum of the college student was almost entirely prescribed. Then, around 1870, President Charles W. Eliot introduced a new system at Harvard. Students were required to take some courses and were permitted to choose others. In varying degrees this practice was adopted by most colleges. In general, liberal arts students have been permitted more freedom of choice than those enrolled in preprofessional or professional courses. The elective system is found also in secondary schools, although there the student's choice is more restricted. In all schools the decline of the strictly prescribed curriculum facilitated the addition of new courses.

The popularity of the ideas of progressive education is a second factor which has contributed to the growth of the curriculum. Expansion of educational offerings follows from the logic of progressive education. If the abilities, needs, and motives of individuals are different, and if education must be adjusted to the individual, then a great variety of courses and activities must be provided to meet the great variety of individual needs. Freedom of the student to choose according to his needs and interests is likewise consistent with the thinking of progressive education.

The third trend which has made for the multiplication of courses is vocationalism. The schools have tried to meet the demands of parents, students, and employers for education to prepare young people to earn a living. They have attempted to provide training in every type of skill and occupation. Progressive education, although not the cause of the trend, has been interpreted to give support to the vocational movement. If learning is to be related to needs and to life experiences, it must be related to training for an occupation.

In recent decades many educators have been casting a critical eye upon the "educational jumble." They have been inquiring about the meaning of the multiplicity of courses to the student who is working his way through the maze. They have expressed two basic concerns. First, it is possible for students to go through the whole process of formal education and arrive at the finish without having any common intellectual ground and without having a basic understanding of the culture which is their heritage. Second, it is possible for students to complete their formal education having learned something about how to earn a living, but having learned very little about how to live. Moreover there is a suspicion that sometimes the student's freedom to choose his subjects may not be freedom in a positive sense, but only haphazard and helpless capitulation to circumstances.

It has been argued, therefore, that in addition to adjusting to individual needs and in addition to providing vocational preparation, the schools have a responsibility to transmit to the younger generation certain common knowledge and an integrated view of their culture. It is maintained that there is knowledge that should be acquired by all persons, as well as specialized knowledge that may be acquired by some persons.

The programs that are proposed to counteract educational and cultural confusion are variously labeled. Both on the secondary and on the college level there is discussion of and experimentation with *balanced* and *general* education. The relation between *liberal* education and *vocational* education has been widely debated. It is interesting to note that the same Harvard that took the lead in introducing the elective system has participated prominently in reevaluating education; a Harvard committee published a report in 1945 under the title *General Education in a Free Society*. Scientific and technical schools are giving more attention to liberal arts. No serious consideration is given to the abolition of the elective system, nor to decreasing the attention given to individuals, nor to the discontinuance of vocational training. The problem is to maintain these and at the same time provide an integrated, humane, and socially relevant education.

Special Education

By drift and by design education in the United States has tended to become specialized in terms of occupational objectives. The trend is indicative of the nature of our society. No individual is self-sufficient. There is a division of labor, and each person succeeds according to his ability to perform special tasks. In this setting, much of the responsibility for selecting and training youth for particular occupational roles has fallen to the schools. The problems of occupational education are many. In certain respects the responsibility is more difficult to discharge than in the case of general education. For, important though general education is, there is often the possibility of making up for a deficiency after formal education has been completed. But to the very degree that specialized training is essential in the first place, it is difficult to correct educational errors later. If the errors can easily be corrected, the demands are not highly specialized and the training is not extremely necessary from the outset. If the demands are truly specialized there is usually only one opportunity to acquire the essential preparation. The schools are thus presented with a number of definite and practical problems.

How, for example, can a student be aided in choosing vocational goals which are appropriate for his abilities and his personality? If he starts in a wrong direction he may spend years of frustration attempting to achieve the impossible when he could have done well in other fields. Occupational maladjustment is costly to the individual involved and to the persons with and for whom he works. Moreover the choice cannot simply be made for him. If he is not to be robbed of all motivation, even under guidance, the choice must be his own.

Then too, the demand for services is not determined by the number of persons who receive training in a particular specialty. Are specialized courses, departments, and schools to limit and select their students according to actual possibilities for employment, or are they to take all who come and let competition act as the selector?

The Federal Government and Education

Since the founding of this nation, the Federal government has been involved in education. In 1787 the Federal government set aside a section of land in every township in Ohio for the maintenance of schools. Land grants were made to every state thereafter admitted to the Union. Under the provisions of the Smith-Hughes Act of 1918, Federal funds have been provided for vocational education on the secondary level. During the depression of the 1930's the Federal government granted funds for programs such as the National Youth Administration and the Civilian Conservation Corps. Support for the school-lunch program, started during the depression, increased from $12,646,000 in 1940 to $92,200,-000 nine years later. After the Second World War Federal support was given for the education of veterans. During the fiscal year ending in June, 1948, the Federal government appropriated nearly $3 billion for education in the states, territories, and District of Columbia.

The support that has thus far been granted indicates that the Federal government recognizes a responsibility for education. Further extension of Federal assistance to education has been prevented by a deeply rooted fear that Federal aid could mean Federal control. Actually, up to the present, the Federal government has interfered very little with control of education by the states. Nevertheless the opponents of Federal aid have been able to point to Federal supervision under the Smith-Hughes Act. For several decades there has been constant combat between the advocates and the opponents of Federal appropriations for education.

Growing awareness of the inequality of opportunity from one state to another has increased the demand for Federal funds to be used to equalize education. The demand comes not merely from those areas which would benefit most, but from all sections. The problem acquires national proportions inasmuch as the differences cannot be attributed so much to unwillingness to pay for education as to inability to pay.

Insofar as the legislative battle is concerned, it appears that the obstacle which for years stood in the way of equalization appropriations was overcome after the Second World War. A study of congressional opinion and voting records seems to show that the lawmakers decided that funds could be provided without taking control out of the hands of the states. A new block, however, was set up by religious groups. Protestants were determined that Federal appropriations should not include aid for parochial schools,

and Catholics were equally determined that there should be no
Federal aid without aid to private schools. Together these groups
made it politically inexpedient to deal directly with the equalization problem.

Education and Social Change

The function of the school in relation to social change is an issue
that underlies many others, for it touches on the nature and purpose of a valid educational program. One of the fundamental
questions concerns the role of education in transmitting the cultural inheritance and its responsibility for criticism and reconstruction of that inheritance. Traditional transmissive education
is both defended and attacked in groups concerned with education.

According to the time-honored concept of the place of the school
in society, the function of education is conservative. It is this
theory of education that has generally been carried out in practice.
The school is a channel for passing on the knowledge and patterns
of behavior which have been accumulated and handed down from
the past. The school accepts the social order of which it is a part.
In any particular community the school gives support to common
customs and ideas, attempts to correct obvious deviations from the
status quo, and disregards practices and beliefs the challenge of
which might cause controversy. In exercising its conservative
function in a highly complex culture, the school may concentrate
on the preservation of selected customs, ideas, and values which
are felt to be in danger of being displaced or of being lost by
neglect.

There are very few educators who protest against the transmissive and conservative role of the school as such. This function
appears obvious. There are, however, many educators who object
to an exclusively conservative purpose in education. For them the
school is not only a transmissive vehicle; it is an agent of social
change. The school should therefore review, evaluate, and criti-
cize the culture of the past and thus stimulate change. They hold
that in a changing society culture is not merely preserved; it is

constantly being remade. Since education is committed to enlightenment, it should actively participate in the reconstruction of culture.

There is another position which is probably more imaginative than real. This is the neutral position. Its exponents argue that the school should remain entirely aloof and detached. Educators, they say, should take no interest in the use of knowledge, in the clashes of culture, and in the everyday affairs of men. This is a philosophy honored more in word than in deed. Perhaps there are a few such truly esoteric creatures, but the much-publicized variety is largely fictional. Insistence that one qualifies for the neutral role often only indicates an inability to recognize one's own preconceptions.

Indoctrination

The view that one holds on the question of the relation of the school to social change will have bearing on one's thinking about indoctrination. The two are closely related. There is a sense, however, in which the indoctrination issue has specific significance. Hence the question: Should the schools mold opinions and shape attitudes?

There was a time in the history of American education when this question would not have had much meaning. It was expected that schools would teach the prevailing beliefs. And why not? Education was sponsored by religious groups. Indoctrination in the "right" beliefs was one of the purposes for which the schools were founded. Even after education moved out of the hands of the church and into the hands of the state, indoctrination continued. The tradition of local supervision was strong. The schools were a possession of the community. Again, the generally accepted attitudes and values were taught in the schools. In fairly homogeneous communities in which there was a rather high degree of consensus of opinion and belief, there seemed to be no reason for objecting to this approach.

The situation in modern communities is quite different. Homogeneity has disappeared. Families of many backgrounds, beliefs, and customs live in the same locality, and their children attend the same schools. It is difficult to discover social consensus. Attitudes and opinions differ decidedly on matters of religion, morals, economics, and government. The mobility of the population tends to disturb consensus that might develop. Teachers are not necessarily born, raised, and educated in the communities in which they work. They are often "outsiders" who bring with them their own ideas. Under these circumstances spontaneous unanimity among families, communities, and teachers with regard to attitudes and values does not always emerge. The question, therefore, is not simply: Should the schools indoctrinate? but: If the schools assume a responsibility for teaching attitudes and values, on what basis shall they be selected and who shall select them?

The indoctrination issue has been vitalized by the interest in propaganda. Although academicians say that propaganda may be either good or bad, honest or dishonest, the word has a bad odor. The general public has become somewhat aware of the influence of propaganda. There is a widespread feeling that to be propagandized is to be exploited. Educators, watching schools being used for propaganda purposes in other countries, have been made to realize what a powerful tool the schools could be if someone were to control them for the promotion of partisan or political objectives. The words *propaganda* and *indoctrination* are frequently associated, and both are suspect among most educators.

One method of dealing with the problem has been to attempt to define it out of existence. It has been held that to indoctrinate is to teach what to think, while to educate is to teach how to think. The function of the school is to teach students how to think; therefore where the true educational function is being performed there is no indoctrination.

More realistic educators recognize that nearly all education has some indoctrinational aspect. They recognize that in the process of training in skills, transmitting knowledge, and teaching "how to think," attitudes and values are inevitably transmitted. In fact they consider the absence of such transfer as regrettable. For this group of schoolmen the problem is not the teaching of attitudes and values as such. Their chief concern is to prevent any particular party, class, race, or religion from using the schools for its own purposes.

SUMMARY

The educational philosophy of early America was religious and aristocratic. Education was a responsibility of the church or of the family, and formal education was for those who could afford it. Free public education developed slowly. It was not until the 1830's that the first state made tax-supported schools mandatory. Within fifty years most states had taken similar action. The upward extension of education was achieved first by the establishment of academies, then by the organization of high schools, and by an increase in the number of colleges and universities. As education expanded the trend was toward greater equality of educational opportunity. Elementary and secondary education became progressively less formal, and higher education moved steadily in the direction of more scientific, vocational, and professional training. The structure of education became somewhat standardized.

Education today is a huge enterprise still growing larger. Enrollments and expenditures are advancing rapidly. As the proportion of persons in schools of higher education increases, reorganization of the prevalent educational structure may be anticipated. Although education has been widely extended many inequalities persist.

The regulation of education rests chiefly with the various states. For the administration of public schools states are divided into smaller units. The tradition of local influence on schools is strong. In recent decades educators have shown a heightened desire to integrate schools with community life.

Ideas and beliefs about education are subject to considerable change. For some years a controversy over the importance of general education has been going on. The advocates of such education hold that there is some knowledge that should be acquired by all persons. On the other hand, the trend has been toward specialized education. The problem appears to be one of striking a satisfactory balance between general and special education. Another issue has to do with the part that the Federal government should play in equalizing educational opportunities.

The functions of the school have always been transmissive and conservative. Many modern educators believe that the school should also be an agent of social change. They assert that the school cannot remain aloof from change. At the same time there is concern in many quarters that schools could be used by partisan groups to serve their own ends.

SELECTED REFERENCES

American Journal of Sociology, vol. 48, May, 1943.

Conant, James B.: *Education in a Divided World*, Cambridge, Mass., Harvard University Press, 1948.

Cook, Lloyd Allen, and Elaine F. Cook: *A Sociological Approach to Education*, New York, McGraw-Hill, 1950.

Edwards, Newton, and Herman G. Richey: *The School in the American Social Order*, Boston, Houghton Mifflin, 1947.

Harvard Committee: *General Education in a Free Society*, Cambridge, Mass., Harvard University Press, 1945.

Hutchins, Robert M.: *Education for Freedom*, Baton Rouge, La., Louisiana State University Press, 1943.

Kilpatrick, W. H.: *Philosophy of Education*, New York, Macmillan, 1951.

Mead, Margaret: *The School in American Culture*, Cambridge, Mass., Harvard University Press, 1951.

Moore, Clyde B., and William E. Cole: *Sociology in Educational Practice*, Boston, Houghton Mifflin, 1952.

Ogburn, W. F.: *Social Education*, Stanford, Calif., Stanford University Press, 1939.

President's Commission on Higher Education: *Higher Education for American Democracy*, 6 vols., 1947.

Warner, W. Lloyd, Robert J. Havighurst, and Martin B. Loeb: *Who Shall Be Educated?* New York, Harper, 1944.

CHAPTER EIGHTEEN

Religious Institutions

There were in the United States in 1952 about 230 religious bodies with an estimated 325,856 churches and an inclusive membership of 81,355,494. Of this number 48,853,367, or 60 per cent, were Protestant; 29,407,520, or 36 per cent, were Catholic; and 1,485,000, or almost 2 per cent, were Jewish. All others constituted about 2 per cent. The twelve largest denominations accounted for 95 per cent of the church members.

Table 12. Church Membership, Twelve Largest Denominations, United States, 1952

Denomination	Membership
Roman Catholic	29,407,520
Baptist	17,500,734
Methodist	11,398,057
Lutheran	4,460,159
Presbyterian	3,571,738
Protestant Episcopal	2,478,813
Disciples of Christ	1,945,607
Eastern Orthodox	1,609,168
Jewish	1,485,000
Congregational Christian	1,241,477
Latter-day Saints	1,150,956
Churches of Christ	1,100,000

SOURCE: *The World Almanac*, 1953, pp. 705–706.

A statistical introduction to this chapter is not altogether inconsistent with the beliefs of organized religion in the United States, for the number of church members is often regarded as a measure of the influence of religion in our society. This belief, of course, is not wholly valid. Membership counts do no reveal the

442

degree of control that religious institutions have over the behavior of persons affiliated with churches. Nor do they tell anything about the influence of religious institutions over persons who are not church members. A full analysis of the regulatory functions of religious institutions calls for a consideration of church and of nonchurch groups. Nevertheless membership statistics do give some indication of what proportion of the total population comes most directly under the influence of religious institutions.

EARLY CHARACTERISTICS OF ORGANIZED RELIGION IN THE UNITED STATES

Although religious institutions have changed in many ways, there are certain characteristics which have marked religion in this country since the beginning of the national period. These early characteristics have had an important influence on the growth and development of organized religion in the United States. They have helped to distinguish religion in the United States from religion in the parent countries of Europe.

Separation of Church and State

The provision for separation of church and state which was written into the First Amendment of the Constitution was not the result of merely casual consideration. Congress was fully aware of the importance and implications of its action. The First Amendment was the result of a long series of experiences and events. State-sponsored religion had disappeared from most of the separate colonies. The idea which was widely accepted in the colonies was expressed in the Virginia Declaration of Rights, adopted in 1776. It declared:

"XVI. That Religion, or the Duty which we owe to our Creator, and the Manner of discharging it, can be directed only by Reason and Conviction, not by Force or Violence; and therefore, all Men are equally entitled to the free Exercise of Religion, according to the Dictates of Conscience; and that it is the mutual Duty of all to practice Christian Forbearance, Love and Charity, towards each other."

Ten years later Virginia defined the relationship of church and state more specifically in the Act for Establishing Religious Freedom. Thomas Jefferson was the author. In describing this action W. E. Garrison writes: [1] "The 1776 declaration had freed the consciences but not the purses of citizens from compulsion by the state on behalf of the church. The 1786 act laid down these principles: (1) that the state has no right to compel the citizen to support with money the propagation even of those religious opinions which he believes, much less those which he disbelieves; (2) that 'civil rights have no dependence on our religious opinions'; (3) that eligibility to public office ought not to be conditioned upon the profession or renunciation of any religious opinion; (4) that all men are free to worship as they will, or not to worship at all, without restraint or penalty; and (5) that all are equally 'free to profess, and by argument to maintain, their opinion in matters of religion'—which would even include antireligious opinions. . . . The effect of this act was not only to disestablish the Episcopal Church but to reject decisively the proposal, strongly urged by some, that Christianity should be declared 'the religion of the state' and that ministers of all denominations should be supported by taxation."

Out of this background of precedents, public opinion, and legislative debate came the First Amendment. It provided that "Congress shall make no law respecting an establishment of religion." In the years since its ratification there has been considerable discussion and some difference of opinion over its specific meaning and application. There has been rather general agreement of interpretation, however, on at least two points: first, no one church shall be established by the Federal government; and second, several or all churches shall not be supported with funds raised by the Federal government.

[1] Winfred E. Garrison, "Characteristics of American Organized Religion," *The Annals*, vol. 256, March, 1948, p. 16.

The American decision to keep government apart from the affairs of religion acquires additional significance when it is noted that there was no European precedent for it. Organized religion unrelated to government had not existed in the Western world since the fourth century. It was believed by rulers that religious solidarity was essential to social and political stability. It was believed by churchmen that state support of the church was required for the welfare of religion. The association of church and state in Europe developed not so much because of the insistence of the rulers, but rather because of the desire of the church to use government as a means of control and of support. In America the protest against the association was carried through by lay statesmen and secular philosophers, with most of the religious leaders concurring.

The Drive for Expansion

Religion in America has been characterized by an unceasing drive to expand. Every local congregation attempted to add new names to its rolls. Each denomination organized for the purpose of increasing its membership. More churches were built in old communities, and new churches were formed in developing communities. Indeed many came to consider the "churching of the unchurched" to be the highest expression of religion. The first duty of the religious person was to persuade others to accept his beliefs.

This expansive mode of practicing religion did not have its source in religious doctrines alone. It was encouraged by the circumstances in which the churches found themselves. When it is recalled that in 1800 fewer than 10 per cent of the people of the United States were members of churches, it is apparent that there was ample opportunity for expansion. Although this figure cannot be taken as an index of the degree to which early Americans were or were not religious, it does indicate that there was no scarcity of potential recruits for the churches. This situation in America was somewhat unique. It may well be that the people in Great Britain or on the Continent were no more devout than the Americans, but most of them were counted as church members. The state-church system had produced this result in both the Protestant and the Catholic countries. But in the United States church membership was more a matter of choice than of default. Since the nation began with 90 per cent of the population unaffiliated with churches, it is not surprising that church people have been highly motivated to increase their numbers. This is one of the reasons why revival meetings, evangelistic campaigns, and membership drives have had such a prominent place in the activities of American churches.

Then too, just as the frontier, ever moving westward, presented economic and political challenges, it was an irresistible invitation to religious conquest. In 1800 about 90 per cent of the population of the United States lived east of the Alleghenies. As the population moved westward the evangelists, the camp meetings, and the churches moved also. The frontier provided some of the most fertile soil on which the seeds of popular religion fell.

With the rapid growth of cities after the middle of the nineteenth century, the churches worked to keep up with population and territorial increases. The country-to-city migration supplied new persons to be enlisted by urban churches. Wavering members, emancipated from the social control of rural communities, had to be reclaimed and brought back into the fold before they had "backslidden" too far. The steady stream of European immigrants, many of whom located in cities, provided still another source of recruits for religion.

Immigration contributed notably to the growth of the Catholic Church in America. At the time of the first Federal census, in 1790, the United States was predominantly Protestant in background. Less than 1 per cent of the population was Roman Catholic. The first immigrants to come in large numbers were the Irish, most of whom were Roman Catholics. There were Catholics among the German immigrants also. The greater number of the immigrants who entered this country during the first part of the present century, when immigration was at its height, came from the Catholic countries of Europe.

Immigration, and the resultant growth of the Roman Catholic Church, made religious expansionism more competitive. From the Catholic point of view increased numbers created a consciousness of a new position and of the possibility of maintaining and enhancing that position. From the Protestant point of view the growth of the Roman Catholic Church loomed as a threat to the position of Protestantism. Thus there developed in both groups a heightened awareness of relative numbers of members.

Only American Judaism has remained largely uninvolved in the competitive aspect of religious growth. This is because Judaism has been regarded as the religious expression of historical experiences which are transmitted through the family, and because it affirms the validity of other religions. It holds that its religious mission is to provide an example rather than to gain converts. There is some competition for adherents among the various branches of Judaism.

Denominationalism

The characteristic of religion in America which has impressed foreign observers more than all others is its denominationalism. The existence and the acceptance of a great number of denominations and sects has seemed strange to persons accustomed to the domination of one established church. The visitor to the United States finds three major religious groups, Jewish, Catholic, and Protestant, none of which receives preferential treatment by the state. Within the Protestant group there are hundreds of denominations claiming recognition. Judaism is divided into Orthodox, Conservative, and Reform groups. Nowhere else in the Western world has there been such a multiplicity of religious denominations. How is this innovation to be explained?

Religious diversity has to a large extent been the result of nationality and linguistic diversity. From the beginning each migrating national and language group brought its own church. Since no legal restraints were placed on these religious transplantings, they thrived and flourished in the new soil. As the United States became nationally more heterogeneous, it acquired more religious bodies. The church was not only an agency by which religious doctrines were transmitted; it was a means by which the culture of the past was maintained. Thus, although there are more than twenty Lutheran bodies in this country, they are divided more by language than by doctrine.

Denominationalism is primarily a Protestant phenomenon. In the case of Catholic immigrants, nationality differences were counteracted by other factors. There have been disagreements among Irish Catholics, German Catholics, Italian Catholics, and English Catholics in America. Among the clergy representing the various nationalities there has been some rivalry for influence. But these contentions have been kept within the church. The long-established unity of Catholicism and the nature of its organization have prevented national loyalties and cultural differences from causing schisms.

Important though they were, cultural backgrounds alone cannot account for Protestant proliferation. The growth of many new religious groups was in response to a favorable environment. Life in the New World was conducive to individualism and independence. This was no less true in the field of religion than in other areas. There was no strong state, no dominating church, and no consensus to check the founding of new churches. When a religious leader, either because of personal ambition or because of religious conviction, rose up to ask why he should not start another church, there was no voice raised in protest. On the contrary, such nonconformity was often looked upon as the manifestation of a national virtue. At times the nonconformity was superficial, for the rebellious faction turned out to be only slightly unlike the conventional group from which it departed. In other instances the results of religious experimentation were unusual and even bizarre.

The events associated with the freeing of Negro slaves provided a signal opportunity for the assertion of religious independence. Sectional differences on the slavery question created disharmony within the churches. In some of the largest denominational groups the break between South and North was complete. Emancipated Negroes, because of a combination of forced segregation and preference for their own organizations, added to the divisions by forming their own churches within the traditional denominational structure. Because the church was one of the chief avenues of self-expression open to the Negro, he demonstrated his own genius for creating new religious groups.

PRESENT PATTERNS OF DIVERSITY AND UNITY

Religious Unity

Notwithstanding the fact that America has been the seedbed of a multitude of religious groups, in some ways the diversity of organized religion in this country is more apparent than real. A second look at the statistics reveals that more than two-thirds of all church members are Roman Catholic, Baptist, or Methodist. Within Protestantism the variety is by no means so great as the long list of denominations suggests. More than 90 per cent of all Protestants in the United States are members of ten denominational families —Baptist, Congregational Christian, Disciples, Episcopalian, Lutheran, Methodist, Presbyterian, Churches of Christ, Evangelical and Reformed, and Evangelical United Brethren.

In many ways traditional Protestant denominationalism has lost its meaning. A survey of the membership of many churches would show a thorough mixture of denominational antecedents. Former Baptists, Presbyterians, Methodists, Congregationalists, and others are found in the same congregation. Even the minister may have started his career with another denominational group. A typical attitude is: "I do not think it makes any difference what church you go to." Many persons have changed from one denomination to another without ever thinking that changing churches might be considered changing religion. Such an attitude is quite in contrast to that of earlier years, when denominational loyalty was regarded as a test of true faith.

The church member can go into almost any regular Protestant

church and find enough that is familiar to make him feel at home. The differences that he finds have little to do with denominational differences. If the architecture is different it is because of the preference of the local congregation, and not because the particular denomination has developed an architecture which distinguishes it from all others. Variations in the order of worship can be identified only vaguely along denominational lines. The type of sermon will be determined less by denominational affiliation than by the theology and ability of the individual minister. In Protestant churches of different denominations may be found ministers who studied at the same seminary. The fact is that among churches of the same denomination there is frequently as much variation as among churches of different denominations.

Many factors have contributed to this grass-roots interdenominationalism. As cultural assimilation has proceeded, so has religious assimilation. Denominational differences have diminished as language, nationality, and sectional differences have diminished. Intermarriage of persons from different churches has encouraged changing church affiliation. But probably the largest contributive factor has been the mobility of our population in the present century. When an individual leaves his old community, friends, and church, old ties and loyalties become weaker and lose some of their power to influence decisions. In choosing a church he may look for one of his own denomination, but if he does not find one to his liking or if there is none nearby, denomination may cease to be important. He will probably choose a church because it is convenient, or because some of the neighbors attend there, or because his children like the Sunday school, or because the "people seem friendly," or because there is a "good" minister. As these exchanges of church members occur, attitudes are modified and differences decrease.

The grass-roots decline of denominationalism has been paralleled by another unifying trend. Since 1906 organic church union has been achieved in the United States in at least fourteen specific cases affecting thirty-two separate bodies. Among the mergers were

the union of a number of Lutheran bodies in 1917, 1918, and
1930; the merger of the Congregational churches and the Christian
churches to form the Congregational Christian Churches in 1931;
the merger of the Methodist Episcopal, the Methodist Episcopal
South, and the Methodist Protestant Churches to form the Methodist
Church in 1939; and the merger of the Evangelical Church and the
United Brethren in Christ to form the Evangelical United Brethren
Church in 1946. Almost all the major Protestant denominations
have participated in one form of union or another. It should be
noted, however, that in most cases the unions were *reunions*, that
is, a return to the parent or original body. The mergers have usually been within the same family of churches. Several have been
absorptions, in which the larger group took in the smaller group.

Interdenominational cooperation is carried on through city,
state, and national councils of churches. From 1908 until 1950
the most important organization for Protestant cooperation was the
Federal Council of the Churches of Christ in America. At the time
of its dissolution the Federal Council was composed of twenty-four
Protestant and three Orthodox denominations, having a combined
membership of twenty-eight million. The work of the council was
carried on by more than twenty committees and departments. In
1950 the Federal Council of Churches and seven other major interdenominational organizations joined to form the National Council
of the Churches of Christ in America. This organization is now
the embodiment of united and organized Protestanism in the United
States.

While in the main organized Judaism, Catholicism, and Protestantism go their separate ways, there are numerous expressions of
unity and cooperation among them. In local communities they work
together to promote social services and political, economic, and
social reforms. On the national level they join forces to secure the
enactment of legislation. One of the outstanding national organizations which attempts to foster cooperation and understanding
among Jews, Catholics, and Protestants is the National Conference
of Christians and Jews.

Religious Diversity

It would be a distortion to present a one-sided picture of religious unity and cooperation in the United States. There is another side to the picture. It is true that Protestants, Catholics, and Jews carry on their religious affairs interfering with each other but little. They accept each other; they have agreed to disagree without malice; and they attempt to cooperate where possible. There are more Christians than Jews, but there is no flagrant persecution of Jews. There are more Protestants than Catholics, but Catholics are rarely oppressed. Nevertheless there are Protestant-Catholic-Jewish conflicts.

It is difficult to know to what extent these conflicts and tensions can be attributed to religious differences and to what extent they can be attributed to other cultural differences. Both are involved. It is to the credit of the churches that when religious-cultural conflicts occur, they usually are not fostered and supported by church groups as such. Even so it must be recognized that there are movements, sects, and cults which are motivated by anti-Judaism, or by anti-Catholicism, or by anti-Protestantism.

Within Protestantism may be found various examples of religious separatism, but one case is outstanding. The Southern Baptist Convention, the second largest Protestant denomination, has not associated itself with the movement for religious unity and cooperation. It did not join the Federal Council of Churches, nor has it become affiliated with the more recently formed National Council of Churches. Indeed Southern Baptist ministers have been known to preach sermons on the subject: "Are Southern Baptists Protestants?" This case is cited because it is a somewhat unique instance in which sectionalism, traditional independence, and sectarianism have combined to preserve religious separatism in a large denomination.

Although most church members belong to the larger and better-known denominations, the members of other religious groups constitute a significant segment of the church population. These groups are usually referred to as *sects* rather than denominations. Of the total of 256 religious bodies counted in the 1936 religious census, some authorities classified 237 as sects. There is no universally accepted definition of a sect, but in general the sect stresses specific beliefs or practices which distinguish it from other groups; it is not so large as the leading denominations; it is local or regional rather than national in scope; it does not have a highly trained ministry; and it keeps apart from other religious groups. Throughout our history many sects have appeared and disappeared, but the net result has been an increased number of sects. Among the sects which have received a considerable amount of publicity are the Church of the Four Square Gospel, Jehovah's Witnesses, and the Father Divine Peace Mission. Among the little-known sects are groups such as the Two-Seed-in-the-Spirit Predestinarian Baptists, Christ's Sanctified Holy Church, Church of Daniel's Band, Pentecostal Fire Baptized Holiness Church, Apostolic Overcoming Holy Church of God, and Defenseless Mennonites.

There are other religious groups which in some ways do not conform to the description of a sect as given above, but which have been regarded as different from the major religious groups. The Christian Science Church, the Mormon Church, and the Society for Ethical Culture are of this type.

Sectarianism by nature is divisive rather than unifying. The sect is formed because its members feel that their religion is different, and because they want to emphasize this difference. The difference is recognized by other religious groups. For this reason the movements toward church union and cooperation have reached the sects only to a small degree. As sects grow larger, give up some of their distinctive ideas and practices, and otherwise begin to take on the characteristics of denominations, they tend to become more cooperative.

Church Membership and Social Stratification

There is some differentiation of church membership, though not clear-cut, along class lines. In most American communities the class structure is evident in the churches. All the denominations have members from all social classes, but individual churches tend to draw their members from one class. There is some evidence that the influence of religion is weakest in both the highest and the lowest social classes.

An analysis of a number of public-opinion polls made by the Office of Public Opinion Research at Princeton University indicates that more Protestants and Jews come from the middle and upper classes than do Catholics. Catholics are more typically workers than are Protestants and Jews. Protestants and Jews are more frequently found in the business, professional, white-collar, and service occupations. There is a significant difference in the number of Protestants, Catholics, and Jews in agriculture. Protestants have the highest percentage of farmers and Jews the lowest. Among Protestants the Episcopalians are least agricultural. Protestants and Jews have had more education than Catholics.[2]

Each Protestant denomination tends to be associated with a particular social class, regional and community variations notwithstanding. The Congregational, Episcopal, and Presbyterian denominations are associated with the middle and upper classes. The Methodist, Baptist, and Disciples of Christ denominations are generally associated with the middle classes. The major Protestant denominations have members from the lower classes, but the fundamentalist, Pentecostal, and holiness sects have become increasingly representative of the least privileged groups.[3]

Very little has occurred to change the patterns of religious segregation by race. Segregation in the churches is practiced much the same as in the community as a whole. If there are few Negroes in a neighborhood, Negroes join white churches; if there are many Negroes, there is segregation. Less than 1 per cent of the Protestant white congregations have Negro members, and this is usually in communities where there are only a few Negroes. Of the more than 6.5 million Negro Protestants, more than 6 million belong to

[2] Liston Pope, "Religion and the Class Structure," *The Annals*, vol. 256, March, 1948, pp. 86–88.

[3] *Ibid.*, p. 89.

Negro denominations. The others belong to predominantly white denominations in which segregation is generally maintained on the local level. Of the some 300,000 Negro Catholics, approximately two-thirds are in segregated or separate churches.

ACTIVITIES OF THE CHURCHES

It would be impossible to consider here all the activities of the churches. Nor may all the churches of the same denomination be placed in one category as engaging in like activities, since their efforts vary greatly both in number and in kind. It is proposed only to note certain trends and to indicate in general the extent to which various types of churches have been involved.

Protestant Congregations

By the end of the nineteenth century Protestant churches had acquired a somewhat settled and standard set of habits. Church life centered around Sunday services, and Sunday services centered around sermons. Orders of worship were simple and by many were regarded as merely a necessary preliminary to preaching. Only the Episcopal Church and a few others placed more emphasis on ritual and less emphasis on preaching. Church auditoriums were opened for morning and evening Sunday services; other rooms were used as the occasion demanded. Sunday school preceded the Sunday morning service. Prayer meeting was on Wednesday night, and sewing circle on Tuesday or Friday. Most churches had the customary cluster of missionary societies, guilds, and young people's societies. The programs of these groups were related to the distinctly religious purposes of the church. Families of the church assembled for "socials," although in some churches the more conservative members frowned on "social affairs" in the church. The duties of the minister were clearly cut out. He preached; he made pastoral calls; he attended or paid his respects to most of the marginal meetings. In the larger and more prosperous churches the minister had an assistant to help him. In the smaller and more isolated churches the program described here was reduced to a minimum.

Around the beginning of the present century a change began to take place in the activities of city churches. The traditional program was greatly modified, and a new type of urban church emerged which came to be known as the *institutional church*. All churches did not turn into institutional churches, but the innovations introduced in these churches influenced the life of most Protestant congregations to a greater or lesser degree.

In the new program Sunday morning remained much the same except that the sermon was shortened and the order of worship gradually changed. Sunday evening was what the minister could make of it by thinking of ideas to give it popular appeal. But it was the weekday enterprises that revolutionized the ways of the church. Instead of being opened only when necessary during the week, the church was open all the time. An amazing array of events was promoted. There was religious education on Sunday and during the week, a modified survival of prayer meeting on Wednesday night, church dinners, missionary societies, guilds, ladies' aids, bridge clubs, young people's organizations, men's clubs, Sunday school class meetings, Boy Scouts, Girl Scouts, dramatics, basketball, lectures, libraries, dancing, luncheon clubs, suppers, teas, choirs for all ages, orchestras, bands, forums, sewing classes, employment offices, visiting nurses, health classes, clinics, day nurseries, and innumerable meetings of officers, boards, and committees to keep the machinery going.

The new approach required new equipment: studies, offices, files, telephones, typewriters, mimeographs, addressographs, stereopticons, moving-picture machines, calendars, newssheets, robes, uniforms, dressing rooms, stages, drinking fountains, billiard tables, bowling alleys, electric signs, bulletin boards, illuminated crosses, and more.

Equally striking was the effect on church budgets. Much money was required to finance the expanded enterprise. An increasing budget was looked upon as a sign of advance, but it presented additional problems. Methods of soliciting funds had to be reorganized in order to meet the greater demands. Carefully planned systems for canvassing every member to secure a pledge of financial support were devised. "Budget Sunday" became one of the outstanding days in the church year.

At the center of all this was the minister. He was at once preacher, teacher, counselor, friend, arbitrator, budget maker, public-relations man, civic leader, administrator, and promoter. Whether assisted by a small or a large staff, the responsibility was his. To be a success he had to attract more people to Sunday services, increase the membership, add new activities and keep the old ones from lagging, make a good impression in the community, expand the budget, and raise enough money to pay the bills. Standards for the selection of ministers were altered accordingly. The cloistered cleric was not well suited to give leadership to the institutional church.

The type of church that we have just described was a product of the urban way of life. The responsiveness of many city dwellers indicates that it filled an important place in their lives in other than strictly religious ways. For the isolated individual it provided a group in which a sense of belonging could be acquired. For the anonymous person it offered an opportunity to achieve recognition and status. Help was given to persons in economic need. Families with limited means found in the church an inexpensive outlet for their social and recreational interests. Parents with more than adequate means favored church activities for themselves and for their children because the environment was wholesome and respectable.

Further, keen competition from other organizations forced the church to make an adjustment. With so many things for the urbanite to do, the church had either to grow accustomed to having many of the interests of its members turned away from the church, or it had to try to compete for their time. The institutional church chose to compete by providing as many activities as possible within the church.

The spirit of the times contributed to the development of the

seven-days-a-week type of church. It was one of the most characteristically American organizations. Cities were growing; industry
and business were expanding. The church included among its members men who in their work were involved in expanding operations.
They liked to help to make things go; they wanted to see growth;
they preferred success to failure for the enterprises of which they
were a part. To these men and to others who wanted to be doing
things, the activism of the church was appealing.

To be sure, only a limited number of churches functioned to the
maximum of their capacity. Activities varied greatly from one
church to another. While a few churches sponsored as many as
thirty activities, most churches had half that number or less. It
would be difficult to find much resemblance between the small,
struggling churches and the large, active, high-powered churches.
The importance of the trend, however, is not to be measured by
merely making a count of activities. It is significant that, whether
successfully or unsuccessfully, the institutional church was imitated. It came to be regarded as a model. The over-all effect was a
change in approach and in attitudes.

The change was much less evident in rural churches than in
urban churches. Rural churches were smaller and their members
were scattered. The rural way of life was not so well adapted to
incessant church activity. In the more isolated rural areas diffusion
of ideas, attitudes, and practices which originate in the city is
sometimes slow. Even so some rural congregations went all out
in developing a full-time program.

The desire to imitate the new program was not unanimous.
There was opposition both in the country and in the city. Many
churchmen continued to define the work of the church in strictly
religious terms. They found it altogether objectionable for churches
to sponsor activities which they regarded as not distinctly religious.
Among some groups this point of view still persists.

The institutional church probably reached the peak of its popularity in the 1920's. Though many such churches are functioning
as strongly as ever, there have been a number of reasons for re-

adjustment. Some churches have retreated slightly because they have come to question the capacity and the necessity for competing with nonchurch organizations in all areas of activity. The movement toward the suburbs of many of the strongest leaders and best contributors has left some central-city churches without the leadership or the money to carry on an active program. Suburban churches, which have been growing rapidly in recent years, provide numerous activities without attempting to account for all the hours that their members spend away from home and away from work. Suburban churches also are more family-centered than mid-city institutional churches. Instead of struggling to emulate the ways of urban churches, progressive rural churches are trying to create a program which is better adjusted to the needs and interests of rural people.

Catholic Parishes

The local unit of the Roman Catholic Church is the *parish*. There is a significant difference between the Protestant concept of a congregation and the Catholic definition of a parish. Most Protestant congregations are made up of persons who are joined together for religious purposes by preference and convenience. An individual may join a church as near or as far from his home as he chooses; for Protestants the term *congregation* usually does not have a territorial connotation. A Catholic parish, on the other hand, is a district, the bounds of which are rather definitely defined and may not be changed except by the bishop. Catholics are expected to associate themselves with the church in the parish in which they live.

A pastor or priest is placed in charge of each parish by the bishop. The parish priest celebrates the mass on all Sundays and feast days; hears confessions; performs general pastoral functions; and conducts baptisms, catechisms, confirmations, marriages, and funerals. Wherever possible the priest is to establish parochial schools. He is responsible for raising funds and for administering parish property. In addition to distinctly religious observances the parish sponsors a variety of social-welfare projects as well as "benefits," dances, and other recreational activities.

The place of the parish church is bolstered by a central belief of Catholicism concerning the function of the church. On this matter there is a basic difference between Protestantism and Catholicism. Protestantism has stressed the direct relationship between the individual and God, without the necessity of an intermediary agency.

Table 13. Adult Church Attendance in the United States

	Don't attend %	Once a month or less %	About twice a month %	About three times a month %	Every Sunday or Sabbath %
Total U.S.	*32*	*11*	*12*	*13*	*32*
Religion					
Roman Catholic	18	6	6	8	62
Protestant, total	32	14	13	16	25
Baptist	26	13	15	18	28
Methodist	37	13	14	16	20
Lutheran	36	12	17	18	17
Presbyterian	31	14	14	23	18
Episcopal	30	25	12	13	20
Congregational	42	30	7	11	10
Other denominations	34	13	10	12	31
Jewish	56	11	17	4	12
Other and none	81	9	2	3	5
Sex					
Men	36	12	11	12	29
Women	29	11	12	15	33
Age					
18–24	30	14	12	10	34
25–34	31	12	11	14	32
35–44	32	14	11	13	30
45–54	32	11	14	11	32
55–64	32	11	11	15	31
65 and over	42	5	8	14	31
Race					
White	32	11	12	13	32
Negro	31	12	12	17	28
Education					
0–8th grade	39	9	11	11	30
1–3 years high school	33	11	11	15	30
High-school graduate	29	13	13	14	31
1–3 years college	31	14	12	15	28
College graduate	25	15	9	15	36

The church from this view is regarded as an aid to the religious life of the individual rather than the sole arbiter of salvation. In contrast Catholicism emphasizes the essential role of the church as the authoritative agency by which morals and religious observances are defined and through which religious salvation is gained. For this reason attendance at mass and observance of other sacraments are matters of surpassing importance for Catholics. Church-attendance statistics seem to reflect this emphasis. One survey showed

Table 13. Adult Church Attendance in the United States (*Continued*)

	Don't attend %	Once a month or less %	About twice a month %	About three times a month %	Every Sunday or Sabbath %
Occupation					
Professional	23	14	12	13	38
Proprietor or manager	33	12	11	17	27
White-collar worker	29	15	10	14	32
Service worker	34	13	9	16	28
Manual worker	35	10	12	12	31
Farmer	30	11	14	15	30
Other	43	8	7	13	29
Income					
Upper	25	15	10	17	33
Middle	31	12	12	15	30
Lower	38	9	11	12	30
City size					
Over 1 million	35	11	9	9	36
100,000–1 million	38	15	11	12	24
25,000–100,000	32	11	11	9	37
10,000–25,000	31	14	12	16	27
Under 10,000	30	11	11	15	33
Rural	28	10	14	16	32
Region					
New England	27	8	11	9	45
Middle Atlantic	31	11	10	13	35
South Atlantic	29	12	13	20	26
East South Central	30	12	13	17	28
West South Central	23	9	16	15	37
East North Central	32	13	12	12	31
West North Central	35	11	12	16	26
Mountain	30	21	7	9	33
Pacific	50	12	7	9	22

SOURCE: "Do Americans Go to Church?" *Catholic Digest*, December, 1952, p. 5.

that among Roman Catholic adults 62 per cent attend church every Sunday, 8 per cent attend about three times a month, 6 per cent about twice a month, 6 per cent once a month or less, and 18 per cent do not attend. Among Protestant adults 25 per cent attend church every Sunday, 16 per cent attend about three times a month, 13 per cent about twice a month, 14 per cent once a month or less, and 32 per cent do not attend.[4]

Jewish Congregations

The synagogue or temple is the center of Jewish religious life. Regular public worship is conducted there along with a program of education for children, youth, and adults. A variety of recreational, cultural, and philanthropic activities are also carried on. The synagogue frequently has a number of affiliated organizations, and it provides a meeting place for Jewish organizations not directly attached to the synagogue. In some places the Jewish community center is sponsored by the synagogue, although the tendency is to keep the community center apart from the synagogue.

Jewish congregations are not centrally controlled and they are not territorially defined. Unless Jews are organized in integrated communities, each synagogue is an independent unit, formed by a voluntary association of members. Within the same area there may be a number of synagogues representing different groups and different shades of belief and practice. Each congregation has its own bylaws and its own officers elected by the members.

It is difficult to evaluate the influence of synagogue activities. What proportion of the synagogue constituency is served by the synagogue depends upon how that constituency is defined. Jewish religious leaders prefer to regard the Jewish population as a whole, about five million persons, as belonging to the Jewish religious group. On this basis the adult attendance survey referred to earlier showed the following results: every Sabbath, 12 per cent; about three times a month, 4 per cent; about twice a month, 17 per cent;

[4] "Do Americans Go to Church?" *Catholic Digest*, December, 1952, p. 5.

once a month or less, 11 per cent; do not attend, 56 per cent.[5] In evaluating these statistics, however, it must be considered that about half of the Jews in the United States do not regard themselves as belonging to the constituency of any synagogue. This is about the same ratio of churched and unchurched as for the population as a whole.

Schools

The Roman Catholic Church in the United States has a sizable school system. In 1950 a nationwide study of Catholic education showed that Catholic elementary schools are conducted in each of the 126 dioceses and in all the states. The Diocese of Reno had 1 school and the Archdiocese of Chicago had 400 schools. Among the states New York was first with nearly 900 elementary schools. In 1948 there were a total of 8,289 Catholic elementary schools with 2,349,049 students and 2,150 secondary schools with 485,000 students. The enrollment in Catholic secondary schools increased approximately 350 per cent between 1920 and 1948. In 1950 there were approximately 350,000 students in Catholic colleges and universities, 25,000 in seminaries, 10,000 in normal schools, and 100,000 in specialized schools and institutions.[6]

Among the larger Protestant denominations only the Lutherans have a significant elementary- and secondary-school program. Most of the schools under Protestant sponsorship are on the level of higher education. In 1947 there were 550 Protestant church-related universities, colleges, and junior colleges in the United States. In 1946 the American Association of Theological Schools reported 66 accredited schools and 28 unaccredited schools in its membership. Some of the theological schools were divisions of the colleges and universities.

The relationship between Protestant groups and their colleges varies greatly. Some churches maintain direct control over their

[5] *Ibid.*
[6] Reported by Benjamin Fine, *The New York Times*, June 5, 1950.

schools. Other schools are related to the churches only nominally. One study shows that since 1900 significant changes have taken place in the relationships between Protestant churches and their colleges. Boards of trustees include a larger proportion of persons from nonreligious occupations. There has been an increase in the proportion of board members and faculty members who are not affiliated with the related church. Also much of the financial support has shifted from the churches to nonchurch agencies.[7]

Jewish schools of higher education include six schools for rabbinical training, nine schools for training religious-school teachers, a training school for Jewish social workers, a college for advanced Jewish studies, and various other colleges and institutes.

Foreign Missions and Relief

Foreign-mission work is one of the leading activities of religion in America which extends beyond local churches. Protestants began sending missionaries out of the country in 1812, and they now have representatives in all continents and in many islands. There have at times been thirteen to fourteen thousand American Protestant missionaries, supported by contributions which have reached $40 million a year. These missionary efforts are carried on by a large number of interrelated societies. Almost every denomination has its own national missionary society, which usually cooperates with various interdenominational missionary organizations. In addition to winning converts and starting churches, missionaries have founded schools, including colleges and universities. They have established hospitals and medical schools, trained nurses, promoted public health, fought famine, organized cooperatives, and improved methods of agriculture.

Since 1914 American Catholics have been giving increasing attention to missions. The work is conducted by a large number of societies and orders. One of the best-known agencies is the Catholic Foreign Mission Society of America. Catholics also have organized

[7] C. A. Baugher, *A Determination of Trends in Organization, Finance, and Enrollment in Higher Education in Church-related Arts Colleges since 1900*, Ph.D. thesis, New York University, 1937.

schools, hospitals, and social services, but they have given less time to these activities and have concentrated more on conversion to Christianity and establishing churches. They have founded many orphanages, and along with other groups have been active in famine relief.

The Second World War affected both Protestant and Catholic mission work. Many missionary activities were disrupted and dislocated. After the war a tremendous problem of reconstruction was faced. As a result more church money was used for foreign relief, and more aid was given to the people of Europe. Most Protestant relief was coordinated under Church World Service, an interdenominational organization operating in Europe and Asia.

Social and Political Action

Church interest in social problems is not a recent innovation, but activity in this area has been increasing during the present century. The trend is evidenced by the formation of committees and commissions to deal with social problems, by the quantity of resolutions and pronouncements on social issues, and by the direct participation of the churches in economic and political affairs. The National Catholic Welfare Conference, founded in 1919, devotes a large share of its effort to social action. The social conscience of American Judaism has been expressed periodically through the Synagogue Council of America and other groups. From the time of its formation in 1908 the Protestant Federal Council of Churches took a lively interest in social issues. The same is true of the present National Council of Churches. A number of Protestant denominations have created social-action departments within their organizations. Among these are the Methodist Board of Temperance, founded in 1912; Congregational Christian Council for Social Action, formed in 1934; Division of Social Education and Action of the Presbyterian Church in the U.S.A., established in 1936; Council on Christian Social Progress of the American (Northern) Baptist Convention, organized in 1941; and Friends Committee on National Legislation, created in 1943.

The churches have differed on social issues, but on the whole they have agreed more than they have differed. The strong humanitarian motivation is indicated by interest in civil rights, health, housing, aid for European countries, refugees and displaced persons, and social security. In general, religious groups have opposed universal military training, favored disarmament, and given their moral support to the United Nations. Catholic, Protestant, and Jewish declarations on economic matters have been concerned especially with the rights and duties of labor, Catholic statements being most specific. Some differences are outstanding. For example, religious groups are not agreed on the ethical implications of the use of military power. Protestants and Catholics have differed on the kind of Federal aid that should be given to education.

Separation of church and state has never been interpreted as requiring the churches to refrain from political action. Churchmen played a prominent part in the political struggle over slavery. In the second half of the nineteenth century a variety of movements such as the Christian Amendment Movement, Know-Nothing Party, Woman's Christian Temperance Union, Knights of Columbus, and Lord's Day Alliance were willing to use the machinery of government to achieve their ends. In the present century the most conspicuous political activity of the churches was the drive for national prohibition, under the direction of the powerful Anti-Saloon League. Between the First and Second World Wars religious groups were active in the peace movement and opposed governmental action which might lead toward war. Since the end of the Second World War the trend has been to form agencies which represent their respective denominational or interdenominational church bodies before the Federal government. These agencies have offices in Washington. They attempt to inform, advise, and persuade legislators and administrators; and they channel information concerning legislation and governmental actions to the church public.

PERSISTENT FEATURES OF AMERICAN RELIGION

Inasmuch as there are several hundred religious denominations in the United States it may appear to be presumptuous and improper to try to generalize about American religion as a whole. There is, however, considerable justification for making the attempt. Even though the United States has been the scene of unrestrained religious differentiation, there are some attitudes, values, and beliefs which pervade much of the practice of religion in our society. Moreover these attitudes and values have been, to a significant degree, characteristic of Americans in their various pursuits. This is both because the values of religion have influenced the total culture and because the nonreligious traits of culture have had a profound effect on the mood of religion.

Individualism

Religion in the United States has been marked by individualistic values and beliefs. Protestantism has championed the concept of a direct relationship between man and God without the necessity of an intermediary person or organization. With regard to the use of Biblical literature individualism has meant that each person is to be free to interpret and to apply sacred writings "in his own light." Concerning non-Biblical matters also the idea prevails that each individual is entitled to his own opinions, and even more that each individual is his own authority. The ethical concomitant is the right of private conscience. The individual must do what he believes to be right. Moreover each person, being free to determine the "will of God for him," must face divine judgment individually. In the practice of religion it is once more evident that a society frequently does not fully conform to its own values. Thus religious folk have wanted to regulate the beliefs of their associates, and they have created opportunities to act as judges of conduct.

Individualism is reflected in the independence of American

churches. There is no central national regulation of religion. There is no established church which is supported, controlled, or even given preferential treatment by the state. Judaism, Catholicism, and Protestantism have no specific legal status. In Protestantism and Judaism the lack of central control is further evident within denominations. Some denominations control their local churches more than do others, but usually each congregation has a large degree of independence. It raises its own funds, determines its own activities, and selects its own leaders. In some denominations the local congregation is almost entirely self-sufficient. Even the denominations that provide for some central control of local churches frequently defend the right of any group to form a new church. When the independence of many American churches was pointed out to one European observer he commented,[8] "Yes, I think I see what you mean. But this congregationalism of yours is not what the world has hitherto called a church; it is anarchy!"

What are the present trends? Is the belief in religious self-determination gaining or losing significance? Is the demand for creedal conformity increasing or decreasing? As the churches become more highly organized do they exercise stronger control over local congregations? Is the church union movement in the direction of more or of less church independence? We shall not attempt to answer these questions. However, in view of the past prominence of religious individualism and independence, it would be desirable to have some means of measuring them. Such measures would be an aid to the analysis of trends in religion and in American culture as a whole.

Activism

Religion in the United States has been activistic rather than speculative. Americans have placed more emphasis on "doing something about one's religion" than on theological thinking and consistency of beliefs. With characteristic utilitarianism and a bent

[8] Quoted by Willard L. Sperry, *Religion in America*, New York, Macmillan, 1946, p. 246.

toward the practical they have showed only limited interest in the farther reaches of doctrinal distinctions. Indeed, they have often regarded preoccupation with anything beyond elementary theological considerations as a deflection from the earnest practice of religion.

The unreflective nature of much American religion is evidenced by the contradictions which it has ignored. In their religion Americans have demonstrated a remarkable facility for disregarding incongruities among beliefs and between belief and practice. The evil nature of man and the wickedness of this world have been proclaimed with passion and affirmed by succeeding generations, but this has never seriously impeded optimistic endeavors. Although singing "earth's joys grow dim," religious Americans have advocated joyful living and have set themselves to the pursuit of earthly goods. Unmindful of the avowed wickedness of this world they have looked upon national well-being and prosperity as a reward for righteousness and have committed themselves to its further promotion. Thus while theology has often been pessimistic, undespairing behavior has been a religious norm.

The unspeculative character of American religion helps to explain why modern science has disturbed religion so little. The science-religion controversy is kept alive only with great difficulty. There was a period during which science was regarded as an adversary of religion. Its challenge was met in some quarters with ebullient protest, if not with logic. In academic circles views on religion were significantly modified by the scientific approach. But only a modicum of the revised thinking reached the great majority of persons. The popular controversy was carried on without benefit of more sophisticated attempts to harmonize science and religion. Eventually the controversy subsided. This was not because the issues were rationally resolved, but because they were treated with indifference. The campaign against science became passé. Without knowing exactly how or why, many persons concluded that there is no necessary conflict between science and religion. Moreover, the belief in "doing" again prevailed. It was held that, after all, what an individual does is a better measure of his religion than what he thinks.

The deeds prescribed for religious action are innumerable and varied: attendance at church; teaching classes; visiting the unchurched; organizing societies and clubs; contributing money; soliciting money; building churches, schools, and hospitals; contributing to the poor; founding missions; leading reforms—these and many more have been the tangible ways of professing religion. The perpetuation and expansion of churches has always been a primary task. It is assumed that an earnest espousal of religion will result in some contribution of time and money for the fostering of religion.

Absorption with the promotion of churches is found both among Protestants and among Catholics. A few decades ago André Siegfried wrote of the Catholic clergy: [9] "The priest who tries to save his congregation from over-rapid Americanization is himself a complete American in his outlook on life and in his daily habits. He is a business man who dominates his church on the same lines as the most practical modernists. . . . Like all good Americans, he believes that the intensity of business life is measured by the cubic contents of church buildings. . . ." Such was the impression of a foreign observer.

Humanitarianism

In American religion the unity of religion and ethics is axiomatic. Indeed, being good and doing good are regarded by many persons as the essence of religion. Theologians have attempted to make a distinction between the ground of religion and the fruits of religion. Still, for theologian and layman alike, man's relationship with God is viewed as being inseparably involved with man's relationship with man.

We have indicated that the church assumes that religious living will result in efforts in behalf of the church. Such efforts are

[9] André Siegfried, *America Comes of Age*, New York, Harcourt, Brace, 1927, p. 52.

regarded as ethically imperative. Since it is believed that religion is fostered primarily through the church, the importance of the church is taken as self-evident. Support of the church is a service to both man and God. Thus most types of church work, whether conducting a class, counting the offering, or planning a picnic, are regarded as good behavior.

But the ethical requisites of religion do not end with the church. While at times service to the church is treated as the full expression of religion, the demands of religion are usually more inclusive. Religion claims the right to be censor and guide in nearly all areas of living. In this orientation the humanitarianism of religion is manifest. The American religious ethic has many facets, but probably humanitarianism is its most typical feature. (Humanitarianism is used here not in the doctrinal sense but in the popular sense to mean concern for the welfare of other people.) To "love thy neighbor as thyself" is a primary ethical requirement, and the injunction is interpreted broadly. Religiously motivated persons have often stopped short of their highest values, and American culture has produced many strong values that restrain and conflict with the basic humanitarianism of religion. Even so, the emphasis on doing good remains.

Modern society has made some types of doing good more complex, and for that reason perhaps more difficult. The application of a humanitarian ethic in a simple agrarian society is not the same as in a heterogeneous, urban, industrialized society. Religion no less than other phases of social life has been confronted with altered social relations and a changing social structure. In this situation the problem of humanitarian religion is organizational as well as ethical.

We began this chapter with an array of church-membership statistics. This is in keeping with the emphasis of organized religion on numbers of members. But it may be that in this religion does itself an injustice. If it is true that the importance of membership figures is overevaluated, it is probably also true that these figures underevaluate the influence of religion. Some of the values which religion has fostered are not only in the church; they are in the total culture.

SUMMARY

Although religious institutions have changed in many ways, there are some characteristics which have marked religion in this country since the beginning of the national period. Among these characteristics are separation of church and state, the drive for expansion, and denominationalism.

America has produced a large number of religious denominations and sects. But in some ways religious diversity is not so great as it appears. Two-thirds of all church members are Catholic, Baptist, or Methodist. Also, Protestant denominationalism has lost much of its traditional meaning. Denominational differences have diminished. At the same time religious diversity continues. Doctrinal, ceremonial, and class differences separate the churches. Religious differences are still a source of group conflict.

In the present century church life in Protestant congregations has been influenced by the institutional type of church. The traditional program was greatly modified and the number of activities was increased. To a large degree the change was an adjustment to the urban way of life. Although some churches changed far more than others, most Protestant congregations were influenced by the innovations. Protestant, Catholic, and Jewish groups all sponsor numerous activities which are not defined as strictly religious.

The churches have a long history of involvement in education. Today the Roman Catholic Church has a large school system. It conducts schools on all educational levels. Most of the schools under Protestant sponsorship are on the level of higher education.

The activities of religion extend beyond local churches. For many years foreign-mission work has been a leading nonlocal endeavor. In recent years the churches have promoted and supported a significant foreign-relief program. Social- and political-action interests also frequently extend beyond local congregations. Church concern about social problems is not a recent innovation, but in the last few decades church participation in economic and political affairs has become more official and more highly organized.

Even though many kinds of religion are found in the United States, there are some values and beliefs which characterize much of the practice of religion in our society. Among these are individualism, activism, and humanitarianism. Americans have valued individual freedom in religion, and they have emphasized doing in the practice of religion.

SELECTED REFERENCES

Abrams, Ray H., ed.: "Organized Religion in the United States," *The Annals*, vol. 256, March, 1948.

Bates, Ernest Sutherland: *American Faith; Its Religious, Political, and Economic Foundations*, New York, Norton, 1940.

Clark, Elmer T.: *The Small Sects in America*, New York, Abingdon-Cokesbury, 1949.

Dewey, John: *A Common Faith*, New Haven, Conn., Yale University Press, 1934.

Douglass, H. Paul, and Edmund de S. Brunner, *The Protestant Church as a Social Institution*, New York, Harper, 1935.

Kirkpatrick, Clifford: *Religion in Human Affairs*, New York, Wiley, 1929.

Niebuhr, H. Richard: *The Social Sources of Denominationalism*, New York, Holt, 1929.

Pope, Liston: *Millhands and Preachers*, New Haven, Conn., Yale University Press, 1942.

Smith, Rockwell C.: *The Church in Our Town*, New York, Abingdon-Cokesbury, 1945.

Sperry, Willard L.: *Religion in America*, New York, Macmillan, 1946.

Sweet, William W.: *Story of Religion in America*, New York, Harper, 1939.

Wach, Joachim: *Sociology of Religion*, Chicago, University of Chicago Press, 1944.

Yinger, John Milton: *Religion in the Struggle for Power*, Durham, N.C., Duke University Press, 1946.

Conclusion

CHAPTER NINETEEN

American Society in Process

We have been viewing American society in the perspective of continuity and change. The fact of continuity may be reemphasized. Even though a society is always changing, it remains linked with its past. What it can and does become depends in part upon what it has been. Culture and patterns of social relations are cumulative. The new is added to and develops from the old. Thus to a degree a society does not cease to be what it has been before.

Still there is change. We have seen that change has touched practically every part of our society. The make-up of the population, the relationships of persons, patterns of group interaction, the organization of communities and classes, the structure and functions of social institutions, social values—these and more have undergone change. And each type of change has been interrelated with other types.

For our purposes one thing remains. This is to identify some of the major processes which have effected the transformation of our society. Many of the occurrences that we have considered may be seen as interrelated sequences of events. A classification of the most important of these sequential occurrences will serve to delineate the patterns of social change. It will serve also as a summary-conclusion for our study. We shall consider ten processes as they have operated in American society: invention, industrialization, urbanization, centralization, specialization, bureaucratization, stratification, mobility, secularization, and assimilation. We shall also consider the nature of social change.

INVENTION

Social change in American society has been much influenced by the rapid rate of invention during the last two centuries. Although no culture is ever stationary, in earlier periods cultural change occurred somewhat slowly. At times changes have been so slight and gradual as to be practically imperceptible to the people who adopted them. Cultural innovations within our society, however, have been strikingly perceptible. They have been huge in number, rapid in occurrence, and vast in consequence. In some measure all the processes that we are considering in this chapter have been influenced by invention.

In the usage of social science the term *culture* refers to the learned ways of doing and thinking which are accumulated and transmitted from generation to generation. It includes also the material and nonmaterial products of man's learned behavior and knowledge. *Invention* may be defined as the bringing together of existing elements of culture to form something new and different. Every invention is an outgrowth of things already present in the culture. The complex develops from the simple. This is one of the reasons why invention has been so rapid in our society in recent centuries. Invention led to invention. Preceding inventions provided the basis for new inventions, and these in turn made possible still further invention. As the number of cultural components increased, the number of potential combinations increased also. The effect was an acceleration of the inventive process. It must be remembered, of course, that many of the inventions that contributed to this process in American society had their origin in other parts of the world.

Inventions may be either material or nonmaterial. Words, customs, and social institutions are inventions just as are dishwashers, medicines, and bulldozers. We shall not enter into a discussion of the relative importance or the causal priority of material inventions as against nonmaterial inventions. Material and nonmaterial innovations have been mutually influential. It is necessary, however, to emphasize the immense effect which material inventions have had on social change. It is evident that American society would not have many of its present characteristics if the process of invention had been less rapid and if it had taken a different trend.

The inventions that have contributed significantly to social change in our society are many. Innovations in the field of economic production and distribution are outstanding. Agriculture, the extractive industries, manufacturing, construction industries, distribution services, transportation, and communication have been revolutionized by inventions. In all areas of living the effects of new material equipment are apparent. Family life, entertainment and recreation, travel, and scientific pursuits have been transformed by new appliances, tools, instruments, and power devices.

The process of invention itself has been altered by invention. Much of our modern material culture was created in the same way as the material culture of centuries ago. Inventions were then largely the result of accident or of haphazard trial and error. Given a particular cultural base, new objects and devices appeared from time to time without plan or design. But in the modern era something new has been added. While accidental and haphazard invention continues, many modern material creations are the result of planned, systematic, and orderly effort.

The new factor in the process of invention is science. Science as such is not new. It has a long developmental history. But the revival in the modern era of interest in science and the eventual refinement of the scientific method helped to open the way to an era of rapidly expanding discovery and invention. One phase of science is concerned chiefly with the accumulation of knowledge as an end in itself. This is sometimes referred to as *pure* science. By an orderly procedure of observation, classification, generalization, and verification the scientist attempts to understand the phenomena of the universe. The other phase of science is concerned with using scientific knowledge as a means to an end. This is referred to as *applied* science. If such a distinction is made the men who for years accumulated knowledge about the structure of atoms were pure scientists and those who made the atom bomb were applied scientists. Although the distinction between pure and applied science is legitimate, they are not mutually exclusive spheres of activity.

Together pure and applied science have measurably modified the process of invention. The acceleration of changes in the material culture cannot be attributed alone to an increase in the size of the cultural base. It must be attributed also to the invention and utilization of a method of discovery and control—the scientific method.

INDUSTRIALIZATION

The onset of industrialization was marked by the shift from handicraft to power-machine production. Methods of producing and distributing goods were radically altered. Simple tools and hand-powered equipment gave way to innumerable minute and massive machines, powered by water, steam, electricity, and internal combustion. Machines and power were the beginning of industrialization. They were and continue to be the prime movers of the process. But machine production initiated an extensive series of changes. It helped to reshape the habits and organization of industrial life. Many of the cultural and social changes that accompanied machine production may be regarded as inherent parts of industrialization.

In agriculture machine production has caused marked effects. Many types of farming are less laborious. The number of acres that one man can cultivate has increased. Improved methods have raised production per acre. Specialized and commercial agriculture have tended to replace self-sufficient farming. The farmer has become more money-dependent. The greater productivity of farm labor has brought about an increase in the size of farms. Also it has decreased the proportion of workers required in agriculture. Farm families have helped to supply needed workers in other occupations.

In nonagricultural industries the changes have been tremendous. More efficient methods have been developed for locating, extracting, and refining the huge quantities of minerals required in modern production. In almost every type of manufacturing reliance is placed on machines to do rapid and laborsaving work. Many tasks are performed which without machinery would be impractical or impossible. In addition to revolutionizing traditional kinds of manufacturing, power machinery has given birth to hundreds of new industries. Industrialization has involved an expansion in the variety as well as the number of industries.

One of the momentous results of power-machine production was the factory system. This system of production has a number of rather definite characteristics. It involves the bringing together of workers to one place to carry on related activities. In factory production an attempt is made to organize work so that each operation is efficiently geared to all others. The system of organization results in a detailed division and subdivision of labor. The factory method is the antithesis of individual effort and has been applied to nearly all kinds of production.

In some types of production the factory system has acquired additional characteristic features. Systematic, specialized, repetitive work led to standardization and mass production. It is convenient and economical to make large quantities of an article at one place. In early factories the tendency was to try to concentrate as many manufacturing processes as possible. But standardization and mass production have resulted in the establishment of different factories for the making of different parts of a commodity. The manufacture of any product, whether automobile, milking machine, or tape recorder, involves a vast organization of factories each performing a more or less specialized function. Under the influence of the factory system industrial units have tended to become large. Still the industrial system with its specialized units and subunits includes both large factories and small.

Improved transportation for economic purposes may be regarded as an important factor in industrialization. The many thousands of economic units are connected by every means of mechanical conveyance. Raw materials are brought to processing and manufacturing centers. Parts are assembled from widely scattered places. Finished products are distributed throughout the country. In consequence the local type of industrial organization has been replaced by an organization of national dimensions, tied together by power-impelled transportation.

Industry has acquired a position of extensive influence in American society. No segment of the economy is insensitive to the pulse of industrial production. The number of workers employed, the wages paid, the quantity and rate of production, the types of goods manufactured, the trends of industrial expansion—these are all matters of large consequence not only within industry but for the entire national population. The widespread importance of industry gives to it great power. The whole economy reacts to the independent and the joint decisions of industrial power groups. Today the great power groups involved in industrial control are management, labor, and government. The inclusion of government is a telling indication of the effect of industrialization. In our society neither management, labor, nor the public at large are willing to keep government aloof from the regulation of production. The joining of economic and political affairs has been decidedly influenced by industrialization.

URBANIZATION

We have applied the term *urbanization* to the extension of city influence and to the spread of the way of life which is characteristic in cities. Urbanization in our society is evident in two ways: first, in the increase in the proportion of the total population living in areas of population concentration; and second, in the diffusion of the urban way of life beyond cities.

The first manifestation of urbanization is probably the more conspicuous. Cities in the United States have grown rapidly both in number and in size. The number of cities of over 25,000 increased from 2 in 1790 to 484 in 1950. In 1950 about three out of five persons were living in places of 2,500 or more. The urban trend has resulted in a notable concentration of population. In 1950 somewhat less than half of the people in the United States were living in cities of more than 50,000 or immediately adjacent to these cities. More than seven-tenths of the total urban population was in such areas.

The factors involved in the growth of cities are many. With regard to the functioning of society as a whole the causes are primarily economic. Population concentration is a necessary condition in order to carry on certain activities and in order to provide many services. From the point of view of the people who have moved cityward the reasons for urban growth are also primarily, but not solely, economic. Cities are centers of employment and of economic opportunity, and therefore the flow of population has been toward them. Cities are also the centers of entertainment, commerce, and education. They provide a great number of activities and a high degree of convenience. The lure of the city derives from many attractions, the importance of which vary with individuals.

The urban way of life has distinctive characteristics. In big cities the manifestations of urbanism are maximized. Social life in large population centers is characterized especially by marked social differentiation, by much impersonal social interaction, and by social solidarity based on a division of labor rather than on awareness of common traits and attitudes. The city is the meeting place and the origin of innumerable different racial, nationality, occupational, religious, class, and interest groups. In the ongoing life of the city much social interaction is necessary, but a high proportion of social contacts are impersonal. The many different individuals and groups are not joined by a feeling of being one people, but by mutual interdependence in the achievement of their separate and common ends.

When, then, we speak of the urbanization of our society we refer to the increase in the proportion of people who work in urban occupations, receive urban services, and practice the differentiated and impersonal way of life of the city. The present century has seen a remarkable expansion of the area in which urban conditions prevail. The influence of the urban way of life reaches into places surrounding cities, into large towns, and even into many rural places. The transportation, communication, markets, financial services, and entertainment of the city are available over wide areas. Many services are provided away from city centers. Urban attitudes, manners, and customs are not limited to cities.

Inasmuch as urban services and opportunities are more widely available, are we to conclude that reasons for urban growth have disappeared? The answer appears to be in the negative, for the urbanward trend of population is continuing. The functional advantages of population concentration remain. Some types of economic activity are mutually dependent upon their near location, and more people can provide more services for each other when they are in relatively close proximity. While the areas in which urban advantages are available have been greatly enlarged, the flow of people is still in the direction of population centers.

Many of the centers, however, are not circumscribed as they once were. This is a major trend of urbanization in the twentieth century. Cities have lost their limits. They sprawl over large territories. Still, they are population centers, vastly and irregularly extended. Their functions are not unlike those which they performed when their bounds were more definite. While the urbanism that emanates from these centers is also not circumscribed it is not evenly distributed. It is at a maximum where the density of population is greatest and it declines as population density declines.

CENTRALIZATION

There are at least two important manifestations of centralization in our society: (1) the centralization of activities, and (2) the centralization of authority and control.

Centralization of activities results in a drawing together of people. It is manifested, among other ways, in the concentration of people in urban areas. Both large and small urban communities are centers of integrated activity. The concentration of population in large cities is especially indicative of centralization. In massive numbers people cluster in metropolitan areas to perform myriads of interrelated activities. Within cities the pattern is further evident. The enterprises which cause population concentration are not evenly distributed throughout cities. Urban inhabitants converge on centers and subcenters to carry on their occupational, trading, educational, and recreational pursuits. The zenith of centralization in metropolitan areas is the "downtown" or central business district, with its almost constant in and out flow of people. Within this district probably one of the most conspicuous symbols of centralization is the giant department store.

It is necessary to keep in mind that the first type of centralization involves a convergence of activities. Although it is epitomized by cities, it is not limited to cities. No matter what the location, centralization is operating wherever merchandising is concentrated. It is functioning too wherever manufacturing processes are integrated in one place. Likewise the closing of one-room schools to establish large rural consolidated schools is a form of centralization.

The second type of centralization consists of the bringing of activities under one system of authority and control. This type frequently accompanies geographic concentration of units as in the case of a huge department store, a large factory, or a consolidated school. In many instances and to a significant degree the appearance of centralized control has been a result of geographic centralization. On the other hand, centralized patterns of authority may emerge apart from territorial centralization of units. For example, a widely dispersed business organization may have a highly centralized system of control.

The trend toward centralized authority and control is apparent in many areas of modern society. In economic affairs it is seen in the growth of large corporations which control vast financial and industrial empires. It is seen too in the emergence of big centrally dominated labor organizations. In government, centralization has increased along with the extension of governmental functions. As government has taken on more responsibilities the tendency has been to form central agencies to administer new programs. Centralization in the Federal government has been influenced by the broad scope of the problems with which it deals. Many present-day problems are of nationwide importance and call for plans of action which are centrally coordinated. In education centralization is evidenced in the establishment of state departments of education and in the formation of national education associations. Through these organizations education on nearly all levels is regulated, standardized, and supervised. In organized religion too there are indications of stronger central coordination and control.

Although the process of centralization has been prominent, it should not obscure the continuing existence of much uncentralized and subcentralized authority and control. Local churches cherish and practice a great measure of self-determination. In education also the tradition of local control is strong and is adhered to within certain limits. Even though large, highly centralized corporations tend to dominate the economy, there are many smaller, less centralized, and relatively independent business units. Also the large centralized units themselves may be regarded as subcenters of control within the total economic organization. In government, in which centralization is often assumed to be greatest, state and local governments are important units of subcentral control. Centralized control is real in our society, but the process is not so complete as is sometimes supposed.

SPECIALIZATION

Specialization is found in every society. The parts that are played, referred to as *social roles*, are not the same for all members of a society. Differences in behavior, duties, rights, and privileges are defined on the basis of factors such as sex, age, physical and mental abilities, education, occupation, and class. Further, the institutions of a society tend to be differentiated in terms of ends to be achieved. Thus family, economic, governmental, educational, and religious institutions perform specialized functions. This specialization of roles and functions brings into existence a *division of labor* by which a society fulfills its needs and achieves its ends. Although some kinds of common behavior are expected within a society, social organization does not function because all the members of a society do the same things, but rather because different individuals and groups do different things.

The type of specialization with which we are primarily concerned here is occupational. Such specialization is not at all new. Ancient societies divided their members into groups such as rulers, soldiers, farmers, and merchants. Colonial America had a division of labor among farmers, shippers, professionals, merchants, artisans, and others. What is new in modern society is the extraordinary extent to which specialization has developed. An occupational division of labor has been created which includes an almost immeasurable number of specialized tasks.

The chief occupational categories are not extremely difficult to identify. The Bureau of the Census, in 1950, classified employed persons into twelve major groups: professional, technical, and kindred workers; farmers and farm managers; managers, officials, and proprietors, except farm; clerical and kindred workers; sales workers; craftsmen, foremen, and kindred workers; operatives and kindred workers; private household workers; service workers, except private household; farm laborers, unpaid family workers; farm laborers, except unpaid, and farm foremen; laborers, except farm and mine. These twelve categories provided the basis for a more detailed classification consisting of 469 items.

The full measure of specialization, however, is not indicated by such a classification. This is only the beginning of the breakdown into specialized tasks. The automobile assembly line is frequently used as a symbol of modern specialization. Here the occupational division of labor seems to be carried as far as possible. Even so there are many other kinds of minute division of labor. Although their work is of a different type, the newspaper reporter who specializes in sporting events and the botanist who spends a lifetime classifying mushrooms also stand along "assembly lines."

BUREAUCRATIZATION

Bureaucracy is a product of large-scale organization, and the dominance of large-scale organization has been steadily increasing in modern society. A high proportion of manufacturing is under the direction of big industries. Workers bargain with their employers through big unions. Large financial corporations administer the flow of capital within our economy. Goods are marketed by big-scale enterprises. Education is conducted by large elementary schools, secondary schools, and universities. Governmental functions are performed by sizable city and state agencies and by a colossal Federal establishment. Many other types of organizations might be named. Individuals are affected by big organizations and therefore by bureaucracies, both by being employed in them and by being otherwise influenced by their decisions, programs, and power.

Essentially bureaucracy is a method of operation. Contrary to one popular conception it is not limited to government; it applies to nearly all organizations of considerable size. A business employing a thousand workers who perform specialized tasks cannot be managed in the same way as one employing ten workers all of whom do the same things. The management system employed in the larger business is bureaucratic. As the size of the organization and the degree of specialization increase, the system of operation becomes more complex; it becomes more bureaucratic.

As an organizational method bureaucracy has certain typical features. Its structural design is pyramidal. From top to bottom the layers of personnel become progressively larger. Also from top to bottom specialization increases; responsibilities and duties are departmentalized, divided, and subdivided many times. Ideally the division of labor among departments, divisions, subdivisions, and individuals is definite and precise; and activity in each unit is integrated with that in all other units. Selection of personnel is impersonal and is based on qualification for specific assignments. Authority within the structure is hierarchically arranged. The organization is joined by a chain of command and responsibility which extends downward throughout the system. The duties, rights, and powers of individuals who occupy positions in the hierarchy of authority derive from the offices they hold and not from the persons themselves. The entire system is regulated by rationally formulated rules, procedures, and practices. This is of course an ideal-typical representation of bureaucratic organization to which particular bureaucracies show varying degrees of conformity. Many smaller organizations have imitated the patterns of the large.

Bureaucracy appears to be inevitable. Large-scale organizations are firmly established, and in such organizations bureaucracy is a necessity if value is to be placed on efficiency. Indeed it is difficult to imagine how some large organizations could achieve anything at all, either efficiently or inefficiently, without bureaucratic operations.

The effects of bureaucracy are experienced differently by different individuals and under different circumstances. For many persons bureaucracy means security. They are habituated to the routinized requirements of their positions; they are unconcerned about promotions; and they count on continuing benefits upon retirement. For other persons the bureaucratic organization appears to be a web in which they are helplessly caught. They are forever frustrated by an impersonal control of standards and rules which seems cruelly indifferent to their special circumstances. To some persons who have opportunities for promotion, bureaucracy presents a constant challenge. They strain to do the things that will make them useful and acceptable to their superiors and thus enhance their chances of advancement. To citizens who come with requests, the procedures and regulations of public bureaucracies often seem to be deliberately calculated to induce irritation. Some observers see large bureaucracies as power centers which threaten personal liberty. But whether experienced as frustration, security, efficiency, or power, nearly everyone is in some way affected by bureaucratization.

STRATIFICATION

The population of the United States, like that of all other societies, is divided into groups which occupy different levels in the prestige structure. Identification with a particular stratum, or social class, is a result of the manifestation of certain characteristics which society as a whole evaluates as being high or low. The characteristics which confer a particular status are determined primarily by wealth and income, occupation, power, birth, and personal qualities. The differential distribution of socially valued traits is the source of social stratification.

As the American population has become more highly differentiated the system of stratification has become more complex. There was a time perhaps when there were only three major social classes—lower, middle, and upper. But the structure is no longer so simple. The processes of industrialization, urbanization, specialization, immigration, and bureaucratization have all combined to produce a more highly differentiated type of society. Thus as the basis for making distinctions has increased, the basis for stratification has also increased. In our society viewed as a whole a six-level structure has emerged. In some communities there are more than six classes and in others there are fewer than six, but the long-time trend has been in the direction of more complex stratification.

Although the class structure is a social reality, the identification of many individuals with their class is often indefinite. The method of self-classification could not be relied upon in discovering American social classes. Feelings of class solidarity tend to be weak. Class consciousness is most pronounced in the upper group; however, here too unity is lacking. When strong feelings of class unity exist, it is usually within local communities rather than nationwide. But even in local communities there are many individuals who have little awareness of belonging to a self-conscious social class.

However complex the structure, a system of open rather than closed classes is supported by the American ideology. Even though rewards are not equally distributed it is held that opportunities for reward seeking should be as nearly equal as possible. Americans have rejected the idea of fixed statuses and fixed advantages. They have believed in mobility up the social scale, and in great numbers they have practiced their belief. In the past the ideal and the practice of mobility were promoted by factors such as the frontier culture, the traditional rural way of life, opportunities for getting ahead provided by the new industrialism, the arrival of immigrants who by taking the lowest positions pushed other workers upward, and the elevation of the general level of living of large segments of the population.

Some of the factors that in earlier periods fostered indefinite stratification and rapid mobility have diminished in importance. There is some indication of less movement out of one class and into another. The evidence, however, is not conclusive, and the full effect of social change on the amount of vertical mobility is not well known.

MOBILITY

In sociological usage mobility is of two types: spatial, or physical, mobility and social mobility. Spatial mobility includes all the physical movements of people from place to place. Residential changes and the daily movements of individuals are in this category. Social mobility involves movement from one social position to another. Movement from one social position to another on the same level is referred to as horizontal social mobility. Movement from a social position on one level to a position on a different level is referred to as vertical social mobility.

A society characterized by a lack of mobility would be one in which persons did not move from the locality in which they were born. Day-to-day movements would be within a circumscribed area, and only rarely would there be occasion for anyone to go outside the community. Moreover positions within the society would be relatively permanent. There would be very little shifting of group memberships, and class positions would be fixed by birth. Under these circumstances an individual would continue to be in association with the same people in a limited orbit of social relationships.

It is obvious how little this description applies to modern American society. The United States never has been the scene of such extreme immobility. There always has existed a considerable amount of both spatial and social mobility. But social change in our society has included an immense increase in mobility. The trend has been farther and farther away from the above model of immobility and in the direction of the opposite extreme.

Physical mobility may be observed on every hand. The daily movements of city dwellers take them to many different places. The downtown center is the focus of much mobility, but in all parts of the city there is constant coming and going. In rural areas, too, the daily movements of people have expanded. Rural people move about freely from place to place in carrying on their occupational, trading, and recreational activities. Throughout the nation a network of railroads, bus lines, airlines, and highways facilitates an enormous amount of intercommunity and interstate travel.

Residential mobility is also on a vast scale. Within communities most families change residences several times, and some families and individuals make frequent moves. Residential changes which involve going to new communities have greatly increased.

Interregional and rural-to-urban and urban-to-rural migrations have taken millions of Americans into new areas to live.

Social mobility is no less important than spatial mobility. Much of the social mobility is a result of spatial mobility. When, for example, a family moves from one community to another it is necessary for the family members to break relationships in the first community and to establish relationships in groups in the new community. On the other hand, social mobility may be unrelated to residential changes. Horizontal shifts in group affiliations occur freely as needs and interests change. There is evidence that the frequency with which such shifts are made has increased. We have said that vertical mobility involves movement from a social position on one level to a position on a higher or a lower level. Although it is not clear whether vertical mobility has increased or decreased, it is well known that there is much social mobility of this type.

The existence of spatial and social mobility has made large numbers of American citizens accustomed to changing social relations. They meet new people, join new groups, participate in new communities, encounter new customs, and are exposed to new values. In adjusting to changing situations they frequently adopt different behaviors. In any specific situation the influence of other and previous relationships is not absent, but people who are mobile tend to be less attached to particular groups, customs, and ideas than are people who are immobile. This tendency toward *mental mobility* is one of the most noteworthy aspects of the increase in mobility during the last hundred years.

SECULARIZATION

In describing secularization it is helpful to make the distinction between sacred and secular societies. *Sacred* in this instance does not refer singularly to things religious. A *sacred society* is one in which a sacred quality is attributed to a high proportion of the existing social practices and beliefs. This applies to economic, family, political, educational, religious, and other social usages. Prevailing ideas and ways of doing things have been transmitted from the past and are time-honored. They are accepted uncritically and are passed on to the next generation relatively unchanged. The necessity for present patterns of conduct appears to be self-evident. They are the best ways, the right ways, and the only ways. The details of custom and belief take on a sacred character along with the major patterns.

There are a number of reasons why social practices become sacred in societies of this type. The effect is in part a result of habituation. Whenever conduct is learned early and reenforced repeatedly, discomfort is experienced when an attempt is made to behave differently. Deviation produces apprehensiveness and fear. When, in addition, nearly all the members of a society share common culture traits, the possibility of turning from the customary is doubly painful. To the psychological distress which accompanies departure from the habitual is added the threat of social disapproval. Moreover, because the members of the society have a common culture, practices different from their own are either unknown or are treated as inferior. Present practices are regarded as essential to the welfare of the group, and any repudiation of the usual and the expected is taken as an affront to the society. Violation of custom is a threat to group integrity and solidarity.

In contrast, a *secular society* is one in which the bonds of tradition are weak. Some practices and beliefs transmitted from the past are accepted, many are questioned, and some are rejected. The basis for accepting or rejecting culture traits is inclined to be utilitarian. They are evaluated in terms of the question: Of what use are these practices and ideas? Within the society individuals and groups observe many different customs and practices and hold many different beliefs. Old ways are constantly challenged by influences from within and from without the society. Innovation and change are expected. Secularization, however, is always a matter of degree. No society becomes fully secularized, for the sacred quality always adheres to some usage, beliefs, and values.

American society is increasingly secular. It is a society of weak traditional controls, of utilitarian standards, and of rapid cultural change. In many areas of activity formal, rational, and legal controls have taken the place of custom. Some of the causes of secularization may be seen in the reversal of factors which support sacred societies. Thus individuals do not become deeply habituated to some customs because they are repeatedly exposed to new and different ways. To a degree they actually become habituated to the expectation of change. But more important as as a causal factor is the diversity of groups which make up our national population. Many different groups have had many different customs. Mobility and urbanization bring these groups in contact with each other. It is difficult to preserve the belief that there is only one right set of practices and ideas when people having diverse culture traits live together. They become tolerant of or indifferent to many variations. Violation of the practices of a particular group is not regarded as a threat to the entire society. Such tolerance of cultural alternatives reduces the inevitability of any particular set of customs and opens the way for change. Furthermore adjustments have had to be made to technological changes. People who are accustomed to having their patterns of living altered by technological innovations are not well trained for the transmission of a a sacred culture.

ASSIMILATION

The population of the United States is composed of people of varying racial and ethnic backgrounds. From many places and through many groups came multifarious languages, customs, beliefs, and values. To what extent are these peoples now one people, and to what measure do they share a common culture?

The least assimilated groups are designated as *minority groups*. These are the groups which are assigned inferior status and which are not permitted the privileges of full participation in American society. In this category are American Indians, Orientals, Spanish-speaking Americans, and Negroes. One thing these peoples have in common: they are racially distinct from the rest of the population. Their racial visibility is an important factor in accounting for their continuing separateness. They are easily identified as belonging to groups which historically have been held in social segregation from the white majority. Furthermore assimilation has been prevented by taboos against interracial marriages. Regardless of the degree of similarity between their cultures and that of the white majority, physical visibility and the ideology of race have kept these groups from becoming assimilated. Race has been a less important factor in the case of American Indians than it has been for the other minority groups.

The position of European immigrants and their descendants is not the same as that of the racial minorities. To a much greater degree the European groups have become assimilated. With regard to these groups there have been three main concepts of what their place should be in American society. They may be identified as the *Americanization, melting-pot,* and *cultural-pluralism* concepts.

The purpose of Americanization is to make European immigrants and their descendants "like Americans." They are to acquire American customs, language, manner of dress, interests, beliefs, and values. The American way of life is defined in terms of a somewhat static idea of American culture as uninfluenced by outside groups. For the most part the adjustment is thought of as being one-way. The varied ethnic groups are to discard the culture of their past and as quickly as possible are to lose their identity by acquiring a new culture.

The melting-pot idea also calls for the disappearance of ethnic identities, but the process is different. The United States is seen as a country in which many cultural groups have come together. As a result of their mingling and mixing all groups are to lose their original characteristics. A new cultural product is to emerge which is different from any one of the components, but to which all have contributed.

Cultural pluralism presents a contrast to both of the above concepts. Instead of anticipating the disappearance of ethnic differences, it advocates the preservation of cultural individuality. Distinctive patterns of behavior, beliefs, and values which do not conflict with the broader social norms are to be cultivated. The goal is not a merging of cultures but a society in which ethnic diversity is maintained within an over-all structure of common culture.

In reality relationships among diverse groups in American society do not conform to any one of the three proposals, but each of the patterns is present. Americanization has occurred in most groups. They have been eager to acquire "American ways" and they have been influenced by American values. The great majority from nearly all groups are characteristically American in behavior and thinking. This is true of some of the racial minorities as well as of white immigrants and their children. Indeed the culture of the Negro in the United States, although deviant in some respects, never has been any less American than that of the native white population.

The flow of cultural influence has not been as one-way as the early advocates of Americanization had hoped. The original culture has undergone some modification as a result of the presence of diverse groups. In many respects incoming ethnic groups changed American culture less than they were changed by it, but the melting-pot effect has not been absent. A great variety of elements combined to form the present culture. Certainly our culture would be different today if the relative ethnic homogeneity of the early 1800's had never been disturbed.

Americanization and the melting-pot effect have not destroyed all ethnic-group identification and pride. Cultural pluralism is a reality as well as a proposal. Groups which think of themselves first as Americans and in which American patterns are ingrained nevertheless manifest prominent characteristics which are directly related to their ethnic origins. Moreover these characteristics are perpetuated by the more frequent association of the members of the respective groups with each other than with other persons.

But even though diverse ethnic influences are active in our society, Americans have achieved notable unity. There are still clashes of culture which arise from differences in ethnic backgrounds. Some religious friction is of a similar source. Certain social distinctions are based on ethnic-group membership. Even so the population of the United States has become a somewhat homogeneous ethnic group. It has also become a highly self-conscious national group. In culture and in identification, Americans have to a remarkable degree become one people.

CHANGE

We proposed at the beginning to view American society in the perspective of continuity and change. The existence of continuity should be evident. Our society has moved from its past to its present form by successive transformations. It is impossible for any society to make a full break with its past and still function as a society. While becoming something different it must continue to be what it has been. This is continuity, and it exists in American society as in all others.

The existence of change should also be evident. We have said that society may be seen as a social system. It is a functioning unit consisting of interdependent parts. When social change occurs the structure and the functioning of the social system are altered. The alteration of the system involves changes in patterns of behavior and changes in patterns of relations. The expected and predictable behavior of the members of society is modified as is also the organization of society.

Society is always changing. It is by nature dynamic. The mutual responsiveness which binds the members of society together does not permit a static condition. Society must constantly be reconstructed in order to survive, and the process of reconstruction entails change. In some societies change proceeds more swiftly than in others. The nature of the social components and the manner of their interaction may result in many and marked modifications as society reconstructs itself. Ours is such a society. The social forces within the system have induced relatively rapid change. We have detailed population, community, class, and institutional changes, and in the present chapter we have outlined major processes involved in change.

But what happens to the operation of the system as change occurs? How can an organization of interdependent parts function when the parts and their relations to each other are changing? It must be remembered that the kind of system to which we are referring is social. It is more comparable to an organic system than to a mechanical system. Still the functioning of one part affects other parts and thus the entire system. In terms of social change this means that a modification of one part requires an adjustment among other parts. Change in one part results in disequilibrium within the system until an adjustment has been made throughout. The system continues to function because social forces are constantly tending to restore equilibrium. This characteristic of society which permits it to function while it is changing is referred to as a *moving equilibrium*. By definition a moving equilibrium is never perfect. The restoration of equilibrium is sometimes rapid, sometimes slow. Change in our society has not occurred without stress and strain, resistance and conflict. But to the present the process has been reconstructive. The essential continuity and integration of American society persists.

Index